Looking Down on Human Intelligence

OXFORD PSYCHOLOGY SERIES

Editors

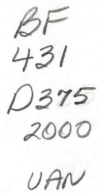

Looking Down on Human Intelligence

From Psychometrics to the Brain

IAN J. DEARY
*Department of Psychology,
University of Edinburgh*

OXFORD PSYCHOLOGY SERIES
NO. 34

OXFORD

UNIVERSITY PRESS

OXFORD

UNIVERSITY PRESS

Great Clarendon Street, Oxford OX2 6DP

Oxford University Press is a department of the University of Oxford.
It furthers the University's objective of excellence in research, scholarship,
and education by publishing worldwide in

Oxford New York

Athens Auckland Bangkok Bogotá Buenos Aires Calcutta
Cape Town Chennai Dar es Salaam Delhi Florence Hong Kong Istanbul
Karachi Kuala Lumpur Madrid Melbourne Mexico City Mumbai
Nairobi Paris São Paulo Singapore Taipei Tokyo Toronto Warsaw

with associated companies in Berlin Ibadan

Oxford is a registered trade mark of Oxford University Press
in the UK and in certain other countries

Published in the United States
by Oxford University Press, Inc., New York

A catalogue record for this title is available from the British Library

Library of Congress Cataloging in Publication Data
(Data available)

1 3 5 7 9 10 8 6 4 2

ISBN 0 19 852417 X

Typeset by Florence Production Ltd., Stoodleigh, Devon.
Printed in Great Britain on acid free paper by
T.J. International Ltd,
Padstow, Cornwall

To Ann, Elayne, Joanna, and Matthew

But that which *Galen* noteth more particularly, touching this, is, that Philosophie and Phisicke, are the most uncertaine of all those wherewith men are to deale. And if this be true, what shall we say touching the Philosophie whereof we now intreat, where with the understanding, we make an anatomie of a matter so obscure and difficult, as are the powers and faculties of the reasonable soule? In which point are offered so many doubts and arguments, that there remains no cleare doctrine upon which we may relie.

(Huarte 1575, p. 70)

Prolegomenon

The theme of this book is the search for the origins of human intelligence differences in terms of brain functioning. Each topic within the field is covered in an essay-type style. That is permissible because the writer makes reference to the principal empirical reviews of each field, and wrote some of them. Giving the reader the undigested mass of facts is like a layperson being handed raw scores from the Wechsler Adult Intelligence Scale, or the NEO-Personality Inventory-Revised; it's the interpretation of the disinterested expert that one is paying for, not the raw materials, just as you want a builder to construct a house and not dump the materials in piles on the site and leave you to assemble them. In other areas of scientific endeavour, especially medical science, the be-all and end-all of the topic is the meta-analysis; impressionistic judgement calls are derogated. But many important decisions in our field demand such judgement calls. The proximity between a test and a theoretical construct, whether or not an association is large enough to be 'interesting', whether a line of investigation is worthwhile at all, what a correlation between two samples of human behaviour (psychometric test score versus putative information processing component) means; all these and more are the decisions we make in our daily work.

The main discoveries and insights, historical and contemporary, are covered. The principal concern, however, is to show how an area of research has gone about its business. So there is a particular interest in historical precedents of current research fields. There is an emphasis on the way constructs are considered and how associations are viewed. There is a focus on the place of theory and with the balance between available evidence and allowable speculation. To be frank, there is a strong dislike of theory such as it is manifest in the field, and a lot of the book is an appeal to go with the data and to be quick to give up on so-called theory which, in psychology, is rarely the well-aimed headlight that, at best, it can be in the physical sciences.

I wrote the book about the origins of psychometric intelligence differences because I know about this area, but the book could have dealt with many topics in psychology that are used for prediction and are also mysterious with regard to the origins of their differences. Personality, some aspects of memory, attention, all might have been topics about which a book with a similar structure and comparable concerns could have been written. So don't be too smug when it is shown how little researchers in intelligence know of the history of their topic, how poor are some of their data sets, how unsupportable are some of their conclusions, and how little they have advanced in terms of process understandings since the early 1900s. This is a book whose form and general points are meant for the psychological everyman, and the criticisms apply beyond human intelligence research.

Some paragraphs ago I mentioned that the reader was paying for the voice of a disinterested expert commentator. Disinterested voices are not legion in the field of intelligence differences. And the reader must be warned that, since the rebirth of the topic of information processing from the 1970s to date, there have been writers of books and articles who view some facets of this area of research as near moribund and/or fruitless (e.g. Ceci 1990; Lohman 1994) and some who see mostly promise (Matarazzo 1992; Brand 1996; Jensen 1998*a*). In addition, there are those who may be characterized as honest brokers, people not hugely active empirically within the field but who have reviewed the evidence and passed even-handed judgement. In this category sit, for example, Brody (1992) and Mackintosh (1998), although Brody's spectacles have a just-noticeable rose-sanguine tint and Mackintosh moves between choleric-yellow and melancholic-blue lenses. With regard to this writer, there is a noticeable change from the tiro medical undergraduate infected with Chris Brand's conquering enthusiasm (Brand and Deary 1982). Scales have fallen from the eyes; procedures, samples, analyses, constructs, theories, all have generated cause for complaint.

In the course of composing this series of related essays I abused the good nature of many valued colleagues. Elizabeth Austin, Peter Caryl, Fergus Craik, Ted Nettelbeck, Aljoscha Neubauer, Robert Plomin, and Lawrence Whalley provided valuable comments on earlier drafts of chapters. My University of Edinburgh colleagues Peter Caryl and Alasdair MacLullich contributed equal shares to the writing of Chapter 9. Janice Sutherland translated Wolff's Latin in Chapter 2. Alan Bedford read through the entire proof. Roy Welensky drew the figures. The conclusions and opinions hereinafter are mine.

May 2000   I. J. D.

Contents

Contents

1 Little *g* and friends

An exposition of psychometric intelligence differences. The anatomy (or geography) of that which has to be explained

SUMMARY

This chapter covers essential background to the psychology of human mental ability differences. The structure, stability, heritability, and utility of psychometric intelligence tests are described. There is a converging consensus about the structure of human ability differences. Human cognitive abilities form a multi-level hierarchy, with a general factor (Spearman's *g*) at the pinnacle, many very specific abilities at the bottom, and separable but correlated group factors of ability in between at one or more levels. Thus many apparently contradictory theories of human psychometric intelligence are partly reconciled. These substantial advances provide merely a taxonomy of psychometric intelligence/IQ-type tests' contents and subjects' performances, affording no necessary insight into the causes of human intelligence differences. The psychometric approach allows individuals to be ranked, and mental ability test scores to be classified. It is a descriptive contribution, with practical applications. The main argument in this chapter is that psychometric intelligence differences are indeed reasonably well described by the hierarchy, have substantial stability and heritability, and have predictive validity. The further argument is that this is incomplete, because the origins (social, psychological, biological) of psychometric intelligence differences are not understood. The remaining chapters cover the main attempts to construe psychometric intelligence differences in terms of lower-level psychological and even biological constructs. Hunt (1980*a*) compared the search for the information processing origins of intelligence to the search for the Holy Grail. It is a critique of this quest or hunt for the foundations of psychometric intelligence differences that continues through this book.

THE SHAPE OF HUMAN INTELLIGENCE DIFFERENCES

It is a favourite debating ploy in discussions about human intelligence to ask for a definition of the construct. One meaning of 'define' in the Oxford English Dictionary is 'give the exact meaning of'. If differential psychologists are daft enough to attempt this, they will find they have been tricked into delivering a hostage to fortune, the premature issue will be rent by inquisitors. When being asked for a definition of human intelligence, an answer can address the Dictionary's other meaning, namely 'mark out the boundary or limits of'. That is the purpose of this chapter. Incidentally, luminaries in the area of intelligence have felt the need to slay the definition dragon at the start of their accounts. Spearman (1927), Jensen (1980, 1998a), Eysenck (1982), and Mackintosh (1998) all refused to be halted by demands for an exact meaning-style definition, deciding that there was a sufficient corpus of research findings to be described and explained without worrying unduly about premature verbal formulations. Flynn (1999) agreed:

> even the hardest sciences did not give elaborate pretheory definitions of their key concepts. Newton did not wait to refine the concept of celestial influence before embedding it in his theory of gravity. (p. 12)

There must be a structure for proceeding to examine the construct validity of human psychometric intelligence differences. Before that, a word or two about the terminology that will be used in this book. The term 'intelligence' was viewed as so fraught with problems that both Spearman (1927) and Jensen (1998) discarded it pointedly from their *magna opera* on the topic. Both adopted what they considered to be the more precise and less stained term '*g*' to capture the essence of their subject's treatise. That approach engendered its own problems; some attention must go to things other than *g* in providing an account of humans' mental ability differences. Those who addressed mental abilities without having *g* as a principal player cast Hamlet without the prince (e.g. Gardner 1983; Horn 1994), and those who focused only or unduly on *g* produced the play without the supporting cast (Jensen 1998a; Brand 1996). Surprisingly, although Guilford (1956) did not subscribe to the importance of *g* or any other single, important aspect of mental ability differences, he retained the term 'intelligence':

> The term 'intelligence' is useful, none the less. But it should be used in a semipopular, technological sense. It is convenient to have such a term, even though it is one of the many rather shifty concepts we have in applied psychology. (p. 290)

In the present book, when referring to measurements made using mental ability tests, the term 'psychometric intelligence differences' is used. For variety they are sometimes called 'mental ability differences' or 'IQ-type test scores' or some such. These measured human differences are presented as something to be explained, not as explanations of anything in themselves. After this chapter, they are treated as dependent variables. This chapter addresses the measurement and some uses of mental ability differences; the rest of the book is about the more interesting and incomplete job of understanding human psychometric intelligence differences (Deary *et al.*, in press).

As was stated above, there should be a structure for the construct validity of human intelligence differences. Figure 1.1 is at once a comprehensive and concise description of the enterprise and of this book. It endorses and enlarges Hunt's (1983) summary to the effect that,

The study of intelligence has historically revolved around three questions: what does intelligence do, what causes it, and how should it be measured? (p. 146)

Moreover, it agrees with Burt's (1940) separation of the three tasks of mental ability researchers:

> we may, I think, clarify and harmonize the conflicting views put forward on the reality and causal efficacy of mental factors, if we recall the three distinct aims of reasoned analysis—prediction, explanation and description. (p. 227)

Measuring and describing human mental ability differences

At the centre of Fig. 1.1 are the phenomena to be described and explained. These are individual differences in some mental abilities of humans, as measured typically by a large number of diverse mental tests. As with any other scientific phenomenon, it must be asked whether there is an agreed taxonomy of the phenomena. That is, how many types of ability difference are there that require explaining? There are other basic questions at this, the psychometric level, such as: are the individual differences stable across the lifespan; how do they change as people grow older; and, do men and women differ on some of these abilities? These psychometric data form the substrate of our discussions. In so far as they cover key mental functions they are important; in so far as they omit others they are incomplete (Sternberg 1999).

Looking up from human intelligence

It is conceivable that psychometric intelligence might have an agreed taxonomy—and even, in addition, that individual differences on the various constructs within the taxonomy might be stable across much of the human lifespan—but that ability test scores are unimportant with respect to life achievements. If that were so, there might be recourse to stating that mental differences are still of interest because they reflect aspects of the brain's operations that are worthy of study in themselves. Maybe, but if psychometric intelligence differences were not able to predict anything important in people's lives they should attract much less scientific study, polemic and non-specialist scrutiny. This aspect of mental test differences is the predictive validity of psychometric intelligence or, from Fig. 1.1's structure, 'looking up from human intelligence'. Researchers in this field ask questions such as: do mental test score differences predict some of the variance in educational and work-related outcomes; and do psychometric intelligence differences account for some variance in people's social life and health?

Looking down on human intelligence

If there is sufficient agreement concerning a taxonomy of the phenomena captured in the term psychometric intelligence differences, and if aspects of the taxonomy

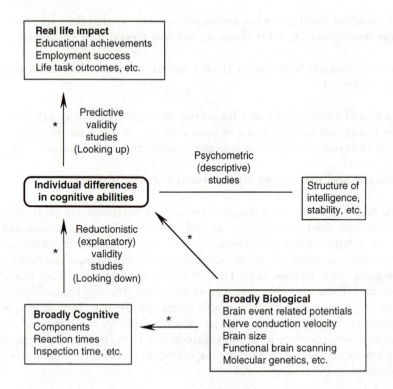

Fig. 1.1 A structure for thinking about the validity of human intelligence differences. There are at least three types of research: psychometric (descriptive) studies, predictive validity (looking up) studies, and reductionistic validity (looking down) studies. The taxonomy and stability of intelligence differences is a descriptive enterprise that forms the platform for assessing validity. Predictive validity of psychometric intelligence is the degree to which mental test differences account for variance in various important aspects of human lives. Reductionistic validity is the degree to which differences in psychometric intelligence can be accounted for in terms of lower-level cognitive and/or biological constructs. *The arrows indicate the usual assumptions about the direction of causation, but in most cases the reverse direction is possible and tenable, or individual differences in both variables might be caused by a third variable. Adapted from Fig. 2 in Deary and Caryl (1997*a*).

account for some variance in important aspects of people's lives, then we are bound to ask: what brings about these differences? This question will not be answered by factor-analytic approaches. Cooper (1999), though, is more equivocal, suggesting that factor analysis might reveal valid, explanatory constructs. Burt (1940), however, agreed that the scope of factor-analytic studies of mental abilities was limited largely to description. He saw the need to discover the origins of psychometric intelligence differences outside of the psychometric approach:

As a mathematician the factorist merely asks: what are the fewest and simplest postulates I can make in order to describe the phenomena I am observing? And from these postulates he tries to reconstruct the facts observed. But when he has completed his reconstruction, he seeks to check and verify his inferences; and so turns again to the empirical world. (p. 214)

Understanding human ability differences is a task outside the framework of taxonomic statistics; it proceeds by tying ability differences to validated empirical constructs of the biological, cognitive, and social spheres. Arguably, asking about the origins of ability differences is the most interesting question, because scientifically it is the most basic. It is what the chapters in the present book, after this first one, are about. Figure 1.1 shows that this is the reductionistic validity of human intelligence differences, or 'looking down on human intelligence'. Looking downwards does not ignore social influences on mental ability differences; another book may be written on that, but it's just not what this one's about. Looking downwards does not insist upon mental ability differences arising from lower-level psychological or biological origins. Looking downwards merely enquires whether these latter sources account for some variance in measured aspects of behaviour. Moreover, there is no undue binding of lower-level causes to heredity. The environment's effects are biological too. Reductionists in human mental ability research are excited by breast feeding as well as by breeding (Willatts *et al.* 1998). As far as possible, the book's aims are to weed out what Dennett (1995) called 'greedy reductionism' in research on human ability differences, and to identify the green shoots of any surviving 'good reductionism'.

A TAXONOMY OF HUMAN MENTAL ABILITY DIFFERENCES

In discussing psychometric intelligence differences, how many abilities must be considered? The answers offered in response to this essential question are, at first blush, contradictory: one, a few, many, or very many! With an appropriate choice of psychologist, one may claim the existence of as many human mental abilities as one's favourite number. If this were the whole story, and the taxonomy of human intelligence differences were in such anarchy, the search for any underpinnings of human intelligence differences would be pointless. The variable to be explained would be too poorly characterized, without the necessary taxonomic structure to afford targetable pools of variance. In empirical fact, such large-scale, apparent disagreement about the psychometric structure of human intelligence differences is illusory.

Taxonomies should not be confused with theories. Competing suggestions as to the taxonomies of mental ability differences are sometimes referred to as theories (Bickley *et al.* 1995; Bouchard 1998). A better term, one that does not lend itself to inducing expectations of causal accounts in the reader, is 'model' (Carretta and Ree 1995). This term emphasizes that psychometrics can help in describing the structure of ability differences. Theories are collections of constructs and their relations that allow prediction and control of aspects of the world. Models of human ability differences are alternative ways of construing covariance pools in mental test responses. At this point it is better to avoid the term 'theories of intelligence differences' and to focus on crucial findings that models must recognize and would-be explanatory accounts must address. *The* surprising and consistent empirical finding in psychometric intelligence research is that people who do well on one mental task tend to do well on most others, despite large variations in the tests' contents. That is, if a largish, representative sample of a population completes a number of diverse mental tests under the same conditions (be the tests speeded and unspeeded, verbal and spatial, easy and difficult, simple and complex), the correlations among the mental test scores will be almost entirely positive, and often moderately large. This was Spearman's (1904) discovery, and is arguably the most replicated result in all psychology.

The structure of the Wechsler Adult Intelligence Scale

For example, consider the Wechsler Adult Intelligence Scale-Revised (WAIS-R; Wechsler 1981). This is one of the most widely used batteries of mental ability tests. It is not based on a theory of human mental functions, but it comprises 11 subtests that are heterogeneous in content. *Information* asks general knowledge questions. *Digit span* involves remembering and repeating lists of numbers both forwards and backwards. *Vocabulary* inquires about the meanings of words. *Arithmetic* involves mental arithmetic problems. *Comprehension* requires the person being tested to explain various facts, actions, and concepts. *Similarities* asks about the ways in which different-seeming objects or abstract things are similar. *Picture completion* involves noticing the missing parts of a number of line-drawings. *Picture arrangement* requires the subject to organize a series of line drawings so that each one forms a story. In *Block design* the testee constructs set patterns from cubes with different-coloured faces. In *Object assembly* jigsaw-like puzzles have to be constructed. In *Digit symbol* the subject must enter a code below a number according to a coding system printed at the top of the page.

These 11 mental tests have quite different surface appearances. Scrutinized by someone inclined to believe in the existence of many independent cognitive functions, they would appear in part to be completed by different mental modules. And so they might be. They are not paper-and-pencil-tests; only one of them (Digit Symbol) involves the testee in writing anything. Yet, as Table 1.1 shows, when the tests were given to a representative sample of the Scottish population (on age, sex, and social class) all 11 subtests correlated positively. Subjecting subjects' scores on the subtests of the WAIS-R to principal components analysis produced the results in Table 1.2. First, note that the result is highly congruent in the two large samples, one in the USA and one in the UK. Second, note the large proportion of the variance accounted for by the first unrotated principal component. It accounts for over 50% of the variance in the tests, and all of the subtests have high loadings on this component.

Table 1.1 Correlations among the 11 subtests of the Wechsler Adult Intelligence Scale-Revised from a representative sample of the Scottish population (data from Crawford, personal communication, $N = 365$)

	Information	Digit span	Vocabulary	Arithmetic	Comprehension	Similarities	Picture completion	Picture arrangement	Block design	Object assembly	Digit symbol
Information	–										
Digit span	0.36	–									
Vocabulary	0.72	0.46	–								
Arithmetic	0.55	0.47	0.48	–							
Comprehension	0.59	0.36	0.70	0.45	–						
Similarities	0.59	0.40	0.67	0.43	0.58	–					
Picture completion	0.52	0.23	0.49	0.30	0.46	0.52	–				
Picture arrangement	0.50	0.31	0.51	0.41	0.42	0.53	0.48	–			
Block design	0.45	0.32	0.45	0.44	0.39	0.46	0.45	0.43	–		
Object assembly	0.32	0.14	0.32	0.33	0.29	0.40	0.41	0.36	0.58	–	
Digit symbol	0.26	0.27	0.32	0.28	0.30	0.33	0.26	0.28	0.36	0.25	–

Table 1.2 Principal components analyses of the Wechsler Adult Intelligence Scale-Revised in the UK and the USA (Crawford *et al.* 1989)

	First unrotated principal component		Rotated Factor I		Rotated Factor II		Rotated Factor III	
	UK	USA	UK	USA	UK	USA	UK	USA
Information	0.78	0.82	0.87	0.81	0.18	0.21	0.16	0.29
Digit span	0.65	0.65	0.25	0.27	0.17	0.11	0.86	0.83
Vocabulary	0.77	0.86	0.88	0.82	0.11	0.22	0.21	0.34
Arithmetic	0.74	0.78	0.40	0.49	0.30	0.28	0.64	0.59
Comprehension	0.78	0.80	0.82	0.79	0.18	0.23	0.25	0.26
Similarities	0.84	0.81	0.65	0.75	0.32	0.30	0.47	0.25
Picture completion	0.75	0.73	0.48	0.48	0.64	0.64	0.10	0.11
Picture arrangement	0.79	0.68	0.53	0.51	0.52	0.49	0.28	0.13
Block design	0.71	0.74	0.22	0.26	0.82	0.72	0.21	0.38
Object assembly	0.62	0.64	0.20	0.14	0.80	0.85	0.05	0.19
Digit symbol	0.53	0.64	0.04	0.23	0.73	0.37	0.32	0.61
Variance %	52.9	55.3	31.5	31.7	25.8	21.4	15.7	17.7

The trouble with *g*

This is, of course, a version of the result first reported by Charles Spearman (1904). Spearman christened this empirical result 'general intelligence' and, in order to avoid misinterpretation, gave it the more neutral signifier *g*. *g* is precisely that—an empirical result; it should be thought of as no more and no less than this, in so far as we are considering psychometric data. It is an interesting and counterintuitive result, for most people's first assumptions would be that some mental abilities are unrelated or negatively correlated with others. Spearman's attempt to give this result a neutral marker did not keep the psychology profession neutral, because *g* is probably the most controversial single result in psychology, as well as being one of the most important (Gould 1981; Brand 1996; Jensen 1998*a*).

g can evoke extreme reactions. It is used either to explain almost everything about human ability differences or it itself is explained away, leaving it explaining nothing. Spearman's (1927) best-known book—*The abilities of man*—is a rhapsody to *g*. Although group factors and specific factors are entertained therein, and the latter found a place in his two-factor model (see Chapter 2), only *g* was given the burden of much explanatory variance and causal attention. Two *g*-encomia in the late 1990s were called *The g factor* (Brand 1996; Jensen 1998*a*). All three books are, in fact, about human psychometric intelligence differences in the round, but they focus pretty exclusively on the fact that the first unrotated principal component accounts for a large proportion of the variance in mental test batteries given to samples of the population. Thus, there is a reaction to *g* that all but says that it is almost the only thing worth bothering about when it comes to investigating human ability differences.

The opposite reaction occurs too. There are writers who see it as their quest to exterminate *g* and/or to explain it away. Gardner's (1983) much-mentioned theory of multiple intelligences finds little room for *g*. In the popular book *The mismeasure of man*, Stephen Jay Gould (1981)—an evolutionary biologist—told his audience in purple prose that *g* is a statistical artefact, a happenstance of the particular analytic method used to examine the associations among mental tests. He went on to criticize those scientists interested in *g* for having reified this artefact. Although there are other important aspects of Gould's writings on human intelligence differences that are overstated or partly in error (Jensen 1982a; Michael 1988; Rushton 1997), here it is shown that *g* is neither an artefact (à la Gould) nor, necessarily, the only aspect of human intelligence differences that matters (à la Spearman, Brand and Jensen).

g is not a necessary artefact of factor (or principal components) analysis, because it need not occur. If, in fact, there were mental abilities that were independent of others they would be uncorrelated and they would not load on *g*. Compare the situation in personality traits (Matthews and Deary 1998, Chapter 1). In that field, people's responses to questions about their dispositions are often uncorrelated, or correlated negatively. Consequently, orthogonal personality factors such as neuroticism and extraversion are isolated using the same statistical machinery that produced *g*. And the rotation of mental ability factors does not, as Gould (1981) incorrectly suggested, make *g* disappear. If the rotation of the components or factors is orthogonal, there arise cross-loadings of the tests on the factors, indicating commonality among all tests despite forcing out orthogonal factors. If the rotation of factors or components in a battery of mental ability tests is oblique, the general component is found in the correlations among the factors themselves. A general factor may then be extracted by performing a hierarchical factor analysis or other latent trait analysis on the factor scores. This is explained clearly by Gustafsson (1984). A more detailed exposition of Gould's errors of omission and commission regarding factor analysis and *g* was written by Carroll (1995, p. 131), who concluded that,

> Gould's statements and accusations about factor analysis are incorrect and unjustified, and should not be regarded as constituting an authoritative guide to evaluating this technique.

Gould's (1981) comments on the factor analysis of ability scales are an unhelpful diversion, but *g* might be a siren too, as discussed later. Immediately below, there is a summary of some evidence on the ubiquity of the general factor among the variance in mental test score differences. And, emphatically, *g* is far from being the whole story; there are other important aspects to psychometric intelligence differences.

Spearman and Thurstone: *g* and friends

Away from popular polemic on psychometric intelligence differences (e.g. Howe 1997) and accounts in introductory psychology textbooks (e.g. Gleitman *et al.* 1999), there is more agreement about the psychometric structure of intelligence differences than there is dissent. Gould (1981) made much of Thurstone's finding several Primary Mental Abilities (PMAs) in opposition to Spearman's monolithic *g*, but this apparent disagreement dissolves to non-difference when investigated. As far back as 1939, H. J. Eysenck—in his first published paper—demonstrated that Spearman's *g* and Thurstone's PMAs were correct. How so? Eysenck examined the associations among 56 cognitive tests that Thurstone and his colleagues chose in order to measure different cognitive factors and had administered to 240 subjects. He applied an early factor-analytic procedure, developed by Burt, that extracted any general variance from the matrix of correlations and then apportioned variance among any group factors that might be found among the matrices of residuals. This is what Eysenck (1939, p. 272) found in Thurstone's own data:

> The first or general factor is responsible for 31 per cent of the variance. On eliminating its effects, there are six submatrices containing significant positive residuals. The group factors derived from these contribute about 2 to 6 per cent of the total variance only. Thus, the general factor is five times as significant as any other.

> Professor Spearman, in a paper read at the recent Reading conference, has maintained that Thurstone's table could be fitted by a two-factor analysis and that this procedure would reveal a single general factor. Thurstone, on the other hand, declares: "We cannot report any general common factor in Spearman's sense in the 56 tests that have been analysed." This is rather surprising, since, in selecting the tests, "special emphasis was laid on those tests which are used as measures of intelligence." Now his Table III does, as a matter of fact, show a 'general common factor in Spearman's sense', i.e., a column of saturation coefficients, all positive, and larger than those in any other column; and its subsequent disappearance is plainly an inevitable result of his method of rotation: this aims, not only at abolishing negative saturations, but also at maximising the *zeros in every column*, even where the saturations are large and positive throughout. No general factor could survive such a procedure. An analysis by Burt's procedure appears to reconcile the two conclusions: for, with Spearman, we discover a general factor, accountable for more of the total variance than any other, and with Thurstone we discover a number of group-factors having a clear psychological meaning.

The general factor in Eysenck's (1939) analysis accounted for 31% of the test score variance but, in fact, 57% of the common factor variance, a similar proportion to that found in the above examination of the WAIS-R battery. The compromise between multiple factors and *g*—appreciated at such an early stage by Burt and Eysenck—was the late-ripening fruit of the next 60 years of psycho-metric research. By the 1980s there were, on the face of it, several viable models of psychometric intelligence differences that did not appear to be reconcilable: Spearman's (1904, 1927) *g*; Thurstone's (1938) Primary Mental Abilities; Guilford's (1956, 1967) 'structure of intellect' with 120 separate abilities; Burt (1940) and P. E. Vernon's (1950, revised in 1961) models that recognized group as well as general factors; and the Cattell–Horn (Horn and Cattell 1966; Horn 1994) model that recognized primary and secondary factors but did not postulate a superordinate *g*. These models are summarized by Gustafsson (1984) and Carroll (1993), and their independent successes in unifying these only-superficially different models brings the story nearly up to date with the psychometric structure of intelligence differences.

Hierarchies of human mental ability differences

Gustafsson (1984) advanced the study of the structure of mental abilities from an exploratory to an hypothesis-testing exercise. Employing confirmatory factor analysis he examined the psychometric structure of 13 tests of ability and 3 of achievement in 981 Swedish 11-year-olds. Figure 1.2 shows the hierarchical model that provided the best fit to these data. Gustafsson referred to 'this unifying model' (p. 193) and summarized its characteristics as follows:

> The Spearman, Thurstone, and Cattell–Horn models may, in a structural sense at least, be viewed as subsets of the HILI [Hierarchical, LISREL-based] model: the Spearman model takes into account variance from the third-order factor; the Thurstone model takes into account first-order variance; and the Cattell–Horn model takes into account both first- and second-order variance. The Vernon model comes close to the proposed model: the *g*-factor is included in both models, and at the second-order level v:ed [Vernon's (1950) verbal–educational factor)] closely corresponds to Gc [crystallised intelligence], and k:m [Vernon's spatial–mechanical factor] corresponds to Gv [general visualisation].

Perhaps the only well-known model of psychometric intelligence differences that found no support in this model was Guilford's (1967) 'structure of intellect', which was posited upon there being orthogonal first-order factors. Carroll (1993, p. 59) agreed and called Guilford's model 'fundamentally defective'.

There are some important features defining Gustafsson's (1984) model of psycho-metric intelligence differences, apart from the fact that it integrates most of the then-extant, apparently contradictory models. It confirms the existence of factors of different degrees of generality, especially a very general factor. Note, too, that the third-order G factor (Spearman's *g*) has a loading of 1.0 on the second-order factor named Gf (fluid intelligence), indicating their being identical. Moreover, the influence of the general factors at times far outweighs the first-order factors in terms of their explanatory power. For example, look at the number series and letter grouping tests in Fig. 1.2. They appear to be accounted for principally by

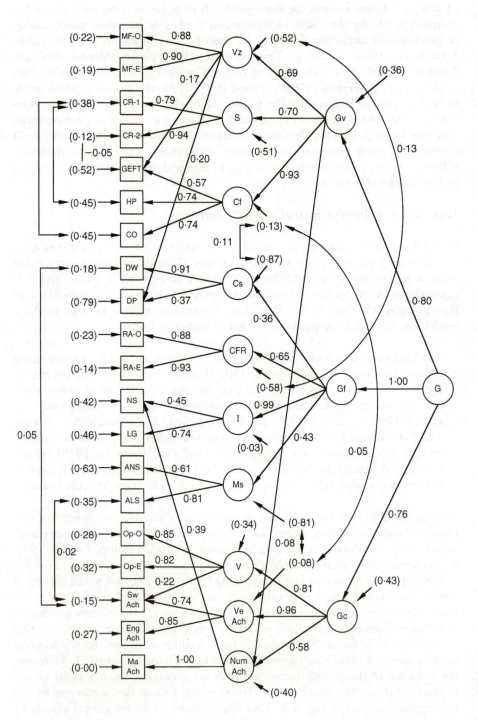

individual differences in the first-order (Thurstonian) factor *I* (induction), but following the trail further up the hierarchy shows that individual differences in *I* have a 0.99 loading on Gf which, in turn, is perfectly correlated with *g*. Thus individual differences in these two tests are explained largely by the most general (G) variance and the lower-order factors contribute only trivial amounts of non-*g*-based variance. The physical proximity of the first-order factors to the tests themselves in the diagram can easily obscure this important result. A further feature of Gustafsson's (1984) model is that, below the level of the third-order factor *g*, there are broad, group factors related to verbal abilities on the one hand and more spatial–visualization abilities on the other.

That's enough of the points that can be made with illustrative single studies. Attention turns now to the magnum opus of Carroll (1993). He collected the correlation matrices of over 450 important datasets involving mental ability test scores and subjected them to a consistent method of exploratory factor analysis. Briefly, he used principal factors analysis, and analysis of the scree slope (and other criteria) to determine the number of factors. Orthogonal rotation solutions were inspected to discover whether an oblique solution was required to achieve simple structure. If so, the correlations among the oblique factors were subjected to a further factor analysis to discover the factors at the next level. This was continued until oblique rotation no longer appeared to be necessary. No analyses were carried out beyond the third level. With this stage complete the solutions were subjected to Schmid–Leiman orthogonalization.

These data sets were selected from a starting number of over 1500, and were considered to be of the best quality (e.g. those using three or more dissimilar variables to measure a given higher-order factor) and to be relatively broad in their sampling of abilities. According to Carroll (1993, p. 78), 'it represents all or nearly all of the more important and classic factor-analytic investigations of the past fifty years or more, as well as numerous others of potential interest'. These included datasets from the laboratories of Thurstone and Guilford. The

Fig. 1.2 A structure of mental abilities derived from confirmatory factor analysis. *Test abbreviations*: MF-O, MF-E, metal folding (odd and even items); CR-1, CR-2, card rotation (parts 1 and 2); GEFT, group embedded figures test; HP, hidden patterns; CO, copying; DW, disguised words; DP, disguised pictures; RA-O, RA-E, Raven progressive matrices (odd and even items); NS, number series; LG, letter grouping; ANS, auditory number span; ALS, auditory letter span; Op-O, Op-E, opposites (odd and even items); Sw Ach, Swedish achievement; Eng Ach, English achievement; Ma Ach, mathematics achievement. *First-order factor abbreviations*: Vz, visualization; S, spatial orientation; Cf, flexibility of closure; Cs, speed of closure; CFR, cognition of figural relations; I, induction; Ms, memory span; V, vocabulary; Ve Ach, verbal achievement; Num Ach, numerical achievement. *Second-order factor abbreviations*: Gv, general visualization; Gf, fluid intelligence; Gc, crystallized intelligence. *Third-order factor abbreviation*: G, general intelligence. Numbers beside the arrows represent parameter estimates for a well-fitting model. The square of the number represents the variance shared by the two variables linked by the arrow. Arrows without origins and numbers in parentheses represent unaccounted-for variance (test-specific and error variance). Note the perfect link between the third-level G factor and the second-level Gf factor, and its subsequent very high association with induction. Redrawn from Gustafsson (1984).

subject samples in the studies were diverse: from infants to old people, from college students to the learning disabled and physically and mentally ill.

From the datasets that were employed, 459 analyses produced factors interpreted as 'General abilities (this includes factors interpreted as *g*, Gf, Gc at 1st, 2nd, and 3rd orders, as well as miscellaneous factors of cognitive development, style and learning ability' (Carroll 1993, p. 138). Thus, general variance, reflecting the overlap in performance rankings on even quite diverse mental abilities, appeared almost everywhere. In order of their numbers of appearances, more specific factors were extracted related to the following ability domains: visual perception, language, memory, reasoning, idea production (of words, ideas, figural creations), mental speed, number, knowledge and achievement, psychomotor abilities, and auditory discrimination. Other factors were extracted less frequently.

The higher-order structure of human mental abilities that emerged from Carroll's (1993) many analyses is shown in Fig. 1.3. Carroll required three strata to describe mental ability test score variance. At the top and most general level—Stratum III—appeared general test score variance—Spearman's *g*—reflecting the fact that mental abilities show near-universal positive correlations. Stratum II contained a number of correlated group factors. Each group factor comprised associations among several or many specific abilities found at Stratum I. To demonstrate the generality of the Stratum III general cognitive factor (which Carroll named G), here are its median loadings from *first*-order factors, in decreasing order: induction = 0.57, visualization = 0.57, quantitative reasoning = 0.51, verbal ability = 0.49, flexibility of closure = 0.45, numerical facility = 0.45, associative memory = 0.43, word fluency = 0.43, speed of closure = 0.42, sequential reasoning = 0.41, spatial relations = 0.40, ideational fluency = 0.38, originality = 0.37, lexical knowledge = 0.37, perceptual speed = 0.37, memory span = 0.36, sensitivity to problems = 0.34, mechanical knowledge = 0.26, and reaction time = –0.08. Thus *g* contains substantial loadings from many diverse, important human mental abilities. Inevitably, the *g* (or G) factor derived from different data sets is coloured by the tests that went into its derivation. This reminds us that general intelligence is a finding, albeit a surprising and important one, but not an identifiable thing (P. E. Vernon 1961). This caution notwithstanding, the *g* factors from quite different-looking sets of mental abilities correlate very highly (Jensen 1998*a*), indicating that such shared variance does not arise from very different sources in different studies.

A feel for the content of each of the second-order factors in Carroll's (1993) analysis may be gained from Fig. 1.3. Reasoning plays a large part in Gf (fluid intelligence). Carroll characterized Gc (crystallized intelligence) as 'a type of broad mental ability that develops through the "investment" of general intelligence into learning through education and experience' (p. 599). Language skills play a sizeable part in this factor, as do various types of knowledge. These two second-order factors are correlated—both load highly on the Stratum III factor G—and at times Carroll was unable to separate them at the second level, resulting in a hybrid factor. Progressing along and inspecting the other *correlated* factors at Stratum II there are many human cognitive abilities that, in cognitive science

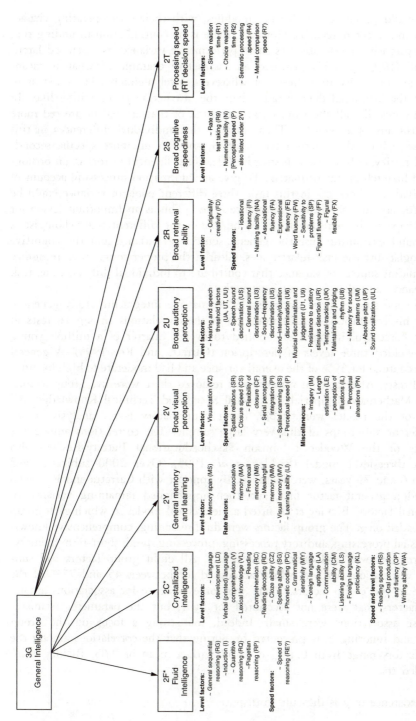

Fig. 1.3 'The Structure of Cognitive Abilities' according to Carroll, who analysed over 450 extant data sets involving diverse cognitive functions using a consistent method of higher-order factor analysis to discover their structure. The three-stratum model has Spearman's *g* at the highest level with group factors between that and narrower ability factors. Redrawn from Carroll (1993).

terms, would be viewed as distinct modules, with their own operating characteristics and research agendas. However, there is no contradiction in finding that these apparently diverse abilities share performance variance, as discussed later.

Carroll (1993, p. 623) provided an instructive example of what it means to conceive of ability in a three-, or whatever-, level hierarchy. He asked us to consider the ideational fluency task where the instruction is something like, 'In three minutes, list all the things you can think of that are red or are red more often than any other colour'. Then consider that individual differences in this task load 0.5 on the Stratum III factor G, and 0.5 on more specific second- (general retrieval ability) and first-order (ideational fluency) factors in an orthogonalized hierarchical factor matrix. To give an information processing account of the individual differences in this task, three different pools of variance could be addressed, not just the task performance *in toto*. This is an important lesson for future chapters. If there are faults to be found, the differential psychologist is often found examining just the general sources of variance and the cognitive psychologist just the task-related ones. Clearly, the proper course is to recognize all significant sources of variance that contribute to individual differences on task performance, and then to investigate each.

Large-scale studies since Carroll's (1993) massive integrating study generally support his conclusions. An examination of the correlations among 16 tests in the Air Force Qualifying Test, applied to over a quarter of a million young adults, yielded three levels of description (Carretta and Ree 1995). A general factor accounted for 59% of the overall variance and had moderate to high loadings from all tests. After general variance was removed there were five group factors: Verbal, Mathematical, Spatial, Perceptual Speed and Technical Knowledge. All aspects of the model were stable, using confirmatory factor analysis, across the different subgroups of this very large sample. The correlations among the 16 tests of the Woodcock–Johnson Psychoeducational Battery-Revised also fitted a three-level model (Bickley *et al*. 1995). Over 2000 subjects, aged between 6 and 79 years, were included. By contrast with Carretta and Ree, who extracted a general factor first, and then apportioned remaining variance to orthogonal factors, Bickley *et al*. fitted a hierarchical model in which each group factor loaded on *g*. The group factors were fluid reasoning, comprehensive knowledge, visual processing, auditory processing, processing speed, short-term memory, long-term retrieval, and quantitative ability. All eight group factors had substantial associations with *g*, which accounted for between 45 and 77% of the variance in the group factors. There was some evidence for associations among group factors that were not accounted for by *g*, but the parameter estimates for these associations were small. Indeed, too strong a focus on the group factors, and ignoring *g*, is prevented by noting that the correlations among the group factors range from 0.471 to 0.757 with a mean of 0.63. Bickley *et al*. concluded that,

the existence of *g* is difficult to dispute. . . .

many alternative models are possible within the boundaries of this three-stratum theory (Carroll 1993; Gustafsson 1984; Undheim and Gustafsson 1987). In fact, one of the reasons it is such a useful and appealing model is its flexibility. As a point of reference, however, this study provides compelling evidence that the three-stratum theory may form a parsimonious model of intelligence. The fact that it is grounded in a strong foundation of vast, previous research also lends strong support for the acceptance of the model . . .
this model of intelligence provides a sound theoretical [I should beg to differ] and empirical base to continue research in the field of mental abilities. (pp. 324–326)

It is hoped that some semi-settled consensus around different levels of ability can obviate otiose arguments about contradictory descriptive models of human intelligence differences. The issue cannot be settled definitively, because there is no guarantee that factor analysis can deliver constructs either at the 'correct' level or validly cut the as-yet fairly seamless robe of test performance differences. Nevertheless, there is enough stable structure across models of ability differences to begin exploring the causes of ability at different levels of generality. Such a consensus view was available over half a century ago and a perverse delight in scientists' emphasizing their differences rather than working to find agreements appears to have let it slip. For example, Burt's (1940) four-factor solution to human ability differences was very similar to, perhaps even more general than, the one that attracts some agreement now:

Four kinds of [mental ability] factors may be formally distinguished – (i) general, (ii) group or bipolar, (iii) specific, and (iv) error factors, i.e. those possessed by all the traits, by some of the traits, by one trait always, or by one trait on the occasion of its measurement only . . .

From the four-factor theorem (as it may be termed) all the familiar factor theories may be derived. (p. 249–250)

That remains largely true. Vernon (1950), too, had recommended a hierarchical model of mental ability differences from *g* through major and minor group factors to specific factors, although he later revised this (1960). With such a model he presaged current thinking, and did much at the time to reconcile British, *g*-oriented models with American models that ignored *g*.

What the hierarchies of mental ability differences do not achieve

A psychometric model of human intelligence differences—even one whose shape is converging convincingly to a series of more or less general factors—is not an external realization of anything in our heads. It is a record of the pools of inter-individual variability in the performance of mental tasks. It is just a system of classification and, as Burt (1940) warned,

So far as it seeks to be strictly scientific, psychology must beware of supposing that these principles of classification can forthwith be treated as 'factors in the mind,' e.g. as 'primary abilities' or as 'mental powers' or 'energies'. (p. 251) [It is interesting to see Burt's aiming criticism equally and specifically at Thurstone and Spearman.]

Similarly, Vernon (1961) was concerned that,

the best-established factors, such as Thurstone's, represent the external qualities or materials of the tests—verbal, numerical, spatial, etc.—rather than central mental functions. It may be that statistical analysis alone is incapable of yielding these more fundamental functional components of the mind. (pp. 138–139)

To repeat, *g* is an empirical result—a robust and intriguing one—and the same may be said for all of the other factors, at different levels in the hierarchy. There is no art to read the mind's construction in confirmatory or exploratory factor analytic diagrams. Nevertheless, these results do assist the search for the causes of human intelligence differences. They insist that there are sources of variance that are more or less general. There is no need to hunt for a specific series of mental mechanisms for every conceivable mental task. On the other hand, the hierarchical models can make life quite complicated. When investigating associations between psychometric test scores and cognitive and/or biological variables researchers must ask whether the correlation arises because of the general or specific sources of variance captured by the mental ability test scores (Stankov and Roberts 1997). A passage by Jensen (1985) forcefully captures the need for the research addressed by later chapters:

For some time there has been a growing consensus among differential psychologists that the traditional methodology of studying mental ability in terms of classical psychometrics, factor analysis, and external validation, over the last 75 years or so, has accumulated an impressive amount of solid empirical facts on the range, correlational structure, and practical consequences of IDs [individual differences] in ability, but has not contributed to the further development of theoretical explanations of the main abilities identified by factor analysis of psychometric tests. In the traditional framework, explanations of IDs have not advanced beyond statements that, to put it in the simplest form, individuals A and B differ in performance on task X, because X is highly saturated (or loaded) with ability factor Y, and A and B differ in ability factor Y. But ability Y is a hypothetical or mathematical construct that is not invariant to the method of factor analysis used to identify it. There is unfortunately nothing in the raw psychometric data that can compel the factor theorist to explain A's and B's difference in performance on task X in terms of their differing on factor Y. Factor rotation could displace the IDs variance on factor Y and divide it between two other factors P and Q, so that the difference between A and B would be attributed to their differing in factors

P and Q. And factors P and Q would be different from factor Y, according
to the usual method of psychologically describing factors in terms of the characteristics of those content-homogeneous tests that show the highest loadings
on the factor. This, in essence, is the theoretical blind alley that differential
psychologists find themselves in if they confine their methodology to traditional
psychometric tests and factor analysis. The measurements and methods of
psychometry reveal only the end products of mental activity, and, by themselves, cannot expose the processes between problem presentation and a subject's
response.

g is hardly more than a tautology, not an explanation, as the emergence of
the *g* factor merely reflects our original observation that scores on all the tests
are positively correlated with one another. (pp. 59–60)

THE STABILITY OF HUMAN MENTAL ABILITY
DIFFERENCES

Interest in the mechanisms underlying human mental ability differences is not
predicated on their stability. Other domains of human variability are unstable,
and yet still attract cognitive and biological reductionist research. There is much
interest in the mechanisms of, say, moods and changes of moods, and variability
is their chief characteristic (Gold *et al.* 1995; Russell and Barrett 1999). Traumatic
brain damage, dementias, psychoactive drugs, cardiac bypass surgery, and a regi-
ment of other causes can effect permanent and/or temporary cognitive decline.
The stability of mean levels of mental abilities is discussed in Chapter 8, which
is devoted to ageing and psychometric intelligence. Here, the stability of individual differences is addressed. If there is considerable stability of individual
differences in mental abilities across the human lifespan, questions follow about
the sources of both the permanence and change.

Whatever period of human life is examined, there is moderate to high stability
of individual differences in mental abilities. Table 1.3 lists some key studies
reporting the stability of psychometric intelligence test score differences from
age 2 to almost 80 years. The table demonstrates that stability of mental ability
differences may be found within childhood, from childhood to adulthood, from
young to mid-adulthood, and in old age.

An unusually long follow-up study of mental ability test differences was the
repeat testing in 1998 of 101 subjects who originally took part in the 1932 Scottish
Mental Survey (Deary *et al.*, 2000). On June 1, 1932, all Scottish children attend-
ing school who were born in 1921 sat the Moray House Test (*N* = 87,498). This
survey was carried out under the auspices of the Scottish Council for Research in
Education (1933), its aim being to obtain data about the whole distribution of the
intelligence of Scottish pupils from one end of the scale to the other.

The test comprised a range of question types including: following directions,
same–opposites, word classification, analogies, practical items, reasoning, proverbs,

Table 1.3 Summary of some key studies of the stability of individual differences in psychometric intelligence (from Deary et al., 2000)

Study	Mean initial age (years)	Mean follow-up age (years)	Correlation	Test used
Humphreys (1989)	2	9	0.56	Wechsler Preschool and Primary Scale of Intelligence and Wechsler Intelligence Scale for Children
Kangas and Bradway (1971)	9	15	0.47	Stanford Binet
	2	15	0.78	
	4	42	0.41	
	14	42	0.68	
	30	42	0.77	
Eichorn et al. (1981)	17–18	36–48	0.83 (men)	Stanford Binet or Wechsler Bellevue (initial) and Wechsler Adult Intelligence Scale (follow-up)
			0.77 (women)	
Plassman et al. (1995)	Approx. 18	Mid-60s	0.46	Army General Classification Test (initial) and Telephone Interview for Cognitive Status (follow-up)
Owens (1966)	19	50	0.79	Army Alpha
	50	61	0.92	
	19	61	0.78	
Letz et al. (1996)	Approx. 20	40	0.86	General Technical score from the Army Classification Battery
Nisbet (1957)	22	47	0.48	Simplex Group Test
Schwartzman et al. (1987)	25	65	0.78	Revised Examination 'M'
Tuddenham et al. (1968)	30[a]	43	0.64–0.79	Army General Classification Test
Mortensen and Kleven (1993)	50	60	0.94	Wechsler Adult Intelligence Scale
	60	70	0.91	
	50	70	0.90	
Deary et al. (2000)	11	77	0.63	Moray House Test

[a]Subjects were probably seven years younger than this, making the follow-up interval 20 rather than 13 years.

arithmetic, spatial items, mixed sentences, cypher decoding, and a few other items. One thousand children from the survey were individually tested on the Stanford Revision of the Binet–Simon scale. The Moray House Test correlated 0.8 with the Binet–Simon scale, demonstrating criterion validity. Deary and colleagues (2000) established contact with 101 people who took part in the 1932 Survey and read-ministered the same test on June 1, 1998, exactly 66 years to the day after the original diet. The raw correlation between the two testing sessions was 0.63. The people retested were restricted in variance when compared with the original population (all of whom had been tested and their data were still available), and the corrected correlation between the two sessions was 0.73. Therefore, in relatively healthy individuals, free from neurological damage, there is considerable stability of mental ability test score differences across almost the entire human lifespan. Data presented in Chapter 8 suggest that verbal ability test scores are more stable across long periods than are performance/spatial ability type test scores, probably because the latter are more sensitive to factors that damage neurons.

The origins of both stability and change in mental ability levels are sought in reductionistic research. Contrary to easy but mistaken assumptions, genetic sources can affect individual differences in cognitive change, as well as in cognitive stability (Chapter 9; Plomin *et al.* 1997). Moreover, aspects of the environment can contribute to stability as well as to change.

THE UTILITY OF HUMAN MENTAL ABILITY DIFFERENCES

Tests of mental ability were originally devised for a practical purpose, namely to identify those children that might not benefit from standard schooling in France. Binet's (1905) test and his account of it were not motivated by theory. Most of that famous publication merely described the tests' items and their administration.

> Binet and Simon's 1905 articles had been written specifically to supply guidance for an educational commission appointed by the Paris Minister of Public Instruction in 1904 to set standards for 'special class' admissions. And while acknowledging that this was actually 'a work of administration, not a work of science,' Binet nevertheless took it seriously. (Zenderland 1998, p. 94)

Zenderland's (1998) account of the early years of ability testing details the conster-nating problem of diagnosing 'feeble-mindedness' at a time when schooling was newly compulsory. An American teacher-turned-psychologist, H. H. Goddard, was responsible for introducing the Binet test to the USA. He had tried medical, sociological, and experimental–psychological approaches to diagnosing mental handicap and found them all wanting. Then,

> his most provocative find was a short list of mental tests given to him by a Belgian doctor and special educator, Ovide Decroly. The tests had been published three years earlier by Alfred Binet . . . (Zenderland 1998, p. 92)

Fuelled by Goddard's energetic promulgation, mental tests caught on because they were so useful,

> they tell us in an hour what otherwise it takes us six months or a year to find out; and they tell us more accurately and consistently. (Zenderland 1998, p.102)

There were several hundred scientific papers on the Binet tests by the time of the First World War. The development of the Army alpha and beta tests for World War I personnel selection brought mental testing to over one million men. Zenderland covered in detail the misapplication of the Binet tests, much of it appreciated by Goddard himself after early overenthusiasm.

Despite mental test usage having a history that makes painful reading, the arenas of education and work remained the foci for the predictive validity of psychometric ability test scores. Neisser *et al.* (1996) declared IQ-type tests to be useful predictors in schools, in the work place, and in society more widely:

> The relationship between test scores and school performance seems to be ubiquitous. Wherever it has been studied, children with high scores on tests of intelligence tend to learn more of what is taught in school than their lower-scoring peers. There may be styles of teaching and methods of instruction that will decrease this correlation [typically about 0.5], but none that consistently eliminates it has yet been found . . .

> Scores on intelligence tests predict various measures of job performance: supervisor ratings, work samples, etc. Such correlations, which typically lie between $r = .30$ and $r = .50$, are partly restricted by the limited reliability of those measures themselves. They become higher when r is statistically corrected for this unreliability: in one survey of relevant studies (Hunter 1983), the mean of the corrected correlations was .54 . . .

> Psychometric intelligence is negatively correlated with certain socially undesirable outcomes . . . The correlations for most 'negative outcome' variables are typically smaller than .20 (pp. 82–83)

Summaries of the predictive validity of psychometric intelligence test scores tend, as above, to focus on school, work, and society. Further support for the above associations can be found in *The bell curve* (Herrnstein and Murray 1994), in which the predictive validity of the Armed Forces Qualification Test was studied in thousands of people from the white population in the USA tested between 14 and 22 years. They were followed up over a decade later when many educational, work, and social data were collected. Although effect sizes were typically not high, there were significant effects of ability level on poverty, schooling, education, marriage, welfare dependency, children's health, and crime. Invariably, the direction of association was such that higher-ability test scorers had better outcomes. These differences were maintained after controlling statistically for parental social class. The so-called 'ultimate validity' of mental ability tests is their significant, though modest, association with survival in adulthood and old age (Deeg *et al.* 1990; O'Toole and Stankov 1992; Korten *et al.* 1999).

Hunter and Hunter (1984) presented a meta-analysis of thousands of studies examining predictors of job success. Tests of general mental ability predicted success in almost all jobs studied, had coefficients that were highly stable across different studies for any given test–job pairing, were best at predicting cognitively complex jobs, and,

> if general cognitive ability alone is used as a predictor, the average validity across all jobs is .54 for a training success criterion and .45 for a job proficiency criterion. (p. 81)

To put the value of mental ability test scores in context as predictors of job success, here are the relative validity coefficients for some of the commonest hiring criteria (Hunter and Hunter 1984):

- Mental ability composite = 0.53
- Job tryout = 0.44
- Biographical inventory = 0.37
- Reference check = 0.26
- Experience = 0.18
- Interview = 0.14
- Training and experience ratings = 0.13
- Academic achievement = 0.11
- Education = 0.10
- Interest = 0.10
- Age = –0.01

The authors encouraged the use of proven additional predictors for jobs in which they could be shown to possess incremental validity. However, using any currently-studied predictor instead of mental ability tests across entry-level selection as a whole was likely, they insisted, to involve massive costs (billions of dollars when applied to the US economy as a whole), arising from lowered productivity. The effect sizes and conclusions largely stood unchanged when Schmidt and Hunter (1998) updated these analyses to include almost a century's research findings in job selection:

> Today, the validity of different personnel measures can be determined with the aid of 85 years of research. The most well-known conclusion from this research is that for hiring employees without previous experience in the job the most valid predictor of future performance and learning is general mental ability ([GMA], i.e., intelligence or general cognitive ability) . . . GMA can be measured using commercially available tests. However, many other measures can also contribute to the overall validity of the selection process. These include,

for example, measures of conscientiousness and personal integrity, structured employment interviews, and (for experienced workers) job knowledge and work sample tests. (p. 262)

In this update, involving the review of a massive research literature, the univariate predictive validity coefficient for GMA tests and job performance was 0.51, by comparison with 0.02 for graphology. Although other predictors of job performance and job training were quite good, Schmidt and Hunter (1998) considered mental ability tests to be especially valuable because they were applicable across all job types, by contrast with other measures which were often applicable in specific situations or jobs, they were very low in cost and time to the employer and interviewee, had massively more research evidence than other predictors, and had a better theoretical background than other predictors. Combining tests of mental ability with any one of work sample tests, integrity tests, or a structured interview achieved validity coefficients above 0.6. Gottfredson (1997) also reviewed research in which mental test scores are used successfully to predict job success. In addition, beyond the scope of this account, she addressed the causes for this association with a particular focus on the cognitive complexity levels met in different workplaces.

The above fields all concern psychometric intelligence differences as a predictor variable. There is also a large usage of mental ability tests as outcome variables, especially in medicine. In this area mental ability test scores are used as indicators of brain integrity that are differentially responsive to brain insults and improving treatments as caused by, to name just a few examples,

- Cardiac bypass surgery (Selnes *et al.* 1999)
- Vitamin and mineral supplementation (Benton and Roberts 1988)
- Lead exposure (Fulton *et al.* 1987)
- Very premature birth (Stewart *et al.* 1999)
- Brain irradiation for childhood malignancy (Silber *et al.* 1992)
- Intestinal worm infestation (Watkins and Pollitt 1997)
- General surgery (Moller *et al.* 1998)
- Severe hypoglycaemia caused by insulin overtreatment in diabetes (Austin and Deary 1999)
- Cushing's syndrome (Whelan *et al.* 1980)
- High blood pressure (Waldstein *et al.* 1991)
- Major depression (Sackeim *et al.* 1992)
- Head injury (Brooks *et al.* 1980; Teasdale and Engberg 1997).

The continued and increasing usage of mental ability tests in practical settings, such as medicine and personnel selection, reflects the fact that tests are found to be useful summaries of brain functioning. Although omnibus tests are used frequently, that does not mean that more specific abilities, in some circumstances, would not be better predictors or outcomes. However, *g* is often the best predictor (Gottfredson 1997; Jensen 1998*a*). Note that mental tests are not invariably employed as stable indicators of outcomes. The role as a measure of trait-like competence is balanced by a role in which mental tests are seen as state-like indicators of performance in instances where brain function is changing, such as dementia. What is important, as first discovered by Binet, is that hotchpotch tests of mental ability (not infrequently and not least because they reflect *g*; Jensen 1998*a*) are useful, being related to success in many aspects of life, and being indicators of brain impairments.

Objections to the use and/or utility of mental ability tests may be made on at least four grounds:

- *Objection*: mental tests do not account for all of the variance, or even the majority, in the variables they predict. *Answer*: that is a straw man. Where mental tests are successful in prediction, they are often the best single variables. The social sciences are not an arena in which single variables fully or even largely determine others.

- *Objection*: mental tests are at times used inappropriately and/or for objection-able purposes. *Answer*: like tools from potato knives to nuclear power tech-nology, they may be put to humanitarian or misanthropic purposes. A common worry about misuse, which combines this and the previous objections, is that an erroneous value judgement will be formed about a single person on the basis of an ability test score in a case where the test is at best a moderate predictor of the criterion variable. Research typically indicates modest effect sizes between tests and outcomes. Such associations would be meaningful if applied to a large sample of people, but not very helpful or fair when applied to any one person. For example, Hunter and Hunter (1984) computed that the cost to the USA of not using, or ignoring the results of, cognitive test scores in workplace selection would be a sum equal to total corporate profits, or about 20% of the federal budget. Gottfredson (1997, pp. 130–132) explains in clear language why even quite small effect sizes matter when applied to decision making with groups of people, e.g. in hiring situations.

- *Objection*: specific tests are sometime better predictors. *Answer*: fine, if there is a proven, better test then it should be used. For example, psychomotor tests, alone or in combination with general cognitive ability tests, can improve pre-dictive validity for selection in some manual jobs (Hunter and Hunter 1984).

- *Objection*: if people's abilities can change with illness or medication, that contradicts the stability of psychometric intelligence differences. *Answer*: not at all. Psychometric ability test scores are approximate indicators of brain function. For most healthy people there will be considerable stability in their cognitive performance, within certain limits given aspects of both the situation and their mental state. That stability is a reflection of the brain's similarity in performance across time. When the brain's efficiency changes, through illnesses such as dementia or treatments such as cardiac bypass surgery, mental tests are expected to be sensitive to the new level of brain function. The real surprise, and further usefulness of ability tests, is that some indicators of ability remain stable indicators of 'pre-morbid' mental ability in the face of some brain insults (O'Carroll 1995).

ENVIRONMENTAL AND GENETIC CONTRIBUTIONS TO HUMAN MENTAL ABILITY DIFFERENCES

If mental ability differences are substantially heritable then there is a warrant to investigate which genes and their products relate to ability differences and how they do so. By 'substantially heritable', perhaps any estimated heritability above 20–30% will do. There is no need to be precise about the heritability level before pursuing those putative origins of human ability differences that involve paths from genes to behaviours. If there is any heritability at all there is investigative work to be done. The obverse is true, too; so-called heritability studies are informative about the relative contribution from the environment. Heritability estimates below 100% warrant the search for environmental mechanisms of mental ability differences. Two further comments are necessary. First, genetic contributions to ability differences do not mean that these are lifelong, or unchangeable; the example of phenylketonuria, the treatable genetic cause of mental handicap, is a well-worn and effective counter-example to such an error. And evidence from adoption and twin studies suggests that genetic contributions to psychometric intelligence change over the lifespan (Loehlin *et al.* 1989; Pedersen *et al.* 1992; Alarcon *et al.* 1998). Second, genetic contributions to mental ability test score variance do not equate to the biology of intelligence. Environment is biology too, in two senses. Environment is biology in the trivial sense that all effects of the environment (so-called social, psychological, and biological effects) on mental abilities must be caused by changes in the biology of the body that affect the brain's functions. Environment is biology in a less trivial sense in that drugs, illnesses, traumas, toxins, and foods that affect mental ability differences are biological effects and are potentially informative about the causes of ability differences. Only one example is needed to make the point. Experimentally altering the blood glucose concentration of a person has widespread and entirely reversible mental-ability-lowering effects (Deary 1998).

A book such as the present volume, devoted to furthering the understanding of any cognitive and biological causes of mental ability differences, could proceed with or without any heritability being demonstrated, because there would still be mechanisms to uncover. Therefore, the purpose of this section is to indicate in broad terms whether the genetic–environmental studies of human ability differences give leads to follow. Traditional behaviour–genetic (–environmental) studies of ability differences do not offer much information about the brain mechanisms of mental ability differences. (That is why this discussion appears here rather than in the chapters which are devoted to mechanisms.) They can point to some heritability, but not to which regions of which chromosomes are responsible. This latter, more interesting contribution is the province of molecular genetic studies which are discussed in Chapter 9.

Behaviour genetic studies of mental ability differences use what are termed experiments of society (adoption) and of nature (twinning) to estimate the relative contributions of genes and environment (Bouchard 1998; McGuffin and Martin 1999). An especially accessible summary of the genetic–environmental literature on general and specific cognitive abilities is provided by Plomin *et al.* (1997). Family studies might indicate that members of the same biological family have similarities in mental ability scores and that these are proportional to their shared genes, but in this type of study the degree of genetic likeness is confounded with the environments shared by the people in question. Studies of twins capitalize on the fact that monozygotic twins have the same genes whereas dizygotic twins share on average 50% of their genes. Therefore, comparing the correlations of mental ability scores in pairs of monozygotic and dizygotic twins can suggest whether or not variation in a phenotypic measure has some genetic bases. Care must be taken in such studies not to confound genetic and environmental similarity. It is quite possible that monozygotic twins, because they look more similar, might have more similar environments, perhaps as a result of being treated in similar ways. These could be a partial or total cause of higher phenotypic correlations in monozygotic over dizygotic twins. It is often assumed that the environments of the two types of twins are the same with respect to similarity, although in some studies care is taken to measure the environment and in other types of study it is not normally a confounding variable. Examples of the latter, i.e. reports which are not so affected by the equal environments assumption, are studies of twins who were separated in early life and studies of adopted children. An additional tool available to the investigator of environmental and genetic sources of variance in mental ability differences is a set of statistical model-fitting procedures. These allow the same genetic–environmental models to be tested competitively for goodness of fit in the different types of study mentioned above (Loehlin 1992).

Monozygotic twins show greater similarity than dizygotic twins on several psychological outcomes, including schizophrenia, autism, depression, attention deficit hyperactivity disorder, and mental ability test scores (McGuffin and Martin 1999). Data from twins reared together and apart suggest that the heritability of mental ability differences is between 50 and 70% (Plomin and Loehlin 1989). For example, the Minnesota Study of Twins Reared Apart examined Wechsler Adult Intelligence Scale, Raven's Matrices, and other mental ability test scores in monozygotic twins reared apart and compared them with monozygotic twins reared together (Bouchard *et al.* 1990). Especially for non-verbal mental tests, the two groups had similar correlation coefficients where twin pairs' scores were examined. They estimated the heritability of mental ability differences at about 70%. There was little evidence to support the possibilities that similarity in mental ability test scores was caused by similarity of rearing environments or by the amount of contact the twins had during their lives.

Bouchard (1998) summarized results from several types of behaviour genetic study concerning mental ability differences. Bouchard usefully explained the bases of the modelling techniques used to assess environmental and genetic contributions to mental ability differences. He considered, and largely refuted, some of the objections to results obtained from behaviour genetic–environmental studies. Five studies from 1937 to the 1990s tested monozygotic twins reared apart. The weighted average twin pair correlation was 0.75. Two studies examined dizygotic twins reared apart, both from the 1990s, and the weighted average twin pair correlation for mental test scores was 0.38. These data suggest a heritability of 0.76 (76%). Data concerning the similarities of unrelated people's mental abilities when reared together found that there is a correlation of 0.28 (nine studies, total N = 689) in childhood and 0.04 (four studies, total N = 398) in adulthood. Bouchard summarized thus:

> Genetic factors strongly influence the expression of general intelligence in adult populations. In addition, although common environmental influence on general intelligence clearly expresses itself in childhood, it appears to dissipate in adulthood. There are fewer comprehensive studies of special mental abilities, but here also the findings from various studies converge. Genetic factors strongly influence special mental abilities but less than for general intelligence. General intelligence, however, mediates much of the genetic variance found in special mental abilities and other genetic phenomena, such as inbreeding depression and the correlations between collateral relatives.
>
> These findings apply to the broad middle class in industrialized Western societies (the group from which most of the samples have been drawn). They should not be generalized beyond that population. (p. 272)

Readers are sometimes presented with two estimates of heritability proportions, namely narrow and broad heritability. Narrow heritability is that proportion of the variance in a measure that is thought to be caused by additive gene effects, those shared by parents and offspring. Broad heritability includes, in addition, non-additive genetic effects that are not shared by parents and offspring and are dependent on genetic background, such as dominance and epistasis effects. A meta-analysis of 212 studies on the heritability of mental ability differences suggested values of 34% and 48% for narrow and broad heritabilities, respectively (Devlin *et al.* 1997). These values indicate sufficiently interesting genetic contributions to begin a search for specific genetic influences employing molecular genetic techniques. Moreover, this study also demonstrated how sui-disant 'heritability' studies are often just as interesting concerning environmental contributions to mental test scores. Devlin and colleagues found that maternal environment, a neglected factor in many such studies, might contribute as much as 20% of the covariance between twins and 5% between siblings. Bouchard (1998) discussed alternative interpretations of these data, and McGue (1997) summarized the implications as follows:

> That the IQ debate now centres on whether IQ is 50% or 70% heritable is a remarkable indication of how the nature–nurture debate has shifted over the past two decades. The anti-hereditarian position that there are no genetic influences on IQ has crumbled for want of any empirical data that would support such a radical view. Equally remarkable is the increasingly dominant view that the major environmental influences on IQ occur within the first few years of life, or in the womb, and directly affect the development of the brain.

If there is specific and substantial environmental influence on mental abilities in early life, there is also some evidence that heritability is not constant throughout life and might increase in middle and old age. Data from the Colorado Adoption Project suggest that the heritabilities for verbal, spatial, perceptual speed, and memory abilities are higher at age 12 years than at 4 years (Alarcon *et al.* 1998). A combined adoption/twin study (the Swedish Adoption/Twin Study of Aging from the Swedish Twin Registry) examined mental test performances of old monozygotic and dizygotic twins who were reared together and apart (Pedersen *et al.* 1992). An interesting single result is that scores on the general factor correlated 0.78 in monozygotic twins reared apart (*N* = 45 pairs) and 0.80 in monozygotic twins reared together (*N* = 63 pairs). Heritability for the general ability factor (the first unrotated principal component derived from all mental test scores) was 81%, and about 58, 46, 58, and 38% for verbal, spatial, perceptual speed, and memory ability, respectively. There was evidence for non-additive genetic variance in the general ability factor, and in verbal ability and perceptual speed. These genetic and the environmental contributions were stable across the second half of life in both cross-sectional and longitudinal analyses (Finkel *et al.* 1996).

Monozygotic and dizygotic Swedish twins (the OctoTwin project from the Swedish Twin Registry) aged 80 years and older were tested on mental tests covering general ability and group factors of verbal, spatial, speed of processing, and memory abilities (Petrill *et al.* 1998). The model that fitted the data is shown in Fig. 1.4. A, C, and E are the commonly-used terms for, respectively, additive genetic sources of variance, common/shared (family-based) environmental sources of variance, and non-shared environmental variance (that which is not shared by full siblings; this term also contains error variance). The results indicate that additive genetic effects on general mental ability in what are termed old–old people rise to over 70% of the variance, and that the majority of the environmental contribution to general ability comes from non-shared environment. Verbal, speed, and spatial ability are closely linked with the general factor, and the independent additive genetic contribution to these group ability factors is quite small, except for memory. Spatial, speed, and memory factors have sizeable, non-shared environmental contributions that are independent of the general factor. The sample sizes for this study were modest (52 monozygotic twin pairs, 65 same-sex dizygotic), although the results, except for speed ability, were in close agreement with other studies of old twins. A larger study of Swedish twins aged 80 years and older (110 monozygotic pairs and 130 dizygotic same-sex twin pairs) found heritability estimates of 62% for general cognitive ability, and 55, 32, 62, and 52% for verbal, spatial, speed of processing, and memory abilities, respectively (McClearn *et al.* 1997). There is enough positive evidence, therefore, to look for the mechanisms of genetic contributions to cognitive ability levels, in old people especially, and also enough to target both general and specific ability factors. There is more about ageing and mental abilities in Chapter 8.

Some related leads for researchers interested in the bases of human ability differences were provided by Luo *et al.* (1994), who examined the performances

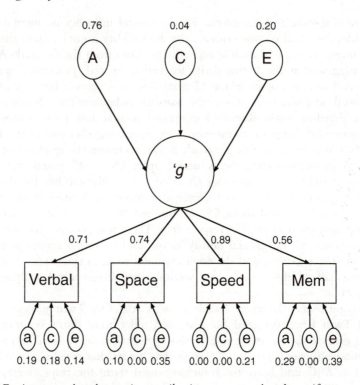

Fig. 1.4 Environmental and genetic contributions to general and specific mental ability factors in Swedish twins aged 80 years and older. *g* is the general factor from the mental ability test battery and there are verbal, spatial, speed, and memory group factors. The letter A (or a) represents contributions from additive genetic variance, C (c) represents shared (between-family) environment, and E (e) represents contributions from non-shared (within-family) environment and error. Numbers represent variance components. Redrawn from Petrill *et al.* (1998).

of 148 monozygotic and 135 same-sex dizygotic school-age twins from the Western Reserve Twin Project. They addressed two questions. Do genetic influences on test scores exclusively influence the *g* component of a mental test, or are there genetic influences on non-*g* aspects of mental tests? How similar is any common genetic influence on specific mental abilities to phenotypic *g*? Confirmatory factor analysis was used to structure the tests of the Wechsler Intelligence Scale for Children into a general factor common to all tests and to verbal, performance, and freedom-from-distraction group factors. The Specific Cognitive Abilities battery of tests was fitted to a similar nested structure with a general factor common to all tests and specific verbal, spatial, perceptual speed, and memory factors. There were genetic influences on the general factor and on the specific cognitive factors. The latter were orthogonal to the general factor. Shared environmental influences were also important. The implication for, say, molecular genetic researchers was that genes must be sought for both common and specific cognitive test variance. Chapter 9 describes how the same research team began this search (Petrill *et al.* 1996).

In a brief review of studies using the methods described above, Plomin and Petrill (1997) concluded that,

> Regardless of the precise estimate of heritability, the point is that genetic influence on IQ test scores is not only statistically significant, it is also substantial. It is rare in the behavioral sciences to explain 5% of the variance. For example, despite the interest in birth order, it accounts for less than 1% of the IQ variance. Finding that heredity accounts for 50% of the variance is a major discovery about intelligence. (p. 59)

These writers insist that this important discovery is just the beginning of the interesting questions that may be asked about the genetics of mental ability differences. There are questions still to be addressed about the relative heritabilities of different mental abilities (some aspects of memory differences appear to have quite low heritabilities; Thapar *et al.* 1994), including information processing indices (see Chapter 6), the different genetic contributions to mental abilities across the lifespan and the part played by genetics in cognitive changes, and the part played by genetics in the overlaps between mental ability differences in different areas of ability. Plomin and Petrill (1997) emphasized how informative genetic studies can be about contributions from different aspects of the environment.

In summary, it does not matter for present purposes what exact percentage of heritability obtains for mental ability differences. A slab of variance in mental ability differences is contributed by pathways that begin with genes, perhaps more so for some aspects of mental ability than others, and perhaps more so as people grow older. This distant link from DNA differences to differences on metal test scores is probably owed to many genes, their products, and their interactions. Heritability studies will not unravel these mechanisms, but molecular genetic studies might (or might not) eventually discover some, and the beginnings of such attempts are discussed in Chapter 9.

RÉSUMÉ

Chorney *et al.* (1998) brought together the themes covered in the present chapter, and viewed the collation as a mandate for research that 'looks down' on human intelligence differences:

> the most exciting direction for genetic research on complex traits such as *g* is to harness the power of molecular genetics to identify some of the genes responsible for this genetic influence ... The high heritability of *g*, its high reliability and stability, its key role in cognitive neuroscience, and its social importance as the best predictor of educational and occupational attainment make *g* a reasonable target for such a programme of research. (p. 159)

That short quotation serves as a good summary of the present chapter, with my insisting on emphasizing factors other than g also, and a foundation from which to explore causes. However, with respect to the authors' opinion that g is central to the concerns of cognitive neuroscientists, that may be hope rather than present reality. Cognitive neuroscience texts and research progress without much explicit mention of this important human characteristic.

Although there has been attention, here, to different levels of mental ability other than g, Carroll's (1997) resume of psychometric research on human intelligence differences harmonizes with broad themes developed above:

> Most experts agree that there *is* a general factor g on which human beings differ. It is measured to some degree by most tests of cognitive aptitude and achievement, but more accurately by tests designed to measure it. It corresponds to most people's conceptions of intelligence. It is quite stable over the life span, and properly constructed and administered IQ tests are not demonstrably biased against different social groups. It is substantially influenced by genetic factors, but also by environmental factors . . . there are many other cognitive abilities besides g. (p. 25)

The job of mapping the structure of psychometric intelligence differences is done to a sufficient degree. As in other areas of science, description must be followed by explanation. The task for the remainder of this book is to examine critically attempts to explain and understand human psychometric intelligence differences. Psychometric intelligence has predictive validity. Mental ability test score differences predict significant amounts of the variance in real-life outcomes, such as educational achievements and work performance. Psychometric tests thus gain credibility, because test scores relate non-trivially to variables outwith their frame of reference. Establishing predictive validity for IQ-type tests is described as *looking up from human intelligence*; looking up in the sense that psychometric intelligence is being related to still more molar, complex aspects of human variability. This allows one escape route from the much-repeated charge that intelligence is 'what the tests test' (Boring 1923). Potentially more important and profound, though, are attempts to explain intelligence by appealing to differences in lower-level psychological and biological processes. This is called *looking down on human intelligence*; thus the title of the book. Succeeding chapters describe and evaluate attempts at cognitive and biological reductionism in intelligence research. Some space and discussion is devoted to articulating the recurring problems of understanding intelligence differences by means of such reductionism (Chapter 4).

Chapter 2 presents and discusses ideas concerning the bases of intelligence differences posited between antiquity and the early years of the twentieth century. Chapter 3 describes and evaluates the first empirical studies in the area, concentrating on the period between the 1880s and the First World War. Chapters 5 to 9, respectively, contain critical discussions of empirical results from psychometric, cognitive–experimental, psychophysical, ageing, and biological research on psychometric intelligence differences. Several individual studies are described in each chapter, as are semi-quantitative reviews and meta-analyses of particular areas of research. However, a dry list of experimental details and results is sterile. Exposition is therefore spiked with the condiment of commentary. The narrative for each topic integrates as much of the best, relevant research as possible, including:

(a) an account of the historical accidents and scientific premises that drove research in a given direction
(b) a description of relevant theories, constructs, techniques, and variables
(c) an attempt at a fair summary of the main results, with failures, successes, retrenchments, and points of growth all represented
(d) any available integration with research covered in other chapters
(e) relevant evidence from developmental, gerontological, and clinical research in addition to the more usual studies on normal young adults
(f) a sceptical evaluation of the area, with theoretical and empirical critiques.

2 Four intelligent reductionists

Looking down on human intelligence from Socrates to Spearman

SUMMARY

Psychologists began to measure mental ability differences using psychometric tests just after 1900. Even before that, they were exploring whether human ability differences had origins in putatively simpler aspects of human cognitive and brain functions. Thus, they wondered whether brighter individuals might also have finer sensory discrimination, faster reaction times, bigger heads (putatively indicating bigger brains), and so forth. The usual historical accounts of these efforts begin with the work of Francis Galton and recount the apparent failures of his approach at the bridge between the nineteenth and twentieth centuries. This chapter begins earlier, with an exposition of three writers' accounts of the origins of human ability differences. They are Juan Huarte, Thomas Hobbes, and Christian Wolff, who spanned the time between the renaissance and the enlightenment. They wrote extensively about the biological and cognitive mechanisms of human ability differences, although none appears in intelligence's current 'hall of fame'. Spearman's two principal, book-length contributions about the origins of human ability differences are discussed from a theoretical standpoint. Huarte and Spearman speculated at a biological level of reduction, and Hobbes, Wolff, and Spearman theorized at a more molar, cognitive level. Thus, thinking about the causes of human mental ability differences is covered from antiquity to the establishing of scientific psychology.

ANTIQUITY TO ENLIGHTENMENT: HUARTE, HOBBES, AND WOLFF ON HUMAN ABILITY DIFFERENCES

In *The g factor* Jensen (1998a) stated that, whereas interest in intellect extends back across many centuries of recorded human thought, interest in the individual differences in intellectual powers is more recent. Historical interest in ability differences was not absent, though. In this section three thinkers are discussed. Writing in the pre-scientific period of psychology, each attempted to give an account of human intellectual differences and their possible causes. None of the following sources is a typical historical reference to the originators of ability research. They are not the standard reference to the fact that the ancient Chinese used a form of ability testing for their civil service, nor a reference to Plato's discussion of the differently precious metals that constituted humans' souls in the *Republic*, nor yet the mentions of ability made in the Hippocratic and Galenical works based on the theory of the humors. They are thinkers whose ideas on intelligence were worked out to a degree that make them seem more modern and place them as forerunners of Galton (1883) and Spearman (1923, 1927). They are three Europeans from different countries, and different centuries, writing from different traditions and for different audiences: Huarte, in sixteenth-century inquisitional Spain, a medical man writing a book on selection for the professions; Hobbes, in seventeenth-century England, writing before and after the commonwealth and the restoration, a philosopher, political theorist, and theoretical psychologist; and Wolff, in eighteenth-century enlightenment Germany, a pre-Kantian philosopher, mathematician, and scientist whose rationalist works included a systematic psychology. These three are hereby nominated for more prominent places in the lineage of thought about the origins of mental ability differences.

THE SIXTEENTH CENTURY: JUAN HUARTE (OR JUAN HUARTE DE SAN JUAN) AND *EXAMEN DE INGENIOS*

Juan Huarte de San Juan, a medical doctor and 'renaissance savant', lived from the third to the ninth decade of the sixteenth century and has been named as the 'father of differential psychology' (Carpintero 1995; Pueyo 1996). Huarte's (1575, translated and reprinted 1594, reprinted 1969) book, *Examen de ingenios* (translated into English as *A triall of wits*, or *The examination of men's wits*), was built around the theses that among men there are individual differences in wits (by which he meant cognitive abilities), and each person has a natural ability for only one vocation, or for none at all. The note to King Philip II, with which his treatise begins, contains a summary of the book's aims:

> But none hath cleerly and distinctly delivered what that nature is which maketh a man able for one science [profession], and uncapable of another, nor how many differences of wittes there are found in mankind, nor what arts or sciences do answer each in particular, nor by what tokens this may be known, which is the thing that most importeth.

Thus Huarte was concerned with the nature of mental ability differences, their number and structure, which abilities link with which jobs, and how to test abilities. Indeed, he posed most of the questions that were given part-answers in Chapter 1. Congruent with Binet (1905, 1916), he put ability testing and practical prediction to the fore. And, as was the case with Binet, the principal setting of ability testing was in education and thereafter occupations. More specifically, with respect to Binet's original remit for developing mental tests, Huarte thought that mental ability testing could discover those people for whom teaching might prove fruitless:

> before I received any scholer into my schoole, I would grow to many trials and experiments with him, until I might discover the qualitie of his wit, and

if I found it by nature directed to that science whereof I made profession, I would willingly receive him, for it breeds a great contentment in the teacher, to instruct one of good towardliness: and if not, I would counsaile him to studie that science, which were most agreeable with his wit. But if I saw, that he had no disposition or capacitie for any form of learning, I would friendly and with gentle words tell him; brother, you have no means to prove a man of that profession which you have undertaken, take care not to loose your time and your labour, and provide you some other trade of living, which requires not so great an habilitie as appertaineth to learning. (p. 4)

Although his principal interest was in practical prediction of educational and occupational outcomes, Huarte also addressed the number, structure, and mechanisms of human ability differences. Spearman's (1904) first empirical studies used data from school examinations and resulted in the discovery of g. Huarte used anecdotal school achievement data also, but employed them to argue against a g-type idea. Instead, he emphasized the independence of different abilities.

But my selfe am at least a good witnesse of this truth; for there were three companions of us, who entered together to studie the Latine toong, and one of us learned the same with great facilitie, the rest could never make any commendable composition; but all passing on to Logicke, one of those who could not learne Grammer, proved in that art a principall Aegle, and the other two, in the whole, never learned one ready point; then all three coming to heare Astrologie, it was a matter worthy of consideration, that he who could no skill of Latine or Logicke, in a few daies knew more in Astrologie than his maister taught them, and the rest could never learne it. I then marvelling hereat, began forthwith to make discourses, and play the Philosopher hereon, and so I found that every science required a speciall and particular wit, which reaved from that, was little worth in other sorts of learning. And if this be true (as verely it is, and we will prove it hereafter) he that at this day should enter into the schooles of our times, making proofe and assay of the scholers wits, how many would he change from one science to another, and how many would he send into the fields for dolts unable to learne? And how many would he call back of those, who for want of abilitie are occupied in base exercises, and yet their wits were by nature created only for learning? (p. 5)

There are more modern resonances in the above. Huarte's theory appears to contradict Spearman's g, but note that Spearman's was a two factor theory of intelligence. There are similarities between Huarte's idea that everyone has an aptitude for only one 'science'—or none at all—and Spearman's special abilities (or s's). Huarte, when writing about aptitude, clearly meant aptitude for high-level learning, which would require high general ability. The extracts printed above indicate his belief that some people had insufficient wit for any of the professions. Among those of sufficiently high ability, he detected individual differences in aptitude for each area of learning. Spearman (1926) was referring to the normal rather than the highly educated population when he wrote, with reference to the distribution of the specific abilities:

> Every normal man, woman, and child is, then, a genius at something as well as an idiot at something.

> It remains to discover what—at any rate in respect of the genius. This must be a most difficult matter, owing to the very fact that it occurs in only a minute proportion of all possible abilities. It certainly cannot be detected by any of the testing procedures at present in current usage. But these procedures are capable, I believe, of vast improvement.

> The preceding considerations have often appealed to me on looking at a procession of the Unemployed, and hearing someone whisper that they are mostly the Unemployable. That they are so actually I cannot help concurring. But need they be so necessarily? Remember that every one of these, too, is a genius at something—if we only could discover what. (p. 8)

Huarte and explaining human ability differences

Huarte's (1575) key chapters—which are a renaissance occupational/personnel psychology manual—dealt with the abilities required to excel at law, divinity, medicine, warfare, and in the office of the king. Before those, there are chapters with the following titles:

2 That Nature is that which makes man of abilitie to learne.
3 What part of the body ought to be well tempered, that a yoong man have abilitie.
5 It is prooved that from the three qualities, hot, moist, and drie, proceed all the differences of mens wits.

These and the associated early chapters in the book are progenitors of the present volume and the research it represents and discusses. The first half of Huarte's book might with accuracy be called 'the biological basis of human mental ability differences: a critical review'. The authors he reviewed in detail wrote in classical Greek and Roman times: Socrates (*c.*470–399 BC), Hippocrates (*c.*460–*c.*377 BC), Plato (428/7–348/7 BC), Aristotle (384–322 BC), and Galen (AD 129–216). The theoretical framework was that of the humors, and the key explanatory constructs were the degrees to which brains are dry, moist, and hot. In his Chapter 2, Huarte complained that the phrase 'nature makes able' was repeated from ancient times, yet there was little evidence about the nature of this nature. He distinguished the normal bases of human ability from those direct gifts of God—as given, for example, to the Apostles, whose intellectual achievements belied their rude backgrounds according to Huarte. He reckoned that the soul could not be the basis of human ability differences, because all souls were equally perfect; no point, therefore, in seeking individual differences there. Some other natural causes of ability differences must be identified:

> But all soules being of equal perfection (as well that of the wiser, as that of the foolish) it cannot be affirmed, that nature in this signification, is that which makes a man able, for if this were true, all men should have a like measure of wit and wisdome: and therefore Aristotle found out another signification of nature, which is the cause, that a man is able or unable; saying, that the temperature of the foure first qualities (hot, cold, moist, and drie) is to be called nature, for from this issue all the habilities of man, all his vertues and vices, and this great varietie of wits which we behold. And this is clearly produced by considering the age of a man when he is wisest, who in his childhood is no more than a brute beast, and useth none other powers than those of anger and concupiscence; but comming to youth, there begins to shoot out in him a marvellous wit, and we see that it lasteth til a time certaine, and no longer, for old age growing on, he goes every day losing his wit, untill it come to be quite decaied.
>
> This variete of wits, it is a matter certaine that it springs not from the reasonable soule, for that is one selfe in all ages, without having received in his forces and substance any alteration: but man hath in every age a divers temperature, and a contrarie disposition, by means whereof, the soul doth other workes in childhood, other in youth, and other in old age. Whence we draw an evident argument, that one selfe soul, doing contrarie workes in one selfe bodie, for that it partakes in every age a contrarie temperature, when of young men, the one is able, and the other unapt, this growes for that the one of them enioies a divers temperature from the other. And this (for that it is the beginning of all the workes of the reasonable soule) was by the Phisitions and the Philosphers, termed Nature; of which signification, this sentence is properly verefied, that *Nature makes able.* (p. 20)

Thus Huarte referred to Aristotle's identifying nature as having a basis in the four qualities. Also, Huarte mentioned their interactions with age to account for age differences as well as individual differences in mental abilities. His theorizing was economical: the same biological factors that produced individual ability differences produced age differences also. Nowadays, similar economy is achieved by replacing temperature with ideas of 'speed of information processing' (Chapter 8). Moreover, alterations to Huarte's causal factors, for example by illness or change of climate, were hypothesized to produce state changes in mental ability levels. The theory, though tending to biological reductionism, as originated by Galen, was environmentalist rather than nativist. The reasonable soul was the same in everyone. Variations in the brain's temperature—Huarte's hypothesized origin of individual and age differences and state changes in mental abilities—arose from differences in the climate, food and drink, and so forth, of the region inhabited. Many geographical differences in ability, personality, and body build were cited as evidence. Huarte was open in basing his reductionist ideas on those of Galen, and he indicated that Galen also approved of mental testing prior to entering the professions:

> he understood that it was necessarie to depart the sciences amongst yoong men, and to give each one that which to his naturall habilitie was requisit, in as much as he sayd, That well ordered common wealths, ought to have men of great wisdome and knowledge, who might in their tender age, discover ech ones wit and naturall sharpness, to the end they might be set to learne that art which was agreeable, and not leave it to their owne election. (p. 23)

Huarte and the biological bases of intelligence differences

The key reductionist account in Huarte's book appears in Chapter 3: 'What part of the body ought to be well tempered, that a yoong man have abilitie'. And here is the introduction, that could serve well to introduce Chapter 9 of this present book:

> For there is none of these philosophers [especially, he meant, Hippocrates and Plato] that doubteth, but that the braine is the instrument ordained by nature, to the end that man might become wise and skilfull, it sufficeth only to declare with what conditions this part ought to be endewed, so as we may affirme, that it is duly instrumentalized, and that a yong man in this behalfe may possesse a good wit and habilitie. (p. 24)

It is notable that Huarte did not stop *en route* from wit to brain to invent intermediate-level (cognitive) constructs. He indicated those constructs of the brain's make-up that are the sources of individual differences in mental abilities:

> Foure conditions the braine ought to enjoy, to the end the reasonable soul may therewith commodiously performe the workes which appertaine to understanding and wisdome. The first, good composition; the second, that his parts be well united; the third, that the heat exceed not the cold, nor the moist the drie; the fourth, that his substance be made of parts subtle and verie delicate.

> In the good composition, are contained other foure things: the first is, good figure: the second, quantitie sufficient: the third, that in the braine the foure ventricles be distinct and severed, each duly bestowed in his seat and place: the fourth, that the capableness of these be neither greater nor lesse than is convenient for their workings. (pp. 24–25)

Huarte's thinking and theorizing were close in content to Galen and other classical thinkers, whom he cited as though they were current authorities; yet their writings were more than a millenium's distance away. His writing occasioned the twofold dangers of questioning the dogmas of the classical thinkers and arousing the suspicions of the then-inquisitional Spanish Roman Catholic church authorities as he mused on the nature of the human 'reasonable soule'. The antiquated language of the book (as available to me via a near-contemporary English translation) and the constant references to classical authorities, whom he criticized using his own empirical observations, make it tempting to treat his work as a mere historical curiosity. However, it is an interesting exercise to ask how many of his hypotheses could pass muster today, in theorizing about the biological seat(s) of intelligence differences. In Chapter 9 associations between brain size and psychometric intelligence differences are reported, as are ideas about the source of intelligence existing in metabolic efficiency, myelinization, connectedness, and so forth. All are close to, and frequently no more specific or enlightening than, some of Huarte's guesses. Modern techniques of brain investigation are only now assisting our slow progress out of the scientific dark ages with regard to ideas about the biology of human ability differences. Even now, with regard to explanatory biological accounts of psychometric intelligence differences, the field is not much further from Hippocrates and Galen than was Huarte (Deary and Caryl 1997a). Associations among brain size, head size, and human psychometric intelligence have been much discussed and are a source of recent controversy, as Chapter 9 recounts. They were, too, in the sixteenth century. Huarte stated that,

> The quantitie of the braine, which the soul needeth to discourse and consider, is a matter that breeds feare, for amongst all the brute beasts, there is none found to have so much braine as a man, in sort, as if we ioine those of two greatest oxen together, they will not equall that of one onely man, but he never so little. And that whereto behooves more consideration, is, that amongst brute beasts, those who approch neerest to mans wisdome and discretion (as the ape, the fox, and the dog,) have a greater quantitie of braine than the other, though bigger bodied than they. For which cause, *Galen* said, that a little head in any man is ever faultie, because that it wanteth braine; notwithstanding, I avouch that if his having a great head, proceedeth from abundance of matter, and ill tempered, at such time as the same was shaped by nature, it is an evill token, for the same consists of bones and flesh, and contains a smal quantitie of braine, as it befals in very big orenges, which opened, are found scarce of juice, and hard of rinde. Nothing offends the resonable soul so much, as to make his abode in a body surcharged with bones, fat, and flesh. For which cause *Plato* sayd, that wise mens heads are ordinarily weake, and upon any occasion are easily annoied, and the reason is, for that nature made them of an empty skull, with the intention not to offend the wit, by compassing it with much matter. (p. 25)

The size of the brain correlates more strongly with mental ability scores than does the size of the head (Chapter 9). Thus Huarte was correct to focus on the brain's size and its composition, and to see beyond the big head. He had the distinction of, beyond theorizing, making experiments and noting medical and other evidence in order to check his ideas. He chided Aristotle, who reckoned that man's head was quite small compared to other animals by comparison with the size of the body. Aristotle, he wrote, should have opened the head and observed the size of the brain whereof,

> he should have found, that two horses together had not so much braine as that one man. (p. 26)

Huarte went on to write that the same applied to the stomach. He quoted Galen's proverb, 'a gross bellie makes a grosse understanding', and reckoned that the brain and the stomach were connected with sinews and their functions were related: 'when the stomach is drie and shrunke, it affoords great aid to the wit' (p. 26).

Huarte reckoned that smaller men needed relatively big heads, and bigger men smaller because there was a certain absolute amount of brain needed for the reasonable soul to operate optimally. The need of four ventricles for discoursing and philosophizing was discussed. Huarte then demonstrated some knowledge about brain injury and the disturbance of the brain's connected systems in producing neuropsychological deficits:

> But it sufficeth not, that the brain possesse good figure, sufficient qualtitie, and the number of ventricles, by us forementioned, with their capablenesse, great or little, but it behooves also that that his parts holds a certaine kind of continuednesse, and that they be not divided. For which cause, we have seene in hurts of the head, that some men have lost their memorie, some their understanding, and others their imagination: and put case, that after they have recovered their health, the braine re-united it selfe again, yet this notwith-standing, the naturall union was not made, which the brain before possessed. (pp. 27–28)

The third quality of a good brain, temperature, was discussed at length later, but Huarte's fourth quality, that the brain be made of subtle and delicate parts, resulted in an interesting hypothesis about the nature of interspecies differences in ability:

> But here encounters us a difficultie very great, and this is, that if we open the head of any beast, we shall find his braine composed with the same forme and manner, as a mans, without any of the fore-reported conditions will be failing. Whence we gather that the brute beasts have also the use of Prudence and reason, by means of the composition of their braine, or else that our reasonable soule serves not it selfe of this member, for the use of his operations; which may not be avouched. (p. 28)

Driven by this logic, Huarte reviewed classical evidence—experiments by Plato and Aristotle—that animals do engage in reasoning, discourse (without speech), and syllogisms, something that comparative psychologists today have rediscovered (McGonigle and Chalmers 1992). And he stated that the sources of among- and within-animal differences in 'wit' are the same as those among men:

> I dare boldly affirme, that even the very Asses (who notwithstanding seeme most blockish of all beasts) have this from nature. (p. 29)

He mentioned also that Aristotle and Galen agreed,

> That the difference which is found between man and brute beast, is the selfe same which is found between a foole and a wise man; which is nought else than in respect of the more and the lesse. This (truly) is not to be doubted, that brute beasts enjoy memorie and imagination, and another power which resembles understanding, as the Ape is very like a man, and that his soule makes use of the composition of the braine, it is a matter apparent: which being good, and such as is behooffull, performes his workes very wel, and with much prudence, and if the braine be ill instrumentalized, it executes the same untowardly. (p. 30)

Huarte's most powerful explanatory construct was temperature, arriving via the conduits of the arterial blood. This applied not just to the brain. Thus, anger, sexual stimulation, and the contemplation of food all had important associations with the heat delivered by the arterial blood:

> For if a man begin to imagine upon any injurie that hath bene profered him, the blood of the arteries runs sodainly to the heart, and stirs up the wrathfull part, and gives the same heat and forces for revenge. (p. 31)

> If a man stand contemplating any faire woman, or stay in giving and receiving by that imagination touching the venerious act, these vitall spirits run foorthwith to the genitall members, and raise them to performance. The like befals when we remember any delicat and savourie meat, which once called to mind, they straight abandon the rest of the body, and flie to the stomacke and replenish the mouth with water. (p. 32)

This was in part why Galen thought sick people should not be fed: the vital spirits went from their proper work to the diversion of the digestive organs. Huarte envisaged the application of this principle to the brain's functioning:

> The like benefit and ayd, the braine receives of these vitall spirits, when the reasonable soule is about to contemplate, understand, imagine, to performe actions of memorie, without which it cannot worke. And like as the grosse substance of the braine, and his evill temperature brings the wit to confusion: so the vitall spirits, and the arteriall blood (not being delicat and of good temperature) hinder in a man his discourse and use of reason.

Chapter 9 inquires whether such reasoning has progressed much further in modern studies of cognitive function using positron emission tomography, single photon emission tomography, and magnetic resonance imaging. Using these new technologies, psychologists' subjects are engaged in mental activity and the experimenter reports those parts of the brain which, as a result, metabolize more or less actively. Blood flow is often used as a surrogate for the metabolic activity. In Huarte's thinking the temperature was such a powerful explanatory tool that he suggested that sudden changes in it should bring about changes in the ability to reason and discourse, as if the level of mental ability had been altered. Huarte recounted some interesting medical cases to support and illustrate his point. The descriptions indicate that the patients might have been in the manic phase of manic-depressive disorder, and Huarte did mention melancholy in this context. He stuck to temperature of the brain as the explanation, to bring together quite different phenomena, such as those children who speak soon after birth and then not until the proper time. He took a lot of time to refute the hypothesis that the devil had a part in this, and was keen always to construe mental phenomena as a part of nature. In this he seems quite modern, and might have found difficulties in inquisitional Spain (Carpintero (1995) suggested that some sections of the book were censored by the inquisition). The idea of economy of theorizing and the idea of 'reducing' some phenomena to lower-level causes run throughout the piece. Thus, he rebuked Plato for stating that one of a man's sons, who could write poetry without any teaching, while the other could not do it despite teaching, must be possessed,

> In which behalfe, *Aristotle* had good cause to find fault with him, for that he might have reduced this to the temperature, as else where he did. (p. 46)

Huarte and the modularity of mind

Huarte, in addition to reducing individual differences to biology, concerned himself with matters closer to current psychometric–cognitive psychology discussions, namely the number of abilities that the brain subserves. His immediate answer was a modular, multi-factor theory which posited three main abilities, understanding, imagining, and remembering, thus:

> With this selfe power of the soul, we understand, imagine and remember. But if it be true, that every worke requires a particular instrument, it behooveth of necessitie, that within the braine there be one instrument for the understanding, one for the imagination, and another different from them for memorie: for if all the braine were instrumentalized after one selfe manner, either the whole should be memorie, or the whole understanding, or the whole imagination. But we see that there are very different operations, and therefore it is of force that there be also a varietie in the instruments. But if we open by skill, and make an anatomie of the braine, we shall find the whole compounded after one maner, of one kind of substance, and alike, without parts of other

kinds, or a different sort; onely there appeare four little hollownesses, who (if we well marke them) have all one selfe composition and figure, without any thing coming betweene which may breed a difference. (p. 52)

Here Huarte reminds us of the faculty psychologists, or modular theorists of mind, such as Gardner (1983) or Fodor (1983). He started from behavioural phenotypes and invoked backwards to suggest the number and types of operations of the brain isomorphic with the functions seen from the outside. Also, akin to psychometricians interested in mental ability, he appreciated that he first had to sort out the divisions of activity of the organ within which he was seeking to explain individual differences. Huarte's further reflections led to his rejecting a simple modular account of the brain and moving to an appreciation of the interdependence of different mental activities:

Now the difficultie consists, to know in which of these ventricles the understanding is placed, in which the memorie, and in which the imagination, for they are so united and nere-neighboured, that neither by the last argument, nor by any other notice, they can be distinguished or discerned. Then considering that the understanding cannot worke without the memorie be present, representing unto the same the figures and fantasies agreeable thereunto, it behooveth that the understanding part busie it selfe in beholding the fantasmes, and that the memorie cannot do it, if the imagination do not accompany the same (as we have already heretofore declared) we shall easily understand, that all the powers are united in every severall ventricle, and that the understanding is not solely in the one, nor the memory solely in the other, nor the imagination in the third, as the vulgar philosophers have imagined, but that this union of powers is accustomably made in mans body, in as much as the one cannot worke without the aid of the other, as appeareth in the foure naturall abilities, digestive, retentive, attractive, and expulsive, where, because each one stands in need of all the residue, nature disposed to unite them in one selfe place, and made them not divided or sundered. (p. 54)

In this rejection of biological modularity Huarte might not have disagreed with Lashley's (1950) principles of mass action and equipotentiality in brain functioning. Just a little later he finally rejected accounts that would posit isomorphism between phenotypic ability divisions and brain structures:

Seeing then al the three ventricles are of one selfe composition, and that there rests not amongst them any varietie of parts, we may not leave to take the first qualities for an instrument, and to make so many general differences of wits, as they are in number. (p. 56)

Huarte also appreciated the interdependence of reasoning and what we should now call working memory, and his account invokes comparison with Kyllonen and Christal's (1990) merging of the two constructs:

And we call memorie a reasonable power, because without it, the understanding and the imaginative are of no value. It ministreth matter and figures
to them all, whereupon they may syllogise conformably to that which *Aristotle*
sayth, It behooves that the understander go beholding the fantasmes; and the
office of the memorie is, to preserve these phantasmes, to the end that the
understanding may contemplat them, and if this be lost, it is impossible that
the powers can worke; and that the office of the memorie is none other, than
to preserve the figures of things, without that it appertains thereto to devise
them. *Galen* expresseth in these words, Memorie (verely) laies up and preserveth
in it selfe, the things known by the sence, and by the mind, and is therin as
it were their storehouse and receiving place, and not their inventer. And this
be the use thereof, it fals out apparent, that the same dependeth on moisture;
for this makes the braine pliant, and the figure is imprinted by way of strayning.
(pp. 60–61)

This discussion of the cognitive mechanisms that conjoin reasoning and working
memory sits comfortably with current thinking about the importance of working
memory in mental ability differences (Chapter 5). Huarte's thesis, though, did
possess isomorphic thinking. He associated imagination with the quality of heat,
understanding with dryness, and memory with moisture. Understanding accrued
with age, as the brain became dry, and memory was at its best in the younger
brain, which was moist and more ready to take impressions from the world.
Recalling that Huarte stressed interdependence among the abilities, he also recognized that the brain has limitations in its processing resources:

the understanding and the memorie are contrary powers, and that the one
chaceth away the other. (p. 72)

His theory of the division of human abilities was hierarchical. Thus,

the principall works of the understanding are three: the first, to discourse; the
second, to distinguish; and the third, to chuse. Hence comes it that they place
also three differences in the understanding: into three other is the memorie
devided: one receives with ease, and suddenly forgetteth; another is slow to
receive, but a long time retaineth; and the last receiveth with ease, and is very
slow to forget.

The imagination containeth many more differences, for he hath three, no lesse
than the understanding and memorie, and from each degree ariseth three other.
Of these we will more distinctly discourse hereafter, when we shall assigne to
each, the science which answereth it in particular. (p. 65)

The identification of distinguishing as a capacity within understanding recurs in
later thinkers' ideas about the origins of mental ability differences. The separation
of memory into what appear to be short- and longer-term stores, in the case of

the first two divisions, is prescient also. Huarte discussed that Aristotle wished to add remembrance and common sense to the above three abilities, reminding us that argument about the number of separable mental abilities has a long and honourable tradition.

Huarte and cognitive styles

Without touching upon the main bulk of Huarte's thesis—concerning the varieties of imagination (ability) in man and the vocations to which they point—there are forerunners of a great many issues that exercise contemporary scientists in the field of human mental ability differences. There are few modern concerns that he does not mention at some point: the number and hierarchical structure of mental abilities, the biological causes of ability differences, the interactions among the cognitive processes underlying thought, cross-species comparisons of intelligence, the development and ageing of ability differences and their causes, and the effects of illness on mental abilities. Even modish-seeming ideas about cognitive styles—the grey area between personality and intelligence—are presaged by Huarte. Sternberg's (1997) theory of mental self-government and thinking styles includes two styles: legislative people who prefer to discover an original path; and executive people who prefer the well-worn trail blazed by others. Compare these with Huarte's goats and sheep:

> Wits full of invention, are by the *Tuscanes* called goatish, for the likenesse which they have with a goate, in their demeanure or proceeding. They never take pleasure in the plains, but ever delight to walke alone thorow dangerous and high places, and to appproch [sic] neere steepe down-fals, for they will not follow any beaten path, nor go in companie. A propertie like this, is found in the reasonable soul when it possesseth a braine well instrumentalised and tempered, for it never resteth settled in any contemplation, but fareth forthwith unquiet, seeking to know and understand new matters. Of such a soule is verefied the saying of *Hippocrates*, The going of the soule is the thought of men. For there are some, who never pass out of one contemplation, and thinke not that the whole world can discover another such. These have the propertie of a beast, who never forsakes the beaten path, nor careth to walke through desert and unhaunted places, but only in the high market way, and with a guide before him. Both these diversities of wits, are ordinarie among professors of learning. Some others are of high searching capacities, and estranged from the common course of opinions, they iudge and entreat of matters with a particular fashion, they are franke in delivering their opinion, and tie not themselves to that of any other. Some sorts are close, moist, and very quiet, distrusting themselves, and relying upon the iudgement of some grave man whom they follow, whose saying and sentences, they repute as sciences and demonstrations, and al things contrarying they reckon vanitie and leasings.

The two differences of wits are very profitable if they be united; for amongst a great drove of cattell, the heardsmen accustome to mingle some dozen of goats to lead them and make them trot apace, to enioy new pastures, that they may not suffer scarcitie; so also it behouveth, that in humane learning, there be some goat-like wits, who may discouver to the cattell like under-standings, thorow secrets of nature, and deliver unto them contemplations not heard of, wherein they may exercise themselves, for after this manner, arts take increase, and men dayly know more and more. (pp. 67–68)

Thus, in agreement with Sternberg (1997), Huarte recognized the benefit to society and scientific progress of these two styles of wit.

Huarte: an assessment

How should Huarte's contribution be assessed in the science of mental ability differences? His work contains the equivalent of a *Psychological Bulletin*-style crit-ical review of the period between classical Greece and the late-sixteenth century. Building upon this, he developed a major applied psychology scheme based on his own theory of the number, nature, and biological bases of human mental ability differences. His ideas on the biology of intelligence have a humoral hue, and are resultingly quaint and archaic, but the brain constructs he targeted as the sources of mental ability differences were frequently similar to those presented later in Chapter 9. His thinking was reductionistic and mechanistic. Mental qual-ities are never left floating in mid-air after being invoked; all must be tied to some principle of the brain's biology. In a typical comment he stated that,

we have made the Understanding an instrumentall power, as the Imagination, and the Memorie: and have given drinesse to the brain, as an instrument with which it may worke. (p. 70)

This last comment, about finding a construct that can explain the mechanism of correlations between psychological differences and brain biology, reaches exactly where most modern studies fall short. In Dennett's (1995) terms, Huarte used cranes rather than skyhooks in his reductionism.

Unlike Galton and Spearman, Huarte's book led to no continuing stream of empirical or theoretical works, and Carpintero (1995) reflected that Spain, having begun serious work on human differential psychology thus substantially, later became an importer rather than an exporter of ideas. The many reprintings and translations of Huarte's book suggest that it did attract and retain some atten-tion. Among differential psychologists within Spain (Pueyo 1996) Huarte is celebrated as a distant father. Among those in the rest of the world he is almost unknown, save for the occasional recognition that his ideas sound 'strikingly modern' (Detterman 1982, p. 101). If bound together with Spearman's (1927) *The abilities of man*, the resulting volume would be a comprehensive review covering the period from antiquity to the establishment of scientific psychology, and would pose almost all of the important questions currently being addressed in mental ability differences.

THE SEVENTEENTH CENTURY: THOMAS HOBBES AND *LEVIATHAN*

Leviathan by Thomas Hobbes (1651) is a broad-ranging book about political philosophy. The first part of the book is entitled 'Of Man' and is a philosophical psychology. Chapter VIII is entitled 'Of the Virtues, commonly called Intellectual; and their contrary Defects'. In it, Hobbes discussed what it means to be intelligent, the bases of human intelligence, and intelligence differences. (Earlier chapters on the scientific method contain valuable material on human thinking also). In doing so, he provided a structure to his thinking that we see in the present book and in Huarte's: mapping an area of human interest, noting that it has individual differences, and then musing on the bases of those differences. For Hobbes, individual differences were almost the first feature he raised when he addressed human intellect:

> Virtue generally, in all sorts of subjects, is somewhat that is valued for eminence, and consisteth in comparison. For if all things were equal in all men, nothing would be prized. And by 'virtues intellectual' are always understood such abilities of the mind as men praise, value, and desire should be in themselves; and go commonly under the name of a 'good wit'; though the same word 'wit' be used also to distinguish one certain ability from the rest. (pp. 38–39)

Thus Hobbes identified two of the reasons that the study of intelligence is at once so prominent in psychology and so controversial: individual differences are easily noticed, and whatever that difference comprises is a highly valued quality or set of qualities. (It is often quipped that many people complain about their defective memory but few people complain about their lack of intelligence.) Note, too, that he used 'wit' as a coverall term and to capture different types of mental ability. He then inquired after the bases of these individual differences, and declared the intellectual virtues to be of two types: natural and acquired.

> By natural, I mean not that which a man hath from birth: for that is nothing but sense; wherein men differ so little from one another, and from brute beasts, as is not to be reckoned amongst virtues. (p. 39)

Hobbes and natural wit

It may be deduced from the above comment that Hobbes had a different view of individual differences in mental abilities from those formed over two centuries later by Galton (1883) and Spearman (1904), who sought the bases of human intelligence differences in the senses and more specifically in powers of sensory discrimination. Instead, by natural 'wit' Hobbes meant,

> That 'wit' which is gotten by use only and experience; without method, culture or instruction. (p. 39)

It is tempting to read this as an early progenitor of the idea of fluid intelligence, but Hobbes' ideas are not so fully articulated as to make the comparison convincing. In suggesting the causes of differences in 'natural wit', Hobbes (1651) called upon psychological-level constructs involving (i) some form of psychological speediness and (ii) strategy formation:

> This 'natural wit' consisteth principally in two things, 'celerity of imagining', that is, swift succession of one thought to another, and steady direction to some approved end. On the contrary, a slow imagination maketh that defect, or fault of mind which is commonly called 'dulness', 'stupidity', and sometimes by other names that signify slowness of motion, or difficulty to be moved. (p. 39)

Hobbes' further analysis of the nature of mental ability differences was redolent with Spearman's (1923) later armchair philosophical methods which resulted from his attempt to dissect the 'Nature of Intelligence and the Principles of Cognition'. There is missing in Hobbes' writing the attraction towards a biological level of explanation that was seen in Huarte. Nevertheless, Hobbes did engage in cognitive-level reductionism:

> And this difference of quickness, is caused by difference of men's passions; that love and dislike, some one thing, some another: and therefore some men's thoughts run one way, some another; and are held to, and observe differently the things that pass through their imagination. And whereas in this succession of men's thoughts, there is nothing to observe in the things they think on, but in either in what they be 'like one another', or in what they be 'unlike', or 'what they serve for', or 'how they serve to such a purpose'; those that observe their similitudes, in case they be such as are rarely observed by others, are said to have a 'good wit'; by which, in this occasion, is meant a 'good fancy'. But they that observe their differences and dissimilitudes: which is called 'distinguishing', and 'discerning', and 'judging' between thing and thing; in case such discerning be not easy, are said to have a 'good judgement' (p. 39)

The invoking of (i) the eduction of similarity between two apparently dissimilar things and (ii) the discrimination of difference between two like things as the heart of the nature of human intelligence and its differences heralds some aspects of Spearman's (1923) much later solution. Both writers placed the ability to discriminate among the objects of experience at the heart of intellectual differences. Spearman's 'eduction of relations and correlates' concords with

Hobbes' notions of 'good fancy'. In his 1927 book, *The abilities of man*, Spearman stated that,

> On the whole, the conclusion seems irresistible, that *g* is more or less involved in educing relations of likeness.

Hobbes thought that good judgement was a virtue in itself, but that good fancy was only virtuous when combined with good judgement or steady direction toward some end. Fancy uncontrolled by this steady direction would lead men toward undue digressions and parentheses, and to see great new things where others correctly saw mundanity. Fancy controlled by judgement led to, for example, the creation of novel and apt metaphors. Hobbes' expansion in this way makes fancy appear like creativity and judgement appear like reasoned discrimination. Fancy without judgement Hobbes deemed to be a kind of madness and, though he said he could find no name for it, it sounds like hypomania:

> Judgment therefore without fancy is wit, but fancy without judgement, not (p. 40).

He saw fancy as more important in good poetry and judgement to the fore in good history, suggesting a Sternbergian (1997) realization of different intellectual styles. Like Binet who followed, Hobbes put judgement centre-stage in his account of mental ability differences. Like Huarte before him, Hobbes thus had occupational recommendations for ability differences.

Hobbes and acquired wit

In his discussion of acquired wit Hobbes viewed reason as its only constituent, 'which is grounded on the right use of speech and produceth the sciences'. Hobbes thought too about the sources of individual differences in this field of intellect and was obviously different from Huarte in his conclusions:

> The causes of this difference of wits, are in the passions; and the difference of passions proceedeth, partly from the different constitution of the body, and partly from different education. For if the difference proceeded from the temper of the brain, and the organs of sense, either exterior or interior, there would be no less difference of men in their sight, hearing, or other senses, than in their fancies and discretions. It proceeds therefore from the passions; which are different, not only from the difference of men's complexions; but also from their difference of customs, and education.

Two notable things emerge from Hobbes' discussion of acquired wit, which may be compared with modern ideas about crystallized intelligence. He envisaged individual differences arising from people's personalities, their education and their culture, ideas that would not be out of place in present-day discussions of knowledge and wisdom (Staudinger and Baltes 1994). Second, he considered the possibility that differences in both natural and acquired wit might have their origins in the brain and in the senses, putting his hypotheses in the same court as those of Spearman (1904) and Galton (1883) and present-day investigators (Raz *et al.* 1987). He ruled out these possibilities—he and Binet (1905) concurring in not observing obvious deficits in the senses (such as hearing and sight) of people possessing less wit, as would be expected if these were the bases of differences in wit. Huarte and Hobbes shared a concern to base their ideas about ability differences on only those constructs that showed variance. For Huarte, the soul was equally perfect in all of us, and so could not be the source of differences in wit. For Hobbes, the lack of individual differences, as he saw it, in the senses sent him seeking elsewhere for sources of variance.

Hobbes' writings on ability differences show a similar set of concerns to those of Huarte and to differential psychologists more recently. He recognized individual differences in mental ability differences. He separated these differences into two types—natural and acquired wit—arguably, as a herald of psychometric separations of ability groupings. He separated natural wit into what appear to be construable as 'convergent' and 'divergent' thinking. He then sought causal explanations for those differences using constructs which he viewed as more basic, such as 'celerity of imagining' and processes related to the discrimination of likeness and difference. His emphasis on differences in men's passions appears to relate to differences in what we would now call personality and motivation, or conation, or thinking styles. His use of explanatory constructs is more purely psychological or cognitive than that of Huarte, and his writing on intellect shows little of the humoral-based biology preserved and developed from antiquity.

THE EIGHTEENTH CENTURY: CHRISTIAN WOLFF AND *PSYCHOLOGIA EMPIRICA*

A concern to articulate the nature of human intelligence, and the origins of its individual differences may be seen in the early eighteenth century writings of the philosopher, early psychologist, and general polymath Christian Wolff (1732). Chapter II of his *Psychologia empirica* is entitled 'On intellect generally and difference of cognition'. The chapter focuses on the ability to represent the things in the world, and the use of language in representing the things in the world. Intellect, according to Wolff, was 'The ability to represent things distinctly' (p. 197). He envisaged two sources of individual differences in the human intellect. First, there were differences with respect to the contents or the products of human intelligence:

> The more things, therefore, that someone can represent distinctly to himself, the greater is his intellect. (p. 198)

Second, he envisaged individual differences in the processes or mechanisms that gave rise to the products of human intelligence:

The more things that someone distinguishes in the same subject, the greater is his intellect. (p. 198)

Wolff imagined something that should be considered rather odd today: what it might be to have the greatest possible level of intelligence:

> Since in intellect we distinguish only the object, which is represented, and the method by which it is represented, and the first degree that is taken from the object and the other from the form, a greater intellect cannot be conceived than that which succeeds in representing to itself everything possible distinctly; consequently, the intellect representing everything possible distinctly will be the greatest of all, or absolutely the highest. (pp. 198–199)

This model of the human intellect as the internal building of a picture of the world has parallels with the young Wittgenstein's (1922) view on human knowledge from the *Tractatus*:

> The world is the totality of facts (p. 5)
> We picture facts to ourselves (p. 8)
> A picture is a model of reality (p. 8)
> The totality of true thoughts is a picture of the world (p. 11)

Wolff's account of human intelligence differences has, therefore, some modern resonances. His notion that more knowledge—the representation of more things— is more intellect would sit quite well with the notion of crystallized intelligence (Chapter 8), or what Lindenberger and Baltes (1994a) called the 'pragmatics of intelligence'. And he conceived the idea that intelligence differences arise from the how as well as the what of intelligence—that process differences as well as bulk knowledge could be discerned. The process he chose as the source of individual differences—the ability to distinguish more things in the same object—harks back to Hobbes, who founded intelligence differences in terms of the ability to discriminate likeness and difference, and to Huarte who hypothesized that distinguishing was one of the components of understanding. And Wolff's ideas presage the first empirical stabs at uncovering intelligence differences: Galton (1883) and Spearman (1904, 1927) sought intelligence differences in the faculty of discrimination, in both sensory and cognitive terms.

HUARTE, HOBBES, AND WOLFF: SOME FINAL THOUGHTS

The writings of Huarte, Hobbes, and Wolff on the mechanisms of human intelligence differences are omitted from most accounts of the history of intelligence research, though Spearman (1927) made references to Wolff. These writers' ideas demonstrate that musing about the origins of human intelligence differences is not a new phenomenon; the sources of such differences were a concern for many centuries of Western thought. The concepts they employed have similarities with the theories of intelligence differences seen in modern times. The ideas of Hobbes and Wolff, translated into modern parlance, would sit comfortably alongside the ideas of Hebb (intelligence A and B), Cattell and Horn (fluid and crystallized intelligence), Lindenberger and Baltes (mechanics and pragmatics of intelligence), and Eysenck (biological, psychometric, and social intelligence). Compare Wolff's ideas above with this statement about two sources of individual differences in intelligence from Hebb (1949):

> The hereditary factor [intelligence A] is essentially the capacity for elaborating perceptions and conceptual activities; the experiential factor [intelligence B] is the degree to which such elaboration has occurred (p. 294)

Like Wolff, Hebb envisaged individual differences in (a) the mechanisms that represent the world, and (b) the products of those mechanisms. These accounts contain the hypothetical origins of intelligence differences spelled out at a psychological level. Like Huarte and, later, Spearman, Hebb tended to reduce these hypothetical mechanisms to the physiology of the brain as he ventured that differences in intelligence A had their origins in, 'the possession of a good brain and a good neural metabolism' (p. 294) (see Chapter 9). One may ask whether Hebb was much more specific about neural constructs than Huarte.

Which among the three accounts above contributes most to the theme of the origins of mental ability differences? Huarte's. Hobbes and Wolff were both polymaths, writing about matters from mathematics and biology to philosophy and politics. Hobbes' controversies with members of the nascent Royal Society of London and Wolff's attempts to systematize the thinking of Leibnitz showed that both were in a rational, non-empirical tradition. Huarte's book is solely about human mental abilities, it is sometimes restrained by classical ideas, but it showed a willingness to criticize and refute them using empirical observations. The constructs used by Hobbes and Wolff to explain ability differences are principally psychological, or cognitive, and bear comparison with Spearman's (1923) largely non-empirical work, *The nature of intelligence and the principles of cognition*. Huarte also used psychological constructs, but always tried to root them in, or reduce them to, biology. This and the frequent use of empirical observations, educational and medical, place his work alongside Spearman's (1927) empirical–polemical tour de force, *The abilities of man*.

THE TURN OF THE TWENTIETH CENTURY: CHARLES SPEARMAN'S CONTRIBUTIONS

Spearman's empirical contributions to the search for the underpinnings of human mental ability differences are discussed in the next chapter, as are Galton's ideas and data. Here, Spearman is discussed as the successor to Juan Huarte, as someone who had a rounded vision of the science of mental abilities. Examining Spearman's ideas, separately from some of his results, provides a neat completion to this historical survey of the causes of human mental ability differences, because Spearman's writing and thinking straddled the period where psychology moved from a philosophical to a scientific endeavour. Spearman's principal manifestos in the field of intelligence were *The nature of intelligence and the principles of cognition* (1923) and *The abilities of man* (1927).

The nature of intelligence and the principles of cognition

The first book of Spearman's pair was reckoned to be the first textbook of cognitive psychology (Gustafsson 1992). It is largely an armchair book, showing Spearman's philosophical side as he searched for the laws of thought. His concerns in the book were the same as those differential psychologists of the 1970s and after, who attempted to map individual differences onto models of mental processing provided by cognitive psychologists (e.g. Hunt 1983), except that Spearman had no substantial cognitive models from which to poach his mental parameters. His view was that understanding individual differences could not progress without an understanding of the mechanisms of thought:

> Any search after 'the nature of intelligence' has shown itself to have a prospect of success when, and only when, it becomes merged into the greater quest after the scientific 'principles of cognition' (p. 32)

Spearman set out to enumerate the principles of cognition and was guided by three further principles, the first of which was clear thinking. The second was a search for ultimate laws, which Spearman considered necessary for anticipation and control. Last, he wanted to reap the benefits of the experimental procedure:

> The great modern point of vantage is the experimental procedure, long the chief tool of the physical sciences, now at last brought by Weber, Fechner, and Wundt—in rising order of genius—to the aid of mental science also. Here is a lever which, upon occasion, can make a modern pygmy as strong as an ancient giant. (p. 34)

His aim was to set research on intelligence within the science of the mind's operations and to base this on sound scientific principles, eschewing impressionistic and common sense views about the mind:

> As regards the anecdotal exemplifications from ordinary life, there is no reason why these—even when the events have really occurred at all!—should be any whit more fitted to prove psychical than physical laws. (p. 35)

But Spearman foresaw problems ahead, because of the nature and reputation of the material he was bound to rely on:

a large proportion of our examples will be sought in what many of the older authorities still regard askance, or even condemn as superficialities, artifacts, if not downright quackeries, but which we here, on the contrary, must uphold as the most live and futureful shoot of all contemporary psychology, to wit, mental tests. . . . For these tests are, as it were, miners excavating forward into wonderfully rich new ground, but repeatedly missing the correct direction on account of labouring in darkness. The light they need is just that which irradiates from principles—from these alone. (pp. 35–36)

Spearman's effort in the book was naïve in conception, and rather quaint. Like Newton, who took bodies in motion and rendered many apparently chaotic phenomena lawful under the yoke of a few constructs and their connecting equations, Spearman attempted to corral our entire mental life into a few laws. One of the problems he first encountered in so doing was the correct level of description to choose. Thus, if he were to explain mental operations, should he rely on a *prêt-à-porter* set of constructs—perhaps from physiology—or does the mind need its own level of explanation? At this stage Spearman took a view akin to many cognitive psychologists of a passing generation, that the mind could be mapped without reference to the brain. Spearman decided to go for a cognitive architecture. The problem then became to decide what was and was not elementary:

An ordinary percept, especially if visual, will be regarded as including far more than any mere mental state. Instead of furnishing a starting point from which to explain the laws of cognition, it is something very complex, which needs laws for its own explanation. (p. 47)

This is an admirable thought, and may be applied to many phenomena in intelligence research, and beyond, today. In many cases findings are taken as coming ready-packed with explanations, when, in fact, they require explaining in themselves. Examples abound in later chapters. Spearman, aware of the power afforded to physical and, more recently, biological science consequent upon discovering their units of explanation, was itching for the new mind science to achieve the same maturity:

Whenever the make-up of any cognitive operation has to be analysed, this is best done by resolving it into the unit-processes as its basal constituents. . . . Psychology, to obtain the much fuller measure of success awaiting it, must evolve toward a mental cytology. (p. 59)

'Mental cytology'—the phrase is pregnant with implications! One can see in it Spearman's envy of the then newly-abled biological sciences, and his desire to organize the mind along lawful lines. It brings to mind Sternberg's (1977*a*,*b*) attempts to find the mental components that performed cognitive tasks such as solving analogies (see Chapter 5). And thus were delivered Spearman's noetic principles, i.e. those cognitive processes that were generative of new mental content. They are quite well known, at least by name.

The first principle was 'experiential apprehension'.

Any lived experience tends to evoke immediately a knowing of its characters and experiences. (p. 48)

The second principle was the 'eduction of relations'

The mentally presenting of any two or more characters (simple or complex) *tends to evoke immediately a knowing of relation between them.* (p. 63)

The third principle was the 'eduction of correlates'

The presenting of any character together with any relation tends to evoke immediately a knowing of the correlative character. (p. 91)

At first sight these might not seem especially impressive. Their origins were more rational than empirical, despite Spearman's concern with the experimental method. Spearman, though, was inventive in applying the principles in two ways. First, he envisioned them as having applications across a staggering range of mental work, and he thereby united under his principles very disparate-seeming mental tasks. Thus, the discrimination of two tones differing in pitch and the finding of a relation between two terms in an analogy—for example, in the question, 'sugar is to sweet as lemon is to ?'—were, according to Spearman, the same task in essence: that of educing a relation. Educing correlates could be applied just as widely and, famously, Raven (1938) used Spearman's laws as the principles of construction for the progressive matrices tests. Second, Spearman was inventive in seeing how much mental content could be built from these two laws. Beyond simple acts of thinking Spearman built models for the completion of more complex inference problems and, in some of his diagrams, he came close to something that might pass muster as a neural network today. Therefore, the mental content to which these laws applied, and the mental content which they could produce, were diverse. Spearman (1927) later commented on these laws:

> together the three make up absolutely all the cognition (other than purely reproductive) of which the human mind is ever in any circumstances capable. (p. 184)

Spearman's most-mentioned reductionistic construct is his vague biological 'mental energy', but his works also showed this desire to rend thinking into cognitive atoms. The route to achieving this was rational, like the efforts of Hobbes and Wolff. Like some other cognitive constructs, they appear neat within their own frame of reference. Limiting their usefulness, they appeared to drift in an impotent, would-be reductionist space between psychometric measurement of behaviour and brain biology, without making convincing contact with either. They have found little explicit application in intelligence research since their inception.

The abilities of man

Beyond their being used as principles for Raven's matrices and their similarity to some of Sternberg's (1977*a,b*) components of reasoning, Spearman's noetic principles did not enjoy much adoption elsewhere, even by Spearman (1927). In *The abilities of man*, Spearman's greatest work on human intelligence, he thought about the nature of intelligence. The noetic principles play only a tardy bit-part, one that is not essential to the plot. This later book is much more empirical, and its concerns are the proper description of individual differences in terms of what later came to be called psychometric factors, and the possible causes of these differences in terms of brain processing. Although Spearman is reductionist by inclination it is not at all clear how the noetic principles fit into any hierarchy of reduction, in the way that, say, biology sits on chemical laws and chemical phenomena rest on physics. The noetic principles seem disconnected, as though they were a hermeneutic rather than an experimental triumph. Another remarkable aspect of *The abilities of man* is its tone. The writing heaves with metaphors and rhetorical flourishes; Spearman made no effort to douse the controversies surrounding intelligence research with the cold water of scientific writing—they leap off the pages. In opening the book Spearman reiterated his commitment to explanation by reduction, and the first separation he commended was the separating of cognition from conation and affect:

> Every science, physical no less than psychological, is obliged to dissect its subject matter, to deal with the different aspects of it in succession, and finally to bring each of these into relation with all the rest. Only by first dividing can the scientist eventually conquer. (p. 3)

As discussed in more detail in Chapter 3, the setting of Spearman's research was important. He conducted research aimed at understanding the nature of human mental abilities when, just as he got going, the world was about to be swept by Binet's (1905) success in devising a set of mental tests. From then until the present there has been more professional and public concern with testing issues in mental ability differences than in seeking their origins. Here is Spearman's (1927) reflection:

> High as was this status attained by the concept of intelligence in biological territory, it later on became quite eclipsed by the reputation which the concept won for itself in the domain of mental tests. During a prolonged incubatory period, these had been cultivated in the seclusion of several psychological laboratories. Then, suddenly, Binet transformed such theoretical work into live practice. The success was astounding. Teachers found in tests of intelligence something that they could handle; and the public got what it believed it could understand. (p. 7)

Spearman was correct; even until now the interest surrounding the measurement of intellectual differences eclipsed the efforts to understand them (Deary *et al.*, in press).

Much of Spearman's prefatory chapter ran through problems concerning mental abilities that had achieved chronic status. He listed the increasing scepticism surrounding the testing of intelligence in the face of the tests' successes, the inability of expert psychologists to decide upon a verbal definition of intelligence, and the problem of whether to include tests of memory, imagination, language, attention, and motor ability in 'intelligence' tests. He concluded, with undisguised exasperation, that:

> In truth, 'intelligence' has become a mere vocal sound, a word with so many meanings that it finally has none. . . . We shall have to give over the fun of arguing words and begin to face facts. Our intellectual joust is over, it is time to plant some beans. (p. 12)

The problem of not having a definition for intelligence was dismissed in Chapter 1, as it is frequently set up as a bogus toll-gate to block further discussions about human ability differences. Spearman considered the attitude that one may measure and engage in research without a full definition; he cited Terman's view that this was how work on electricity was done. He was not entirely convinced, feeling that although one might not need to know the essence of the construct in advance, one did need some guide concerning what to put in the measures. Spearman was not content to claim that, since the tests 'work', one may proceed from that. He discussed the possibility that the content of mental tests might have been chosen to conform to school success, making their main claim to validity a sham:

> On the whole, the chronicle of modern 'intelligence' has been dramatic. The first act shows it rapidly rising to a dazzling eminence. But in the second, there begin to be heard notes of criticism, which soon swell into an insistent hostile chorus. The most enthusiastic advocates of intelligence become doubtful of it themselves. From having naively assumed that its nature is straightway conveyed by its name, they now set out to discover what this nature really is. In the last act, the truth stands revealed, that the name really has no definite meaning at all; it shows itself to be nothing more than a hypostatized word, applied indiscriminately to all sorts of things. (p. 24)

Models of mental function

Spearman's bean-planting began with his clearing the ground by uprooting a number of then-extant models of mental function. The idea of independent mental faculties was discussed first. Akin to cognitive psychology's constructs, faculties were devised to capture what made people similar in mental make-up. Spearman found mental ability differences rarely touched upon in his historical review, though he was aware of Wolff's writings. He found little consistency in different accounts of faculties and cited two key faults. First, they made a pretence of explaining the mind but were in truth devoid of meaning. Second, they contradicted the unity of mind which, to Spearman, was its most essential characteristic.

Spearman evidently found it frustrating that the idea of independent faculties of mind continued to flourish despite evidence for the unity of mental functions:

> One curious feature about these formal faculties has yet to be mentioned. The doc-trine loses every battle—so to speak—but always wins the war. It will bend to the slightest breath of criticism; but not the most violent storm can break it. (p. 38)

Faculty psychology is still alive and well in the shape of Gardner's (1983) multiple intelligences. According to Chabris (1998), mainstream psychometric research on intelligence, which emphasizes *g*, has the opposite fate: winning the empirical battles but losing the communication war.

Among other problems with faculty psychology, Spearman mentioned errors of thought that needing shouting very loudly and repeatedly at many of today's psychologists, not least those of us working in the area of mental ability differ-ences. The first is the problem of investing too much in a word that becomes applied to some conception of mental function, which Spearman referred to as,

> the old illusion whereby words are taken as real coin instead of mere counters. Having fashioned for ourselves such a name as, say, judgement, then—because the name remains the same—we fall into the belief that we are treating of an entity always the same. (p. 39)

Words like intelligence, attention, concentration, motivation, and so forth, come to mind as having these problems, and so do quack-constructs used in the study of mental ability differences, not least 'mental speed' and 'speed of information processing' which are frequently used as cloaks to cover naked ignorance. In the course of the rest of this book one of the most recurring grouches will be precisely this one of Spearman's, that we humans tend to furnish ready epithets masquerading as explanatory constructs. And we continue to commit his second-named error of thinking we are dealing with a similar entity because a similar name is applied (see jingle and jangle fallacies in Chapter 4). Another complaint from Spearman, aimed again at faculty psychologists, was,

> *Dicto secundum quid ad dictum simpliciter.* You can test the power of attention. For you can test the ticking-off of numbers, and this ticking-off is done by the power of attention.

This completes the sins that psychologists commit all the time in studying cogni-tion; not only do psychologists invent epithets for mental functions, they sometimes state that their mental tests and procedures tap directly these mental components. This applies not just to traditional psychometric tests, but also to experimental–cognitive tests (Chapters 6 and 8), psychophysical tasks (Chapter 7), and psychophysiological procedures (Chapter 9).

Having finished off faculty accounts of mental functions—one can almost see Spearman dusting himself down after the scrap—he turned to what he called the 'anarchic doctrine', or sampling theory (see Thomson 1939). These psychologists wished to assert that there were many cognitive abilities, but also not to deny their correlation, yet only to admit that there was some complicated connection between them. Spearman's put down of this idea was that,

> the bare proposition that the intellectual aptitudes stand in complex relations to one another says nothing wrong only because it says almost nothing at all.

However, he did concede that huge numbers of independent, very specific abilities could give rise to correlations among tests. In a key section that revealed some tensions of the times, Spearman discussed how there was a trend towards finer and finer analysis of tests but that, as correlational theory developed, it became clear that it would be just as profitable to take many tests of different types and,

> Throw all the scores for them indiscriminately into one common pool.

> A little more than a year afterwards [he cited his 1904 paper, p. 274, as evidence for the above suggestion] appeared the great work of Binet and Simon. Here, the paradoxical recommendation to make a hotchpot was actually adopted in practice. Nevertheless the elaborate correlational theory which had in point of fact generated the idea, and had supplied the sole evidence for its validity, was now passed over. The said authors employed a popular substitute. 'Intelligence', as measured by the pool was depicted as a 'general level' of ability. So far as doctrine is concerned, this is the only thing introduced by them that was novel. And most surprisingly Binet, though in actual testing he took account of this 'general level' alone, still in all his theoretical psychology continued to rely altogether upon his old formal faculties, notwithstanding that these and the 'general level' appear to involve doctrines quite incompatible with each other. (p. 60)

> When Binet borrowed the idea of such promiscuous pooling, he carried it into execution with a brilliancy that perhaps no other living man could have matched. But on the theoretical side, he tried to get away too cheaply. And this is the main cause of all the present trouble. (p. 70)

The 'present trouble' remains the trouble addressed by this book; psychometric testing never did provide a cheap route to understanding mental ability differences. Spearman continued in this vein as he began the next chapter of his book which addressed his own two-factor theory of intelligence:

> Whilst Binet, followed by psychologists in all civilised countries, was busy culling the first fruit of the doctrine—that is to say, the procedure of miscellaneous pooling—the originators of the doctrine chose the path of developing the tree from which the fruit had grown. (p. 72)

In an earlier paper I stated that there was no war between Binet's and Spearman's approaches to mental ability differences (Deary 1994*a*). These extracts support that statement—Spearman supported Binet's approach but thought the more important issue was the nature of (or understanding of) rather than the testing of intelligence differences—but there were clearly sour grapes on Spearman's part, an apt metaphor given Spearman's piqued horticultural reference above. He explained the law of tetrad differences of correlations and how this device helped him to develop the idea that each mental task was completed by the mind's applying its general mental factor, which was invoked for all mental tests, and a specific factor for the given test. This brings the discussion of Spearman's book to the most relevant section for present purposes, as he examined the nature of these mental constructs:

> But notice must be taken that this general factor g, like all measurements anywhere, is primarily not any concrete thing but only a value or magnitude. Further, that which this magnitude measures has not been defined by declaring what it is like, but only by pointing out where it can be found. It consists in just that constituent—whatever it may be—which is common to all the abilities inter-connected by the tetrad equation. This way of indicating what g means is just as definite as when one indicates a card by staring at the back of it without looking at its face. (p. 75)

Thus Spearman did not reify g, did not call it 'general intelligence', and kept it as a regularity to be explained rather than an explanation, although,

> Eventually, we may or may not find reason to conclude that g measures something that can appropriately be called 'intelligence'. Such a conclusion, however, would still never be the definition of g, but only a 'statement about' it.

He then spent much space addressing possible routes towards understanding the nature of g *and* the s abilities:

> Even the most complete demonstration . . . that g and s certainly exist, would not itself afford the smallest indication as to the nature of what these two factors represent. (p. 87)

That nature is the single issue addressed by this present book. Spearman explicitly wondered about different possible constructs and different levels of explanation. At the psychological level of explanation he dismissed 'intelligence' as a construct (cf. Howe 1988; Jensen 1998*a*) because there was no agreed definition of the term. He dismissed 'attention' as an ambiguous concept, and decided that there was more to mental ability than 'what the tests test' (Boring 1923) because of their predictive validity. He then took what he denoted an adventurous step by,

Deserting all actually observable phenomena of the mind, and proceeding instead to invent an underlying something which—by analogy with physics—has been called mental energy.

At the physiological level Spearman offered up the explanatory constructs of 'mental energy', this time in biological rather than psychological terms, and 'plasticity'. By plasticity he did not mean mere speed of nervous transmission (see Chapter 9), but something more subtle that would enable the more plastic nervous system to,

> Shape out with time in all psycho-physiological territories finer and more subtle complexes of conductors. In this way, it would function with more precision and constancy (in the sense of systematic regularity); the eventual advantage would be a greater speed and also exactness of the normal much practised abilities. A nervous system whose development has been favoured by a superior plastic function would in its performances surpass other nervous systems in much the same way as a machine made of steel would surpass one similar but made of iron. (p. 91)

By contrast with some of today's researchers who have gone looking for an understanding of ability in terms of mere speed (and been chided on several counts; Stankov and Roberts 1997), Spearman showed some subtlety in seeking a function that might deliver both a fast and an accurate brain (cf. Raz *et al.* 1987). 'Finer and more stable complexes of conductors' is more in the mode of neural network thinking (Rabbitt and Maylor 1991). Eventually, Spearman concentrated for quite a time on ideas of 'energy' and 'mental span', the latter concept being quite close to the present-day conception of working memory, which is now popular as a possible explanatory construct for psychometric intelligence differences (Chapter 5). Spearman's scholarship was impressive, and the authorities he cited span many centuries and languages. He was uncomfortable with the vagueness of the 'mental energy' construct but pleaded to be allowed it on the same basis that physicists are allowed their hypothetical constructs; ironically, one of the constructs that Spearman mentioned is the now-archaic 'ether'! At times, the idea of energy, when expressed in more psychological terms, has similarities to the concept of resources. Despite the scholarship, it is difficult to divine from the text exactly why Spearman settled on the idea of energy. Having taken it on board, however, he reckoned that,

> Such an energy would seem to be just what is wanted to explain *g*, whilst the engines might go far towards explaining the *s*'s. (p. 135)

This was metaphor rather than explanation, and the choice of metaphor reflected the steam/industrial age. To account for the same phenomena Anderson (1992) invoked a 'basic processing mechanism' to explain *g* (people with better overall psychometric test scores were reckoned to have faster information processing generally) and software-type modules to account for more specific abilities. The two accounts mostly recapitulate psychometric findings in terms popular at the respective times. Spearman, however, persisted in his keenness to emphasize that psychometric results were not explanations and he stated that g was only,

> a name for the factor—whatever it may be—that is common to mental tests
> . . . This is the very definition of g. All else about it—including the question
> as to whether it has the least right to be regarded as a genuine measure of
> 'intelligence'—lies still before us to ascertain. (p. 161)

More of Spearman's contributions, especially his empirical works, are discussed in Chapter 3. His contribution to thinking about the origins of mental ability differences spanned levels of description from psychometric (the concept of g and the s's), through experimental (sensory discrimination; Spearman 1904), to physiological (the notion of mental energy driving modular mental engines; see Chapter 9), bound together by a cognitive philosophy (the noetic principles; Spearman 1923). It is at once a disparate and a complete scheme. Disparity and completeness arise from his employing such different levels of description fully to account for individual differences in mental abilities, and never convincingly pulling the constructs together. Although he provided many psychometric data to establish the robustness of the g factor and the slightness of group factors, the power of the noetic principles to bind together all cognition was generated by rational argument. Burt (1940), writing not much later, was critical about Spearman's mental energy, and his suggestion about the way forward in explaining mental ability differences had a more modern ring:

> Intelligence, I regard, not indeed as designating a special form of energy, but
> rather as specifying certain individual differences in the structure of the human
> nervous system—differences whose concrete nature could be described in histo-
> logical terms. But in any case, whether it is a 'real' property in either of these
> senses or in some other remains a question that cannot be solved by factor-
> analysis as such. Just as we cannot deduce the essential character of the
> elementary processes in the retinas from a mere analysis of colour equations,
> so we cannot determine the nature of intelligence without supplementary
> evidence from anatomy, physiology and genetics, to be accumulated by research
> that is only just beginning. (pp. 216–218)

CONCLUSION

All four writers discussed above—Huarte, Hobbes, Wolff, and Spearman—share the views that humans evince individual differences in mental abilities and that these differences demand some explanatory account. In Spearman's evocative phrase, they have all sought a 'mental cytology': a set of constructs at whatever level of description that will provide the source of some fraction of the individual differences. The constructs range from complex psychological processes to aspects of brain biology, and it is this same range that is found in present-day research. The reductionistic ladder may be followed downwards from Chapters 5 to 9. Part of the value in acknowledging these early contributions is in comparing them to present-day ideas, and another part is in beginning the process of filling in two millennia of history concerning scientific conjectures on the origins of cognitive ability differences.

3 The discriminating mind

*Intelligence and sensory discrimination in the early twentieth century,
and the more recent rise of joint experimental–differential approaches to
human mental ability differences*

SUMMARY

The beginnings of the scientific investigations into the origins of mental ability
differences followed Galton's and Spearman's ideas about sensory discrimination as
one element of human intellectual variation. Their empirical efforts are written off
as failures by some of psychology's historians. However, there are inaccuracies in
the historical accounts of this research. A re-examination of the key research papers
and reanalyses of data sets produced between 1900 and World War I reveals a
consistent association, of small effect size, between psychometric intelligence and
acuity of sensory discrimination, especially for vision and audition. The distinction
between measuring and understanding ability differences, as emphasized by
Spearman, was largely lost from the 1920s until the rise of cognitive psychology
in the 1970s. The gathering force of a new spirit in mental ability research, one
that sought a combined cognitive–differential approach and a redirection towards
understanding psychometric intelligence differences, is adumbrated.

THE MODERN ERA: ASKING SCIENTIFIC QUESTIONS

Much that is contained within the writings of Huarte, Hobbes, and Wolff might be
seen as cheques that were never in danger of being cashed. Until the late-nineteenth
century ideas on the bases of human intelligence differences were worked out by
rational thought, and not submitted to telling experiments. Huarte stands out as a
partial exception, because he made use of more empirical evidence than did the other
two, probably because of his medical training. Attention turns now to the beginning of the scientific phase of research into human intelligence differences. Human
ability differences as a field of scientific research was incubated between the period
when Galton (1883) was writing his hypotheses and impressions and 1904 and
1905, when Spearman reported his discovery of *g* and Binet and Simon assembled
the first psychometric test of mental ability for children. From the first few years of
the twentieth century until now there have existed two streams to the story of
human ability differences. On the one hand there are the developments in the
psychometrics of cognitive abilities; constructing and refining tests, finding the
psychometric structure of mental abilities, and assessing the predictive validity of

Some material in this chapter appeared previously in Deary (1994a and 1997).

the tests. That has been dealt with in summary form in Chapter 1. There are quite full and absorbing accounts of these developments in intelligence testing in other books (Fancher 1985*a*; Jensen 1998; Zenderland 1998). Binet (1905, 1916) identified his contribution as existing within this applied stream:

> The scale [the Binet–Simon scale] that we shall describe is not a theoretical work; it is the result of long investigations, first at the Salpetriere, and afterwards in the primary schools of Paris, with both normal and subnormal children. These short psychological questions have been given the name of tests. The use of tests today is very common, and there are even contemporary authors who have made a specialty of organising new tests according to theoretical views, but who have made no effort to patiently try them out in the schools. Theirs is an amusing occupation, comparable to a person's making a colonising expedition to Algeria, advancing always only upon the map, without taking off his dressing gown. We place but slight confidence in the tests invented by these authors and we have borrowed nothing from them. All the tests which we propose have been repeatedly tried, and have been retained from among many, which after trial have been discarded. We can certify that those which are here presented have proved themselves valuable. (p. 193)

Perhaps one would have rushed to counsel Binet that colonizing might better be done both by actual travel and by taking (and making, and improving) a map. It shortly becomes clear that Spearman's opinion was that Binet was travelling blind.

This book focuses on a second stream of intelligence research; the attempt to understand any identifiable cognitive and biological elements of human mental ability differences. Using the word stream as a metaphor is in danger of conveying a false impression that there was an organized body of continuous research directed to this end. It was not so. There was a flurry of ideas and activity from around the end of the nineteenth century until the First World War. After that, whereas the intelligence testing enterprise greatly enlarged, the attempts to seek the origins of psychometric intelligence differences were sporadic until about the 1970s, with the rise of cognitive psychology and the development of new methods in biological psychology.

To understand what happened during the first scientific wave of activity in seeking the bases of mental ability differences, four matters are discussed hereinafter: (a) the typical historical account of the period, (b) errors in the typical historical account, (c) the actual empirical results obtained, and (d) what the data from the period can tell us.

HUMAN INTELLIGENCE DIFFERENCES AND SIMPLE PSYCHOLOGICAL PROCESSES: THE TYPICAL HISTORICAL ACCOUNT

The essence of what was written about the first scientific attempts to examine the origins of intelligence differences would read as follows: 'Whereas Binet and his co-workers successfully sought a test of "intelligence" among the higher cognitive abilities, people such as Galton and Spearman sought, without success, indicators of and explanations for intelligence differences in lower level, simpler psychological functions. Especially damaging to the ideas of Galton were the studies of Sharp in 1898–1899 and Wissler in 1901.' Thus, while Binet was measuring mental ability differences, others focused more on trying to understand them. To begin this work, they made guesses at the possible simpler psychological functions that might be the partial bases of higher-level cognitive variation. First, though, follows some idea of what contemporary sources suggest went on in those early studies.

Some accounts from a range of psychological sources illustrate the above summary. In an introductory text on psychology Bernstein *et al.* (1988) wrote:

> In the late 1800s, Sir Francis Galton tried, unsuccessfully, to develop a test of intellectual ability by measuring people's perceptual and motor abilities, such as how fast they responded to simple stimuli and how sensitive they were to pain. Other researchers soon concluded that these abilities had very little to do with intelligent behavior (Wissler 1901).

Blum (1978) wrote in a similar way about associations between sensory-level measurement and higher cognitive differences:

> He [Galton] could not find any clear relationship between simple sensory acuities and the more global phenomenon of mental ability. Likewise, J. McKeen Cattell, who studied with Galton, attempted similar kinds of measurements in the United States, and elaborate statistical analysis of his data failed to show any dependable relationships with course grades of college freshmen. (p. 44)

Galton did hypothesize that ability differences might originate in the senses. Spearman (1904) described Galton's idea as follows:

> men of marked ability [appear] to possess on the whole an unusually fine discrimination of minute differences in weight. (p. 206),

but knew that,

> [Galton] was a suggestive writer . . . [who] appears to have been diverted from the point by other interests, and to have contented himself with the above general impression without clinching the matter in systematic investigation. (p. 206)

Spearman was correct. Galton's (1883) description of his evidence for a connection between sensory acuity and human mental ability differences was in part merely anecdotal:

The trials I have as yet made on the sensitivity of different persons confirms the reasonable expectation that it would on the whole be highest among the intellectually ablest . . . as a rule . . . men have more delicate powers of discrimination than women, and the business experience of life seems to confirm this view. The tuners of pianofortes are men, and so I understand are the tasters of tea and wine, the sorters of wool, and the like . . . Ladies rarely distinguish the merits of wine at the dinner table, and though the custom allows them to preside at the breakfast-table, men think them on the whole far from successful makers of tea and coffee. (p. 20)

Of Galton's ideas on the senses, Sternberg (1990) wrote that:

He [Galton] also discovered that people are inferior to cats in their ability to perceive tones of high pitch. This finding presents a problem for any psychophysically based theory of intelligence that subscribes to a notion of evolutionary continuity. This suggests that, in at least this one respect, cats are superior in intelligence to humans. (p. 70)

Sensory range was indeed one of the measures collected by Galton (Johnson *et al.* 1985) but Galton's theory of intelligence differences focused more on discrimination within the range. Galton formulated the hypothesis about an association between differences in higher mental abilities and fineness of sensory discrimination. He did not report a decisive experiment. It is not clear why some writers thought otherwise. In the later 1880s Galton collected anthropometric data in laboratories in South Kensington, first at the International Health Exhibition and later at the Science Galleries of the Museum. Data from thousands of subjects were collated and were concerned mainly with physical measurements, although there were some data on visual acuity, highest audible tone, and simple reaction time. Recent analyses of these data show that there were social class variations in the sensory and reaction time measures—and in many of the physical measures—but the data have little bearing on Galton's earlier, discrimination-based ideas about human intelligence differences (Johnson *et al.* 1985).

Galton was not the first writer to muse on the psychological underpinnings of differences in cognitive abilities. Huarte, Hobbes, and Wolff (Chapter 2) had done much the same, along similar and sometimes more developed lines of thought, hundreds of years earlier. The difference that marks Galton was his writing on the threshold of psychology as a science; it makes an easy narrative step to move on to the empirical studies of his ideas. He did collect some data, but they were not reported or analysed to a sufficient degree to pronounce upon his ideas. The 'typical historical account' continues by stating that Galton's ideas were refuted by two influential studies conducted in the USA across the bridge of the nineteenth and twentieth centuries.

The two studies were conducted by Clark Wissler (1901), supervised by McKeen Cattell at Columbia, and by Stella Sharp (1898–1899) supervised by Titchener at Cornell. Fancher (1985*a*), in his history of intelligence research, told as a sequence of biographies of the central players, wrote of 'Wissler's devastating results' (p. 48) with regard to the hypothesis that human intelligence differences might be related to simple psychological characteristics. Eckberg's (1979) opinion of Wissler's results was that they were

> so dismal that they directly caused Cattell to end his own involvement with testing. (p. 138)

After mentioning the results of Wissler and Sharp, Carroll (1982) wrote that from

> the debates in the literature of the times one would think that the mental testing movement was being laid to rest. (p. 33)

> In the early years . . . use was made of relatively simple tasks, usually involving powers of sensory acuity and judgement (e.g., detecting small differences in the weights of two visually similar objects) or speed of reaction time in responding to stimuli (e.g., naming colours) . . . perhaps only one has survived in the current measures of intelligence—the memory span test. (p. 36)

In his influential history of experimental psychology, Boring (1950) commented on this era of human intelligence research as follows:

> As early as 1898 Stella Sharp at Cornell was able to show that Binet had won out over Cattell—if we may put this complex matter so simply. Sharp's conclusion was a decision of Titchener's laboratory that the Wundtian variables of experimental psychology are less adequate for a description of those human abilities which make for success than are Binet's devices, which he made up and did not, in general, come directly out of the laboratories. Perhaps Titchener felt even then—as he did later—that applied psychology is scientifically unworthy and that failure of 'pure' experimental psychology to meet the requirements of functional use was not disparaging to the Wundtian school. Or perhaps he was glad to find Cattell in error. (p. 572)

Eckberg (1979) viewed Wissler's and Clark's studies as important. The following comments from this source also illustrate the unusual language sometimes used when historians of psychology describe this period, having recourse to metaphors of violence and physical injury.

> The final study, which proved a staggering blow to the testing movement, was performed by Clark Wissler (1901) at the Columbia University Laboratories, then under the direction of Cattell. Wissler employed 21 different tests, an elaboration of the tests suggested by Cattell a decade previously. He then used Pearson's new method of correlation to determine the relationships among psychological tests, anthropometric measures and college grades. The

results were so dismal that they caused Cattell to end his own involvement with testing.

It was with the Wissler study that testing entered its period of decline. R. D. Tuddenham (1962) . . . reports that by 1905 the academic movement was 'moribund', so much so that Binet's later work almost did not revive it. The movement waned as a result of a decade of failure to discover important hierarchical mental differences. The negative findings of Sharp and Wissler are commonly cited as the crushing blows to the movement . . . but their studies can better be seen as the culmination of a long line of studies that hardly ever produced the kinds of results expected. Be that as it may, the enthusiasm of testers declined markedly after 1901. (p. 138)

It is difficult to accommodate both Eckberg's gloomy account and the following description of the same period of the testing movement given by Boring (1950):

Thorndike was in a position in his *Educational Psychology* of 1903 to show what kinds of tests were best for predicting educational success. At the end of this decade Goddard had got out his own revision of the Binet–Simon scale, and Whipple had published the first edition of his manual of *Mental and Physical Tests* with his description of fifty-four tests and how to give them. By 1910 mental testing had clearly come to stay. (p. 574)

ERRORS IN THE TYPICAL HISTORICAL ACCOUNT

The typical historical account of the beginnings of research into the bases of human ability differences makes three types of error. First, there are errors in the factual descriptions of the supposedly decisive studies of Wissler and Sharp. Second, this leads to errors in stating the importance of these studies. Third, there is a failure to recognize the difference between those researchers seeking only to measure human intelligence differences and those intent on understanding them.

Factual errors

First, some quotes illustrate factual errors in the historical accounts of the Wissler and Sharp studies. Eckberg (1979) commented that,

In one widely cited study Stella Sharp (1899) found little consistency among schoolchildren as they moved from test to test.

Sternberg (1990) said that,

Sharp (1899) undertook a large-scale experiment to discover the usefulness of the Binet–Simon tests in applied settings (p. 78)

Carroll's (1982) account noted that,

> The results of this [Wissler's] study, as well as those of a somewhat similar
> one by Stella E. Sharp (1898–1899) working under Titchener at Cornell, were
> taken as persuasive evidence that mental tests of simple mental reactions had
> no promise as predictors of scholastic achievement or, for that matter, as
> measures of anything like intelligence. (p. 33)

It comes as a surprise, then, to discover that Sharp's (1898–1899) entire sample
was only seven postgraduate students. She included no tests of simple sensory
abilities. There were no statistical analyses in her paper. The tests used were an
odd, almost unrecognizable, adaptation of some of Binet's ideas for tests. The
importance given to Sharp's report must have been a case of Chinese whispers
in the telling of the history of psychology; a confusion perpetuated by some
people failing accurately to report the contents of their cited sources.

Other writers, though, did not make these errors, and were aware of the limitations of Sharp's study. Cairns and Ornstein (1979) remarked that,

> Despite the fact that Sharp's study was basically inadequate to the task of
> evaluating the Binet approach—she tested only seven subjects (all advanced
> students in psychology), with materials and under conditions different from
> those recommended by Binet—her report was influential and had the effect
> of dampening interest in the assessment of intelligence. (p. 479)

Watson's account of the two studies contained criticisms:

> Most of the investigations of the time were concerned with simple sensori-
> motor and associative functions and were based on the assumption that
> intelligence could be reduced to sensations and motor speed, an attempt which,
> as is now known, was doomed to failure. Furthermore, although more suitable
> verbal material was used, the studies of College students at Cornell, such as
> Sharp's, and the Wissler study at Columbia, were found to be essentially
> non-predictive. What the workers failed to take into account was the fact that
> college students are a highly selected group having a considerably restricted
> range. The negative findings of these studies effectively blocked further inves-
> tigation at the college level for years. (Brozek and Evans 1979, p. 197)

Spearman (1904) criticized Wissler's study for trying to collect too many data
too quickly:

> No less than 22 tests were carried out, many of a most difficult character,
> besides measuring the length and breadth of each reagent's head; that during
> the leisure moments afforded him in the course of these tests the observing
> 'student officer of the department' had to note in writing the contour of
> the reagent's forehead, the character of his hair, the nature of his complexion,

the colour of his eyes, the shape of his nose, the description of his ears, of his lips, of his hands, of his fingers, of his face, and of his head—and that this whole procedure is considered to be satisfactorily completed in forty-five minutes. (p. 283)

Misstating the importance of Sharp and Wissler

Sharp's (1898–1899) study had neither the subjects, tests, nor analyses to justify its repeated citing as a 'blow' to the idea that human mental ability differences had a basis in simple mental functions. Wissler's (1901) study was much larger, but used only students with high ability. Additionally, Jensen (1980) noted that Wissler calculated less than 10% of the possible correlations in the study, the range of the subjects was highly restricted, no measurement errors were taken into account, and the simple reaction time measurements used were based on only three to five trials. And there was no suitable test of sensory abilities.

The studies of Sharp and Wissler, if they did dampen researchers' ardour for a Galtonian/Cattellian approach to human mental ability versus that of Binet, had no inherent power to do so. As the next section shows, the 'versus' in the previous sentence is the next error made in the typical historical account.

Misunderstanding measuring versus understanding human intelligence

Sharp (1898–1899), in the introduction to her paper, asked whether one might 'Account for unlike results from the building up of unlike materials' (p. 334). Her study might not have produced any evidence that could be used to decide this issue one way or the other, but the question is central to this present book; it is one about the bases of human mental ability differences, not one about measurement of the phenotype *per se*. Thus, it should be recognized that researchers at the turn of the century did make the measurement–explanation distinction, although commentators on the historical research sometimes seem oblivious to it. To find a practical measure of human mental abilities (Binet's triumph) was distinguished at the time—although often conflated by more recent writers— from the effort to find an explanation for those differences in terms of simpler sensory or other mental or biological differences (Spearman's quest). This theme is enlarged in the next section. If we are to reset our calendar after the false empirical starts of Sharp and Wissler, it must be to 1904 with the publication of Spearman's first and epoch-making paper.

SPEARMAN AND BURT AND REALLY LOOKING DOWN ON HUMAN INTELLIGENCE

Spearman's 'general intelligence' paper of 1904 is still well cited in psychology, and is one of the most important reports in the discipline. It is remembered principally for the discovery of *g*. That would have been discovered anyway, by someone, because it is ubiquitous (Chapter 1). The more attractive part of Spearman's paper is its agenda. It was written to launch a new speciality he called 'correlational psychology' (now called differential psychology or individual differences). This type of psychology sought the simple psychological processes that accounted for higher-level mental ability differences. Spearman knew about Binet's tests and thought they were useful practically. He believed also that these tests would reveal little about the nature of human intelligence differences. There was no competition between Binet and Spearman in terms of their scientific aspirations. They were studying human abilities in complementary ways. Spearman's (1904) launching of a 'correlational psychology' was for,

> positively determining all psychical tendencies and in particular those which connect together the so-called 'mental tests' with psychical activities of greater generality and interest (p. 205)

This statement could easily be the letterhead of today's search for the information processing bases of human mental ability differences. Spearman (1904) commented on the success that Binet was having in producing tests to measure human ability differences, but separated this from his own aim, which was to understand these differences in terms of tractable psychological processes.

> Binet and Henri appear now to seek tests of a more intermediate character, sacrificing much of the elementariness, but gaining greatly in approximation to the events of ordinary life. The result would seem likely to have more practical than theoretical value. (p. 210)

In this statement Spearman in effect reproduced the validational structure of mental ability differences sketched in Chapter 1 (Fig. 1.1). According to Spearman, the Binetian mental tests were intermediate between individual differences in life's outcomes and any brain processes whose differences correlated with test performances. Among other remarkable aspects of Spearman's (1904) article is the literature review it contains. Unlike many of its contemporaries, Spearman's piece reviewed thoroughly previous studies in the area. Considerable detail is offered on relevant studies and he concluded that,

> There is scarcely one positive conclusion concerning the correlation between mental tests and independent practical estimates that has not with equal force been flatly contradicted. (p. 219)

By mental tests Spearman was referring to measurements of basic psychological functions, and by independent practical estimates he was referring to estimates of intelligence using assessments that preceded the Binet-type tests. Spearman concluded that the question of the association between lower-level measures of psychological functions and estimates of higher level cognitive abilities was open:

In spite of the many previous inconclusive and negatory verdicts, the question of the correspondence between the Tests of the Laboratory and the Intelligence of Life cannot yet be regarded as definitely closed. The only thing so far demonstrated is that the old means of investigation are entirely inadequate. (p. 225)

Given the prominence of this paper it is odd that the typical historical account does not include Spearman's conclusion, as it was based on the most thorough review of the work of the period. He knew that, far from having decided the issue of basic processes and mental ability differences, the studies by Sharp and Wissler were among other inadequate investigations of a topic that had yet empirically to get off the ground. Spearman noted in his review that only Wissler's study employed correlation coefficients, with other studies using tabulated results, many studies had included children of different ages, and studies had frequently lacked a clear purpose and had not reckoned with errors of measurement. In stating his purpose, Spearman, again, made a clear distinction between the measurement of intelligence differences and their explanation. In a further passage he stated this along with his intentions, which again appear quite modern and relevant to the aims of this book:

As regards the nature of the selected Laboratory Psychics, the guiding principle has been the opposite to that of Binet and Ebbinghaus. The practical advantages proffered by their more complex mental operations have been unreservedly rejected in favour of the theoretical gain promised by the utmost simplicity and unequivocality; there has been no search after condensed psychological extracts to be on occasion conveniently substituted for regular examinations; regardless of all useful application, that form of physical activity has been chosen which introspectively appeared to me as the simplest and yet preeminently intellective. This is the act of distinguishing one sensation from another. (p. 241)

The Binet and Galton–Spearman approaches to human ability differences were thus distinct, there was no competition towards the same end and therefore no question of one winning out over the other. Spearman acknowledged the utility of higher-level mental tests, but they did not meet the needs of his research programme. He sought to understand human mental ability differences by decomposing or reducing them in part to individual differences in simpler mental processes. He chose sensory discrimination as his measure of simple processing, as Galton had done before him. Binet (1905), however, did not agree with the seeking of the causes of intelligence in the senses:

But here we must come to an understanding of what meaning to give to that word so vague and so comprehensive, 'the intelligence'. Nearly all of the phenomena with which psychology concerns itself are phenomena of intelligence; sensation, perception, are intellectual manifestations as much as reasoning. Should we therefore bring into our examination the measure of sensation after the manner of the psycho-physicists? Should we put to the test all of his psychological processes? A slight reflection has shown us that this would indeed be wasted time.

It seems to us that in intelligence there is a fundamental faculty, the alteration or lack of which is of the utmost importance for practical life. This faculty is judgment, otherwise called good sense, practical sense, initiative, the faculty of adapting one's self to circumstances. To judge well, to comprehend well, to reason well, these are the essential activities of intelligence. A person may be a moron or an imbecile if he is lacking in judgment. What does it matter, for example, whether the organs of sense function normally? Of what import that certain ones are hyperesthetic, or that others are anesthetic or weakened? Laura Bridgman, Helen Keller and their fellow-unfortunates were blind as well as deaf, but this did not prevent them from being very intelligent. Certainly this is demonstrative proof that the total or even partial integrity of the senses does not form a mental faculty equal to judgment. We may measure the acuteness of the sensibility of subjects; nothing could be easier. But we should do this, not so much to find out the state of their sensibility as to learn the exactitude of their judgment.

For some researchers in the USA, after Binet's tests had caught on, there was a realization that mental tests were not linked to basic psychological and/or biological constructs and that this left them wanting. Their concerns were similar to Spearman's. Zenderland (1998), writing about Goddard's experience with mental tests recounted:

'The Binet people, including yourself are not sufficiently self-critical', University of Iowa psychologist Edwin Starbuck warned Goddard privately. He recommended returning to simpler and more well-established psychological procedures, such as sensory discrimination and motor skill—tests for which there was 'some definite measuring stick' (p. 238)

There was no 'final standard' against which to gauge their validity, Fernald complained. Comparing test results with school results did not solve this issue she argued. 'One group of people seem to be using the school as a check on the Binet test', she concluded, while 'another group is using the tests as a check on the school.' To Fernald, the problem was clear. 'Don't we go in a circle?' (p. 240)

Goddard apparently believed that mental test score differences originated in biological differences, though his speculations were vague:

Intelligence [is] . . . dependent upon and correlative with neuron activity . . . [the] more elaborate and complicated the neuron pattern the higher the possible intelligence. (Zenderland 1998, p. 294).

In his first empirical studies Spearman (1904) used tests of sensory discrimination in three modalities: auditory (pitch discrimination), visual (hue discrimination), and tactile (weight discrimination). Estimates of intelligence were of a rough-and-ready kind and were not based upon psychometric tests. He considered school work to represent 'Present Efficiency' and, when corrected for age, could reveal 'Native Capacity' (p. 250). Peer ratings by the most able children were thought to reveal 'common sense', and the general impression that children made upon others allowed them to be classified as 'bright', 'average', or 'dull' (p. 251). Spearman studied five samples of subjects. For the village school sample, nine correlations were given between three estimates of intelligence and the three discrimination measures. Using Fancher's (1985*b*) recalculations—owing to minor errors in Spearman's original hand-calculated correlations—the mean correlation between discrimination and intelligence estimates was 0.39 (range 0.25 to 0.47). Subjects rated as more intelligent were able to make finer discriminations. Spearman estimated that the correlation between general discrimination and general intelligence approached 1.0 when corrections for unreliability of the tests were made. This is a huge correction, and the conclusion is not convincing in the face of a correlation between pitch and light discrimination that was −0.02. Moreover, the sample was small and the confidence intervals on the correlations large. In the preparatory school sample, pitch discrimination correlated with marks received in classics, French, English, and mathematics to give an average correlation of 0.38 (range 0.27 to 0.44). The adult sample he tested included no measure of intelligence.

Spearman's (1904) literature review was exemplary. His stated intent was clear and interesting. His methods of sensory discrimination were better measures of basic processes than had been used before. His rankings of ability used peer and staff reports and marks in school examinations. His analyses were modern for their time, and involved some innovations such as correcting correlations for unreliability. His samples were small. Therefore, the empirical kernel of the article is a curate's egg, and Spearman's experiments may be considered at best as suggestive pilot studies. His conclusions were overstated, although they were interesting as future hypotheses to be tested. To an extent he realized this and he later cooled his claim about the identity between general discrimination and general intelligence in a footnote to Burt's (1909–1910) first article:

> This conclusion of mine was badly worded. I did not mean (as others have naturally taken it) that general intelligence was based on sensory discrimination; if anything vice versa. I take both the sensory discrimination and the mani-festations leading a teacher to impute general intelligence to be based on some deeper fundamental cause. (p. 165)

It is not easy to pick out Spearman's precise meaning in this statement. However, it suggests a search for more basic processes that might account for both intelligence and discrimination differences. And it brings into play Spearman's main contribution to psychology, *g*:

If [the general factor] be mental at all, it must inevitably become one of the foundation pillars of any psychological system claiming to accord with actual fact—and the majority of prevalent theories may have a difficulty in reckoning with it. . . . Thus we are becoming able to give a precise arithmetical limitation to the famous assertion that 'at bottom, the Great Man is ever the same kind of thing.' This Central Function, whatever it may be, is hardly anywhere more prominent than in the simple act of discriminating two nearly identical tones. (p. 273)

Again, this is reading too much into his own data, though Chapter 1 showed that the general factor accounts for much variance in mental test scores. We shall return to Spearman's hunt for the 'central function' presently, but let us continue the history of attempts to relate higher mental abilities to differences in sensory discrimination.

Burt (1909–1910) gave two reasons for conducting his first major empirical study. He reckoned that general intelligence, which was 'above all supreme' in its importance, was under-researched: 'the notice it has received from psychologists has been in proportion astonishingly scant' (p. 94). He rehearsed complaints about earlier studies that echoed Spearman's (1904) strictures, although his intention appeared more like Binet's. Burt attempted to,

Determine whether higher mental functions would not show a yet closer correlation with 'General Intelligence' than was shown by simpler mental functions, such as sensory discrimination and motor reaction, with which previous investigations have been so largely engrossed. (p. 95)

Burt did include simple sensory measures among his tests. He did not emphasize Spearman's (1904) results, and when he cited those who thought that intelligence differences had a basis in sensory discrimination, he mentioned Titchener. Burt's subjects were drawn from a 'high class' (p. 99) preparatory school in Oxford (the Dragon School) and from a nearby school whose children were the sons of local businessmen. The experimental tests were presented in five categories. Sensory tests measured two-point skin discrimination, weight discrimination, pitch discrimination, and visual comparison of the lengths of lines. The other ability test categories were motor, sensorimotor, association, and voluntary attention. As in Spearman's study, the measures of intelligence would be considered unsatisfactory today, being taken from the impressions of the masters at the schools.

Two-point discrimination and the discrimination of weights correlated at near-to-zero levels with intelligence estimates. Pitch discrimination correlated 0.40 and 0.37 with intelligence estimates in the two groups. The ability to discriminate the lengths of two lines correlated on average at 0.29 and 0.31 with estimates of intelligence. Readers might have reservations about entertaining results from Burt, given the suggestions about his scientific probity (Hearnshaw 1979). In support of these data, it can be argued that the results date back long before questions have been raised about Burt's methods, and a parallel data set was collected from the same subjects by J. C. Flugel, with very similar results. Having made little mention of Spearman's (1904) claims regarding sensory discrimination in his introduction, and having announced his greater interest in higher mental functions, Burt (1909–1910) appeared surprised by his results on sensory testing:

> Before actually calculating the coefficients [we] believed we were finding no correlation throughout the sensory region. (p. 131, footnote)

> General Intelligence, then, shows little or no relation to senses which to civilised men are of low cognitive value; but it shows a marked relation to those senses which aid the perception of relations or formation of concepts, and are of high cognitive value. (p. 132)

Thus Burt mused about the sensory bases of intelligence. However, for a figure who is seen as the academic descendant of Galton and Spearman, he did not put these ideas to the fore in this or later writings. Burt's results were undoubtedly supportive of Binet's approach to the measurement of mental abilities; tests of higher mental functions appeared to be the most predictive of estimates of intelligence. Of the 12 tests used by Burt (1909–1910), six resulted in correlations of about 0.5 or below with intelligence estimates, and six correlated 0.5 or above. According to Burt:

> The former six—the simple sensory and motor tests—are thus of little use in the empirical diagnosis of intelligence (p. 157)

If Burt's study was a failure of the simple sensory approach to intelligence, as Burt considered it to be, it was only a failure against the wrong criterion, that of measurement rather than understanding. Burt replicated the modest correlations found between simple sensory measures in the visual and auditory modalities and estimates of intelligence that were reported by Spearman (1904).

Burt (1909–1910) articulated the importance of modest correlations between sensory and intellectual measures in terms of a theory of intelligence:

> The main significance of this hierarchy of experimental performances, is, as it appears to me, that we are led to infer that all the functions of the human mind, the simplest and the most complicated alike, are probably processes within a single system. A process typical of higher psychophysical 'levels' may be concerned with a process typical of lower psychophysical 'levels' far less intimately than either is with a process of intermediate 'levels'. Yet, this relatively small correlation is not a disproof, but a consequence of, their inclusive organisation within a single integrative system of psychical dispositions or neural arcs. The contrary assumption of a radical dichotomy between 'the general mammalian foundation of the central nervous system' and the

'specifically human capacity' of General Intelligence—towards which Dr Archdall Reid, and even Professor Thorndike seem to incline—proves a serious barrier to advance of the biological standpoint in individual psychology. (p. 164)

This interesting formulation is relevant to more ancient and more modern findings in intelligence research. For example, in Chapter 9, there are studies which examine whether nerve conduction velocity, reaction time, and psychometric test scores form a Burtian hierarchy. Burt sketched a hierarchical system of mental and biological constructs, guessing that those at non-adjacent levels of reduction would have lower correlations than constructs at adjacent levels. Also, he raised the question of whether some of the variance in psychometric intelligence differences arises from basic differences in brain structure and functions, or whether intelligence differences largely inhabit higher-level functions. These statistical and conceptual issues will be replayed several times as recent experimental evidence is sifted. Finally, Burt's scheme harks back to Huarte's (1575) opinion that the same aspects of brain biology that caused individual differences in mental abilities among humans also accounted for differences within other species.

Thorndike *et al.* (1909) tested 37 female school students and 25 third-year high-school boys for ability to match lines of different lengths and boxes of different weights. These sensory discrimination task variables were correlated with estimates of intelligence and scholarship. In discussing the results the authors were replying specifically to Spearman's (1904) claim that there was an identity between general discrimination and general intelligence, and they did not spend much time discussing the fact that they too had found a modest positive relationship, similar in effect size to Spearman's, between the two. They estimated that the true correlation between general discrimination and general intelligence was 0.23. Instead of combining the two concordant empirical results and developing the findings by asking about their importance, Thorndike and colleagues reacted to Spearman's theoretical account by proposing the opposite:

The theoretical importance of Spearman's conclusion lies in the support which it would give, if verified, to the hypothesis that the efficiency of what may be called the general mammalian foundation of the nervous system is closely correlated with what may be called the specifically human neurone-connections. The present results support the contrary hypothesis, that the efficiency of a man's equipment for the specifically human task of managing ideas is only loosely correlated with the efficiency of the simpler sensori-motor apparatus which he possesses in common with other species. (p. 367)

In general there is evidence of a complex set of bonds between the psychological equivalents of both what we call the formal side of thought and what we call its content, so that one is tempted to replace Spearman's statement by the equally extravagant one that there is *nothing whatsoever* common to all mental functions, or to any half of them. (p. 368)

This comment is similar to Burt's (1909–1910) musing about what proportion of human ability differences is to be found in basic brain parameters and what proportion in more high-level organizational parameters.

Two further reports offer an empirical verdict on the association between mental ability and sensory discrimination: Abelson (1911) and Carey (1914–1915, 1915–1917). Abelson tried to discover the psychological principles underlying mental test scores. Here was what was said about Binet's tests:

> They do not know what these tests measure or signify. The tests are isolated from the main body of scientific psychology. They neither derive much light from it, nor do they import much to it.

Again, the effort was to understand rather than measure mental ability differences. The subjects tested were 88 girls and 43 boys, the least 'backward' pupils from eight London County Council schools for so-called 'mental defectives'. The following tests were included: tapping; crossing out an irregular line of rings; crossing out groups of four dots from rows that contained groups of three, four, and five dots; performing memory tests for sentences, names, and commissions; discriminating the longer of two vertical lines; pointing to a part of a geometrical figure that satisfies a command such as, 'Point inside the two circles and the triangle but only in one square'; and interpreting pictures.

Measures of reading ability were obtained from the teachers, who provided an estimate of practical intelligence in response to the question, 'Which of these children she would soonest trust on an errand requiring the sharpest intellect' (p. 289). The average correlation among the tests was 0.32 for the girls and 0.26 for the boys. There were a very few, near-zero correlations. The average correlation when tests were correlated singly with global rankings of intelligence was 0.50 for girls and 0.41 for boys. For the lines discrimination task, the average correlation with the other 11 test scores was 0.30 (range 0.20 to 0.43) for girls and 0.28 (range 0.11 to 0.47) for boys (i.e. brighter children made finer discriminations). Abelson concluded that the,

> idea that the tests are mere laboratory artefacts, having no relation to ordinary life, falls to the ground. (p. 303)

In a reanalysis (Deary 1994a) Abelson's final correlation tables were submitted to principal components analyses. Analysis of the boys' correlation matrix revealed a general factor, accounting for 33.6% of the variance, with most tests having substantial loadings on it (mean loading = 0.57). In the girls' sample the general factor, accounting for 37.7% of the variance, had substantial positive loadings for all tests (mean loading = 0.61). The discrimination task loaded on the general factor at similar levels in the boys' and girls' samples, 0.57 and 0.58, respectively. The coefficient of congruence comparing the first unrotated principal component in the samples of boys and girls was 0.98. Therefore, visual discrimination had a moderate loading on g, similar to other mental tests in this battery.

Carey (1914–1915, 1915–1917) examined correlations between intelligence estimates and sensory and memory measures in over 150 schoolchildren. Estimates of school intelligence, practical intelligence, painstaking, and social status were obtained from teachers. Using the pooled results from at least two testing occasions, Carey obtained visual, auditory, and tactile discrimination measures. Several other tests including memory, verbal, and pictorial/spatial tests were included. The mean correlation of all tests with visual discrimination was 0.28 (range 0.00 to 0.51). The mean correlation of other tests with auditory discrimination was 0.22 (range –0.01 to 0.46). Tactile discrimination correlated only 0.02 with other tests on average. This replicated the results of Thorndike *et al.* (1909), Burt (1909–1910), and Abelson (1911) in that there was a significant, though modest, correlation between tests of auditory and visual discrimination and psychometric mental tests and estimates of intelligence. A reanalysis of Carey's results (Deary 1994*a*) revealed a general factor accounting for 34.9% of the variance, with visual and auditory discrimination loading 0.57 and 0.45, respectively.

Some writers of the history of intelligence were taken to task above for their error-prone accounts. They retell the story of the failure to find associations among simpler psychological measures and psychometric abilities. On one interpretation of 'failure' they were incorrect. There were significant associations between sensory discrimination measures and psychometric ability differences; key papers were ignored. The effect sizes were small. On another count they were correct. The movement to explore the bases of human intelligence died as a concerted research programme from about the time of World War I. Psychometric testing grew hugely, but there was comparatively very little interest in the psychological and biological processes underlying test performance, save for behaviour genetic studies.

A FRESH START

From the renaissance and enlightenment thinkers to the first empirical studies on human mental abilities in the late-nineteenth and early twentieth centuries, we have traced an interest in discovering the bases of human cognitive differences. The success of attempts to measure psychometric intelligence differences has at times been confused with the separable effort to understand their cognitive and biological bases. In future chapters the progenitors of inspection time (Chapter 7) and reaction time (Chapter 6) approaches to understanding intelligence differences are discussed. For now, we move from a detailed account of the epoch from the 1880s to World War I and move time at faster speed. Like films where detailed scenes of a character's life are suddenly followed by the comment '50 years passed', little progress was made in understanding human intelligence differences from the 1920s to the 1970s. During this half-century there were sporadic studies of the underpinnings of cognitive differences, but there was no discernible research programme or published body of work on this topic. Some of the studies conducted during these dark ages of intelligence research are recounted in later chapters. During that time the intelligence testing movement had a huge applied effect, growing in its educational, clinical, and occupational presence. Debates raged about the psychometric structure of mental ability differences all through this period. Psychology on a wider front underwent large-scale changes of fashion, with the rise and fall of behaviourism and of psychoanalysis. It was with psychology's rediscovery of mental processes and the rise of cognitive psychology from the late-1960s that one may pick up the story of a solid interest in the nature of intelligence differences.

Earlier in this chapter Spearman (1904) and his student Abelson (1911) were cited as stating that the measurement of intelligence was a practical concern and that experimental work was required to understand intelligence differences. But heed was not taken and, in the same year that Neisser's (1967) *Cognitive psychology* appeared, Eysenck (1967) wrote a manifesto the main purpose of which was to bring differential and experimental psychology together in the study of human intelligence differences. He diagnosed a serious malaise in the study of intelligence with the appearance of Guilford's model of the operations, contents, and products of intelligence in which, according to Eysenck:

> Guilford has truly cut the Dane out of his production of Hamlet. If this is really the best model (1965 style) which psychology can offer of intelligence and intellect, then the time seems to have come to retrace our steps; something has gone very wrong indeed! (p. 82)

> I would suggest that the psychometric approach has become almost completely divorced from both psychological theory and experiment (p. 83)

Within the field of intelligence research, Eysenck was reiterating Cronbach's (1957) call for psychology's two modes of attack to combine forces. Even before that Sargent (1942) had warned that 'factor analysis is not a substitute for the experimental analysis of the individual' and had advocated a 'combined differential–experimental approach to human abilities'. Eysenck wanted to:

> suggest the importance of starting out on a fifth stage of intelligence assessment, a new stage based on theoretical and experimental work, and not divorced from the main body of academic psychology. . . . Investigations should pay more attention to laboratory studies of . . . speed of information processing. (p. 96)

These are all distant echoes of Spearman's cry for understanding against the incoming measurement tide in 1904.

The experimental approach to human ability differences took off properly in the 1970s as cognitive psychology's influence rose and some psychologists began to use new cognitive insights to ask about individual differences. Hunt's series of experiments on the nature of verbal ability, which combined experimental and differential approaches, began then (e.g. Hunt *et al.* 1975). In 1976, Resnick's edited volume *The nature of intelligence* contained several chapters whose writers suggested that cognitive–experimental approaches were needed fully to understand human intelligence differences. In 1977 the journal *Intelligence* began, with Detterman (1977) arguing that there was a need for a focus for research into intelligence. From the first issue it was clear that a substantial proportion of the contributors to *Intelligence* would construe intelligence differences from an information processing point of view. This may be seen as a *marriage de convenance* between the apparently unprogressive, static description of abilities provided by the psychometricians and the promise of cognitive processes being laid bare by the more dynamic cognitivists. An earlier proposed attachment between psychometric intelligence and learning theory had not been consummated (Estes 1974; Bachelder and Denny 1977).

One new line of attack was the study of standard psychometric tasks from an information processing point of view in an effort to understand better the demands they made of cognitive processes. Royer's (1977) study of the Block Design test is one example. This type of approach was carried out with great ingenuity by Sternberg (1977*a,b*) in his studies of reasoning tasks and their basic components (see Chapter 5).

A broader, emerging approach was to ask whether aspects of constructs identified by human experimental psychology might have parameters whose values were associated with individual differences in mental abilities. *Intelligence*'s second volume had two good examples, which asked whether perception and attention, respectively, might be associated with intelligence. Royer (1978) introduced his article as follows:

> The purpose of this paper is to discuss what the role of perceptual processes in intelligence is. . . . If we measure the current status of the question by the indexing of literature . . . it seems that the question does not exist. (p. 11)

Among other issues, Royer examined how altering the information processing characteristics of tasks altered performance on them (cf. the Hick task in Chapter 6). In an anticipation of inspection time research (Chapter 7), and despite his principal interest being stimulus complexity, Royer hypothesized that,

> experimentation on the limits of the perceptual system's encoding processes can provide information about other limits of the information processing system. (p. 33)

Reflecting similar comments made by others since the beginning of the twentieth century he insisted that,

> there is a need to investigate intelligence tasks using experimental techniques rather than correlational ones. I would add that the need is imperative. (p. 37)

Royer (1978) conceded that a critique of his approach was an underemphasis of parallel processing. In the work since then the overwhelming emphasis has been on serial processing. Like the growing number of papers that reflected an awakening to the possibly fecund association of differential and cognitive psychology, Royer's paper was a manifesto—a statement of encouragement and intent—rather than an empirical contribution. It was a call to arms rather than a battle fought. A similarly theoretically suggestive but empirically empty paper was contributed by Zeaman (1978) who urged that the concept of attention could provide a base for intelligence research:

> The general methodological approach I will take to the problem of relating individual differences in attention and intelligence can be described as an experimental process analysis, and may be contrasted with the traditional psychometric approach to the problem. . . .
>
> A quite different approach to the problem makes use of a theoretically guided experimental analysis of tasks in which attention is presumed to play a role. Controls for the intrusion of processes other than attention are arranged experimentally. The requirements of such an approach are first of all a theory in which attention is a major theoretical construct, and secondly a diverse set of experimental operations to anchor empirically the inferences of differential behavioural processes with their accompanying individual differences. (pp. 56–57)

Later in the 1978 volume of *Intelligence* there was a series of articles on the possibilities for unifying psychology's two disciplines in the study of intelligence. The papers had been presented at the American Educational Research Association in 1978 in Toronto, Canada. Snow (1978) provided an informative series of descriptions of the main psychometric factors in intelligence and a survey of some possible cognitive approaches. Perhaps the best article of all was that by Sternberg (1978) who captured and documented the new movement very well:

> There seems to be widespread concurrence among theoreticians and methodologists alike that new approaches to studying intelligence should somehow combine the differential and cognitive (information-processing) approaches that have been used in the past, and that the combination should somehow enable the investigator to isolate components of intelligence that are elementary (at some level of analysis). (p. 196)

That last parenthetical comment, as we shall see later, was well-advised. Sternberg's (1978) piece is full of useful information, tantalizing suggestions, and wisdom, such as the realization that there are many false leads in this area, which are then not replicated. The history of the area, of course, shows that the opposite is common too; there are many positive leads that are not followed up (Deary 1986, 1994*a*). Sternberg outlined some promising approaches to the future study of intelligence such as structural equation modelling, cognitive components of intelligence, cognitive correlates of intelligence, and computer theories of intelligence. Indeed, perhaps little more than promise could be expected at this stage for, as Carroll (1978) stated in the same issue:

the state of the art in individual differences research in an information-processing mode can be thought of as little more than embryonic. (p. 114)

Most of the prophets of the new, combined approach to intelligence had reservations as well as enthusiasms about the enterprise. An example of some measured criticism of the approach may be found in the symposium paper by Hunt and MacLeod (1978). They foresaw some problems for cognitivists who had tried to apply psychometric techniques and for differential psychologists who 'have tried to interpret their measures in terms of theories of cognitive psychology' (p. 129). They suspected that there were 'deep conceptual differences between the differential and cognitive psychology approaches to thought'. Although they made it clear that they could have used several tasks, they place their discussion in the setting of the sentence verification task. For example, they provided a thoughtful discussion on whether average performance on a cognitive task should be considered as a primitive (for example, overall performance on the sentence verification task, although one could equally well insert overall performance on the Hick reaction time task or the Sternberg memory scanning task; see Chapter 6) or whether one should employ parameters derived from within the task. The latter, they noted, involved the application of a model to the task performance, to which one is then theoretically committed. Also, whereas the differential approach tends to use linear models of performance, 'information-processing theories of cognitive processes regard performance as a non-linear function of primitive variables of the model' (p. 139). Moreover, they evinced concern about the qualitatively different ways in which subjects approach cognitive tasks, a concern supported by functional brain scanning results (Chapter 9).

Their worries remain relevant, but not entirely in the ways that were articulated by Hunt and MacLeod (1978). We should ask ourselves whether, if we are troubled by the qualitatively different ways that subjects approach tasks, we have truly made contact with information processing primitives. This raises the issue of the level which researchers have in mind when they are thinking about information processing parameters. If it is at the level of overall cognitive task performance then there is a prima facie case for being very sceptical about whether there is anything primitive about the measure at all. Take the case of the sentence verification task (Clark and Chase 1972). There are lawful changes in reaction time with experimental manipulations of the task, but the task does not offer an obvious decomposition in terms of information processing primitives. Indeed, it appears to be complex, with many possible cognitive processes being involved in its performance. Whether isomorphisms exist between task performance and brain processes remains obscure. At essence, this problem centres on the validity of the experimental task being used to study the bases of individual differences in psychometric test performance. If we respond to Cronbach's (1957) call for a wedding of psychology's two disciplines, and if we accept the strictures of the cognitively-oriented psychologist to the effect that we do not truly understand the nature of intelligence differences, then the burden of parameterization of the human cognitive system falls upon the cognitive psychologist. Therefore, for any task or set of tasks or cognitive theories that we appeal to, we must be firm in asking to what extent they provide a valid model for cognitive performance. We shall see in later chapters that such valid task decomposition is hard to come by.

In the same symposium-based series of contributions to *Intelligence*, Carroll (1978) made the following point:

> Surveying and carefully examining this literature has caused me to conclude that little progress has been made thus far in understanding mental abilities in terms of processes. It can be argued, to be sure, that there has been some success in identifying psychological processes, but the interpretation of these processes often stands or falls depending on whether one can accept the information-processing models on which the identification of a particular process is based. Further, the experimental identification of a process often depends chiefly upon the finding of individual differences in the parameters of the process, which has led, in effect, to the identification of a whole, new series of individual 'traits' that are little related to the mental abilities isolated in classical psychometric studies. Even if the relations are found to be of substantial magnitude, it is not very revealing or informative merely to establish the correspondences between traits and processes that are defined largely on the basis of those traits. There is an obvious circularity in all this. (p. 88)

Perhaps as a way out of such circularity, there are very different levels of task that are used to search for information processing primitives. Whereas some have looked to experimental/cognitive paradigms such as the sentence verification and memory scanning tasks, others have looked to psychophysical procedures and physiological parameters. The latter level may recommend itself, at least in avoiding the problem of subjects' qualitatively different strategies in approaching cognitive tasks. For, if one can identify a basic process which acts as a limiting factor in cognitive test performance, one may argue that it provides a necessary bottleneck through which all cognitive processing must pass. Vickers and Smith (1986) described this notion:

> one major strategy guiding attempts to measure the speed of mental functioning has been to isolate some process sufficiently elementary to be relatively immune from influence by higher cognitive activities or by motivational and social factors. In its focus on a simple, component process, likely to play a limiting role in most (if not all) more complex processes, this strategy resembles the employment of standard algorithms as benchmark tests of the processing speed of a digital computer. (p. 619)

Around the turn of the decades from the late-1970s to the early 1980s, something new was happening in intelligence research; something that had been proposed since its inception, but that had lain dormant for 50 years or so. The feel of this time is captured nicely by Carroll and Maxwell's piece in the *Annual Review of Psychology* for 1979, and the tone of the review, written for the general psychologist rather than the expert audience who read Carroll's *Intelligence* article the year before, was upbeat:

> A discernible new trend, however, is a budding but fitful and hesitant courtship between two traditionally separate disciplines of psychology—psychometricians, on the one hand, and experimental cognitive psychology, on the other . . . .. this current trend represents a coming to full circle of tendencies that were evident already around the turn of the century when J. McK. Cattell, Binet, Spearman and others attempted, with little real success, to measure intelligence through observations of simple processes such as sensory discrimination, choice reaction time, and memory span. (p. 604)

> The fresh wind blowing is that of cognitive psychology and the prospect that its perspective may be able to reform psychometricians and the theory of IDs [individual differences] in a radical way. . . . a Pheonix-like revival of directions that were evident 80 years ago. (pp. 633–634)

Let us ask about the health of the offspring that were the issue of that coy courtship.

4 Vade-mecum

Desperately seeking a mental cytology

This chapter was not an easy one to put together or to place, yet it might be the most important one in the book in so far as its principles have application after the empirical reports in the following chapters have been variously replicated, refined, superseded, and refuted. The comments made here are some guiding principles and caveats behind the search for the causes of individual differences in human intelligence. Such matter tends not to be collected or stated as a corpus. It appears between the cracks of the content of research: in the discussions after symposia at conferences, in the referees' comments to journal submissions—and in the authors' replies—and in the throwaway afterthoughts to lectures. Many of the following comments represent the cold water that needs to be thrown on the discussion sections of journal articles, in which over-the-top claims have become almost mandatory in the competition for publication in a culture where there is a bias towards publishing the positive, novel, and seemingly important. What follows here serves to prevent premature accusations of naïve reductionism by way of getting retaliation in first. The comments are largely obvious, so much so that these principles are frequently violated, ignored, and left unstated. They are offered as an optional vade-mecum to evaluate the research that is presented in subsequent chapters, and to spot the instances where this author forgets his own pious warnings.

This chapter might as easily have been placed after Chapter 9, and served as a general discussion section for the book as a whole. Those familiar with the research addressed in this volume will benefit most from the present placement. Tiros in the field may wish to revisit this chapter after reading the main empirical essays (Chapters 5–9).

A MENTAL CYTOLOGY?

Assuming that 'looking down' to discover some origins of human psychometric intelligence differences is worthwhile and valid, there is the difficulty of deciding where to begin such a search. Below the level of human behaviour captured in the responses to psychometric tests and life achievements, there are many levels of description that are used to capture regularities in the functioning of the brain.

Looking for variables outside of the psychometric domain, to provide parameters that might account for some of the variance in human psychometric intelligence, is to demand that the field from which they are drawn has sorted out its own taxonomy. Spearman knew this; before he wrote his magnum opus on psychometric intelligence—*The abilities of man* (1927)—he wrote what he saw as the foundation of such a work—*The nature of intelligence and the principles of cognition* (1923; see Chapter 2). His reasoning was that one needed to know the structure of thinking before one could isolate the processes that might be the source(s) of individual differences. So, as we saw in Chapter 2, Spearman (1923) advised that:

> Whenever the make-up of any cognitive operation has to be analyzed, this is best done by resolving it into the unit-processes as its basal constituents. . . . Psychology, to obtain the much fuller measure of success awaiting it, must evolve towards a mental cytology. (p. 59)

Metaphors abound in intelligence research, and this is a particularly nice (and sobering) one, evoking a solution to the mind's operations that classifies the units of function, just as biologists were able to classify cell types and their functioning within the bodies of organisms.

Therefore, when visiting an area of brain research to exploit it for variables that might contain individual difference parameters related to psychometric intelligence differences, there must be an assessment of the content and adequacy of that area's mental cytology. It must be asked whether it has a mature classification of component processes. The phrase itself might easily be viewed as betraying post-Victorian overenthusiasm for the power of science. However, as discussed in Chapter 3, the early years of the cognitive revolution in psychology saw similar expectations concerning a periodic table of mental components in whose variance mental ability differences might reside.

WHICH FLOOR FOR INTELLIGENCE?

Armed with the correct level of sceptical inquiry about the area of research which is to be the donor of new performance parameters, which of many possible levels of description should be exploited to account for variance in mental ability differences? The reduction of any psychological phenomenon to lower-level constructs meets this problem. Hettema and Deary (1993) discussed the similar choices that face researchers who are pursuing the origins of personality trait differences in the fields of social psychology, learning theory, physiology, biochemistry, genetics, and evolution.

There is no one area that provides a focus for reductionistic research on human intelligence differences. In the chapters that follow researchers have, in their enthusiastic ignorance, turned to most conceivable levels of description in the cognitive sciences and neuroscience to explain some variance in human intelligence differences.

Some tried to peel apart *psychometric* items to discover their segmentations, and to offer these as an account of mental components (Chapter 5). Robert Sternberg's (1977*a,b*, 1985) componential analyses of analogical reasoning items is an example of this approach.

There are those who appeal to tasks within *experimental–cognitive* psychology for valid measures of basic mental processes (Chapter 6). One of the most prominent illustrations of this path is the work conducted on the Hick reaction time procedure (Jensen 1987*a*).

At a lower level, arguably, there are efforts to seek explanatory variance relevant to psychometric intelligence at the level of *psychophysics*, that is, in the elementary performance parameters of the visual and auditory system (Chapter 7). Among research at this level is work on sensory discrimination (beginning with Spearman 1904) and inspection time (Deary and Stough 1996).

Moving down to *psychophysiology*, there is much work on the associations between the electrical activity of the nervous system and mental ability differences (Chapter 9). Many different procedures in the field of event-related potentials have been used to investigate differences in human intelligence (Deary and Caryl 1993).

At the level of *physiology* and *anatomy* there is, by comparison with the research efforts mentioned above, a small amount of literature on a number of *biological* factors and their relationships with intelligence differences. This includes the conduction velocity of the nerves, the metabolic activity of the brain, and the overall size of the brain (Chapter 9; Deary and Caryl 1997*a*).

There is a great deal of evidence on the genetic contributions to human intelligence differences. Traditional behaviour genetics, using family, adoption, and twin studies, has established that there is a sizeable genetic influence on mental abilities (Bouchard 1998) (Chapter 1). Thus, there are sources of biological variance in ability differences as a result of gene differences, but they do not point to individual genes. That is changing. With the arrival of molecular genetics and the development of the human genome project the research has progressed to a stage where behavioural phenotypes such as psychometric intelligence may be related to specific gene loci (Daniels *et al.* 1998). Therefore, in a reductionist attempt to understand some of the underpinnings of psychometric intelligence differences, the old and new genetics must be seen as important tools (Chapter 9).

YOU CAN ONLY LOOK WHERE THERE IS LIGHT

An area of science cannot progress without the necessary constructs, methods, data, and mathematical infrastructure necessary for its explanation. Those functions and problems of the brain that are based on the excitatory amino acid transmitters could not be understood in the days when the only known neurotransmitters were noradrenalin, dopamine, acetylcholine, and serotonin. And before the dopaminergic system was discovered it was not possible to formulate the current biological theories of schizophrenia. Before methods of single-cell recording in the nervous system were developed it was not possible to understand memory formation in terms of long-term potentiation. It is humbling, and it can induce appropriate patience, when it is acknowledged that understanding in an area of science cannot be rushed by human will, effort, or rational invention. In assessing the topic of the present book it must be accepted that currently there might exist few of the necessary constructs that will do the job. Therefore, the art of compiling a story on human intelligence differences lies partly in assessing the adequacy of the concepts, investigative tools, and statistical modelling techniques that are to hand, and how far they fall short of what will eventually be necessary. Two errors are to be avoided.

First, one should not strain too hard to produce a story from what is known. That way, an edifice is erected with unsound or imaginary foundations and a wonky structure. It soon becomes obsolete, and overtaken by the facts. There is a responsibility not to pull the wool over the readers' eyes by pretending that more is understood than is actually the case.

Second, one must not be too dazzled by tomorrow's toys and start writing off all current knowledge and writing promissory notes based on the 'next big thing'. The responsibility here lies in wringing out what one can from results that have been published and replicated, and not taking the Micawberish route of waiting for something to turn up tomorrow.

Finally, in stating clearly that explaining human ability differences can occur only after the receipt of validated constructs relating to brain function, it must be acknowledged that the research here is accepting the food from others' scientific tables. In this volume it becomes clear that not a little of this food lacks nourishment, is stale, and some of it proves to be incompletely digestible.

PSYCHOMETRIC FACTORS ARE NOT BITS OF THE BRAIN, NECESSARILY

A refrain in this book is to berate those who claim too much for their results when it comes to understanding human intelligence differences. However, because to work in human intelligence is like having one's living-room windows open constantly to noisy and sometimes hostile neighbours, one can tend also to claim too little. The psychometric structure of human intelligence differences is just one way of organizing responses to the particular set of mental tasks that researchers have set their subjects. A g factor emerges, accounting for around half, or a bit more, of the variance in diverse mental tasks; and a number of group factors is found. But that does not mean that there is a brain structure or functional characteristic, or a set of them, that must have isomorphism with elements of the psychometric structure. To assume so is to commit the high sin of reification. Factors are just empirical regularities requiring understanding, they are not things. Gould's (1981) charges of reification would come from too obvious a speaker. Perhaps more surprisingly, Burt (1940) had earlier warned against reifying factors:

> more than one voice in recent discussions has warned the factorist against the temptation to 'reify and deify his factors'. With such a caution I am in close sympathy. Yet, being addressed exclusively to the psychologist, it may seem to deny his working concepts a validity allowed to those of other sciences. . . . The

mathematical part of the factorial argument is for the most part deductive; and therefore, like all deductive reasoning, is admittedly unable to guarantee the reality of the results deduced. In such an argument the factors are notions postulated, not things observed or measured. (p. 214)

And McNemar (1964) found differential psychology's tools wanting when it came to discovering the cognitive architecture from which psychometric intelligence differences sprang:

studies of individual differences never come to grips with the *process*, or operation, by which a given organism achieves an intellectual response. Indeed, it
is difficult to see how the available individual difference data can be used even
as a starting point for generating a theory as to the process nature of general
intelligence or of any other specified ability. (p. 881)

But sometimes psychometrically produced factors do map quite well on to things in the body. And it would be silly to rule out the possibility of a mapping between the psychometric structure of psychometric intelligence and some aspects of the brain's function. An instructive example may be found in research into the psychological aspects of diabetes mellitus. This is the illness in which the pancreas fails to produce insulin and so the cells of the body are unable to import glucose from the bloodstream. People with the disease inject themselves with insulin to reduce the glucose in their blood and supply it to their metabolizing cells. The injection of too much insulin lowers the blood glucose level below normal physiological levels, inducing a state of hypoglycaemia. The brain is unable to use any fuel except glucose. Therefore, when hypoglycaemia is severe, it can result in unconsciousness and seizures and, rarely, death. Before progressing to this level of severity there are many bodily symptoms of hypoglycaemia that are used by people as warnings so that they can take extra sugar to curtail an attack. Since the early days of insulin treatment in the 1920s it was believed that the body's response to hypoglycaemia was generated by two physiological systems. One response was called *neuroglycopenic* and the symptoms of tiredness, mental confusion, loss of concentration, etc., that it comprised were believed to be the direct result of low fuel availability in the cerebral cortex. The second response was called *autonomic* and was believed to be the result of the autonomic nervous system being stimulated by low blood-glucose levels, resulting in symp-toms such as trembling, pounding heart, and sweating. Therefore, there was a universe of symptoms which had been collected and divided into groups by clinical wisdom, and there was a theory about how the symptom reports were generated. However, there was no direct evidence to map the assumed clusters of reported symptoms to functional compartments in the body. In the early 1990s our research group of diabetologists and psychologists took the step of submit-ting patients' reports of hypoglycaemic symptoms to a series of exploratory and confirmatory factor analyses (e.g. Deary *et al.* 1993). From these analyses there emerged a clear psychometric separation of the hypothesized neuroglycopenic and autonomic groups of symptoms. Confirmation that these statistical groupings of symptoms were isomorphic with functional compartments within the nervous system was obtained from experimental studies using induced hypoglycaemia in combination with pharmacological blockade of different parts of the nervous system (Towler *et al.* 1993).

A psychometric structure can sometimes, then, suggest a biological structure or functional arrangement. It will not always be the case, and like a map of unknown quality researchers should apply due scepticism and turn in another direction when the evidence demands it. But the psychometric structure should not be ignored. *g* might have little substance when the empirical dust settles, but its pervasive influence on mental performances makes it perfectly sensible to ask whether this general variance might arise from some source(s) of biological variance in the nervous system. It is not reification merely to recognize that *g* and the group factors in intelligence performance are regularities that require explaining. And it would be bad psychological science if, in the current state of ignorance, researchers did not look at explanatory possibilities in the brain's biology as well as higher-level psychological and social factors.

Intelligence researchers should not be slaves to psychometric structures, and they should not, Nelson-like, turn a blind eye towards them either. They should not swallow *g* whole and stick it undigested into the head in the form of a bogus explanatory foreign body. Spearman (1927) at times approached this error, in so far as he compared *g* to 'mental energy', and began to look forward from there by hypothesizing on the basis of this assumption. Over half a century later Anderson (1992) did this, and *g* was renamed as a Basic Processing Mechanism, the brain's motherboard or Pentium processor, and further hypotheses were formulated on this basis. He went further, and conceived the idea that group factors of intelligence were like software packages running on this master processor. The psychometric structure was thus placed into the head as a theory of intelligence. To be fair, Anderson's monograph usefully brings together developmental and neuropsychological evidence to support the possibility that the main second stratum (Carroll 1993) abilities have a basis in the partitioning of the brain's functions. The opposite error to placing psychometric intelligence inside the skull is to create a theory of intelligence differences that simply ignores much of the psychometric evidence, such as Gardner (1983) did, rendering his theory popular but scientifically incredible (Brody 1992).

MENTAL TASKS ARE NOT MENTAL CONSTRUCTS

This section is a reminder of Spearman's (1927) quotation that was encountered in Chapter 2:

> *Dicto secundum quid ad dictum simpliciter.* You can test the power of attention. For you can test the ticking-off of numbers, and this ticking-off is done by the power of attention.

Human blood can be classified into the ABO blood group types: O, A, B, and AB. In doing this, there is a simple experimental procedure for testing humans' individual differences in phenotypes. These individual differences have behavioural consequences and predictive validity; if a patient is transfused with the wrong type of blood a severe, possibly fatal, reaction might follow. Moreover, the underlying constructs that result in the phenotypic individual differences are known. The ABO blood group phenotypes represent different molecular structures on the surfaces on the red blood cells. Along a reductionist chain it is possible to describe the genetic bases of these molecular differences which produce the test-tube-allocated human phenotypes. This is a case of a 'behavioural' measure (the macroscopic response of blood cells to certain reagents) equating to an underlying construct with a tractable, in this case genetic, origin. ABO blood group differences can be measured and classified, and understood. It was not always like this. ABO blood group differences were measured and classified for a long time before they were explained in molecular terms.

Individual differences in mental abilities can be measured and classified, but they are not understood. Researchers attempting to understand psychometric intelligence differences use mental tasks at supposedly lower levels of description—tasks from experimental/cognitive psychology and psychophysics, say—and it must be asked whether there exists a validated account of the elementary or lower-level psychological processes involved in the performance of such tasks. The research literature is drenched with claims about mental tasks that measure (meaning that they capture variance in a valid construct) information processing speed, mental speed, processing efficiency, processing capacity, one of a dozen or more aspects of memory, working memory, some aspect of language, an aspect of attention, and frontal lobe functioning. The list is as long as it is depressing, dangerous, and disingenuous. It is depressing because one sees that a process of hand-waving is going on whereby mental test differences are being 'explained' on the basis of constructs whose validity is often no better than the mental test differences. It is dangerous, because hypotheses developed from such claims are based on an illusion of understanding. And the claims are often disingenuous because the researchers must know that the claims to understand the constructs assessed by task performances are insupportable.

In succeeding chapters every effort is made to remember not to buy the hand-waving constructs that accompany mental test descriptions (for example, that the Hick reaction time test measures the construct called 'the rate of gain of information' or that differences in functional brain scanning using positron emission tomography measure the brain's 'processing efficiency'). To do so would misserve the trusting reader with an illusion of understanding. On the other hand, an effort will be made to tease out what constructs explanatory tasks are meant to measure and the extent to which they are validated.

MENTAL TESTS CONTAIN MANY REAGENTS AND REAGENTS MAY BE PLANTED IN MANY TESTS

The analogy with blood typing might be extended to make a further point. Some blood-typing sera contain more than one active agent, or antibody. Thus, a positive reaction might be obtained in cases where the person lacks a particular blood group antigen. Useful blood-typing sera contain just one active agent or 'test'. Mental tests are rarely assumed to measure just one elementary brain process. They are messy mixes of different reagents that assess an unknown number of brain processes. The ideal of people like Spearman and later, cognitive researchers was to test elementary mental processes, either by devising a test with just one reagent or by cleverly constructing variants of the test so that the performance of an elementary process might be adduced from the person's reactions.

Therefore, 'pure' mental test reagents that assess single validated brain processes are an ideal (see the hopes for inspection time in Chapter 7). The reality is that most or all current mental tests are assessing many unknown processes. Recognizing that fact more explicitly than is done at present impels some different approaches in research. In exploring a construct that is related to human intelligence differences it should be appreciated that the construct is mixed with others in any mental test. In addition, the same construct can be captured within more than one task. It should be possible to find new tasks, quite different phenotypically from each other, that also contain the construct of interest and also relate to intelligence differences in predictable ways. A good example of this approach, though not ultimately a successful one, is met in Chapter 7 which describes Vickers' attempts to create superficially very different tasks that allow the isolation of a person's 'inspection time'.

MODULES AND *g* ARE NOT CONTRADICTORY

Every schoolboy knows that different bits of the brain perform different psychological functions. There is evidence from neuropsychologically damaged individuals, from functional brain imaging, and one can point roughly to the areas involved in language, memory, perception, spatial ability, and so forth. Yet, every schoolboy should know too that there is much general variance in psychometric intelligence differences, and that test scores of memory and language and spatial ability and so forth all load highly on the first unrotated principal component of a principal components analysis. On the one hand, there are modules and division and, on the other, there is general intelligence and the cohesion of mental test performance across many types of task.

Since both of the above are among the best established facts in psychology there must be an account of mental processes and their individual differences that can explain both sets of findings. It is senseless to be 'for' one or other interpretation—*g* or the specificity hypothesis (Jensen 1984)—because both are correct and to provide a theory of one without the other would leave much of the brain's performance characteristics untouched.

INTELLIGENCE AND INTELLIGENCE DIFFERENCES MIGHT BE TWO DIFFERENT OR OVERLAPPING VENTURES

One solution to the above paradox is to entertain the idea that the performance characteristics of the brain and the sources of individual differences are not areas of psychological research that need to picnic on the same spot. Recall Spearman's two books. In *The nature of intelligence and the principles of cognition* (1923) he sought the design features of the brain that supported higher psychological functions. In *The abilities of man* (1927) he gave an account of ability differences in humans. Two research tasks, therefore. The first is to understand the functional units of the brain and how these interact to produce what might be called intelligent behaviour. For non-brain damaged individuals these are likely to be much the same, in the way that our other organs operate in the same fashion to achieve their tasks. The second is to understand why individuals perform mental tasks at reliably different levels of efficiency within a species and to explain why the pattern of such differences obtains. These are not necessarily closely related tasks, and are currently addressed more or less separately by cognitive and differential psychologists, respectively.

But Spearman (1923), as was discussed above and in Chapter 2, thought that the tasks were related:

Any search for 'the nature of intelligence' has shown itself to have a prospect of success when, and only when, it becomes merged into the greater quest after the scientific 'principles of cognition'. (p. 32)

He described psychometric intelligence tests as,

Miners excavating forward into wonderfully rich new ground, but repeatedly missing the correct direction on account of labouring in darkness. The light they need is just that which irradiates from principles—from these alone. (pp. 35–36)

Spearman, if represented here correctly, was indicating that one needs to know the basic cognitive constructs that are being tapped by psychometric tests. He was urging that there must exist a mental taxonomy so that one can point to a mental test and state that it indexes this, that, and/or the other basic mental process. Without such a taxonomy the tests describe performance differences but the origins of these differences are mysterious and, whereas an ability was measured, there was a failure to understand the nature of the ability tested and the source(s) of its individual differences. Spearman wanted to do cognitive and differential psychology, and saw the former as the basis of the latter.

That's one view, but here is another, from the neo-Spearmanian Jensen (1998*c*):

All but an exceedingly few neuroscientists today are interested in interspecies variation in behavioral capacities. They may well find discovering the brain's general operating principles enough, without having to explore the causes of individual variation in the functional efficiency of the essential design features of the brain and their general operating principles . . . The very existence of the *g* factor (like all other psychometric factors) is only revealed by examining *intra*species individual differences in each of the broad and diverse class of functions we regard as constituting intelligence—discrimination, generalization, learning, memory, insight, abstraction, problem solving, and the like. But before we can begin to research the physical basis of *g*, do we first need to discover all of the brain's design features that make these functions possible? I don't think so. The question of what causes the various cognitive functions of the brain to be positively correlated is a very different question from that of understanding the specific operating mechanisms of each of these functions

I propose the following working hypothesis: individual differences in human behavioral capacities do not result from differences in the brain's structural operating mechanisms per se, but rather are the result of other aspects of cerebral physiology that modify the sensitivity, efficiency, and effectiveness of the basic information processes that mediate the individual's responses to certain aspects of the environment. (pp. 207–208)

What Jensen described as the '"vertical" search for the neurological causes of *g*' is pretty much identical to what is meant here by 'looking down on human intelligence'.

What may be characterized as 'Jensen's guess' about the origins of individual differences in human intelligence is interesting in itself and because of its differences with Spearman's guess. Jensen, in essence, hypothesized that the origins of individual differences in psychometric intelligence will be understood at the level of biological differences in nerve cells and their assemblies and interactions, whereas cognitive science's search for a description of the operating principles of the brain (a functional architecture) will be carried out at a level further up— at a more molar level—and will articulate those processes which run on a fabric with built-in individual differences. According to Jensen, our cognitive clothes will all have the same designs, but different qualities of materials; something like that, because all this supposing takes place in the face of so much ignorance that none of these statements can be accepted as exact hypotheses. Who can be sure that what Jensen vaguely points to as the lower-level fabric is not also something relevant to the operating characteristics of the brain?

In the end, it may be concluded unhelpfully that the search for an understanding of the generic functional architecture of the human brain and the sources of its individual differences might be more or less independent. Cognitive science might discover design features that suggest parameters for individual differences, or individual differences might obtain at an entirely different level of description, or at more than one level. These different levels might be lower ones in the reductionist scheme, as suggested by Jensen, or they might be higher, in terms of the way that basic processes are combined to form cognitive strategies (Sternberg 1985).

CORRELATIONS ARE FINDINGS TO BE EXPLAINED, NOT EXPLANATIONS

Much of the data presented in subsequent chapters comes in the form of univariate or multivariate associations between psychometric test scores on the one side and cognitive or biological variables on the other. It's an old saw that correlation does not imply causation, but people forget it. Or they do something slightly different, by assuming in finding a correlation that they have been given an understanding of something. Correlations should be seen as an opportunity for more work; they are findings that need to be established, explored, and explained. They need to be established because there are rarely studies with such large, representative samples and such meticulously chosen and administered tests and tasks that their replicability cannot be questioned. In discussing the associations found between mental ability differences and physical attributes Jensen and Sinha (1993) exclaimed that,

> The most amazing feature of the research literature on correlations between mental and physical traits is that, until very recently, virtually no attention was paid to the various *causes* of the correlations or to the fact that different types of correlations have quite different theoretical significance. (p. 144)

Associations need to be explored, because it is necessary to know the conditions under which they reappear (replicate), increase in strength, and disappear. Changing aspects of the tasks used, the conditions of administration, and the subject sample might all have effects on the association we have read or reported. These limits to the reoccurrence of associations are quite well studied in the area of inspection time research (Chapter 7) where the strength and occurrence of the association changes depending on a number of variables.

Associations need to be explained. In fact, that is the most interesting part of the enterprise. A phenomenon is understood when there is a mechanistic explanation, and correlations can be the starting point for this by establishing that such a bridge of explanation needs to be built between two different-seeming measures or constructs. Part of the explanation of a correlation is the examination of its direction. When two variables are correlated it is often assumed that one variable explains the variance in another, that is, one variable is more basic than the other. In the field of intelligence research things can be seen the other way round, or both variables might be explained by a third factor, or both variables might just be indices of the same construct going under two different guises.

Jensen and Sinha (1993) offered a useful reminder of the difficulties in interpreting correlations. Some associations are what they called 'functional' and can be the beginnings of a trail of causation from brain mechanisms to behaviours. However, other correlations are 'nonfunctional' and

[a] by-product of a long chain of other causes, often reflecting cultural values, such as the nonfunctional relationship between intelligence and physical stature. (p. 231)

Jensen and Sinha also raised the issue of whether significant correlations between ability differences and other variables exist within families or between families (with no significant within family association). Table 4.1 shows the likely causes of such correlations. This table notifies researchers that a number of reasons for association are explanatory blind alleys.

OUT OF YOUR ARMCHAIR! INTO THE LAB!

It is important repeatedly to warn differential psychologists that correlations do not imply causation, because correlations and their multivariate relations are their currency. It was discussed above that correlations do not mean a particular type of causation. But one may go too far with humility and as a corrective it must be recalled that correlations have causes, and the most important part of the job is to find them. And the causes of correlations will not appear in the hypnopompic reflections that spring from a spell in the armchair. In the study of the causes of individual differences in psychometric intelligence it is common to see the most important part of the job being done without the proper tools. Thus, the reasons for correlations are raised in the discussion sections of journal articles and in review papers, whereas the proper place for them is as new papers that take the correlations as the raw material.

It is depressing to see the loose talk that takes the place of proper experimentation at this crucial part of the enterprise. Armchair explanations are not governed by the stern rules and no-entry signs of empirical research, and the inexact, unvalidated constructs that may be used and combined in rational argument fail to be judged by the criterion of truth. The armchair is for hypothesis generation, not for explanation.

It is the armchair that spawned the vacuous constructs that have held back research in this area—like 'mental speed'—and have generated grandiose theories that block progress because they take so long to dismantle by refutation. A good example of the ease with which ideas spring from the armchair that are then difficult to operationalize is the notion that the correlation between inspection time and psychometric intelligence might be caused by high-level cognitive strategies (Chapter 7). Rhetorically, this idea has great power in debunking the importance of the correlation, but constructing a hypothesis to test this idea proved difficult. A forum for conceiving new hypotheses is needed, but care is needed in deciding how far to proceed without the hard discipline of hypothesis generation and empirical test; in the face of these masters some loose constructs and solipsistic theories will evaporate like Scotch mist.

Table 4.1 Causes of correlations between mental ability differences and indices of information processing (from Jensen and Sinha 1993, pp. 230–232)

Type of association		Explanation
Within family	Genetic linkage	Genes for different traits having loci in close proximity on the same chromosome
	Pleiotropy	One gene that affects the development of two phenotypically distinct traits
	Structure–function relationship	Association whereby mental ability test differences are dependent on a particular information processing index
	Exogenous	Not heritable; prenatal or postnatal factors that affect siblings differentially with respect to the parallel development of both mental and physical traits
Between family (with zero within-family correlation)	Genetic heterogeneity/genetic stratification	. . . of the population with respect to certain mental and other correlated traits
	Selective mating	. . . for each of two genetically independent traits
	Assortative mating	. . . of two distinct traits
	Cross-assortative mating	. . . for both traits
	Common environment	Factors (e.g. nutrition, childhood diseases, etc.) that generally affect all of the siblings within a family but may differ between families

Reduction-prone empiricists can be captives of the armchair too, by restricting their thinking to those possibilities that can be arrived at by rational thought. Those working in the field of intelligence differences must consider making appropriate alliances with computational neuroscientists if they are to capture the parameters that nestle in the complexity of the brain's functioning. Noble (1998), discussing how computational approaches helped the understanding of the heart's functioning, expressed this warning as follows:

> The limits of the reductionist approach are not only that it will fail to account for functional phenomena at a higher level. There is also a technical limit, which is that the network of interactions of individual components in biological systems are frequently so complicated that understanding them requires computing tools, partly in order to explore the interactions quantitatively in a reasonable time, and also because, beyond a certain level of complexity, 'armchair' theorising becomes inadequate to the task. (p. 65)

EXPLANATORY CONSTRUCTS ARE AS CHEAP AS TALK

If the proverbial Martian came to earth and made a study of the different branches of science it might go back with a description of the thing called psychology that portrayed it as a hybrid discipline between an empirical science and the literary genre of magical realism. Psychology has the weaponry and accessories of hypothetico-deductive science—its luminaries invented lots of the machinery of hypothesis testing in the form of statistics—but has a tendency to talk about its findings using terms that defy pinning down. This is odd, because psychologists also invented the ideas of construct validity and the nomological network. These ideas are essential, because they get around the superficiality that a construct is its definition which is, after all, only more words with more constructs. Construct validity and the nomological network tell us that there is only as good evidence for the existence and usefulness of a construct as there is empirical evidence. The true worth of a construct is everything that empirical science has found out about it. Figure 1.1, then, represents a bare bones sketch of the nomological network of intelligence; if it is not a worthwhile construct, it should be scrapped on the basis of the scrutiny of that diagram, not some confusion over semantics.

So, what's the complaint here? There are lots of cases in the search for an understanding of human intelligence differences where empirical findings are explained using constructs that have little validation, sometimes little more than a common-sense meaning. Worse, sometimes entirely new constructs are invoked to account for important findings, in the way that a magical realist might invoke a new law of nature to manipulate a character in a way that suits the development of the storyline (see skyhooks below). One is almost spoilt for choice in terms of examples of the loose use of constructs to explain findings in our area of interest. For example, the association between inspection time and intelligence has been explained on the bases of motivation, attention, concentration, strategies, and so forth, with authors rarely stating the operational rules that would allow a hypothesis to be tested from these ideas (Chapter 7). The appeals are to the common-sense notion of the constructs rather than scientific operationalization. Stott (1983) nicely corrals some implausible and vague constructs which some of the greats in the area thought might underpin mental ability differences:

> For two generations there have been conjectures about what these substrata elements may be. Jensen (1980) reviews them: Spearman's electrochemical energy, Thorndike's modifiable neural connections, Godfrey Thomson's brain elements and Burt's neural complexity—and points out that none of them generate testable hypotheses. (p. 279)

The aforementioned suspect, pseudo-explanatory terms are like those that Dennett (1995), in another scientific situation, called skyhooks; scientific sounding formulations that promise a lift to another level of explanation, but have no empirical foundation. Dennett used the skyhook analogy to apply to faulty thinking about 'design space' with regard to biological evolution, but they apply equally well to design space in thinking about cognitive architectures and their possible individual differences. Thus:

> Skyhooks would be wonderful things to have, great for lifting unwieldy objects out of difficult circumstances, and speeding up all sorts of construction projects. Sad to say, they are impossible. (p. 74)

> There are cranes, however. Cranes can do the lifting work our imaginary skyhooks might do, and they do it in an honest, non-question-begging fashion. They are expensive, however. They have to be designed and built, from everyday parts on hand, and they have to be located on a firm base of existing ground. (p. 75)

In Chapter 9, the work relating apolipoprotein E gene variants to cognitive function is an example of expensive, painstaking 'crane' work. On the other hand, some of the cognitive formulations found in Chapters 5 and 6 hang from skyhooks. Skyhooked 'explanations' of mental ability differences are a cheat; they are not based upon validated constructs that link to the platforms of the brain. And, where explanatory skyhooks are invoked, they may divert attention away from interesting empirical data by providing a dazzling veneer of unproductive theory.

Psychology's explanatory constructs are alarmingly prone to fashion. Resources, working memory, and inhibitory processes are among those that are often invoked with supposed explanatory power. What should be demanded of such invocations? At least that the construct can do some work, either by placing the phenomena being discussed within a well-validated theoretical structure that can make non-trivial predictions about what can be expected in future experiments, or by pointing to where researchers might look for the biological instantiation of ideas. For example, if a finding is thought to be founded upon the attentional system there might be an association with activity in the cingulate gyri of the brain. In a memorable critique of the construct of 'resources' as an explanatory tool in psychology, Navon (1984) asked whether they were a theoretical 'soup stone'. The implication here is that researchers must beware the summoning of constructs that do no work, that add merely spin—the appearance of explanation without its substance—and that are themselves lacking construct validity. Human intelligence differences are pretty well construct-validated, and there is no point in trying to place such an edifice on foundations that are far weaker than the building itself. Resources might enter a competition with strategies as the most-invoked yet least well-operationalized construct in psychology.

At worst, invoking vague but plausible-sounding constructs may be used to prevent or delay progress in an area of research. Scientifically, it is the equivalent of the cry 'I spy strangers' in the UK's House of Commons. If a member of parliament wishes to delay the passing of a piece of legislation he or she may, under an old rule, cry 'I spy strangers' during a debate. The House must immediately suspend its business while the Speaker puts the motion, 'That strangers do now withdraw' before the House.

THE VALUE OF EXPLANATORY CONSTRUCTS MAY GO DOWN AS WELL AS UP

Differential psychologists are probably seen as among the hard men and women of psychology, with their interest in psychometrics and some controversial topics. Yet they are naïve souls whose ventures into other areas of psychology are characterized by faith in the soundness of borrowed tools. No matter how critical they are within their own subdiscipline of psychology, differentialists keen on getting at the bases of cognitive ability differences lift tasks from cognitive psychology, psychophysics, psychophysiology, physiology, brain anatomy, and so forth, and state without a backward look that they measure 'mental speed', 'neural efficiency', 'rate of gain of information', 'working memory', 'attention', and so forth. Until they have a closer look, that is. It then becomes obvious that other disciplines are just as guilty as psychology when it comes to invoking a nice epithet to describe what they think underlies the task.

Discovering that tasks at a supposedly lower level of reduction than psychometric tests fail in their promises to contain elementary processing constructs, and fail to have a reductionistic link to the brain's processing, can leave the differentialist in a dilemma, and with a lot of work that they were not expecting to have to carry out. This can be seen in various chapters, but is exemplified as well as any other in the chapter about the Hick reaction time procedure (Chapter 6). Herein was contained a key information-processing construct that might be used to explain some mental ability variance, namely 'rate of gain of information'. It did indeed prove to be correlated significantly with IQ-type test scores.

However, when buying into this test differential psychologists found they had inhabited a house that needed a lot of basic renovation, and much effort has had to go into exploring what the Hick task actually does measure that is important in terms of brain processes. The Hick reaction time task is far from standing alone in this: differential psychologists who have resorted to psychophysiological and psychophysical measures have had to dally in those areas to explicate the constructs underlying the tasks that they thought were theoretically solid and explicated. Chapters 5, 6, 7, and 9 deliver examples. Thus, whereas the intention within this field of research is to root psychometric ability differences in variance obtained from valid brain parameters, it is discovered often that the supposedly more basic measure needs further understanding too. This makes the research effort more complicated, by requiring iterative development of the constructs at both sides of correlations, and by necessitating mechanistic understandings of the correlations.

A note on the quondam explanatory construct 'mental speed'

Mental speed has become an almost meaningless catch-all term, and sometimes hides under equally beguiling and often meaningless terms such as 'information processing-speed' or '-efficiency'. Why anyone could be for or against a mental speed theory of intelligence is puzzling, because it is not clear what is meant by that undigested statement. Human reactions and propensities may involve speed-iness at many levels of description: time to complete a psychometric test, speed of one of the many of experimental (often reaction time-based) procedures, psychophysical speed, and speed of physiological processes. Speed of processing is just about as meaningless and can be seen to mean any one of these alternatives in different places.

It is not out of the question that individual differences in human abilities might depend on the speediness with which something occurs in the nervous system. However, an operational definition of any speed measure is required and an investigation into those abilities to which it contributes variance. Rarely will the general notion of 'mental speed' help to understand or to generate hypotheses (Stankov and Roberts 1997; Roberts and Stankov 1999). Loose, pseudo-explana-tory terms—mental speed, information processing speed, elementary cognitive tests, neural efficiency, and the like—as well as being Dennetian skyhooks, are the flimsy but sometimes unspotted coverings of the elephant-trap of the scientific jingle fallacy (see the section on pleonasms and oxymorons below).

ISOMORPHISM IN GENERAL

There has been no disguising of the reductionist outlook of this book, in the sense that good science tries to discover whether natural phenomena at a given level are partly understandable in terms of more basic, validated constructs. One of the interesting aspects of this is the way in which one level maps on to another.

Common-sense, or other non-scientific, theories of such mappings from one level to another often assume a false and simplistic isomorphism, because human imagination has no privileged access to the latent structures of nature. Thus, the original natural philosophers divided substances into earth, air, fire, and water because those were what they sensed, whereas the latent structure of matter is explained in the periodic table of the elements and the interactions of elements.

Armchair, common-sense, unempirical theories of the origins of intelligence can be seen in this way too. An example is the way in which Robert Sternberg divided the solving of analogical reasoning items into encoding, mapping, and application components (Chapter 5). So convincing did this division of the psychological activity involved in analogies seem that Kline (1991) thought these components had to be true, and needed no empirical verification. But they are only true in a common-sense way, in so far as that is how we should describe what we do when tackling such a mental problem. There is no guarantee that such a convincing description has any one-to-one mapping in terms of what happens in the brain, any more than the apparently compelling four-elements theory of matter had any explanatory force or isomorphism with the latent structure of matter. To delineate a common-sense taxonomy of mental abilities (see Spearman's principles of cognition in Chapter 2) and then to look for a one-to-one relationship with some series of functional units in the brain is a most unpromising-sounding enterprise. It smacks of the impatience of those unwilling to wait for the brain's functional architecture to be understood, and its sources of individual difference revealed, and it relies, naively or arrogantly, on the unproven power of human rational thought to discover the explanations for mental phenomena. Rational thought often looks to appealing, currently fashionable metaphor (variously steam engines, telephone exchanges, and computers in the case of human intelligence), and as Stoljar and Gold (1998) stated:

> Cognitive neuroscience is a science of minimal commitments; it holds that one ought to take what is known and make an attempt to integrate it with whatever else is known in an effort to develop a more adequate understanding of the mind. It is the view that we should let *science* tell us what the theory of the mind will look like rather than a preconception dictated by metaphor or by technology. And this seems like common sense if anything is. (p. 130)

REALLY, IT'S ALL BIOLOGY?

It might be helpful if we psychologists and other mental philosophers knew a bit more about the human brain. Its workings set the limits to plausible hypotheses about how intelligence differences might come about. And knowing about its structures and their interactions and workings can suggest sources of variance that might be involved in producing psychometric intelligence differences.

Morgan (1998) agreed, suggesting that biological theorizing was more trammelled than psychological speculation:

> Coming back to the fact that I'm a psychologist, I could produce thousands of models of visual perception. However, if I am required to produce something that accords with known properties of nerve cells in the visual system I immediately become extremely constrained, and I have to do a whole lot better. This is the virtue of the idea that there is something fundamental to biology. Understanding the brain at the physiological level is more fundamental than producing a purely verbal account of how it might work. (p. 32)

One wonders to what extent the understanding of psychometric intelligence differences, among other mental phenomena, will need biological-level constructs for their explication. One eventually expects to find cognitive-level emergent properties that help to account for ability differences, and it is surely without doubt that these will be the coin of our mental discourse—in the way that chemists talk a chemical language and not a purely physical one—but to date there are too few validated cognitive-level constructs to prevent our looking to biology concurrently.

This type of reductionism applied to the brain, and especially applied to individual differences in brains' functions, comes in for criticism (Rose 1998; Horgan 1999). We should refer, before we judge reductionists too monolithically, to Dennett's (1995) distinction between reductionism in general (which he deems a good thing) from greedy reductionism:

> greedy reductionists think that everything can be explained without cranes; good reductionists think that everything can be explained without skyhooks.

> There is no reason to be compromising about what I call good reductionism. It is simply the commitment to non-question-begging science without any cheating by embracing mysteries or miracles at the outset. (p. 82)

In the chapters that follow, cognitive- and other-level miracles abound. There are many examples of greedy reductionism, whereby the origins of mental ability differences are found via a skyhook epithet applied to a correlation between a psychometric test and an unvalidated information processing variable. What Rose and Horgan appear to me to be criticizing are what Dennett (1995) called greedy reductionists (see above) and, more usually, another type:

> One side proposes an oversimple crane, at which the other side scoffs—'Philistine reductionists!'—declaring, truthfully, that life is much more complicated than that. (p. 394)

Sometimes, though, the overambitious application of a small crane in explaining mental phenomena should be treated more understandingly, as a failed 'nice try' as Dennett (1995, p. 397) put it. This might apply to the investigation of nerve conduction velocity differences as applied to mental ability differences (Chapter 9); at least such investigations begin with the merit of nerve conduction velocity being a well-conceptualized, biologically-rooted variable.

Part of the query 'Is it all biology?' is driven by recognizing the two fastest-moving tools in psychology at present: molecular genetics and functional brain imaging. To the unwary, both of these might seem to offer a short cut from behavioural phenotypes to biology, with possibly a cutting-out of the mid-level constructs given by psychology. However, there will be a place for psychologists in this new integrated science of mind. There will always be the need for the accurate characterization of phenotypes, and the mechanistic links between the biological and the behavioural will need mapping. Plomin and Crabbe (in press) argued strongly that intermediate, information-processing (cognitive/psychological-level) constructs will be required fully to tell the story, if it ever proves tractable, of how biology, including gene differences, contributes to individual differences in psychometric test scores. So did Flint (1999) in his frank and not very hopeful assessment of the possibilities for links between specific genes and cognitive functions:

> We need a much greater integration of different levels of understanding of cognition in order to exploit the genetic discoveries. In short, a rapprochement between molecular and systems neuroscience is required. (p. 2015)

> without either luck or a sufficiently advanced molecular understanding of the cognitive process it has proved practically impossible to infer how a gene determines cognitive function. (p. 2026)

It is a moot point, though, whether there will be discoverable, valid psychological constructs intervening, say, between individual differences in genes and individual differences in a cognitive test. Perhaps Craik (1943) got this about right when he considered the reductionist approach to psychological phenomena:

> The plea for physical explanation does not mean that it is useless or incorrect to give apparently non-physical clinical explanations of psychological phenomena—for instance, to say that an unpleasant experience or shock may *cause* amnesia or suppression. This is a correct statement of the phenomena as far as it goes; but we are entitled to go further if we can. If we then find a more ultimate physical and physiological train of events to be involved 'in between' the shock and the suppression, we should regard this as a more ultimate part of the mechanism, just as it is correct to say that the pressure of one's finger on the self-starter causes the engine to go, but more fundamental to say that the pressure of one's finger causes current to flow in the windings of the starting motor and still more fundamental to give an account of the flow of current and torque exerted by the motor in terms of electronic and electro-magentic theory. (pp. 4–5)

BIG THEORIES ARE 'A BAD THING'

There is nothing like a theory for blinding the wise (Meredith, 1879)

In Hermann Hesse's novel *The glass bead game* the job of the rarefied academics was to create presentations that alloyed many traditions, including elements from mathematics to music (more on this in Chapter 10). Although there was much reference to somehow trying to get things correct, in terms of modelling nature, in the playing of the glass bead game the worry for the scientifically oriented reader is that, really, the criteria were aesthetic rather than scientific/objective. In fact, it seemed that internal consistency and beauty and other unspecified yardsticks were paramount. This is a template for how not to do ordinary science; autochthonous, grand, beauteous schemes that hang together pleasantly are not the way to understand human ability differences.

In the field of human intelligence so-called theories have done more harm than good. They can have some deleterious effects. For some reason there has been a demand for fairly all-encompassing theories of intelligence differences, looked for as emerging whole from their originators (Guilford 1956; Sternberg 1990). In an area of study like psychology, where the error terms are so large and the valid constructs and laws so rare, it is absurd that one should be expected to come up with a broad theory that requires many constructs and their interrelations. One sympathizes with the ex-president of the United States, George Bush, when he admitted that he lacked 'the vision thing'. Sensible scientists should admit the same failing here, and admit to a kind of sinking feeling when they see a 'big' theory of intelligence and intelligence differences. So little is known about the bases of intelligence differences that it is bound not to be correct. And it typically takes a long time to make sensible progress in more deserving constructs once the theory has obtained a place on the statute book. Like trying to decorate a house while a hyperactive toddler runs around messing things up and forcing one to do trivial tidying instead of long-term renovation, a theory can keep one busy refuting or operationalizing its aspects instead of focusing on less immediately compelling, but fundamentally more important, sensible empirical advances.

Big theories divert people from the available empirical evidence and get them arguing instead about how the evidence can be forced into their scheme. In Chapter 3 there was the situation of Spearman and Thorndike using a near-identical result to support entirely contradictory theories. Therefore, they can act as a diversion from modest facts that are quite clear. Not everyone agrees that big theory is a siren, and Lazarus (1993) is quoted for the purpose of urging the reader to consider the opposite view:

> psychologists were enjoined (this I vividly remember) to avoid 'armchair' speculation in the interests of being empirical scientists. Only in recent years have most psychologists once again been willing to see value in philosophical analyses, to take on large-scale theory, to take seriously observations that are

not obtained through laboratory experiment, to engage problems of subjective meaning, and to avoid the sterile scientism of the recent past.

What are called theories in psychology have a vast range, so it is not clear what type of animal one is dealing with. Theories such as those of Freud or Piaget erected great edifices that spawned so many constructs they proved hard to test and validate in the usual manner. Within intelligence research there are grand theories such as those of Gardner (1983) and Sternberg (1985). These are so far ahead of the empirical evidence that it is difficult to think of them as usual scientific theories that constrain hypothesis testing and at the same time suggest falsifiable tests. Theories can be much more useful, in terms of suggesting modest predictions from existing facts. Theories can be seen as a continuum, from a modest hypothesis that is the next jump ahead of the empirical evidence, to a rambling structure that erects many unvalidated constructs far ahead of the collected facts. A handy measure of a theory would be the 'distance' it ends up from the known evidence. This would need to be combined with the status of the subject. The rigours of physics might allow quite a bit of distance to be tolerated, but the noise involved in social science associations does not. As Flynn (1999) commented:

> Global explanations are suspect without the identification of mediating variables that link them to the phenomenon they are supposed to explain. (p. 13)

REPLICATED FINDINGS ARE PRECIOUS

Within the field of medicine there are two related aspects of methodology that are popular: meta-analysis and evidence-based medicine. The first formalizes the process of comparing a number of related studies in an area and the second frames the common-sense view that if one makes an intervention then there should be empirical backing for doing it. There have been some good effects from what might seen mundanely obvious good scientific practice, but broadly the impact of these methodologies has been to stop people shooting from the hip and force them to come up with the evidence for what they are claiming. Moreover, these pressures have meant that multiple studies with similar methodology are demanded; something that might otherwise be seen as undesirable, since novel studies are prized, often, over replications or failures to replicate.

The field of information-processing approaches to intelligence is an area, like so many others in psychology, where it is hard to collect a body of research that is homogeneous enough to perform a meta-analysis. Supposed replications often have substantial changes in methodology; an example might be in the relations between intelligence differences and event-related potentials (Chapter 9) where there are over a hundred empirical reports, but hardly one that bears comparison with another so that it might be termed an attempted replication. A partial exception is inspection time (Chapter 7), where there has already been a meta-analysis. Do one study and then move on is the more usual guiding principle.

More evidence-based intelligence research is required. At the risk of appearing unutterably dull, and to compound the felony of being against fanciful theory, one has to urge more replicated studies, more interlaboratory agreements on the operationalization of constructs and parameters to be measured, and generally larger masses of data on the same topic so that one may hypothesize from solid ground. To listen to discussions within the intelligence community is sometimes like watching an archaeologist who has dug a trench one-foot square and is speculating from that rather than widening the trench. This demand arises from the same aspect of the social sciences that originated the previous section: there are large error terms and the teasing out of the faint signal in much of this work needs big bodies of evidence. Otherwise, psychologists will spend their research careers chasing straws in the wind. In Chapter 9 the studies relating the brain's pH and mental ability differences are examples of these straws.

YOU NEED TO BE A POLYMATH

To promulgate and understand the material covered in a research topic like the one covered here demands that one becomes something of a polymath. The concepts and techniques cross many levels of scientific endeavour, and there is no way of telling where the next clue to the origins of intelligence differences might come from. Therefore, researchers must gain some knowledge outside of psychometrics and/or collaborate with those who have the appropriate specialist knowledge, whether this be psychophysics, physiology, molecular genetics, or brain imaging. As in much of the rest of biology, the study of human intelligence is becoming increasingly molecular.

Therefore, a psychometric parochialism is not possible in the understanding of human intelligence. Becoming knowledgeable about other areas helps us to integrate those new levels of explanation that might be useful for understanding human intelligence and avoid being overly idealistic, because of our ignorance, about what they might offer.

EXPLANATORY TRACTABILITY: PROXIMITY AND DISTANCE

These two ideas aid thinking about the job that is still to be done when a correlation is discovered between two variables. Take the examples of correlations between brain size, or, within molecular genetics, a QTL, and psychometric intelligence differences (Chapter 9). Each leaves a great explanatory distance, the scientist having to invoke the possible constructs that mediated the correlation and to generate a long chain of reasoning to fill in the blanks. At the opposite extreme one might move much less of a distance from the psychometric data and invoke the components that make up the task (Chapter 5). As discussed above, this gives us no guarantee of finding those components in the brain, and the issue might be the realization that nothing more has been done than to redescribe the tests themselves.

DIFFERENTIAL PSYCHOLOGY'S PLEONASMS AND OXYMORONS: JINGLING AND JANGLING

Sometimes it is hard to tell what level of description is being addressed in studies examining psychometric intelligence and putative information processing measures. Gullible readers are accepting of authors' claims that they are engaging in reductionism. However, it often transpires that they are, in fact, doing something much more mundane, which is to correlate two tasks at the same level (usually psychometric), merely calling one of them a psychometric task and the other one an information processing task. They are committing a scientific pleonasm. Therefore, one must be cautious and critical about claims that tasks are digging below the psychometric surface to the mechanistic underpinnings of intelligence differences. There are not always clear lines to be drawn between levels, but we shall see that some so-called 'experimental' tasks are so complex that they are hard to separate from IQ-test items themselves (Chapter 6). This pleonastic activity, which Kelley (1927) described as the 'jangle fallacy', is the scientific error of having,

> Two separate words or expressions covering in fact the same basic situation, but sounding different, as though they were in truth different. (p. 64)

The field of personality psychology provides one of the clearest examples of the jangle fallacy, where there are many different construct names applied to measurements which tap neuroticism-type differences. A demonstration within the research on human ability differences occurs in Chapter 5, where Kyllonen and Christal (1990) provide evidence that Spearman's *g* and the concept of working memory, though they are studied by almost non-overlapping groups of researchers, are so close that one would struggle to push a cigarette paper between them. This author also hears a jangle within this jangle; some of the tests that Kyllonen and Christal use to examine working memory differences, though they are called working memory tests, look suspiciously like the reasoning tests that are the markers for *g*.

The opposite error to the jangle fallacy is the jingle fallacy; a scientific oxymoron where unconnected things, or things not proven to be connected, are conceptually grouped together as facets of the same phenomenon. Thorndike (1904) described it as,

> unthinking acceptance of verbal equality as proof of real equality. (p. 11)

Rose (1998) referred to this error as the agglomeration fallacy:

Science often proceeds by alternately grouping together different phenomena as aspects of the same (lumping) and recognizing differences between them (splitting) . . . agglomeration lumps disparate activities. (p. 180)

Mea culpa. The test of so-called 'auditory inspection time' was conceptually related to visual inspection time before there was sufficient empirical evidence that they were related (Chapter 7). More broadly and importantly, some of the buoyancy of the information processing approach to psychometric ability differences has been due to scientific jingling. The above-mentioned loose terms of 'mental speed' and 'elementary cognitive tasks' have been used to bring together theoretically measures that are poorly understood (in reductionistic terms) and not necessarily related statistically. The unwary reader might see anything from psychometric tests such as the Wechsler Digit Symbol, through reaction time, inspection time, and event-related potential measures, to nerve conduction velocity described as measures of speed (or efficiency) of information processing and believe that there were well-established empirical relations and theoretical understandings among them. Closer reading of the evidence (Chapters 6–9) demonstrates interesting empirical relations, but no brain-shaped conceptual display cabinet that can assemble these measures as a coherent whole. The jingling has a hollow ring.

FIRST, CATCH YOUR VARIANCE

Following Mrs Beeton's recipe for rabbit pie—which apocryphally begins with the instruction 'first catch your rabbit' [it does not, though the recipe does begin with '1 rabbit' (Beeton 1861)]—one conducts research on psychometric intelligence differences in the presence of such differences. Since the thing which is to be explained is variation in human psychometric abilities, then the study will be most powerful when the sample contains humans who resemble the population and whose abilities vary. It sounds almost too obvious to state, but this essential ingredient is often meagre in studies looking at the bases of human intelligence differences. Frequently, the double problem exists of having range-restricted samples who also have deviant means. The commonest reason is the use of university students as subjects. At once they have: a) a narrow standard deviation by comparison with the population at large, which reduces the size of any expected correlation from the true value in the population; b) high mean scores, which can give problems with ceiling effects in mental tests and reduce correlations again; and c) they are not guaranteed to attack mental tests in the same ways as the rest of humanity, thereby meaning that a restricted view of intelligence differences is examined.

Almost every chapter in this book that addresses empirical work will have this problem. A sizeable proportion of the studies in this field of research rely on university undergraduates. This results in a general depression or failing to find significant associations, rafts of 'corrected' correlations which would have been unnecessary if there had been an adequate sample in the first place, and a focus on a highly aberrant group. After all, if we wished to discover the bases of individual differences in say, extraversion, we should not just recruit party animals, we'd want some bookworms too.

5   Cake-slicing

Cognitive reductionism with self-sufficiency

SUMMARY

Can psychometric-type ability tests be cleaved to reveal cognitive components, those discrete mental offices that the mind performs in solving the tasks? And does interindividual variability in these stages account for people's differences in mental test scores? This type of reductionism—splitting mental tests into mental units without borrowing constructs from lower levels of psychological or biological research—was attempted by R. Sternberg and others. It is self-sufficient, because it extends the remit and discoveries of psychometrics. A critical discussion of Sternberg's componential analyses of analogical reasoning items finds acceptable models of test performance but raises doubts about the cognitive veridicality of the cognitive components. Other researchers emphasized the constructs of 'working memory' and 'control processes' as possible elements of psychometric intelligence. Embretson fits highly acceptable models to test performances, and the latent factors that account for test score variance are concordant with hypothetical mental processes. But there is little independent validity for the latent factors *qua* elements of cognition. Further attempts to discover brain processes within psychometric intelligence tests suggest future lines of research but fail to unveil convincingly the principles of cognition. A persistent question for this level of research is: do putative mental elements merely reflect structural aspects of psychometric test items or have they an existence in people's minds?

INTRODUCTION

This chapter differs from the two that follow in that a cognitive-reductionist approach is adopted without explicitly travelling to another area of psychology and borrowing their tasks, constructs, and theories. The driving ideas of most of the approaches in this chapter are that a method can be found that will cleave into their elements the actual items used in psychometric intelligence tests, and that these elements show isomorphism with information processing stages or modules in the brain. Typically, the researchers here discussed used statistical modelling techniques to isolate mental processes from tasks that are drawn largely from the mental test tradition, although there is some integration with tasks from cognitive psychology.

STERNBERG'S COMPONENTIAL APPROACH TO INTELLIGENCE DIFFERENCES

When Robert Sternberg (1977*a,b*) published his first works on human intelligence differences they must have appeared as the epitome of the new synthesis in human intelligence research (Chapter 3). Here was an author who was historically aware, making explicit connections between his work and Spearman's ideas, was willing to draw upon the ideas and techniques of both cognitive and differential psychology, was interested in speed of processing, was using the newest statistical modelling techniques, had devised a novel method for winkling out the inherent components from mental test items, and was interested not only in atomic components of intelligence functioning but also in larger issues of mental representation and mental strategies and how these linked to basic processes. From a single body of research, therefore, shone the promise of the new approach to intelligence, with the bonus that its protagonist was energetic, rigorous, and a highly skilled communicator of the research.

In examining Sternberg's research and the other programmes that will follow in this and subsequent chapters, one must separate two things. First, there is the nature of what was being attempted in terms of a general approach. This articulates a way of looking down on human intelligence that provides a framework for research activity. Second, there is the empirical success or otherwise of the approach. That is, one can assess the degree to which the approach was implemented in empirical research, whether it was expanded into related approaches and whether it was proved wrong. Often, the empirical implementation of an approach has produced too few studies on which to make valid assessments.

In solving individual mental test items humans might bring to bear some subset of important mental operations. Perhaps, then, mental test problems can be manipulated so that measures of the efficiency of these processes are extracted from individuals. Any individual differences in the efficiency of these processes can in turn be examined for predictive power over more general cognitive performance. Sternberg was not the first to think along these lines. Furneaux (1952) attempted to reduce a person's performance on IQ-type test items to parameters of speed, persistence, and error. He also described a lawful relationship between the log of solution times of an item and the level of difficulty of a problem. The essence of the approach was to focus on the test items themselves and, by manipulating them, squeeze out some value corresponding to a brain process parameter. The assumption was that test items themselves possess, or can be made to possess, a partial isomorphism with brain processes. It is an exciting possibility, although it might prove difficult subsequently to provide evidence for the validity of any putative processes produced from the picking apart of mental test items.

Expanded later into a more general theory of human intelligence far beyond the bounds of psychometric testing (Sternberg 1985), Sternberg's (1977*a,b*) first journal and book-length publications set out his general reductionistic approach and methods. The questions he addressed showed a lineage back to Spearman (1923), and a willingness to embrace issues conjoining cognitive and differential psychology, namely:

1. What mental processes constitute intelligence functioning?
2. How rapidly and/or accurately are they performed?
3. Into what strategies do they combine?
4. Upon what forms of mental representation do they act?
5. What is the knowledge base that is organized into these forms of representation?

In examining individual differences in people's cognitive abilities Sternberg outlined three approaches. There might be qualitative differences, say, between the cognitive contents and structures of novices versus experts in areas such as physics and games such as chess. There might be quantitative differences between people of higher and lower psychometric intelligence on tests of basic information processing—assuming of course that any such processes could be identified (Chapters 6 and 7 address this, the cognitive correlates, area). The third approach was the one that Sternberg set about testing. This, the cognitive components approach, dissects out the underlying cognitive components of complex tasks such as analogies, series completion, and syllogisms.

Spearman (1923) arrived at the conclusions that, after the apprehension of experience, the two principal mental components were the eduction of relations and the eduction of correlates. That is, much of how humans discover regularity in the booming, buzzing, confusion of existence is a result of (a) inducing dimensions of similarity between two things and (b) inducing a new outcome given an object and a relation. For example, one of the items in the Stanford revision of the Binet test is: 'A bird flies, a fish ... ?' We educe the relation 'mode of movement' and we educe the correlate of 'fish and swimming'. Raven (1938) constructed the Progressive Matrices tests following Spearman's principles of eduction of correlates and eduction of relations. In each of the matrix problems subjects must infer (educe) one or more relations among the horizontal and vertical columns of the items and then apply the relations in order to educe an answer (correlate). It was on this form of analogical reasoning that Sternberg first wielded his componential scalpel. In an argument with many Spearmanian (1923) resonances, Sternberg made the case for the centrality of analogical reasoning in human thought. He emphasized that much of our exploratory, cognitive efforts engaged us in extracting general characteristics from the world and applying them to novel objects. Offering the following example:

Sugar is to sweet as lemon is to ... ?

(Answer options: yellow, sour, fruit, squeeze, tea)

he implicitly agreed with Spearman that analogical thinking had a common skeletal structure:

• the *encoding* of the stimuli (apprehension of experience, perhaps)
• the *inferring* of a rule (eduction of a relation)

- the *application* of the rule to a new object correctly to continue the pattern (eduction of a correlate).

He argued that, despite Spearman, Raven, Guilford, and Burt all considering analogical reasoning to be central to human mental abilities, the processes comprising this type of thinking remained poorly understood.

Sternberg (1977*a,b*) was writing at a time, still within the first decade of cognitive psychology, when (largely serial) processing accounts were being constructed for many cognitive tasks. He reviewed various accounts of analogical reasoning but opted to implement and test four models of his own devising. In assessing this highly innovative research programme three separate aspects are discernible. First, there was the identification, enumeration, and operation of the components of analogical reasoning; the componential models of the task. Second, there was the method used to examine aspects of the operation of the components and to assign individual difference values to the operation of the components. Third, there was the larger theory of human intelligence in which this componential 'subtheory' took its place (Sternberg 1985).

First, the componential models. Sternberg (1977a,b) used the following example to illustrate his theory:

Washington is to 1 as Lincoln is to . . . ?

(Answer options: a. 10, b. 5)

In fact, this is probably not a good example, and the sugar/lemon-taste problem given above is better. The relation that has to be educed is the value of the paper money-note on which the respective president's face appears. Most people outside the USA would be unaware of this fact and would opt unprofitably to follow the more widespread piece of knowledge that Washington was the first president. It does not lead on to the correct answer. Such cultural specificity aside, the model states that, to answer this analogy correctly, one must engage four cognitive components: encoding, inferring, mapping, and application. Sternberg's account of the solution runs as follows. One *encodes* the 'Washington' and '1' terms in the problem. Attributes of each of the terms are retrieved from long-term memory and retained as an 'attribute value list' in short-term memory. Using these lists, relations between the two terms are *inferred* (like Spearman's eduction of relations). The 'Lincoln' term in the problem is *encoded*. Relations between the 'Washington' and 'Lincoln' terms are then *mapped* (more educings of relations). Relations are stored as an attribute value list in short-term memory. One then *applies* the inferred relation to the 'Lincoln' term (Spearman's eduction of correlates) to generate the missing term from the analogy. What Sternberg offered here was an account of the atoms making up the molecule of analogical reasoning. He was proposing that the brain 'digested' analogy problems using the mental enzymes of 'encoding', 'inferring', 'mapping', and 'application'. There was also a 'response' component. Later, he would add other components, such as 'comparison' and 'justification' (Sternberg 1985), but, for now, concentrate on the former four, because they offer potentially a reductionistic account of a key human mental ability.

What sorts of objects are they, these components? Kline (1991) examined their nature by referring to the concepts of contingent and non-contingent propositions. Contingent propositions are empirical entities which, depending on the empirical evidence gathered, might be true or false. Non-contingent propositions are necessarily true or false. Empirical evidence plays no role in the truth value of non-contingent propositions because they are a priori and can be known through the making of valid inferences. Kline warned that, on occasion, researchers gather empirical evidence pertaining to non-contingent propositions and that this unnecessary activity should not deceive us into thinking that they are, in fact, contingent entities. Researchers, then, might fool themselves and others into thinking that they are studying causal relations when, in fact, they are dealing with semantic relations. Kline's view was that Sternberg's components were non-contingent propositions, thus necessarily true. It is inconceivable, he argued, that one could analogize without encoding, inferring, mapping, applying, and responding; these, he insisted, are true a priori and do not require the gathering of evidence. Broadening his critique to Sternberg's knowledge acquisition components and metacomponents, Kline also declared them to be non-contingent propositions, not in need of experimental validation.

In summary, Kline's (1991) argument was that Sternberg's components are non-contingent, necessarily true; they were incorrectly being 'validated' by the methods of empirical research. However, perhaps the situation is precisely the reverse. It is arguable that Sternberg's components are contingent, falsifiable hypotheses, but have been ushered in using methods more appropriate for philosophical than scientific discourse. Like Spearman's (1923) three mental principles underlying thought, Sternberg's components were invented rather than discovered. They represent a slicing up of the phenotypically obvious aspects of the performance of a mental task. If we sat in our armchairs we might state that the processes within nutrition consisted of ingestion, digestion, assimilation, and excretion. But that would not take us far. It would not lead us closer to the bodily mechanisms involved. It would not invoke the enzymes at different stages of the alimentary canal, the different absorptive and excretive activities of different cell assemblies, and so forth. So, far from accepting Kline's (1991) conclusion that Sternberg's components are necessarily true, we should ask, as always, about their construct validity. Are they truly recognizable and separable—valid—brain processes. How could we tell? We might look for the appearance of the components in different combinations to solve different problems, as atoms appear in different molecular assemblies, or specific componential deficits as a result of brain damage or psychopharmacological intervention, or specific patterns of brain activity, in event-related potentials and functional magnetic resonance imaging scans, when given processes were active. Before that, we need a method of testing the operating characteristics of the components. The development of such a method was, arguably, Sternberg's most original contribution.

Sternberg (1977a,b) introduced a method called partial cueing for testing models of componential function within analogical reasoning tasks. Before being shown the whole analogy—see the examples above—a subject is shown a variable number of terms within the analogy: none, the first one, the first two, or the first three. In the case of the sugar/lemon analogy one would see, in the different partial cueing conditions: no terms; sugar; sugar and sweet; or sugar, sweet, and lemon. After the cueing, the subject views the whole analogy with the answer options and makes a response as fast as possible. Putting this method together with Sternberg's theory of the components involved in analogical reasoning, a series of simultaneous equations can be constructed and solved to give the timing of each parameter for each person undertaking the tasks. For example, if we assume that subjects undertake processing of all of the componential stages exhaustively before moving on to the next (their times are, therefore, additive) the equations are as follows:

0 cue: solution time $= 4a + fx + gy + fz + c$

1 cue: solution time $= 3a + fx + gy + fz + c$

2 cue: solution time $= 2a + gy + fz + c$

3 cue: solution time $= a + fz + c$

where

a = exhaustive figure scanning and encoding

x = exhaustive inference time

y = exhaustive mapping time

z = exhaustive application time

c = constant response time

f = number of values changed between terms 1 and 2

g = number of values changed between terms 1 and 3

Thus, in a 2-cue item one is assumed to have 'inferred' the relation between terms 1 and 2 (sugar and sweet) and this time drops out from the solution. In a 3-cue item one is assumed to have inferred the relation between terms 1 and 2 and also 'mapped' the associations between terms 1 and 3 (sugar and lemon), and the time for these components consequently is not required in solving the item. Thus, with a large number of items for each of the cueing conditions, we may solve the equations to obtain values for encoding, inference, mapping, application, and response. This method was an original and clever achievement, offering a cognitive-reductionist account of analogical reasoning and an individual differences-oriented parameterization of the components. However, it was based on a number of assumptions. Among these were that people solved the analogies in the same way and that components were not operating in parallel. Most importantly, it assumed that the four components existed. Sternberg's research initially merely tested whether the processes of inference, mapping, and application were gone through exhaustively. To be clear, then, the first major experiments were tests of competing models which were formulated to answer the following question: do people, on average, move on to the next component (stage) as soon as they have got a good relation between terms or do they go through all possible relations before moving on? Now, once one peeks inside any of these components' assumptions we can see other problems. For example, inferring a relation when the first two items of an analogy are, say, (a) large circle with two plus signs within it and a small circle with one plus sign (Fig. 5.1) versus (b) Washington and Lincoln might be a qualitatively different experience, with one being more easily quantifiable into attributes than the other. Still more disparate may be the mapping process. If the large circle with two plus signs becomes a large square with two triangles we see that size and number of attributes remain and that the circle maps to square and the plus signs map to triangles. But, how does that compare with the mapping of Washington to 1? The answer here does not arrive by an observational process; it is the result of a less quantifiable, perhaps capricious, process of hitting on the correct mapping from a possibly unknowable number of possible mappings. Arguably the numbers are quite different between individuals, whereas the simpler geometric analogies constrain the possible mappings. But that is an aside. The key issue is that Sternberg tested a specific hypothesis about process performance—exhaustiveness—whereas he did not test the correctness of the number or nature of the components.

Sternberg's (1977a,b) four models of componential performance were applied to two types of analogy: cartoon people whose physical attributes could be changed, and verbal. The four competing models tested, using the equations based on the

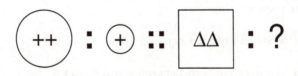

Fig. 5.1 An analogy item similar to that used by R. J. Sternberg in his componential analyses. The format is 'A is to B as C is to what (D)?' There might typically be three answer options. There are two transformations on the left-hand side of the double colon. Large circle goes to small circle and two crosses go to one. If we map the large circle in A to the large square in C and the two crosses in A to the two triangles in C and then apply the two A to B transformations from C to D then we should be looking for a small square with one triangle among the answer options. Another example may be found in Sternberg (1985, p. 143).

partial cueing technique, assumed progressively less exhaustive processing and accounted for the following amounts of solution-time variance in the 'people' and 'verbal' analogies, respectively: model I = 76% and 83%; model II = 85% and 85%; model III = 92% and 86%; and model IV = 91% and 85%. The conclusion was that application was self-terminating after a likely-looking result was achieved by the subject, that mapping was probably self-terminating, and that inference might be exhaustive, although it was unclear. What we can also conclude is that these models are derived from a very restricted set of possible models, and we have no idea how many others with arbitrary variables might perform equally well. There was relatively little to choose between the models tested in terms of their ability to explain solution-time variance. Moreover, the subjects were university students in whom the assumption that 'people perform the analogies in the same fashion' might be safer than in the wider population. Indeed, there was some evidence that, even within this restricted sample, people with better reasoning scores fitted the model better for the verbal reasoning items. They also tended to be faster responders but, paradoxically, slower encoders. However, as encoding time is characterized here it appears more like a kind of error checking than a speed of processing. The multiple correlations between component latencies and reasoning scores were high, greater than 0.7 for both types of analogy. These latter results were obtainable because Sternberg's method allowed an apportioning of the solution time to the various components.

Sternberg's (1977a,b) partial cueing procedure was elegant, and aspects of components can predict reasoning scores and solution times in reasoning tasks. But the question above all others is the validity of the components: do they represent valid aspects of brain function? Alderton *et al.* (1985) suggested that different forms of inductive reasoning tests correlated highly because the same component processes were involved in each; although in view of the promiscuous correlations among mental tests of almost all kinds (Chapter 1) we should be loathe to accept this as a hypothesis in support of components to the exclusion of other possibilities. Still, they proposed two tests that components should pass. First, there should be cross-task correlations between performance parameters of the same components from a sample of subjects. Using more general components than Sternberg, Whitely (1980) did not find impressive cross-task correlation. Second, it should be demonstrated that hypothesized processes do contribute to the success of a task. This demand that components deliver certain results is progress, but still omits the key question of construct validity.

Alderton *et al.*'s (1985) experimental work explored Sternberg's components in the setting of analogy and classification tasks. They examined subjects' abilities in 'inferring' (educing relations) and 'applying' (educing correlates), thus checking whether subjects could generate and apply rules to produce correct answers before seeing answer options. They were interested in the idea of sequential dependency; whether or not, given a correct or wrong processing operation at an earlier stage in a reasoning item, one would then deliver a correct or wrong answer in responding to answer options. They tested three models of reasoning performance. In the first, the only components were stem processing accuracy (correct inference and application) and guessing. In the second, they included a new component named 'recognition accuracy': the ability to respond correctly despite incorrect stem processing once the answer options were inspected. The third model included a component termed 'distraction': responding incorrectly after correct stem processing, having seen the answer options. In analogy tasks, 95% of their higher ability subjects fitted the second model, i.e. they benefited from seeing the answer options. Only 50% of the lower ability subjects fitted model 2, with 25% each fitting models 1 and 3. That is, more of the lower ability subjects did not benefit or were actually impaired by viewing the answer options. In the classification tasks the higher ability subjects were divided 10%, 40%, and 50% across models 1, 2, and 3, respectively, with results for the lower subjects dividing 15%, 5%, and 80%. Therefore, there were still high and low ability differences in the models that fitted their performances, but there were, in addition, clear differences between tasks. Seeing the answer options in the classification tasks was more harmful than in the analogy tasks. Even among students, then, there are differences in task structure on the basis of evidence from componential analysis.

Alderton *et al.* (1985) examined the issue of correlations among components. Across analogy and classification tasks, components with the same label correlated on average 0.57 whereas components with a different label correlated on average 0.42. If a component carries the same label a strong version of componential theory would hold that it is the same mental component. This difference between the correlations, based on the number of subjects in their study, is not significant and, although it was taken as some evidence for components' distinctiveness, it suggests other conclusions too. First, it brings us back to consider a general factor underlying supposedly distinct components. Second, the high correlations between components of the same label do not validate the existence of such components. The correlations might arise simply because people are doing rather similar sorts of work in the same-labelled components, making it a case of the psychometric tests' content overlap rather than componential performance. People's ability to find a relation in the first few terms of analogy and classification tasks might well be correlated, but that is a psychometric issue and does not necessarily reveal any underlying component in the performance of the two tasks. No more so than the more surprising empirical finding of *g* informs us about the mechanisms of intelligence.

The issue of cross-task generalization of Sternbergian components was addressed by Sternberg and Gardner (1983). They extended the componential model to series completion and classification tasks in addition to analogies. Typically, the items did not offer ideal answers but, based upon work done on categories and prototypes in long-term memory, a correct answer was possible. Here are some of their examples:

Analogy

Tiger is to chimpanzee as wolf is to . . . ?

(Answer options: camel, monkey)

Series completion

Squirrel, chipmunk . . . ?

(Answer options: racoon, horse)

Classification

Zebra, giraffe, goat

(Answer options: cow, dog)

In their second experiment, paper-and-pencil and tachistoscopic (partial cueing) versions of these three reasoning test types were employed. Correlations among the three paper-and-pencil tests, where the outcome measure was number of correct solutions, were greater than 0.8. Among the tachistoscopic versions, where the outcome measure was response latency, the correlations were 0.45, 0.65, and 0.72. Correlations across task formats (paper-and-pencil versus tachistoscopic) were a mean of −0.35 for same-type tasks and −0.30 for different-type tasks. Negative correlations are expected because high numbers of correct solutions in paper-and-pencil versions go with shorter latencies in tachistoscopic versions. These data were taken as evidence for similar processes across tasks, but they are also in line with what we know of the near-universal significant correlations among psychometric tests. They do not offer support for components that would distinguish the componential hypothesis from what is known about *g*. Modelling of these data found only four reliable components: encoding, comparison (comparing answer options to an ideal point), justification (when no ideal answer is available one answer must be justified as preferable to others), and response. Other parameters were found in some tasks but not others.

In their third experiment, Sternberg and Gardner (1983) used the three reasoning tasks described above, and devised picture, word, and geometric forms of each. The 18 subjects were individually tested for 25 hours, each one completing 2880 items. In estimating model fits, the inference, mapping, and application components were combined into a 'reasoning' 'component'. A major change from previous work was the necessity for a comparison component that accounted for significant variance. The justification component was not used in the picture task. One way of examining the similarity of components is to correlate their times across different tasks. Collapsing the component times across different task contents (thereby comparing different task types), the mean correlation for corresponding component scores was 0.32 and for non-corresponding component scores was 0.24. Collapsing the component times over task types (thereby comparing different task contents), the mean correlation for corresponding component scores was 0.40 and for non-corresponding component scores was 0.24. This was taken by the authors to be evidence for the convergent and discriminant validity of components. However, some comments on these data make them less than convincing support for the validity of components. In computing these correlations only four components were used: encoding, which often had a poor fit to the data; reasoning, which was a composite variable; comparison, which was not one of the original or key components; and justification, which did not appear in some tasks. Most worrisome of all for this large effort was the necessity to form the conglomerate 'reasoning' as a component of reasoning tasks; not much reductionism there. Indeed, it was an agglomeration of the three components—inference, mapping, and application—which began as the elemental hearts of the reasoning process. The correlations, too, are compatible with a psychometric view in which general ability suffuses all mental tests and in which more similar mental tests tend to have higher correlations.

The componential approach of Sternberg is still widely described and cited in introductory psychology textbooks (e.g. Gleitman *et al.* 1999), in differential psychology textbooks (e.g. Pueyo 1996), and in higher-level texts specifically dealing with human intelligence differences (e.g. Mackintosh 1998). Yet it is described often without any final conclusion as to its validity. Gleitman and colleagues, reaching huge numbers of students at an introductory level, make no evaluative or cautionary comments about the existence (construct validity) of Sternberg's components. And the frequency of citation for the componential approach, especially at introductory and advanced textbook levels, is in contrast to its marked lack of appearance in modern experimental and differential psychology research. This state of affairs is unacceptable. If the components, which form easily the most researched facet of Sternberg's (1985) triarchic theory of intelligence, are real then they are among the most important discoveries in mental science. They would be a partial empirical realization of Spearman's rationalist search for a mental cytology. They would be essential constructs in many types of cognitive brain research. Why then, when they feature in introductory psychology textbooks' chapters on human intelligence differences, do they fail to appear in introductory books that describe cognitive architectures (e.g. Hampson and Morris 1996; Dawson 1998; Gazzaniga *et al.* 1998)?

So, we must decide to praise the componential approach, to bury it, or to urge more research. There have been relatively few studies, mostly conducted on undergraduates, offering little information about whether the componential models fit the population's range of ability. The individual components do not always appear in the models. No model is demonstrably significantly different from others and, in general, a restricted set of models has been tested. The correlations of same- and different-labelled components across tasks is entirely consistent with what we know about correlations among psychometric tests, without our being obliged to invoke the existence of components. Independent components are correlated significantly in speed of processing and in accuracy. The place and importance of the components beyond their inconsistent application in laboratory reasoning tests has not been shown. Ultimately there is little evidence about the construct validity of the components, and the claimed validity of the correlations between component scores and psychometric test scores is not sufficient; this tells us that they are related to mental test score differences (the very phenomenon we are trying to explain), but not what the components mean. Thus, it is hard to believe that much has been achieved that was not already captured by Spearman's $g + s$ theory, despite an ingenious method.

The need for some demonstration of the independent existence of the components has not been addressed. There is, therefore, little evidence that Sternberg's parsing of reasoning is anything more than an arbitrary, variable, and stylish series of cuts in a seamless robe. It is a story being retold in textbooks, but with a limited purchase on the brain's make-up and functioning, and little place on the current agenda of research into the origins of intelligence differences. Kyllonen and Christal (1990) pronounced as follows:

> In the 1970s and early 1980s several researchers developed detailed information-processing stage models of reasoning tasks, such as analogies and series tasks . . . The approach taken in these studies was to isolate stages such as encoding, inference, and application, then analyze the relationship between performance in each stage and performance on the task overall. One of the hopes for this research was that complex cognitive abilities, such as reasoning ability, would be reducible to more elementary components, such as the inference component. Despite some successes . . . in one important sense this research can be looked upon as a modest failure. No one component was ever shown over different studies to be the essence of reasoning ability. In retrospect, this hope for the componential decomposition of complex abilities may have been rather naïve. If our result is correct, if working-memory capacity is responsible for differences in reasoning ability, then it may be that working-memory capacity affects success across the various component stages of reasoning tasks. This would make the attempt to localize reasoning deficiency futile. (p. 427)

The above disquisition addressed only one of the three aspects of Sternberg's triarchic theory of intelligence. That is because the componential subtheory is the segment of the larger theory that is the most relevant to present concerns and it is the part of Sternberg's opus with the most detailed experimental evidence. Theorizing, therefore, in the rest of the triarchic theory will probably be even harder to tie down to brain processes, as Gustafsson (1984) reported:

> Sternberg argues that the g factor in Spearman's Two Factor theory represents individual differences in meta-components; that the Thurstonian I-factor [induction] represents individual differences in a set of performance components; and that Gf reflects individual differences in the execution of performance components generally. It has been shown, however, that g is identical with Gf, and the empirical evidence also indicates that I is virtually identical with these higher order factors. Sternberg thus proposes three different explanations for the same individual difference variance. Even though these explanations are not mutually exclusive, this indicates that the componential theory is much too loose to function as a general psychometric theory.

WORKING MEMORY AND GENERAL CONTROL PROCESSES

Embretson (1995) was another researcher eager to combine the successes of differential and experimental psychology in finding out the origins of individual differences in psychometric intelligence:

> Until the influx of the information-processing paradigm in intelligence research, studying the nature of the general factor was difficult. The information-processing paradigm, however, has provided new theories and methods for studying covert processes in general intelligence. Two contrasting explanations about the basis of individual difference in general intelligence have emerged under the information processing paradigm: general control processing (i.e., global metacomponent functioning) versus working memory capacity. (p. 169)

Why did she alight on these two constructs? First, it became clear that the construct of working memory was coming closer to psychometric intelligence, especially individual differences in the general factor. Thus, Kyllonen (1996*a*) stated:

> The working memory system was developed theoretically not as a label for an individual-differences factor, but rather as a construct to explain experimental results in the memory literature. We know how to characterise working memory limitations of individual-differences results. We know how to manipulate the working memory requirements of a task without even computing correlations. Unlike the case with other conventional psychometric factors, such as reasoning ability and *g*, it is possible, in principle, to measure working memory capacity on an absolute rather than a relative scale. This property carries with it tremendous potential for, among other things, bridging the individual differences and the cognitive engineering literature. (p. 73)

Readers might wonder why working memory is being considered in this chapter and not in Chapter 6, which deals with cognitive-experimental variables. In fact, Chapter 6 is largely reserved for those few cognitive constructs that are produced by the application of the subtractive method; it examines associations between psychometric intelligence and cognitive components isolated from reaction time tasks. There is certainly a theory of working memory, and there are isolatable bits to it (Baddeley 1992*a,b*), but the assessment of individual differences in working memory, for example by Kyllonen and Christal (1990), is done by psychometric tests. Therefore, like Sternberg's componential approach, some research on working memory as an ingredient of human psychometric intelligence differences essays to gain reduction by the application of mental tests and their differences.

Unpacking the components of Raven performance

Raven's (1938) matrices were devised according to Spearman's (1923) principles of cognition, and individual differences on this test are highly *g*-loaded (Marshalek *et al.* 1983). Carpenter *et al.* (1990) sought to identify the processing characteristics needed to attain average versus very good performance in solving items from the advanced set of the Raven problems. Processes were adduced from student subjects using verbal reports during and after performing the task, and studying their eye-tracking patterns during the task. The processes and their differential limitations and architectures were implemented on computer software that was then tested on Raven problems to see whether the models could reproduce human problem-solving ability differences. The program modelling average performance was called FAIRAVEN. Very good performance was implemented on a programme called BETTERAVEN. Carpenter *et al.* concluded that:

> The BETTERAVEN model differs from FAIRAVEN in two major ways: BETTERAVEN has the ability to induce more abstract relations than FAIRAVEN, and BETTERAVEN has the ability to manage a larger set of goals in working memory and hence can solve more complex problems. (p. 404)

Carpenter *et al.*'s (1990) first experiment, with eye-tracking and subject verbalization methods, discovered that: more errors were made on items where more rules had to be induced; items that were, on average, rarely solved correctly took longer to solve in those whose answers were correct; rules were induced one at a time; and rule formation involved pairwise comparison of the pattern's elements. None of these is surprising, nor do they appear to 'reduce' the problems to the brain's functional elements. They do appear to reflect accurately Raven's (1938) intentions in constructing the general type of problem and the differential difficulties across items. From this phenomenological description of item solution in the Raven test, and from individual differences data, the authors adopted the idea that a factor in producing individual differences in Raven test scores was 'keeping track' or 'goal management' (p. 413). The next experiment produced a correlation of 0.77 ($N = 45$ students) between Raven scores and scores on the Tower of Hanoi task (this task was devised with different difficulty levels and subjects were taught a 'goal recursion strategy'). The conclusion from this association between two psychometric tests was:

> These correlations support the thesis that the execution of the goal-recursion strategy in the Tower of Hanoi puzzle and performance on the Raven test are both related to the ability to generate and maintain goals in working memory. (p. 414)

> Probability of an error increases with the number of subgoals to be generated in working memory . . . This pattern of results supports the hypothesis that errors in the Tower of Hanoi puzzle reflect constraints of working memory;

consequently, its correlation with the Raven test supports the theory that the Raven test also reflects the ability to generate and maintain goals in working memory. (p. 415)

Differential psychologists will not be surprised to see a high correlation between two tests that involve tough mental work. Also, the finding that harder items lead to more errors on both of the tests is commonplace. How much further does this analysis go? The authors invoked a seeming explanation of the processes underlying test performance and suggested that these processes are the loci of individual differences. 'Working memory', 'goals and subgoals', 'goal management', and 'goal maintenance' are all posited from a rational look at the data. They also added a construct called 'some shared abstraction processes' (p. 415). No independent measures of these constructs are available, and the methods needed to demonstrate their explanatory power are not provided. That is, these constructs are not tied within this study to known facts about the way the brain tackles information. These explanations have the feel of being restatements of the principles that went into the construction of the test; that is, the tests are looked to for a model of mind rather than the brain itself being interrogated. In later chapters we shall take to task those researchers who invoke a capacity called 'mental speed' or 'information processing speed' to 'explain' correlations between psychometric intelligence tests and measures such as reaction times, inspection times, and nerve conduction velocities. The same criterion of construct explication is applied here. If so-called processes or components are invoked they must do some reductionistic work: their existence must be demonstrable outside the realm of the mental test, or they must have explanatory power.

In constructing computer models of test performances Carpenter *et al.* (1990) stated that:

The primary goal in developing the simulation models was to specify the processes required to solve the Raven problems. (p. 415)

(Perhaps the true test of simulatory success would be the ability to solve the many test-type problems that have high correlations with the Raven.) In constructing a model of the average student performer (FAIRAVEN) the ability to work out one of the rules is left out. The ability to solve a rule in some subjects and not in others is quite an interesting finding, but it does not feel like a model of basic processing when features of a model are so closely linked to the phenotype of test performance. If making some adjustment to a non-obvious aspect of processing were to result in the ability not to find a rule, that would be a better signature of reduction. Adjustments are made to several boxes in the FAIRAVEN box-and-arrow model to produce BETTERAVEN. In fact, a whole new box called 'goal monitor' is added. Perhaps at this stage some real potential for reduction becomes clear and also underscores the poverty of 'working memory' and 'goal management' in this context. The real reduction is in all of the tweaks that were made to the BETTERAVEN program code in order to make it perform better than FAIRAVEN. If there were isomorphism between the program, especially the program differences, and aspects of the brain, then progress would be made. Such work is certainly conceivable but it was not addressed. What the models produce, through their differential success in solving Raven items, is a kind of elaborate restatement of John Raven's test-building principles. The mystery of the structure of mind and its sources of differences is described and some common-sense verbalizations are attempted but understanding goes unaddressed. A sceptical description of what has gone on in this attempt to discover the information processing bases of ability differences is as follows:

- Spearman suggests principles of cognition (after armchair speculation)
- Raven implements these in a test; this test involves the subject finding rules and hard items involve finding more and harder rules and keeping lots of rules in mind and implementing them
- When students do the test they describe, with individual differences in completeness, the rules that make up the items, and find the hard items hard because the rules are more numerous and hard to find and lots of them must be kept in mind while they are implemented
- When computer programs implement these item-construction rules (and the different insights that students gain into them), as seen through the eyes of the test-takers, they replicate the performance of the students

This type of analysis can be helpful in constructing and improving tests and items, and can perhaps instruct subjects how to solve test items, but it does not afford a breakthrough to a new level of description that can explain average test performance or test differences. The conclusion of the article is alluringly named 'cognitive processes and human intelligence' but it is a siren, offering mostly description and hand-waving. The process of 'abstraction' involves mostly the latter, merely stating that abstract reasoning appears in many accounts of human intelligence. 'Goal management' was mentioned as follows:

> One of the main distinctions between higher scoring subjects and lower scoring subjects was the ability of the better subjects to successfully generate and manage their problem-solving goals in working memory. (p. 428)

> Thus, what one intelligence test measures, according to the current theory, is the common ability to decompose problems into manageable segments and iterate through them, the differential ability to manage the hierarchy of goals and subgoals generated by this problem decomposition, and the differential ability to form higher level abstractions. (p. 429)

Readers can judge whether more has happened here than is apparent to this author's eyes. The constructs invoked do not sit on a cognitive architecture, and the computer models were not sold as or correlated with a known human mental infrastructure. In so far as the authors are saying that people working on human mental ability differences could usefully take note of work that is going on in working memory, that is welcome and finds agreement from others (Baddeley and Gathercole 1999). But that was done by rational argument, not by relating aspects of performance to some independently validated indicator of working memory outside the arena of the psychometric test. Indeed, functional brain scanning work reported in Chapter 9 suggests that Raven performance is dependent importantly on brain areas other than those involved in working memory. This latter type of research, with the advantage of another level of brain analysis, offers some possibility for reduction that will not be provided by studies that peer into psychometric tests and common-sensibly muse about the attributes shared by other tests.

Psychometrics reconstrued using cognitive architecture

Kyllonen and Christal's (1990) report makes a good case study for the area of research addressed in this book. First, they proposed a cognitive architecture (a 'mental cytology' in Spearman's (1923) parlance). Second, they proposed that individual differences might exist at loci within this architecture. Third, they measured these individual differences and correlated them with psychometric ability test scores. This is a model of what is required in the area. Their architectural edifice comprises three boxes: declarative memory and procedural memory are two inputs into working memory. The environment is a further input into working memory and responses emit from working memory (Fig. 5.2). Therefore, suggested Kyllonen and Christal (1990), there might be individual differences in the three memory boxes or in the efficiency of inputs and output. Theirs is a recognizable architecture, a simple box and arrow model of different types of memory, but not the only candidate account of cognition, not a full account of information processing, and far from being a model connected validly to basic brain processing. For example, Dawson (1998) listed a sample of 24 distinct candidate cognitive architectures, each with their own structure–process pairings, that attracted 'vibrant debates concerning the merits of each proposal' (p. 170). Were this matter of cognitive architecture to be settled, of course, then the study of the bases of intelligence differences would have a better focus.

Returning to Kyllonen and Christal's (1990) model, they suggested that there might be individual differences in the memory structures (working, declarative, and procedural) and/or the processing cycles (cognitive, motor, and perceptual). Thus, they produced a 'four sources' (p. 390) model of individual differences whereby these can arise from type and extent of knowledge (in declarative and procedural memory), working memory capacity, and speed of processing in the processing cycles. They argued that in psychometric models such as those discussed in Chapter 1, there is an emphasis on g as a putative variable for explanatory focus, and that this is closely allied to abstract reasoning, something with which Carpenter *et al.* (1990) and Sternberg (1977*a,b*) would agree. On the other hand, arguing from cognitive literature covering memory, learning, and reasoning,

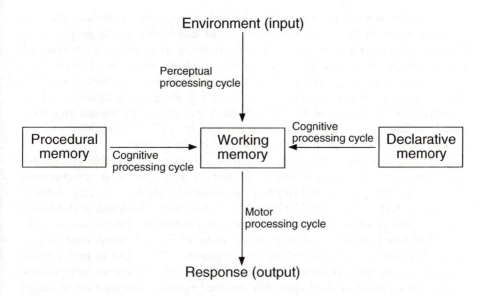

Fig. 5.2 The cognitive architecture used by Kyllonen and Christal to examine associations between working memory and psychometric intelligence. For explanation see text. Redrawn from Kyllonen and Christal (1990).

Kyllonen and Christal preferred to emphasize the centrality of working memory as a key limiting construct.

> Reasoning ability thus has a central role in the conventional abilities model, and working memory capacity has a central role in the four sources model. An important question is, to what degree are these two constructs related?

Tests are then developed and compiled to measure 'reasoning', 'working memory', 'general knowledge', and 'speed of processing'. All were psychometric tests, not based upon validated theories of information processing. Four studies tested a total of over 2000 US military recruits during basic training. Different permutations of 15 reasoning tests (some from the Armed Services Vocational Aptitude Battery, some from the Educational Testing Service's kit of factor-referenced cognitive tests, and some specially developed), six working memory tests, four general knowledge tests, and two processing speed tests were administered. The covariances were construed as structural equation models.

Reasoning tests were sometimes mental arithmetic problems, other mathematical problems, verbal reasoning (e.g. analogies), number series, syllogisms, and so forth. General knowledge comprised two vocabulary tests, a science knowledge test, and a test of paragraph comprehension. Processing speed was tested using a multiple choice arithmetic test and a test of matching codes to words. These are all high-level psychometric tasks requiring unplumbable combinations of who-knows-how-many elementary information processing operations. The tests of reasoning, from their surface content, would load highly on the general factor from a battery of cognitive tests, although reasoning as a process is not dissected or laid bare by the testing. Other supposed tests of processing speed, drawn from experimental psychology and psychophysics, are presented in Chapters 6 and 7. Processing speed is not a settled construct, is has no agreed indicators, and the tests used by Kyllonen and Christal (1990) do not access any known processing speed mechanism, as they themselves discussed (p. 425). In addition, they had mostly very low correlations with other tests in the batteries.

'Working memory' carries more weight as an explanatory variable in Kyllonen and Christal's (1990) account and so the tests require a bit more scrutiny with regard to the transparency of their processing demands. The first 'working memory' test was a test called 'ABCD Grammatical *Reasoning*' (Kyllonen and Christal 1990, p. 398; emphasis added). The test involves transitive inference on the order of ABCD based on information about the order of pairs of letters (and pairs of pairs). The second test involved algebraic equations. These had to be combined to work out the value of letters from the values of other letters set in equations. Third was a version of digit span that involved recalling the position of a digit in different-sized lists presented on a computer screen. Fourth was a test of arithmetic. A fifth test presented subjects with three letters and asked them to respond with a further three letters having added a certain number to the alphabetic position of each (e.g. GNB + 2 = IPD). At a superficial level of analysis all of these tests involve symbol (letter or number or both) storage and manipulation. Although the term 'working memory' was used to corral the tests, it is not possible to say more than there is a family likeness among the tests and that psychometrically one might expect them to share covariance with a very high loading on general fluid ability.

Over their four large-scale studies Kyllonen and Christal (1990) arrived at similar models. The fourth of these is shown in Fig. 5.3 as an example. In each case psychometric test scores were assumed to load on the designated factor (in psychometric test parlance) or structure/process (in the parlance of their cognitive architecture), and on no other. This largely succeeded. Because these were all psychometric tests, none of which had a demonstrated, tractable information processing structure, one may merely say that these latent variables have the same status as any other factor in a factor analysis. They may not be equated with lower-level brain-processing mechanisms. The latent trait analysis informs us that individual differences in tests within a common-sense grouping of tests are mostly due to a common factor. In the case of the 'working memory' tests they concluded that there was a general working memory factor, not domain-specific. But this type of analysis does not lead to the components of processing involved in the tasks or in the factors. Musing about the 'nature' of these—the individual tests and the latent factors—is at the level of rational argument, not scientific explanation. Another feature of each of the models is the lack of a g factor. Each of the latent traits was significantly intercorrelated, with the exception of 'processing speed' and 'general knowledge', but the models seemed better left at expressing

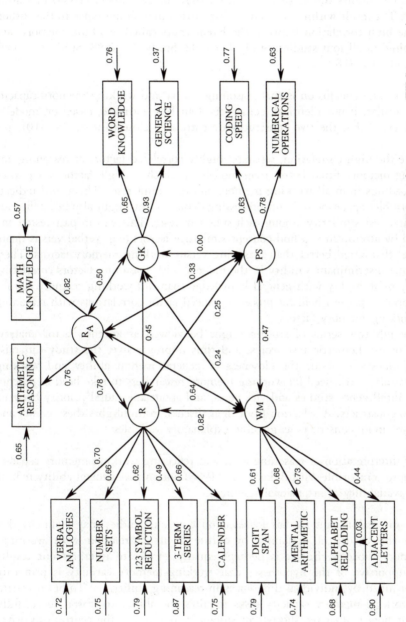

Fig. 5.3 Structural model showing the associations among latent variables of reasoning (R), working memory (WM), processing speed (PS), general knowledge (GK), and armed services vocational aptitude battery reasoning (R_A). Rectangles represent manifest variables (test scores). Redrawn from Kyllonen and Christal (1990).

correlations among various factors rather than having them all load on a general factor. The results differ, therefore, from those of Gustafsson (1984) or Carroll (1993). The result within the models that carried most importance to the authors was the high correlation between the latent traits called 'working memory' and 'reasoning' in all four studies: Study 1 = 0.82, Study 2 = 0.88, Study 3 = 0.80, and Study 4 = 0.82.

> Our second conclusion is that reasoning ability and working memory capacity are similar, if not identical, constructs. Our best estimate, based on model 1 and 1x, is that the two constructs are correlated close to 0.90. (p. 410)

Despite the high correlation, separate, highly correlated factors of reasoning and working memory fitted better than models in which a single factor was posited with loadings from all working memory and reasoning tests. This could indicate a discernible separation of brain-processing demands but might also be a reflection of greater test similarity among each subset of tests. This was in part tested and refuted by attempting to find content-similarity factors (e.g. verbal versus quantitative) that fitted better than reasoning versus working memory factors. There was some discriminant validity in the models, with reasoning factors correlating slightly more highly with general knowledge than did working memory factors. The opposite pattern held for processing speed factor correlations with reasoning and working memory factors.

Although this series of studies might be viewed as another factor analytic model of psychometric test scores, and thus unprogressive, the study did raise helpful questions about the closeness of general mental ability and working memory, about the need for working memory researchers to take heed of psychometric intelligence studies and vice versa, and about any causal priority between the two constructs. A selection from their discussion highlights these points and raises yet more constructs as possible explanatory variables:

> Our interpretation of reasoning ability as reflecting working memory capacity is more compatible with Ackerman's (1988) notion that general ability reflects the availability of attentional resources.

> The discussion thus far has focussed on how our studies may yield insights into the nature of reasoning by virtue of its correlation with working-memory capacity. But it is perhaps equally correct to interpret our results as supportive of the hypotheses that working-memory capacity is primarily determined by individual differences in reasoning ability . . . To be successful in working-memory capacity tasks requires the ability to reason successfully about how to manage short-term storage resources . . . the central executive, which is responsible for overseeing processing and allocating attentional resources, is still largely a mystery. The advantage to our linking of working-memory capacity with reasoning ability is that unpacking the mystery of reasoning is a problem faced by both those who work from the experimental

perspective and those who work from the correlational-abilities perspective. Perhaps our linking these two [mysterious!] concepts will result in insights on the nature of reasoning and the nature of working-memory capacity from adherents of each of these two schools. (Kyllonen and Christal 1990, pp. 427–428)

Kyllonen (1993) examined the 'four sources' information processing model of abilities in more detail and suggested that the most general factor from his cognitive components battery of tests was working memory. Again, in this study, the information processing battery of tests was compared with more standard psychometric ability tests. The working memory factor correlated almost perfectly with a factor derived from arithmetic reasoning and mathematics knowledge psychometric tests. Stauffer *et al.* (1996) criticized Kyllonen's (1993) study on the grounds of incomplete sampling of psychometric intelligence in providing a general factor, restriction of range in the subject sample, omitting the proportion of variance from the general factor in the information processing and psychometric batteries, and failing to extract lower-order factors properly. Stauffer and colleagues examined almost 300 school, college, and university students on the armed services vocational aptitude battery (ASVAB) and Kyllonen's (1993) cognitive component-oriented cognitive abilities measurement (CAM). The CAM is computer based, has 25 measures, and offers scores on four components, namely processing speed, working memory capacity, declarative knowledge, and procedural knowledge. Ten scores from the ASVAB and 25 scores from the CAM showed positive correlations mostly in the range 0.4 to 0.5. A well-fitting structural equation model (Fig. 5.4) extracted three first order factors from the ASVAB (verbal/math, clerical speed, and technical knowledge) and the four expected factors from the CAM (see above). Higher order general factors were extracted from each battery, and all of the first order factors had loadings greater than 0.8, with five of the seven loadings greater than 0.9. The two general factors, ASVAB *g* versus CAM *g* correlated at 0.994. The general factor accounted for 64–80% of the variance in the ASVAB and 48–83% of the variance in the CAM. Stauffer and colleagues commented,

> The near-unity of the correlation between the two higher order factors
> ... indicated that they represent the same general factor. Because of those
> correlations and because the higher order factor in the paper-and-pencil
> battery [ASVAB] is known to be psychometric *g*, it is clear that the higher
> order factor in the cognitive-components battery [CAM] also measures *g*.
> (p. 199)

Our results suggest that measurement of human ability, whether by traditional paper-and-pencil tests or by cognitive components, yields, in large part, a measure of *g*. Although the cognitive components have unique names, they all correlate most strongly with V/M [verbal/math from the ASVAB], the universally accepted measure of *g*. Further, the amount of *g* in the common

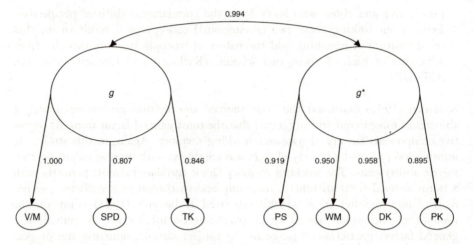

Fig. 5.4 Structural model with maximum likelihood estimates showing the association between general factors obtained from a set of paper-and-pencil tests, the armed services vocational aptitude battery (ASVAB), and the computer-based component-oriented cognitive abilities measurement (CAM). The first-order factors of the ASVAB are verbal/mathematical (V/M), clerical speed (SPD), and technical knowledge (TK). The first-order factors for the CAM are processing speed (PS), working memory (WM), declarative knowledge (DK), and procedural knowledge (PK). Note the almost perfect correlation between the two general factors and the very high loadings of the first-order factors on the respective general factors. Redrawn from Stauffer *et al.* (1996).

> variance among the cognitive-components tests is greater than in traditional paper-and-pencil tests, indicating that the amount of reliable variance attributable to specific abilities is smaller in cognitive-components tests than in traditional paper-and-pencil tests. That finding is contrary to the expectations of some cognitive psychologists. (pp. 200–201)

Frontal lobology incorporates *g*

In agreement with Carpenter *et al.* (1990), Duncan *et al.* (1996) were keen to articulate general mental ability in terms of 'managing goals', although not in exactly the same way. Moreover, Duncan *et al.* had a biological locus for the origin of these goal-relevant *g* differences:

> in large part at least, *g* reflects the action control functions of the brain's frontal lobes. (p. 258)

Cognitive neuropsychologists have warned about the tendency to implant too many human functions in the frontal lobes. Indeed, this tendency has attracted the criticisms that 'frontal lobology' is a new pseudoscience and that placing a mental function in the frontal lobes is about as specific as addressing an envelope with the sole location 'Europe' (David 1992).

Presaging evidence presented in Chapter 9, Duncan *et al.* (1996) countered traditional views that psychometric ability test scores are not decreased following frontal lobe damage. They remarked that, especially with more fluid ability tests, such decline in mental ability is evident. In addition, notwithstanding evidence for modularity of brain functions, there are areas that subserve many functions in a general way, such as the dorsolateral prefrontal cortex and the anterior cingulate areas (Posner and Peterson 1990). Further correlative evidence linking general mental ability and the frontal lobes, according to these authors, is that both have attracted the cognitive processing epithet 'executive function' as being a key process. In a section of rational argument, reminiscent of the style used by Carpenter *et al.* (1990), they thought that:

> The process of shaping behavior by competition between candidate goals or action requirements is basic to both Spearman's g and executive deficit following frontal lesions. In line with the standard distinction between controlled and automatic behavior, the shaping process is most likely to fail under conditions of novelty and weak environmental support. (p. 256)

In fact, the long introduction to Duncan *et al.*'s (1990) piece amounts to drawing some parallels between g and frontal lobe functions. The promise for reduction is that both a biological locus and a cognitive construct are seen as the seat of general ability differences.

The empirical part of the work examines some psychometric ability tasks alongside a new task designed to get at a putative frontal lobe function. The task might look as follows:

WATCH RIGHT

2	3
X	E
B	C
7	2
3	4
H	A
L	Q
4	9
3	8
T	M

+

8	5
N	F
R	Y

The subject's task is to read letters. Each horizontal line in the above list appeared alone on a computer screen for 200 ms with a blank period afterwards (of 200 ms) before the next horizontal line appeared in the same location. The subject follows the top instruction, and so reads 'E, C, A, Q, etc.'. Sometimes, instead of a number or letter pair, a plus (+) or minus (–) sign appears. The plus sign means 'stick to the right or move to the right if you are reading from the left-hand side'. A minus sign means the same, but applies to the left. This plus or minus sign is called the 'second side instruction'. Some people, proceeding correctly with the task, would fail to apply the second side instruction. They knew they had seen it; they just did not do it. This was termed 'goal neglect' (p. 270) by the authors and was thought to be 'reminiscent of frontal patients'. Failing to apply the second side instruction was associated with psychometric ability test level as measured by the Cattell Culture Fair test. If subjects were made to repeat the second side instruction after failing to apply it they would then apply it correctly. After beginning to apply it, people rarely failed to do so thereafter. In 15 out of 90 occasions the second side instruction was not applied in block 1 of testing. The authors diagnosed this fault by formulating as follows:

> a process of goal activation fails in some subjects, even though the verbal description of the task requirements has been understood. The relevant task requirement 'slips the subject's mind' but can be activated by a further verbal prompt. (p. 274)

In a second experiment Duncan *et al.* (1990) examined 41 people on this test. They also took psychometric ability tests. After near universally correct performance up to the occurrence of the second side instruction, 17 did not then apply it. However, only a minority of these subjects reported seeing the second side instruction. There was a correlation of 0.52 between the number of test blocks in which the second side instruction was not applied and scores on Cattell's Culture Fair test. With sufficient prompting almost all subjects correctly applied the second side instruction. A third experiment added a new requirement to the letter-reading task. A dot would at times appear on the left or right above one of the letters/digits and subjects were asked to press a left or right response button, corresponding to the position of the dot. Thirty-eight middle-aged adults were tested and there was a correlation of 0.55 between failure to apply the second side instruction and Cattell Culture Fair test scores. It became clear from the pattern of results that neglecting the second side instruction was concentrated in the lower part of the mental ability distribution. In a fourth experiment 7 out of 10 people with frontal brain damage showed neglect of the second side instruction but only 1 out of 10 posterior lobe brain-damaged patients did so.

Duncan *et al.* (1996) concluded from their data that:

> simple goal activation function involved in our experiments is a central element of Spearman's *g* (p. 293)

Key factors are novelty, weak feedback, and multiple concurrent concerns. (p 298)

To have discovered a central 'element' of Spearman's *g* approximates to Hunt's (1980*a*) 'Holy Grail' of intelligence differences being captured in a single information processing parameter. It is a big claim. It is not justifiable. The behavioural failure identified and measured in Duncan *et al.*'s task does appear, from two modest studies, to have a correlation with psychometric intelligence. However, as will be done with every other such correlation (Chapters 6–9), there must be scrutiny about how far research has gone in explaining what is quite an interesting finding. The name attributed to the test performance—'goal activation function'—is a common sense-based redescription of the task. Parallels with frontal lobe damage are acceptable as circumstantial evidence. But none of this validates the construct measured by the task in terms of a cognitive or biological architecture that touches the brain. That must come from further research, which might take several different lines. The goal activation function should be implanted in phenotypically dissimilar tasks to discover whether it might be extracted from a battery of such tasks. Functional brain-imaging techniques might reveal activation–deactivation signatures of successes and failures in applying the second side instruction. These signatures should also characterize people with high and low psychometric intelligence. There might be a genetic correlation between this ability and psychometric test scores. Psychopharmacological manipulations might alter goal activation and psychometric test scores. And so forth. At present, as with, say, inspection time around the early 1980s (Nettelbeck 1982), all that is known is a test–test correlation. On one side of the correlation is a test with a character that throws up some hypotheses about brain function that seem worth pursuing. The breaking into a conscious activity stream with the second side instruction is central. Working memory might be implicated, but the correction by verbal instruction goes against that. The error of not applying the instruction is made by people in the lower IQ range, raising the issue of whether the correlation can be found across the normal range of ability scores. Quite a number of subjects reported not seeing the plus or minus signs, a problem that requires further investigation in its own right, implying an inspection time limitation (Chapter 7). The second side instruction, therefore, has promise as a task and needs further development. It suggests the kinds of things that people of different ability test levels can and cannot do well. But, then, so does the Carpenter *et al.* (1990) report and so does every other psychometric test that has a modest or better correlation with psychometric intelligence tests. The explanatory value of the correlation depends crucially on the nomological network, the construct validity, of the information processing task. In that regard the second side instruction task is underdeveloped. It is hard to agree that its tractability is such that it presently delivers an 'element' of psychometric intelligence differences.

The paper by Duncan *et al.* (1996) might, in common with other information processing constructs reviewed later, claim too much in terms of the explanatory value of the studies. Moreover, in common with Carpenter *et al.*'s (1990) report there are extended discursive sections that seek information processing accounts by rational argument rather than data, much in the way that Spearman (1923) did.

Excising components using multicomponent latent trait modelling

Embretson acknowledged Sternberg's (1977*a,b*) original contribution in combining differential and information processing approaches to intelligence, but chose a different set of components and, in a technical appendix, explained why she used a new method for modelling task accuracy: multicomponent latent trait models. From a consideration of Sternberg's (1977*a,b*) and Pellegrino and Glaser's (1980) research on reasoning tasks, Carpenter *et al.*'s (1990) analyses of Raven's progressive matrices, and Kyllonen and Christal's (1990) studies of reasoning and working memory, Embretson identified components of 'working memory' and 'general control processes' as important covert mental components that could account for individual differences in general psychometric intelligence. The latent components are extracted from people's performances on an abstract reasoning test, constructed on the principles of Carpenter *et al.*'s (1990) rules of inference in Raven's matrices. Success of inference strategy was hypothesized to be governed by a person's working memory capacity and the memory load of the item. This was manipulated by varying the number of rules that had to be applied across items. Then:

> The second latent response variable ... is strategy application. This variable reflects the rate of implementing the inference strategy in task processing. The latent ability that governs this response is general control processing. (p. 173)

Whereas there is a large amount of literature on the construct of working memory (Baddeley 1986), the evidence for the relatively general, possibly nebulous, construct identified as general control processing is less impressive. The ability to extract such covert performance parameters requires strong prior theory. The memory load variability of the abstract reasoning task appears clearly to manipulate memory requirements, and the contribution of general control processing is then assumed to be equal in all items. The latent performance components extracted from this abstract reasoning test were successfully used as mediators between the scores on the Abstract Reasoning Test and the scores on the factors of the ASVAB: verbal knowledge, quantitative reasoning, processing speed, and technical competency (Fig. 5.5). However, the only contribution of any size is to the quantitative reasoning factor.

As was seen with Sternberg's (1977*a,b*) research, Embretson's (1995) approach is careful manipulation of the psychometric test items in order to extract so-called component scores. In the abstract reasoning task the memory load of the items is varied to allow a memory component to be extracted. The general control processing is a remainder term. Both processes, though, are aspects of test items, and we have no evidence to date that they have validity as identifiable brain

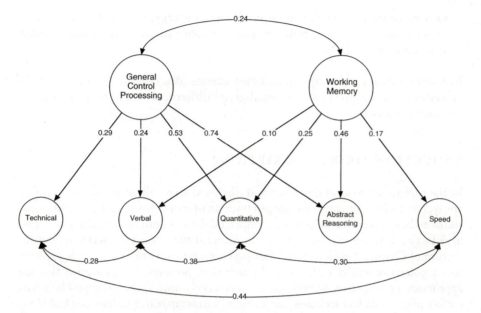

Fig. 5.5 Structural model showing that latent components of 'working memory' and 'general control processing' mediate the associations between factors from the armed services vocational aptitude battery (ASVAB) and scores on Embretson's abstract reasoning task. Redrawn from Embretson (1995).

processes. They account for some variance in other psychometric test items but, despite their being the result of systematic task construction, it is not clear whether they have taken us any further in understanding the nature of intelligence than does an ordinary factoring of ability test scores. Embretson did address issues of construct validity for her factors but her 'construct representation' and 'nomothetic span' dealt with the decomposition of the abstract reasoning task and the relations with the ASVAB, respectively. This much is necessary. And she properly noted that the now-famous study in which Kyllonen and Christal (1990) showed the near identity between working memory and reasoning was limited by the fact that they used phenotypic tasks to operationalize working memory. She continued that:

> It should be noted that operationalising covert processes requires strong prior assumptions. Thus any study, including this study, is limited by the requisite assumptions and associated methods. Further research, with multiple operationalisations of the two processing variables, is needed to further determine the relative importance of these sources of individual differences in general intelligence. (p. 184)

Quite. Embretson ended by describing the continuity between her favoured mental components and two of Spearman's (Chapter 2) constructs:

General control processing, Spearman's mental energy, is the conative directing of attention, whereas working memory capacity parallels Spearman's mental span concept (p. 184)

It is indeed striking that Spearman's two guesses (described in Chapter 2) at the processes founding psychometric intelligence differences should be so prominent in today's research.

REDUCTION OR REDESCRIPTION?

In the various approaches described and discussed above there are similarities that are worth noting. In each case some clever analysis of psychometric ability tests seems to have taken the field toward understanding cognitive operations at a level of reduction beneath psychometric performance differences. They seem to flout the dictum of Chapter 1 which stated that psychometric tests cannot provide explanatory accounts of ability differences. In each case, however, it was argued that the appearance of reduction or explanation was largely an illusion. The psychometric surface of the tests was reckoned not to have been scratched, let alone cracked along the natural fault lines of the brain's information processing systems. In essence, the conclusion was that each approach ended by the author elaborately redescribing the tests with which they began.

Sternberg (1977*a,b*) conceived a new model-fitting procedure, using simultaneous equations and regression, for cutting reasoning performance into components. But the life of the components was not sustained outside the incubator of the psychometric test and a 'reasoning' component to explain reasoning ability differences is not marked progress.

Carpenter *et al.* (1990) accurately reproduced the performance of different subjects on the Raven's Matrices with computer programs based on an architecture related to SOAR, which has promised to deliver a 'general intelligence' (Laird *et al.* 1987; Rosenbloom *et al.* 1991). However, their model was aimed at producing a phenocopy of human performance. No attempt was made to seek isomorphism between the structure–function relations in the computer program and aspects of lower-level human information processing. That is what would be demanded by explanation rather than redescription of mental ability differences. The promise for this approach is that artificial cognitive architectures such as SOAR specify structures and processes whose equivalents might be sought in human brains. This approach still has a long way to go. Any suggestion that a hypothetical cognitive architecture's parameters might be the source of human ability differences requires that the architecture has validity as a model of human brain function, that aspects of the architecture can be specified and then measured in humans, and that individual differences in aspects of the architecture correlate with human performance differences. In neural networks, for example, the possible parameters of interest might be number and structuring of units, learning parameters such as adaptive gain and momentum, parameters that affect the magnitude of the weights or that vary with time, and so forth.

Kyllonen and Christal (1990) fitted complex and convincing structural equation models to large data sets involving mental tests chosen to be markers for structures and functions of a cognitive architecture. The architecture was reproduced in the structure of the latent traits and implied a key role for working memory in reasoning and perhaps psychometric intelligence generally. However, the equating of mental tests to latent constructs reflected the pattern of covariance found in complex, standard psychometric tests, none of which had an information processing account. The naming of the latent traits was a common-sense process of thinking about the overlap between the surface structure of the tests. It is not out of the question that this method might reveal underlying brain processes, but it no better placed to do so than any other psychometric analysis (Chapter 1).

Embretson (1995) showed lawful relations between quantitative aspects of mental test content and quantitative changes in subjects' performances. In addition, latent traits from the tests accounted for variance in the performance differences in other tests. The latent traits were given names which were hypothesized to be information processing characteristics, successors to Spearman's (1927) mental 'energy' and 'span'. It is yet to be demonstrated that the latent traits are isomorphic with processes in the brain and do not just reflect aspects of the tests themselves.

It's probably no fluke that in each of the cases above the analytic tools being wielded were state-of-the-art, complex computational machinery. The grinding of test data through such elaborate data-mincing machines, and the impressively reconstructed output, compel the impression that the mental ability test performance differences must have been understood or explained by the lower-level constructs. However, the apparently explanatory constructs in all cases were applied by reason rather than a breakthrough in explanation. It is suggested that these studies achieved interesting psychometric advances that offer ways to construct new tests and items, ways to construe psychometric ability test differences, and new lines of inquiry as to the sources of ability differences (e.g. the cognitive-neuroscience investigations into working memory and frontal lobe processing). They point to explanatory destinations from a psychometric platform, but they have yet to travel.

Two themes that arose were to do with goal formation and management and working memory. There is an urgent need for an empirical and theoretical conjoining of working memory and *g*, given the weighty and rather different empirical histories of both (Baddeley 1986, 1992*a*,*b*; Jensen 1998*a*). They find a common ancestor in Spearman (1927). Although he is better remembered for his construct of 'mental energy', which he introduced in his Chapter IX, less is said about his preceding chapter in which he discussed the concept of 'Universal Mental Competition' (p. 99). In this chapter and later Spearman mused over the finding that the number of ideas that can be kept actively in mind is about five or six. Spearman traced ideas about a limited-capacity memory system back to the sixteenth century, perhaps even to Augustine (354–430 AD), and made some references to ideas of chunking. A modern researcher into working memory differences might nod at his writing:

> Of all the competitions for existence, of all the wars for 'a place under the sun,' surely none is more relentless than that which is continually waging between the various contents of our own mind. (p. 99)

> But when we compare the multitude of all that the mind of an adult man has collected with that of which he is conscious on any single moment—we must be astounded at the disproportion between the former's wealth and the latter's poverty. (p. 101)

RÉSUMÉ

Sternberg devised an ingenious way of chopping up analogical reasoning tasks to find stages such as encoding, mapping, application, and so forth. Each of these stages could be measured, and individual differences in their timings were assessed. Therefore, this promised a possible isomorphism between identifiable elements in actual test items and processes in the brain. Research thereafter added further stages and found differences in high- and low-ability individuals. There has been theoretical criticism of Sternberg's stages, and more recent research has sometimes failed to replicate the structure that Sternberg originally found. To some extent Embretson and Kyllonen and Christal extended this approach, and the field shows a certain amount of life. The possibility raised in this chapter is that the psychometric tradition might have spawned the means of its own reduction; understanding intelligence, after all, might be possible using tasks and methods familiar to IQ testers. The nagging worry is that this area of research, frequently employing sophisticated modelling procedures, has done little more than neatly and attractively pull apart the layers of the psychometric intelligence layer cake. The slices can all be pushed together to reconstruct the cake, but they have not, in truth, revealed what we wanted: the ingredients and procedures of the recipes for different sponges and fillings. As Stauffer *et al.* (1996) commented:

> Despite theoretical foundations and arguments, cognitive components tests appear to measure much the same thing as traditional paper-and-pencil tests. (p. 193)

One recurring presence as a putative explanation of some general ability differences is that of working memory. Whereas it is not certain that this construct has a lower-level existence than other psychometric ability constructs, it does have a large and burgeoning experimental and biological literature (Carpenter *et al.*, 2000; Smith 2000). In so far as the above literature is saying that people interested in intelligence differences should take more heed of working memory research because of the large shared variance between working memory and *g*, then this conduit to much cognitive and biological evidence about cognition should be travelled, even if it does lack data on individual differences. Baddeley, the originator of the working memory concept, has moved closer to seeing a role for working memory research within psychometric intelligence differences (Baddeley and Gathercole 1999). If working memory does turn out to be *g*'s separated identical twin, with better social skills, entry to cognitive-neuroscience high society, and inordinate empirical and theoretical wealth, then who will cavil at *g*'s being adopted if that is the gain and all that's lost is a name?

6 Faster, smarter?

Reaction times: raking around in cognitive psychology

SUMMARY

In trying to get at the reasons for psychometric intelligence differences, some investigators take the following approach. They acknowledge that one of the aims of cognitive psychology is to discover elementary aspects of human cognitive functioning. These aspects are often called structures and processes, and their performance characteristics can be measured using cognitive tasks. These tasks are often a variation of the reaction time technique, and they may be used to measure individual differences in the cognitive process in question. Therefore, individual differences in putatively elementary cognitive process may be correlated with individual differences in psychometric intelligence tests. If the two are correlated significantly, a possible conclusion is that individual differences in the elementary cognitive task partly explain (account for some variance in) human intelligence differences. Hunt (1983) provided a brief manifesto for this type of research into human mental ability differences:

> My co-workers and I have studied individual differences in the elementary processes of information handling. We refer to these processes collectively as the 'mechanistic aspect' of thought. Our work is based on a strong commitment to theory. We assume a general model of how the mind works as an abstract information processor, and study individual differences in situations that we believe expose the elementary processes of the model. This is analogous to the use of simple programs to test the arithmetical capacities of computers. In both cases the validity of the test depends on the accuracy of the model on which the test is used. (p. 143)

In this mode, the reaction time-based techniques of Hick, Posner, and Saul Sternberg, among others, are discussed. The theoretical rationale for some cognitive tests is presented, with an explanation of how these tasks were intended to yield measurements of low-level cognitive processes. The correlations of these processes with cognitive test scores are summarized. The contribution made to the understanding of intelligence differences is evaluated, and there is reflection on the construct validity of each cognitive task.

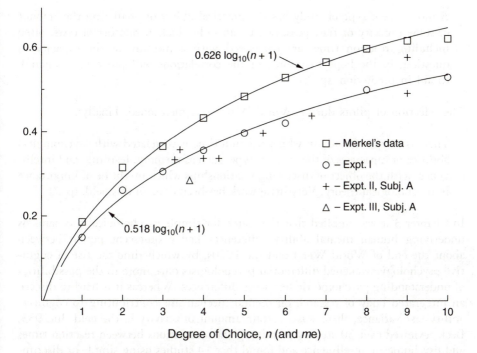

Fig. 6.1 The logarithmic relationship between the number of stimulus alternatives in a reaction time task and the reaction time duration. These are Hick's original data and include Merkel's data from the late-nineteenth century (the open squares). Facsimile reproduced from Hick (1952).

INTRODUCTION

An early study of the association between reaction times and higher mental abilities nicely echoes the structure of the study of intelligence outlined in Chapter 1 (Fig. 1.1). Lemmon (1927) declared that there were three types of study employing reaction time measures:

> Few phenomena in psychology have been studied more than reaction time. In almost all the studies in this field, however, the speed of response has been studied for its own sake, its importance being taken for granted, and there has been little thought of determining its relationship to the principal psychological capacities. (p. 5)

According to Lemmon, this was the typical experimental study of reaction times in which the influences of internal and external factors were examined. In a second type of study using reaction times, other measures were inferred from it. Lemmon cited Henmon's work which used reaction times to get at sensory differences and the earlier work of Helmholtz who used reaction times to infer speed of nerve conduction. A third type of study is what was earlier called predictive validity:

A more recent type of study has the practical object of predicting the amount of some capacity or trait possessed by an individual. A number of tests, often including reaction time, are correlated with a measure of the capacity in question, in the hope that some of the correlations will prove large enough to aid in prediction. (p. 6)

The selection of pilots during World War I was mentioned. Finally:

There is a type of study in which reaction time is correlated with psychological abilities or capacities of the 'higher' type, such as memory, learning, and intelligence, with the object of disclosing relationships which might be of importance in psychological theory. Very little work has been done in this field. (p. 7)

In Chapter 3 it was implied that the search for simple psychological mechanisms underlying human mental ability differences had a quiescent period between about the end of World War I and the 1970s, by which time the rise of cognitive psychology awakened differential psychologists once more to the possibilities of understanding psychometric test score differences. Whereas it is hard to discern an integrated body of research on mental mechanisms contributing to cognitive ability test variance, there was a certain amount of activity in the field. In 1933, Beck reviewed over 30 studies examining the associations between reaction times and psychometric intelligence and found that 14 studies using simple or discriminative reaction time had a median correlation of –0.16 (range 0.32 to –0.90), 14 studies of serial reaction time showed a median correlation of –0.18 (range 0.03 to –0.53), five studies examining speed of reading resulted in a median correlation of –0.30 (range –0.14 to –0.32), and six studies of reflex response had a median correlation of –0.06 (range 0.08 to –0.24). In all instances negative correlations indicate that people with higher psychometric ability test scores had faster reaction times. These results would not induce enthusiasm in those wishing to reduce mental abilities to basic psychological mechanisms, save for the odd, outlying result such as Peak and Boring's (1926) report of a correlation of 0.9 between reaction time and psychometric intelligence (in five senior students). The trail of this type of research goes rather cold until Eysenck's (1967) report of a German study using a new reaction time method.

THE HICK REACTION TIME PROCEDURE

Simple reaction time involves responding to a single stimulus as fast as possible, usually with an instruction to avoid errors. When responding to one of a number of possible stimuli—waiting, say, to react to one of four lights that is about to be illuminated—the reaction takes longer. Hick (1952) was not the first researcher to note that there was a lawful relation between the degree of stimulus uncertainty (waiting to see which one of a number of alternatives one will be asked to respond to) and people's reaction times. Hick replicated the findings of Merkel from 1885.

He noted Blank's (1934) suggestion, made without developing any theory, that there might be a logarithmic association between the number of stimulus alternatives and reaction time durations. Hick recast these classical findings in the then-modern theory of information, as articulated by communication engineers in the years following World War II. He described reaction time events in terms of the probability of a given stimulus occurring: the more alternatives there were, the lower is the information to the subject about which event will occur. The maximum information is available in simple reaction time when the subject knows that only one possible event can occur. Proportionately lower information is on offer as the stimulus set increases. This description is in terms of the *information the subject has* about the likelihood of a given event occurring. As described below, when there are more stimulus alternatives in the display, *the subject needs to make more binary decisions* to effect a correct response. Information in this latter sense is a logarithmic (base 2) function of the number (n) of stimulus alternatives. Hick found that Merkel's data (Fig. 6.1) were well-fitted by the expression

Reaction time (seconds) = $0.626 \log_{10}(n + 1)$

Hick's idea was that a person's 'rate of gain of information' was a constant and might be described by the increment in reaction times as the degree of stimulus uncertainty rises. Note that this lower-level construct is inferred from the equation describing people's response patterns. In his own experiments Hick employed an array of 10 lights linked to 10 morse keys on which subjects rested their fingers in preparation for responding. First using himself as a subject, Hick included some procedural factors that are often missing from more modern 'Hick' reaction time experiments. Thousands of reactions were performed. Practice was given between different degrees of choice in order to abolish the effect of the previous set size. Tests were performed in which the set sizes were (a) increasing in size, (b) decreasing, and (c) random for each subject. Hick's own reactions (Fig. 6.1), using between 1 and 10 choices, were fitted well by the expression

Reaction time (seconds) = $0.518 \log_{10}(n + 1)$

Hick's experiments on just a few subjects showed the hypothesized relation between reaction times and stimulus uncertainty (the inverse of information available to the subject), and he recognized that this lawful association was still far from being informative about brain-processing mechanisms:

> With regard to the mechanism responsible for these results, speculation about neural networks is outside the present scope. There is no objection to trying to depict schematically the component operations, but it must be admitted that what analysis of the data has been carried out does little more than draw attention to the difficulties involved in finding any simple scheme. (p. 20)

Hick's discussion of possible mechanisms took place without reference to brain structures or processes, and was based on abstract choice models which are, in effect, mathematical models aimed at plausibly and accurately replicating the response time relationship with stimulus set sizes. One of the models—and the only one that appears to be mentioned in subsequent accounts of the Hick procedure—proposed that a number of dichotomizing decisions was made concerning which was the target stimulus and, therefore:

> If we can again assume that the component operation—the dichotomising tests—are of like kind and will probably take about the same time, this process of progressive classification agrees closely with the logarithmic relation between reaction time and degree of choice. (p. 22)

Thus, if there is only one stimulus, no binary decisions (0 bits) need be made; the response is determined. If there are two possible stimuli, one binary decision is required; four possible stimuli require two decisions and eight potential stimuli need three.

A more accessible account of the same phenomenon was published a year later by Hyman (1953), who summarized as follows:

> When a stimulus is chosen to which *S* must make a discriminatory response, his reaction time seems to be a monotonically increasing function of the number of possible stimuli from which the stimulus can be chosen.

Using a communication theory metaphor, the reaction time display was a transmitter, stimuli were signals in messages, the space between the display and the subject was a channel, and the subject was a receiver or decoder. Hyman systematically altered the number of stimulus alternatives in a reaction time task in which the response was recorded by a voice key. Only four undergraduates were tested, each undertaking over 15,000 trials. Hyman's first experiment broadly reproduced Merkel's (1885) and Hick's (1952) procedures. In subsequent experiments, stimulus uncertainty was manipulated using different means. First, he altered the likelihood of occurrence of certain choices: for example, in a two-light condition one light was nine times as likely to be lit as the other, and in an eight-light condition two lights came on (individually) in one-quarter of trials, two in one-eighth, and four in one-sixteenth. The other method of manipulating information was to form sequential dependencies between successive choices. Hyman was successful in showing that the uncertainty of the stimulus condition (expressed as the number of binary decisions, or bits, needed to process the correct response) had a linear relation with reaction time. In agreement with Hick (1952) he noted that:

> More important than the shape of this function are the factors which operate to bring it about. This particular study was set up to discover the type of relationship which exists rather than to delve into the causes of this relationship.

Therefore, what became known as the 'Hick' task represents a lawful relation between stimulus characteristics and people's timed responses. As such, it resembles the inspection time procedure (Chapter 7), in which there is a lawful association between the duration of a stimulus and a person's likelihood of correctly making a discrimination. These associations between aspects of the stimulus and human responses were first reported about the same time; Merkel's reaction time data appeared in 1885 and MacKeen Cattell's 'perception time' data (the forerunner of inspection time) appeared in 1886 (Deary 1986). The comparison with inspection time helps to focus on the essential ingredient that makes the Hick reaction time task potentially interesting: there is a straight line association when reaction time is plotted against the base 2 logarithm of the number of stimulus alternatives. A person's slope parameter in the Hick procedure, according to Hick's speculations using a communication theory metaphor, might represent their 'rate of gain of information'. Note from their quotes above how hesitant Hick and Hyman were about implanting this construct in the brain, and how far back they stood from suggesting that anything about the brain had been explained. They clearly separated the empirical finding from the as-yet unknown causes of the finding. To say people had a 'rate of gain of information' was a restatement of the stimulus–response pattern; it was not a reductionistic claim.

Hick's (1952) and Hyman's (1953) studies were small, testing only a few well-educated colleagues and/or themselves. There were no examinations of individual differences in the slope parameter, and both writers emphasized that the mechanisms contributing to the slope were unknown and, at the same time, the most important and intriguing aspect of the finding. Thus, the Hick procedure's slope might characterize something important about a person's information processing efficiency, might provide a site at which to examine individual differences in information processing, and does represent an interesting regularity that requires a mechanistic explanation. This last point is vital: the Hick slope is a regularity yet to be explained; it does not in itself reveal basic brain processing. Anticipating what now follows, there has been much research on procedural aspects concerning how best to implement the Hick procedure (Jensen 1985; Bates and Stough 1998), and much also on correlations between Hick parameters and psychometric ability test scores (Jensen 1987*a*), and some research on extensions to Hick's theory (Beh *et al.* 1994). The necessary research on mechanisms causing the Hick slope and individual differences therein is sparse.

HICK REACTION TIME AND PSYCHOMETRIC INTELLIGENCE: ESTABLISHING THE ASSOCIATION

Eysenck's (1967) report stated that:

> If intelligence is conceived as speed of information processing, then simple reaction time, involving 0 bits of information, should not correlate with intelligence, but the slope of the regression line, showing increase of reaction time with amount of information processed, should correlate (negatively) with intelligence; in other words, intelligent subjects would show less increase in reaction

time with increase in number of light/button combinations than would dull
ones. [This is a slightly more precise way of phrasing Spearman's first nogenetic
principle; see Chapter 2.] Experimentally, the prediction has been tested by
Roth (1964) who demonstrated that while as expected simple reaction time
was independent of I.Q., speed of processing (slope) correlated significantly
with I.Q., in the predicted direction. (p. 86)

Roth's finding a correlation of −0.39 between the slope in the Hick procedure
and scores on a psychometric ability test (the Intelligenz-Struktur-Test) made
little impact until it was taken up by Jensen and Munro (1979). They examined
39 15-year-old schoolchildren on Raven's progressive matrices and an implementation of the Hick-type reaction time task that separated the movement time
(MT) from reaction time. Because the term 'reaction time' is often applied to
the entire response time (including movement time), Jensen's nomenclature can
be confusing. Therefore, the entire response time minus the movement time will
hereinafter be referred to as decision time (DT). The device used to measure reaction times according to the Hick procedure is often called a Jensen box (Fig.
6.2). Eight lights form a semicircular array, and a home button is situated equidis-
tant from each. The subject places a finger on the home button. When one of
the stimulus lights is lit, the subject, as fast as possible but avoiding errors, lifts
the finger from the home button and switches off the stimulus light (in older
versions this was done by having a microswitch situated just proximal to each
stimulus light; in newer versions the light and switch are combined). Subjects'
responses are assessed to different numbers of stimulus sets, typically 1, 2, 4,
and 8; Jensen and Munro added a six-stimulus condition, giving stimulus sets
requiring, according to Hick's (1952) theory, 0, 1, 2, 2.58, and 3 binary decisions. Decision time (DT) is the time between the stimulus light coming on and
the subject's finger being lifted from the home button. Movement time (MT) is
the time between the finger being lifted from the home button and the stimulus light's being switched off by the subject's correct response. The variability
(standard deviation, SD) of DT and MT is also measured. The slope of DT is
measured, according to Hick's original finding, but the slope of MT, being much
flatter, is usually omitted. Decision time takes longer than movement time, with
the former taking more than 300 ms and the latter less than 200 ms for most
subject groups in most conditions. Jensen and Munro (1979) reported the
following correlations with scores on Raven's matrices: total DT (including all
five stimulus set sizes) = −0.39 (p < 0.02); SD DT = −0.31 (p < 0.05); total
MT = −0.43 (p < 0.01); SD MT = 0.07 (ns). The slope of DT, the regression
coefficient of DT on bits of information (Hick's 'rate of gain of information'),
was computed for each subject and its correlation with Raven scores was −0.30
(p = 0.06). Even simple movement time (the MT when there was only one stimulus light and no bits of information) correlated −0.38 (p < 0.05) with Raven's
scores.

There were two expectations of Jensen and Munro's (1979) experiment. First,
that the slope measure of the Hick procedure would have a privileged correlation

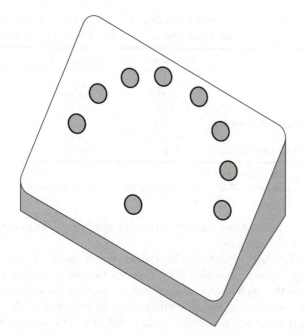

Fig. 6.2 The device used nowadays to measure indices of the Hick (1952) reaction time procedure. It is often called a Jensen box. The semicircular array of buttons/lights is the stimulus set. Some of these may be covered over during an experiment to allow different-sized stimulus sets. The separate button is the home button. The subject places a finger on the home button. One target button/light is lit, usually from a stimulus set of 1, 2, 4, or 8. The first timer starts. The subject lifts the finger from the home button to begin the reaction. The first timer stops and records the 'decision time' (Jensen [1987] called this the reaction time). The second timer starts. The subject presses the button light that is lit (the target button). The second timer stops and records the 'movement time'. Note that in Hick's own experiments there was no such separation of overall response time into decision and movement components. Moreover, Hick used a procedure with multiple response keys on which different fingers were placed.

with psychometric intelligence and, second, that the DT, because it was intended to isolate the cognitive aspects of overall response times, would have a stronger association with ability test scores than MT. Neither expectation was met and they commented that:

> The fact that these specific expectations were not borne out seems somewhat puzzling; at present we can offer no explanation.

The Hick procedure came to the notice of researchers in human intelligence differences because of its potential for quantifying some hypothetical 'rate of gain of information' in individual humans. Roth's (1964) initial findings that the slope of a Hick-type reaction time task correlated significantly with psychometric

Table 6.1 Correlations between psychometric intelligence scores and indices from the Hick-type reaction time procedure (data from Jensen 1987*a*)

	Corrected*	Uncorrected	Total *N*
DT mean	−0.32	−0.22	1195
DT intercept	−0.25	−0.12	774
DT slope	−0.28	−0.11	1558
DT intraindividual variability	−0.48	−0.27	1397
MT mean	−0.30	−0.25	1302
MT intraindividual variability	−0.02	−0.01	1154

DT, decision time; MT, movement time.
*Corrected for attenuation of ability range and unreliability of measurement.

intelligence, whereas simple reaction time did not, were contradicted by Jensen and Munro's (1979) results.

Jensen (1987*a*) later reviewed the results of 33 samples (total *N* = 2317 subjects), many his own, in which Hick-type reaction time measures were studied in association with psychometric ability test scores. The correlations reported are probably underestimates of the true effect sizes, as over half of the samples were university students or above-average ability children. The average fit of the DT data to Hick's law was 0.995, with little indication that MT fitted Hick's law; movement times increase very little as stimulus uncertainty increases. Table 6.1 shows the raw and corrected mean correlations for the main Hick reaction time indices with ability test scores. None of the individual uncorrected correlations is even moderately high, although there is little doubt that significant associations exist. The average correlation between psychometric ability test scores and MT variability is almost zero, but the other five indices correlate within quite a narrow band of effect sizes, between −0.11 and −0.27 (uncorrected).

Jensen (1987*a*) suggested that if the speed and/or efficiency of information processing were related to psychometric intelligence, then the correlation between ability test scores and reaction time should increase as the stimulus uncertainty increased. Data from 15 independent groups supported this in the DT data but not the MT data, as expected. However, the differences between correlations were small, increasing from −0.19, through −0.21 and −0.24, to −0.26 for 0, 1, 2, and 3 bits of information, respectively. In addition, some adequate studies failed to find this association. Jensen correlated the expected rankings of the correlations between set size-based DT and psychometric intelligence with actual rankings of correlation sizes; the coefficient of association was only 0.39. There was no tendency for the correlation between DT variability and test score to increase as the set size increased.

One carefully performed study failed to confirm some of the key theoretical associations between psychometric ability scores and Hick reaction time indices. Barrett *et al.* (1986) examined Wechsler ability test scores and Hick reaction times in two groups of 40 or more young adults whose mean IQ was just above 100 and whose standard deviation was near to normal. Reaction time and reaction time variability were related to psychometric test scores (people with higher psychometric test scores had faster and less variable reaction times), but there was no significant correlation with the Hick regression line slope and no tendency for correlations between ability tests and reaction times to increase as the stimulus uncertainty became greater. Those significant associations that were obtained were improved when people whose reaction time data did not fit Hick's law (more than 20% of subjects) were removed. Therefore, in a study which paid attention to measurement characteristics of the Hick reaction time (RT) data, the authors found moderate associations with response latencies and variabilities, but:

> In a series of tests of four specific hypotheses proposed upon the basis of the expected properties of Hick's Law and its relationship to cognitive perfor- mance, the evidence suggested that the measurement characteristics specifically defining the law are probably correlated only marginally and nonsignificantly with cognitive performance as assessed by the WAIS [Wechsler Adult Intelligence Scale]. Certainly, the slope of the regression line computed . . . does not correlate with the WAIS scale scores; nor do the *SD*s of the RTs have a positively increasing slope in the manner of Jensen's data. In addition, the plot of the median RT x FULLWAIS correlations against each bit of infor- mation does not yield a positively increasing slope as suggested by Jensen's results. (p. 35)

In summary, there are robust but modest correlations between reaction time indices from the Hick procedure and psychometric test scores. However, the original rationale for the Hick procedure was its capacity to quantify humans' 'rate of gain of information' as captured in the slope. The slope does on occasion produce correlations in the expected direction, but they tend not to be the largest of the Hick procedure's correlations with ability test scores. Indeed, the correlation with movement time, even to a single stimulus (no bits of information required), is almost as high. This turn of events is crucial, although it is not always dwelt upon by researchers in the field. The point of entry of the Hick procedure to intelligence research was its supposed ability to index an identified single parameter—an element—of human information processing; now it is found that there are correlations with several aspects of reaction time, including decision time mean and variability, and movement time. Even simple reaction time, it seems, has a significant correlation with psychometric ability test scores. Jensen (1987*a*) discussed these findings and suggested that such widespread correlations might be the result of a general speed or efficiency that suffuses performance in all aspects of the Hick procedure; in which case, one must question why the procedure itself has remained the focus of research, as this evidence would incline one towards more mainstream reaction time procedures and models.

Some of the above findings, which support the existence of correlations between reaction time indices and psychometric test scores, may be seen in studies conducted after Jensen's review. Beauducel and Brocke (1993), studying univer- sity students, found better ability test correlations with the intercept than the slope of the Hick procedure. Both reaction times and variability measures yielded associations from below 0.2 to about 0.4. There was no increase in correlation with increased stimulus uncertainty. Simple reaction time was about as highly correlated as more complex conditions. Crucially, there was no correlation between the Hick slope and ability test scores, and the authors commented that:

> Applying Hick's law is not necessary for finding and theoretically explaining RT x IQ correlations. (p. 635)

These authors were generally pessimistic about what the Hick procedure can add to an understanding of human ability differences. Similar findings, including a near-zero correlation between ability test (WAIS) scores and Hick slope were reported by Deary *et al.* (1992), who tested 85 otherwise-normal young adults with Type 1 diabetes.

HICK REACTION TIME AND PSYCHOMETRIC INTELLIGENCE: EXPLAINING THE ASSOCIATION

There is a pattern to research on information processing correlates of mental test scores. An association is suggested, then established, and then the researchers settle down to the long process of explaining the association. Some of the explanation involves refuting confounding-type explanations, and some of it involves struggling to discover a mechanism that will account for individual differences in the information processing task and bridge the constructs spanned by the correlation. There are few well-developed explanations for reaction time–psychometric test score associations, but Jensen and his colleagues have been busy in refuting what are in essence attempts to 'explain away' the association.

Jensen (1987a) rejected the suggestion that the correlations arise out of a common test-taking factor, especially the need to work quickly. He noted that the correlations arise when the psychometric tests are unspeeded, that the correlations with speeded mental ability tests were not especially high, and that tests of working speedily such as clerical checking and letter cancellation correlated poorly with both psychometric ability tests and reaction time indices. He rejected the suggestion that the results were accounted for by a speed–ability trade-off, such that high-ability subjects sacrifice accuracy for speed. Phillips and Rabbitt (1995) reported that such factors do not account for psychometric test–reaction time correlations. In fact, high-ability subjects are faster and more accurate, and there are very few errors in most Hick-type reaction time experiments.

A more vague, and thus harder to refute, suggestion is that some subjects are more motivated, and that this general drive for success explains the correlation between reaction time and psychometric test scores. Jensen (1987a) invoked the Yerkes–Dodson law and suggested that, at more complex levels, one would expect a negative association between drive and performance. However, this 'law' is not sufficiently precise to formulate such a refutation. The suggestion that some people try harder in all tasks also arises with inspection time (Chapter 7) where it was put to an experimental test and failed. The motivation hypothesis of reaction time–psychometric intelligence associations was tested by Lindley and Smith (1992). The motivation hypothesis suggests that an incentive should reduce or eliminate motivation differences and, therefore, lower the reaction time–psychometric intelligence associations if they are motivation-based. Lindley and Smith studied the associations under conditions in which subjects did or did not receive a reward in the form of a lottery ticket. The same coding speed–mental ability test score correlations were obtained with and without the incentive, providing no evidence for motivation as the causal factor. One limitation of the study is that paper-and-pencil measures of 'reaction time' were used. Although these have moderately high associations—0.4 to 0.5—with standard reaction time procedures (Buckhalt 1991; Neubauer and Knorr 1998), the link is not high enough for paper-and-pencil measures to stand convincingly in the stead of equipment-based tests. Another attempted examination of the motivation hypothesis, this time in children, used only feedback about reaction times which cannot be considered a strong manipulation of motivation (Neubauer *et al.* 1992). As discussed in Chapter 7, Larson *et al.* (1994) used differential financial rewards during laboratory tests and found no evidence for motivation as the cause of information processing test–psychometric intelligence correlations. Although Maylor and Rabbitt (1995) found some evidence that higher-ability subjects' choice reaction times benefited from feedback more than those of low-ability subjects, they concluded that:

> individual differences in this task are largely determined by information-processing rate rather than by factors such as the ability to detect errors or to monitor and control RT. (p. 325)

The factors above were among the suggestions contained in a substantial critique in which Longstreth (1984) sought confounders to explain away the Hick reaction time correlations with ability test scores. He raised three potential problems with Jensen's reaction time technique. First, there might be order effects, because subjects always proceeded from set size 1 to 8 in that order. Second, there might be visual attention effects across set sizes, because the physical spread of the lamps is greater in the larger set sizes, which require greater visual angles. Third, there could be a response bias across set sizes, because moving the responding finger in different directions might take different amounts of time. Jensen and Vernon (1986) suggested that the latter two—visual attention effects and response bias— were unlikely to be responsible for any reaction time–mental ability correlations, it being more likely that they merely added noise. The striking fact then becomes the finding of the correlations in spite of these noise factors. Order effects were potentially more serious. People who scored higher on mental ability tests might also learn faster within the Hick procedure. Therefore, as they move through the set sizes in Jensen's experiments, the slope of their reaction times versus bits of information confounds their practice effects with their information processing.

People with higher-ability test scores might thus have flatter slopes because they learn faster than those with lower scores.

All three procedural factors suggested by Longstreth (1984) were examined experimentally by Widaman and Carlson (1989). Visual attention effects and response bias did not appear important. These were manipulated as follows. In Jensen's experiments, when the number of lights is less than the full set of eight, the target lights are always those at the centre of the display. Widaman and Carlson manipulated this such that the lights of set sizes 1, 2, and 4 were either in the centre (in one condition) or at the extremes (in a second condition). By contrast with Widaman and Carlson, when Bors *et al.* (1993) controlled for visual attention effects in their study, the correlation between reaction times and psychometric ability test scores no longer differed from zero.

Widaman and Carlson (1989) studied order effects by having three conditions: ascending, as used by Jensen, in which the set sizes of lights are encountered by the subject in the order 1, 2, 4, 8; descending, in which the subject begins with set size 8, and proceeds to 4, then 2, then 1; and random ordering of the set sizes. As predicted by Longstreth, the Hick slope was flatter in the ascending condition and steeper in the descending condition, with the random order falling in between. For example, for the grouped versus spread light conditions the increment in decision time for each bit of information was 15.6 ms and 13.9 ms, respectively, for the ascending condition. The respective increments for the descending condition were 26.6 ms and 33.2 ms. The slope of reaction time correlated negatively (−0.26 which became −0.25 after controlling for the effect of grouped versus separated lights) with ability test scores in the ascending condition and positively in the descending condition (0.18, 0.29) and the correlations were significantly different. Random ordering of conditions produced near-to-zero correlations (−0.06, −0.06). These results indicate that the correlation between ability test scores and the Hick slope is confounded with practice. Possibly this correlation, when it is found, is more to do with able people's reaction times' different rates of change with practice than with the stimulus complexity. Widaman and Carlson (1989) suggested that:

> the correlations between SAT [scholastic aptitude test] scores and RT and MT intercept and slope estimates are consistent with the hypothesis that correlations between Hick parameter estimates and measures of mental ability or achievement occur because of ability-related differences in automatization of responding to the task, rather than ability-related differences in the rate of execution of elementary mental operations. The results from the present study call into question the typical interpretation of findings related to the Hick paradigm (p. 84)

By contrast with studies that find some substance to possible confounding factors in the reaction time–psychometric ability test correlations, others failed so to do. Neubauer (1990) designed Hick-type reaction time tasks that avoided attention (retinal displacement) and response bias effects, and found similar if not larger correlations than those in other studies. Kranzler *et al.* (1988) found no worrying effects of visual attention, and failed to find the effects of order on slope that Widaman and Carlson (1989) reported a year later. Widaman (1989), however, cited three factors that made the Widaman and Carslon (1989) result more convincing: a threefold larger sample size, the inclusion of a random-order-of-set-size condition, and the use of a number of trials per condition compatible with previous Hick reaction time–mental ability studies. Larson and Saccuzzo (1986) also found little effect of order of Hick set sizes on the slope of the reaction time latencies.

Neubauer (1991) constructed a modified version of the Jensen-style Hick reaction time device. This eliminated visual attention effects and controlled for response bias. Order of set size was random in order to eliminate learning–automatization effects. Innovatively, the stimulus target light was extinguished when subjects moved from the home button (cf. Smith and Carew 1987); this prevented the strategy of moving from the home button on anticipation of the stimulus, which otherwise might artefactually shorten decision time. Having eliminated many of Longstreth's suggested confounders, the Hick correlations with Raven's advanced matrices scores were: −0.26, −0.31, and −0.39 for 0-, 1-, and 2-bit decision times (all significant); −0.20 for the slope (non-significant); and −0.24, −0.14, and −0.46 for 0-, 1-, and 2-bit decision time standard deviations. There were no significant associations with movement time indices. A similar reaction time task, but with lower stimulus–response compatibility, increased most effect sizes, especially that of the slope (to −0.38). Neubauer concluded that:

> Precautions for controlling the sources of artifact of the classical Hick paradigm presumably had the effect of yielding 'purer' measures of speed of information processing, subsequently leading to higher correlations. (p. 190)

There are refutations, therefore, of some of Longstreth's (1984) suggested confounding effects, and some equivocal support for a learning–automatization view of any slope–psychometric intelligence correlation. What is not stated clearly enough in the literature is that insinuated problems with the Hick procedure tend to focus on the slope phenomenon and/or the separation in Jensen's apparatus of overall response time into movement and decision times. Given that the slope parameter (1) often has a lower correlation with psychometric test scores than mean reaction time and reaction time variability, (2) has no special place in Jensen's (1982*b*, 1993) theorizing about the causes of reaction time–ability test correlations, and (3) that overall reaction/response time (DT + MT) also correlates with ability test scores, there is little need to focus on these arguably peripheral aspects of the Hick procedure. Thus, much of the effort that has examined possible confounds in the Hick task's correlations with psychometric ability concentrates on factors that are not the loci of the most robust associations.

Other, more general and pertinent suggestions are that correlations between reaction times and ability test scores arise because subjects attend better in both types of test, that the correlations arise because the tests in general are unfamiliar, that the cause of the correlation is that high-ability people automatize the processing involved in the tests faster than lower-ability people (Sternberg 1985), and that some people are better motivated in both psychometric and experimental tasks. Neubauer *et al.* (1992) found that partialling attention scores from the Hick reaction time–Raven's matrices correlation in schoolchildren did not substantially reduce the effect size. However, they did find an interaction between sex and feedback (considered to be manipulating motivation) in Hick response and accuracy rates, and their study has limited applicability to the usual literature because of the sample characteristics and the fact that the apparatus was different from Jensen's, leading many subjects to make large numbers of errors. Sternberg's idea concerning automatization was tested by Neubauer and Freudenthaler (1994) using the sentence verification test (Hunt and MacLeod 1978). As their 60 student subjects progressed through 9 hours of contact with the test, the correlations with Raven's advanced progressive matrices remained steadily between about –0.35 and –0.4. Their concluding comments bridge nicely the above accounts, which try to explain away reaction time–psychometric ability associations employing so-called top-down accounts (effectively, however, most explanatory constructs are suggested as confounding/problematic variables), with the following accounts which offer bottom-up accounts of the correlation in terms of brain processing:

> If RTs in an ECT [elementary cognitive task] still correlate with psychometric intelligence after more than 2,000 trials of training (as was demonstrated), then top-down explanations of this relationship on the basis of metacomponential processes (Sternberg 1985) or controlled versus automatic processing (Ackerman and Schneider 1985) seem largely implausible. Instead, from our findings we infer strong support of the biologically based bottom-up explanations of the mental speed theory of intelligence. (p. 214)

Explaining associations between reaction times and psychometric ability test scores consists of research conducted on two fronts. Thus, like good batsmen in cricket, investigators in this area and in other related areas such as inspection times (see Chapter 7) must be able to play off the front (attacking) foot as well as the back (defending) foot. As seen above, the investigators must properly address likely experimental confounds and the possibility that other personological variables (personality, motivation, attention, and so forth) account for any significant associations (Jensen 1987*a*; Larson *et al.* 1994; Neubauer 1997). This process of testing each possible confound as it suggests itself to critics is an incomplete and impoverished way to conduct science. Investigators should also have some positive ideas about the reasons for the associations. Jensen (1993) suggested three possible origins to account for reaction time–psychometric ability associations. Two of these, at least, are explanations at the biological level. First, he hypothesized that speed of transmission of nerve impulses might be one basis of general mental ability and the reaction time–mental ability association. His piece mentioned that one indicator of this speed might be nerve conduction velocity, which is discussed in Chapter 9. As discussed elsewhere, however, an individual difference outcome measure represented by response latency can arise from a number of non-speeded neurological parameters (Rabbitt and Maylor 1991). Second, Jensen reckoned that noise in neural transmission might tally with the finding that intraindividual variability in reaction times correlate with psychometric test scores. As the biological basis for this noise parameter Jensen (1982*b*) appealed to a notion of there being a 'neural oscillator' and hypothesized that longer wavelength oscillations resulted in more variable reaction times and lower general mental ability scores. Jensen's ideas were not substantially backed up with accounts of brain function; they were arguments along the line of 'if there were a brain para-meter to account for this phenomenon it might look like this . . .'. Nevertheless, since his suggestion was mooted, pacemakers have been found in the human brain and have become popular hypothetical entities in accounting for informa-tion processing limitations. Synchronized oscillatory activity has been found in the basal ganglia, though at fairly low frequencies (Plenz and Kital 1999). A faster neural pacemaker, thought to underlie temporal limitations in some cognitive processes, has been posited by Poppel (1994), who gathered clinical, cognitive, physiological, and psychophysical evidence for a neural window of about 30–40 ms within which events cannot be separated temporally. The third entity which Jensen invoked to account for reaction time–ability test correlations was capacity of working memory, although other researchers in this field have viewed reaction times as indicators of mental speed, and have viewed memory capacity as a source of ability-related variance separated from that which is shared with reaction times (Neubauer *et al.*, in press).

THE STATUS OF THE HICK SLOPE

There is an almost odd concern with the Hick procedure given the increasing evidence that its slope parameter has no special correlation with mental test scores. For example, Beh *et al.* (1994) extended the Hick procedure to cover 11 conditions containing between 0 and 6.1 bits of information. They achieved this by having an array of eight potential stimuli (circles on a computer monitor) and between one and four targets; that is, on any one trial between one and four circles would be filled in (indicating a target) and the subjects had to respond to all target circles within one trial. Correlations between Raven's matrices scores and median choice reaction time (DT and MT were not reported separately although they were collected) ranged from −0.33 to −0.61 over the 11 condi-tions, and averaged −0.49. Correlations between Raven's matrices and intraindividual variability of reaction time ranged from −0.15 to −0.58 with an average of −0.37. Correlations at the 0- and 1-bit level were smaller but, beyond that, the associations were similar, from 2 to 6.1 bits. Therefore, Jensen's (1987*a*) idea that correlations increase with increasing stimulus uncertainty was not supported. The slope parameter was not mentioned or reported.

Jensen (1998*b*) argued that the slope variable from the Hick reaction time procedure can be improved upon, and that correlations with psychometric test scores are low because the slope variable has poor psychometric characteristics. Among these, he enumerated small variance, low reliability (a mean of 0.39 in six studies (Jensen 1987*a*); although Neubauer *et al.* (1997) achieved a reliable slope measure and barely improved the association with psychometric intelligence), and an artefactual negative correlation with the intercept. Controlling for the intercept score, aggregating individual measures, and improving the Hick task can, he argued, bring about a better correlation with the slope variable. Jensen's argument here was that the Hick slope has not really been given a fair chance, handicapped as it is by these limitations. His conclusion was that more research must free the Hick slope from its psychometric shackles. Jensen's hope is contrasted by Lohman's (1994, 1999) pessimism on the same matter. However, others agree with Jensen but have with some success sought other solutions, such as eliminating those subjects whose individual reaction time condition means do not fit Hick's law (Neubauer 1991).

One hesitates before endorsing the decision that says the Hick slope can be salvaged by improving aspects of Jensen's instantiation of the Hick procedure. After all, Hick (1952) and Hyman (1953) found the association between bits of information and reaction time without the need for such modifications. Furthermore, Roth's (1964) slope–ability test score result was obtained without such deliberation. Perhaps Jensen's separation of overall RT into DT and MT introduced problems rather than improvements to the Hick procedure. The Hick slope is calculated from DT and, if different people behave such that there are differences in the way mental processing is allocated between MT and DT, then there might be unwanted individual differences in what goes to make up the DT values. For example, some subjects appear to shorten their DT by an anticipatory movement off the home button before they have fully decided which target stimulus has been lit (Smith and Carew 1987). Neubauer (1991) was possibly the first to counter this strategy in a reaction time–psychometric intelligence study by masking target stimuli after the subject moved from the home button. Nettelbeck (1998), however, is not convinced that such modifications to the Hick task truly eliminate higher-level strategies. Stough *et al.* (1995*c*) attempted to prevent such strategies by having the RT stimuli presented for a short time and then masked by illuminating all of the stimuli in the response set. Subsequently, Bates and Stough (1998) employed a modified Hick–Jensen task in which target stimuli were lit for only 50 ms and also masked, and in which subjects were given encouraging verbal feedback for responses two standard deviations below their running mean. A short interstimulus interval (1200–1300 ms) was employed. Their reasoning was that these alterations forced subjects to process information in the given time window and that attention had to be focused more diligently and homogeneously (across subjects) throughout the task. The procedure was limited to two response conditions—set sizes of two and four—in order to avoid effects of spatial attention. Thirty young subjects were divided by median splitting on the Wechsler Adult Intelligence Scale-

Revised (WAIS-R), and the authors found an expected main effect of set size on RT, a marginally significant effect of IQ level on RT, and, crucially, there was an interaction between WAIS-R grouping and RT set size; the higher scorers on the WAIS-R had a flatter Hick slope. The uncorrected correlation between Hick slope and WAIS-R full-scale IQ in this small subject sample was –0.54. Bates and Stough concluded that their modifications to the reaction time procedure increased the accuracy of decision time measurement and produced results that favoured an interpretation of the reaction time–mental ability correlation founded on a construct variously called 'information processing speed' (p. 60), 'mental speed' (p. 61), and 'speed of neural computation' (p. 61) as opposed to 'attentional strategies or personality/motivation effects' (p. 61).

QUO VADIS? WITH THE HICK TASK

Mutatis mutandis, some of the findings emanating from the use of the Hick task will be found in the application of other reaction time-based procedures to human ability research. Some assessment of its position, though, is warranted here. Beauducel and Brocke's (1993) call that,

> A substantiating theory for explaining and integrating positive results, anomalies and prevailing *ad-hoc* assumptions and for integrating them into broader theories of intelligence seems overdue (p. 627)

is still true. The cognoscenti differ in how best to implement this integration. Jensen (1998*b*) conservatively advocated sticking with the original model:

> When the b [Hick slope] x IQ correlation is estimated under conditions that reduce the statistical suppression of this relationship, the correlation is appreciably increased and is consistent with prediction from information processing theory. (p. 43)

Stough *et al.* (1995*c*) disagreed and maintained that:

> the Hick information processing model of intelligence should be replaced. (p. 61)

A mechanistic account of those modest but robust associations found between Hick parameters and psychometric test scores is lacking and, even if the slope benefits from a revival after psychometric therapy has been applied, there are several aspects of performance within the Hick task that such an account must cover. There is no single best way to proceed, but some opinions are offered about approaches that might clarify or muddy the waters.

Two approaches that have been employed for good reasons and with interesting results are perhaps not optimal routes to explaining correlations between reaction times and mental test scores. Complicating the Hick task further can increase correlations with ability test scores, as Neubauer (1991) found when the stimulus–response compatibility was lowered. A so-called 'odd-man-out' procedure can be applied to Jensen's reaction time device. Instead of a single target light appearing, three are turned on simultaneously; two are adjacent lights, and the third is separated by at least one 'off' light. The subject's task is to respond to the 'odd-man-out', the separate light. This procedure appears at times to improve the correlations obtained between single reaction time indices and ability test scores (Frearson and Eysenck 1986; Diascro and Brody 1994). Its drawbacks are that it moves in an uncharted way away from the Hick task, and it results in far longer response times that presumably envelop even more as-yet-poorly-understood processing stages. Using the 'odd-man-out' task allowed Diascro and Brody (1994) to conclude that:

> tasks that assess the ability to rapidly perceive relationships among stimuli are good measures of general intelligence. Although tasks that require subjects merely to notice a difference between stimuli relate to intelligence, increasing the complexity of the discrimination and forcing subjects to make judgements about relationships among elements of a stimulus array increases the correlation with IQ. (p. 92)

Such an account is interesting, and has resonances with Spearman's (1923) cognitive elements of human intelligence (Chapter 2). But it is not what is needed: this account is a common sense-level redescription of the aspects of tasks that aided the correlation with ability test scores. One might just as well describe the aspects of tasks that have high *g*-loadings in order to understand human ability differences. Instead, what is needed is the promise of some more mechanistic understanding of the task demands in terms of validated brain processes. Higher correlations with ability test scores are no bad aim in this line of research, but more valuable still is the proximity to something that looks like a tractable cognitive process. As reaction times lengthen such a realization recedes. Fatter reaction time–ability test score correlations on occasion may be obtained when reaction time-type or other information processing tasks are combined with a competing cognitive demand in dual-task designs (e.g. Roberts *et al.* 1988; Egan and Deary 1992) but, again, the complexity involved appears to militate against comprehending the tasks' fundamentals. Whether or not it is the case that more 'complex elementary cognitive tasks' correlate better with ability test scores (Jensen 1993; Neubauer 1997) is not the key issue; the parenthetical oxymoron reminds us that comprehensibility is more important than effect size. Lastly, the transfer of information processing tasks from computer-based apparatus to paper-and-pencil formats, with the obvious attractions for convenience of testing, again increases confusion by loosening experimental control over individual item responses. However, Neubauer and Knorr (1998) have made progress towards demonstrating that some paper-and-pencil applications can be valid indicators of computerized reaction time differences.

Research that is more helpful includes the attempt to discover those conditions and confounds that enhance and reduce or eliminate the reaction time–mental ability correlation. For example, although their sample sizes were small and un-representative and others have not replicated their findings, the attempts by Bors *et al.* (1993) to eliminate the need for visual scanning in the Hick test provides a model for probing the key ingredients of reaction time tasks that deliver the associations. They were correct in stating that:

> it is possible, after all, that Galton was not wrong in attempting to analyze intelligence in terms of fundamental perceptual-motor elements. But the greatest hurdle in pursuing such an approach is to ensure that the elements are sufficiently isolated in our experiments as to be uniquely identified. (p. 499)

Another approach that might be informative is to gather circumstantial-type evidence about biological correlates of reaction time tasks. For example, a series of studies examined the effects of the brain's cholinergic system (using nicotine/smoking as an independent variable in experimental designs) on many levels of information processing from psychometric tests, through choice reaction time and inspection time to event-related potential indices (Bates *et al.* 1994, 1995*a*; Stough *et al.* 1994, 1995*a*,*b*). This experimental sweep of outcome variables from gross psychometric to physiological indices is praiseworthy, as is the experimental manipulation of neurotransmitter–receptor function. It would be informative to compile a series of replicated results in which neurotransmitter–receptor agonists and antagonists were comprehensively applied and a broad range of cognitive outcomes studied. Evidence already gathered implicates, though equivocally (Petrie and Deary 1989), central cholinergic pathways in some aspects of efficient cognitive processing in normal humans.

The aforementioned approach to teasing apart the processes involved in reaction times involves manipulating aspects of brain function with targeted psycho-pharmacological interventions. Another approach that also spans levels of description in the cognitive domain is to manipulate aspects of cognitive tasks and observe concurrently the effects on cognitive task performance and brain physiology. Houlihan *et al.* (1994) studied decision time, movement time, and the latency of the P300 component of brain event-related potentials. They used a version of the Sternberg memory scan task (see below) rather than the Hick task. They found that decision time and P300 latency, and also move-ment time, were affected by stimulus response processes. Decision time was sensitive to response bias. Their data confirmed others' concerns that stimulus evaluation in reaction time tasks continues after subjects have lifted their finger from the home button in order to begin the execution of their response (Smith and Carew 1987; Neubauer 1991). They concluded that the separation of overall response time into decision and movement times is not achieved and that to a greater or lesser extent both indices reflect the same sources of variance. More research combining psychophysiological and cognitive techniques is described in Chapter 9.

COGNITIVE AND DIFFERENTIAL PSYCHOLOGY: BEYOND THE HICK TASK

It is not profitable slavishly to drag the reader comprehensively through all the results of the other reaction time procedures that have promised components that will explain some variance in mental ability test scores. Probably there is no fully rational account of why some tasks and their putatively extractable components have attracted individual differences researchers more than others. For example, the Hick reaction time test enjoys no great effort of research within experimental–cognitive psychology, was not developed much theoretically beyond the initial reports in the 1950s, and had a successful initial correlation with psychometric ability test scores in an obscure report (Roth 1964), although the pattern of results was not then replicated in the first follow-up study 15 years later (Jensen and Munro 1979). These are not strong credentials for a front-runner among cognitive tasks in accounting for individual differences in mental test scores. Of the other favourite measures, only two have attracted even a reasonable number of empirical studies (Neubauer 1997): they are Sternberg's memory-scanning task and Posner's letter-matching task.

S. Sternberg's (1966) memory-scanning task

Subjects view, successively, at the same location on a computer monitor, a series of single digits. This is the memory set. Each digit appears for the same duration, often just over a second. The number of digits is varied, typically between one and six. There is a gap of about two seconds after the memory set. Then there is a warning, following which the subject encounters a single digit in the same location. This is the target digit and the subject responds as quickly as possible, indicating whether or not the target digit was a member of the memory set. Sternberg found that a linear function fitted the association between the number of symbols in memory (the memory set size) and response latency. Responses to memory set size 1 took 400–500 ms, whereas those to memory set size 6 took more than 600 ms. As the memory set size increased by one digit the response time increased by about 38 ms. He concluded that each member of the memory set was compared in turn with the target stimulus. Because the slopes for the 'yes' and 'no' responses were the same, S. Sternberg (1975) suggested that this comparison process must proceed exhaustively, and then a response was made. Note that unlike R. J. Sternberg's (1977) models of analogical reasoning, in which many processes were self-terminating following a match to target, S. Sternberg's model of memory comparison is less efficient, proceeding to effect all comparisons of target with memory set, even after a match has been found in the case of positive responses.

Neubauer (1997) reviewed 10 studies (total $N > 900$) that correlated indices from the Sternberg memory-scanning task with psychometric test scores. Half of the studies included only students as subjects. The N-weighted mean correlation was –0.27 with mean reaction time, –0.35 with variability of reaction time, and

–0.30 with intercept. However, in the five studies that examined the theoretically-interesting slope variable, the *N*-weighted mean correlation was –0.11.

Posner's letter-matching task

Subjects must proceed through two conditions before the key component of this task emerges. Posner and Mitchell (1967) described their task and its cognitive intent as follows:

> The goal is to find levels of processing which depend primarily upon the physical attributes of the stimulus and levels which depend upon more detailed analyses such as naming or relation to a superordinate. To obtain this goal a single experimental paradigm is developed which provides an opportunity to observe processing at different levels within the same experiment. The stimuli are pairs of letters, digits, or forms and the response is always pressing one of two keys ('same' or 'different'). What is varied is the level of instruction upon which *S* is to base his classification. The instructions used to define 'same' are physical identity (e.g., AA), name identity (e.g., Aa) and rule identity (e.g., both vowels). This technique allows the same stimulus–response combination (e.g., A–B different) to occur with instructions at quite different levels. (p. 393)

Therefore, reaction times are found for confirming the physical identity (PI) versus the name identity (NI) of letters. Example reaction times for these activities in Posner and Mitchell's (1976) experiments were 549 and 623 ms, respectively. (A further condition, confirming that both were vowels, took on average 699 ms.) Thus, the difference between NI and PI might be informative, although Posner and Mitchell were cautious in speculating here. Their model of results was abstract, and merely denoted PI instructions as decision demands at a hypothetical 'node 1' and NI conditions as demands at 'node 2', a level of processing further down the line. Whether the processes were serial or parallel the authors were reluctant to speculate, although they did note that:

> from introspective accounts it seems reasonable that all *S*s derive the name of the letters before proceeding to analyze whether they are both vowels or consonants.

Hunt developed this task and studied it especially with regard to psychometric verbal ability. The epithets applied to the task's key component were speed of lexical access, 'ability to gain access to memory for highly over-learned symbols used in language' (Hunt 1983, p. 143), and decoding, 'the activation of highly overlearned information in long-term memory' (Hunt 1980*b*, p. 113). Hunt (1980*b*) found that the NI–PI measure—the putative speed of lexical access, which he viewed as one of the mechanistic processes underlying verbal ability— was different in different groups, much in the same way that Jensen (1987*a*) reported group differences in the Hick slope. NI–PI differences were as follows:

high verbal university students = 64 ms; normal university students = 75–80 ms; low-verbal university students = 89 ms; young adults not at a university = 110 ms; adults past 60 years of age = 170 ms; 10-year-old children = 190 ms; and mildly mentally retarded children = 310 ms (Hunt 1980*b*).

Neubauer (1997) reviewed 11 studies (total $N > 1000$), carried out between 1978 and 1993, that correlated indices from the Posner letter-matching task with psychometric ability test scores. Only five of the studies reported a correlation between NI–PI difference and psychometric test scores, and three of these focused on verbal ability or crystallized intelligence measures. The *N*-weighted mean correlation between the NI–PI measure and ability test scores was –0.27. The majority of the studies tested students, thus ensuring that the correlations were underestimates of the true values. Just as one finds with the Hick paradigm, however, there were significant correlations with other measures within the Posner procedure. The reaction time for the name identity condition had an *N*-weighted mean correlation of –0.33 with psychometric ability test scores, and the effect size for the least-cognitively interesting physical identity reaction time was –0.23.

PSYCHOMETRIC INTELLIGENCE AND MULTIPLE REACTION TIME MEASURES

Some investigators used all three of the above, most popular reaction time tests in examining psychometric intelligence differences. Neubauer *et al.* (1997) tested over 100 young adults on Raven's Advanced Progressive Matrices (RAPM) and indices from the Hick, Sternberg, and Posner reaction time tasks. For the Hick task only 0-, 1-, and 2-bit conditions were used, and the device was rather more akin to Hick's original fingers-on-keys (though with only four keys) equipment than Jensen's reaction time box. Correlations between RAPM and Hick indices ranged between –0.14 and –0.32, the highest correlation was between mean RT for the 2-bit condition and RAPM, and the RAPM–Hick slope correlation was –0.24 (slope split half reliability = 0.84). In the Sternberg test the correlations of RAPM with reaction times in 1, 3, and 5 set size conditions were –0.22, –0.20, and –0.25, and with the slope was –0.14. PI and NI conditions in the Posner test correlated with RAPM at –0.31 and –0.41, respectively, and the NI–PI difference at –0.20. Many of the subjects were university students, thus probably resulting in smaller effect sizes than would be found in a general population sample. The general findings are those that can be adduced from the broad sweep of the literature; overall reaction times and intraindividual differences in reaction times correlate at between small and medium effect sizes with psychometric test scores, and slope/difference parameters—carrying the theoretical weight of the tasks—do rather more poorly. The discussion of findings focused mostly on matters of psychometrics and procedure rather than construct validity, although among their points is an interesting discovery of a confound between condition and practice in the Posner task. The all-too-obvious conclusion is that a flurry of correlations is achievable between psychometric ability test scores and different aspects of different reaction time procedures, and that we do not have a reductionistic account of the reaction time indices. Neubauer and colleagues refer to the reaction time and other relatively simple tasks as elementary cognitive tasks (ECTs). The term has a somewhat hollow and poignant ring; hollow, because elementary may mean that one understands the elements of the tasks, and this is plainly not so; and poignant because elementary also could mean not decomposable, and this may well be the unintended truth (see Lohman 1994). However, this does not mean that the cause of the correlations must be one or more higher-level confounding variables, such as those discussed earlier. It is perfectly tenable that the cause of the correlations is lower-level processing limitations, although these are as yet obscure in nature. Neubauer and Knorr (1998) bet on the latter alternative:

> This substantial relationship between mental speed or SIP [speed of information processing] and human psychometric intelligence leads us to a final remark. Almost from the beginning this line of research (i.e. the mental speed approach to human intelligence) has been criticised for the relatively weak (though consistent) relationship between ECTs [elementary cognitive tasks] and intelligence. In fact, correlations of up to 0.3 (or at best 0.4) in the majority of studies have led authors to conclude that no single ECT can explain more than about 10 percent of the variance in intelligence tests . . . In our view the relatively low RT–intelligence correlations in previous research are mainly due to the homogeneity of the samples tested. . . . when a comprehensive battery composed of different ECTs is used . . . it is even possible to obtain a multiple correlation of 0.77. In our view such findings do not justify dismissing the mental speed concept of intelligence (cf. Stankov and Roberts [1997]) but rather make the dismissal a dangerous (because erroneous) enterprise. (p. 148)

Sometimes, as evidenced in the previous quotation, in order to predict as much variance in psychometric test scores as possible, researchers had recourse to entering multiple components from information processing tasks and studying the multiple correlations (Vernon 1983; Jensen 1987*b*). The attempt to do so would be understandable if one were assured that the components being entered were to some substantial extent independent and theoretically validated. Neither is the case. The lack of independence in the measures is seen from the fact that the multiple correlations are sometimes not much greater than the largest single zero-order correlation (Neubauer 1997), although Neubauer and Knorr (1998) provide a counter-example. Vernon's (1983) data on 100 students who undertook simple and choice reaction time tasks and Sternberg and Posner-type tasks in addition to psychometric ability tests show moderate to large correlations among all the information processing measures. When the indices from the reaction times of the supposedly different information processing measures were subjected to principal factor analysis, one factor accounted for 65.5% of the variance. There are comparable data in Studies I and II of Neubauer and Knorr (1998). An almost as powerful single factor was found when Vernon entered intraindividual variabilities in a similar analysis. Vernon (1985; Vernon and Kantor 1986) established that the timed nature of the psychometric tests did not account for the correlation with reaction time tests; neither did shared content (verbal or numerical) or test difficulty level:

> Rather, it is the *g* factor common to all psychometric variables that accounts for the bulk of the relationship between IQ and reaction time. Further, given the degree of this relationship, it appears that a moderately large part of the variance in *g* is attributable to variance in speed and efficiency of execution of a small number of basic cognitive processes. (p. 69)

Some further regularities that have emerged from reaction time studies are the findings that more complex reaction time tasks, up to a certain level of complexity (Jensen 1993), have higher correlations with psychometric ability test scores, and that the association between mental test scores and reaction time indices is higher with highly *g*-loaded mental tests (Jensen 1998). The first of these has been dubbed 'the complexity' hypothesis, and has some support (Vernon and Jensen 1984; Vernon and Weese 1993). The interpretation of such a finding is not clear and, even though it is termed a hypothesis, it could equally be termed a result that has emerged from the data and demands an explanation, perhaps indicating that as so-called elementary cognitive tasks approximate the complexity of psychometric test items, they relate more closely to them. The finding may indeed be interesting but one must realize that what this finding means is that tests with reaction times of many hundreds of milliseconds correlate better with psychometric tests than, say, the Sternberg slope, which averages about 38 ms per item. Again, shared variance has been earned at a fearful, perhaps fatal, loss in tractability, because it is stretching language to refer to anything that takes the best part of a second as 'elementary'.

HERITABILITY OF REACTION TIME INDICES AND REACTION TIME–MENTAL ABILITY CORRELATIONS

Human mental ability differences are partly heritable, and are related to reaction time-type tests. One approach that might further our understanding, although it will not necessarily reveal the brain bases of the so-called information processing tasks and indices, is to examine the heritability of reaction time parameters and ask whether their phenotypic correlation with psychometric test scores has a basis in the genes. This information can illuminate to a degree the causes for the correlation. For example, Rijsdijk *et al.* (1998) reported correlations of around −0.2 between Raven and Wechsler ability tests and simple and choice reaction times in adolescent Dutch twins. Heritability of reaction times was about 50–60%. Crucially, the reaction time–psychometric intelligence correlation was entirely due to shared genetic factors. Table 6.2 summarizes several studies reporting a heritable component to various reaction time indices, often of the Sternberg or

Posner type. Some have found evidence of a strong genetic basis for the phenotypic correlation between psychometric test scores and reaction time indices.

The best of the studies shown in Table 6.2, with traditional Sternberg and Posner tasks and indices, and subjects—aged between 18 and 70 years—drawn from the normal population, is by Neubauer *et al.* (in press). They used Raven's advanced progressive matrices (RAPM) and a short form of a German psychometric test battery based on Thurstone's tests of primary mental abilities, the Leistungs-Pruf-System (LPS). Psychometric and reaction time test scores were corrected for age and sex. As with other studies using such 'elementary' cognitive tasks, the actual mean reaction times involved are relatively long, from over 600 ms to almost 1 s (some of Vernon's reaction times are over 1 s). All reaction time measures, even the Sternberg slope, showed between adequate and high reliabilities. A single factor accounted for 58.4% of the variance in the latency measures from the Sternberg and Posner tests; derived (slope or difference) measures were not used in this analysis. Various analyses are of interest from this study. First, the effect sizes between latency measures from the Posner (RTs from PI and NI conditions) and Sternberg (RTs to set sizes 1, 3, and 5 and the intercept) tasks and RAPM, LPS, a general psychometric test factor, and a fluid *g* factor from the LPS were atypically high, being invariably above 0.3 and usually above 0.4. Correlations between Sternberg and Posner measures and the crystallized *g* factor measure from the LPS were markedly lower, ranging from −0.11 to −0.30. The Sternberg slope measure had low correlations with all of the psychometric measures, the largest being an effect size of 0.12 with RAPM. The Posner NI–PI difference score ('speed of lexical access in long-term memory') fared only mildly better, its strongest correlation was −0.22 with the crystallized *g* measure of the LPS. The high correlations found in this study are likely to have arisen from the wide range of ages (age-adjusted scores were not employed for these analyses, only for genetic computations) and the fact that speeded measures and psychometric test scores, especially fluid-type scores, show a falling-off with age (see Chapter 8).

Heritability estimates from the study are not straightforward to report. The shared environment component was rarely significant, yet the authors warned against the power of their study in detecting modest contributions from this source. Additionally, the authors found dizygotic (DZ) correlations that were typically more than half of the monozygotic (MZ) correlation, indicating the presence of shared environmental effects. Therefore, depending on whether this component is or is not accepted, respectively, for each mental test score, the heritabilities range from a low of 0.21/0.39 (space subtest of the LPS) to a high of 0.81 for the *g* factor. Heritabilities for the reaction time tests are shown in Table 6.3. Full genetic–environmental models are shown for all indices but, for all of the reaction time parameters, the best-fitting models were so-called 'reduced models', which did not require additive genetic, shared environmental, and/or individual environmental/error terms for best fitting. Only the additive genetic and individual environment/error terms were required for best fitting of the data from Sternberg reaction times from set sizes 3 and 5, the Sternberg intercept,

Table 6.2 Heritability estimates for so-called elementary cognitive tasks (ECTs) based on reaction times

Study	Subjects	ECTs	Heritability	Comments
McGue et al. (1984)	34 MZ and 13 DZ twin pairs	Posner letter matching, Sternberg memory scan, Shepard–Metzler mental rotation	From 0.16 to 0.80	Only results from MZ twins analysed
Ho et al. (1988)	30 MZ and 30 DZ child/adolescent same sex twin pairs	Two paper-and-pencil-based speed of processing tests	0.52 and 0.49	Correlation between Wechsler scores and speed tests largely due to genetic factors. Speed tests non-standard
Vernon (1989)	50 MZ and 52 DZ twin pairs	Posner letter matching, Sternberg memory scan, sentence verification, combined tests	From 0.23 to 0.98; median 0.52 for reaction times; 0.53 for intraindividual variabilities	More complex tests (longer mean reaction times), more heritable and had higher correlations with ability test scores
Baker et al. (1991)	Reanalysis of Vernon (1989)	Posner letter matching, Sternberg memory scan, sentence verification, combined tests	0.45 for ECT composite	Genetic correlation between psychometric and individual ECT measures ranged from 0.7 to 0.8
Petrill et al. (1995)	149 MZ and 138 same-sex DZ	Thirty measures from cognitive abilities test (Detterman 1986)	'heterogeneous pattern of genetic and environmental influence' (p. 204)	
Neubauer et al. (in press)	169 MZ and 131 DZ twin pairs	Sternberg memory scanning, Posner letter matching	From 0.00 to 0.60 for individual ECT indices: 0.39 for a general ECT factor (see Table 6.3)	'most of the phenotypic correlation between mental speed and intelligence is due to genetic factors'

MZ, monozygotic; DZ, dizygotic.

Table 6.3 Monozygotic (MZ; $N = 169$) and dizygotic (DZ; $N = 131$) correlations and additive genetic (a), shared environment (c), and error/individual environment (e) contributions to individual differences in the Sternberg and Posner reaction time tasks (after Neubauer et al., in press)

	MZ	DZ	Full model			Best reduced model		
			a^2	c^2	e^2	a^2	c^2	e^2
Sternberg memory scanning								
RT for set size 1	0.30	0.27	0.00	0.30	0.70	–	0.30	0.70
RT for set size 3	0.47	0.24	0.35	0.10	0.56	0.45	–	0.55
RT for set size 5	0.51	0.21	0.47	0.00	0.53	0.47	–	0.53
Intercept	0.16	0.10	0.13	0.08	0.79	0.23	–	0.77
Slope	0.13	-0.11	0.11	0.00	0.89	0.11	–	0.89
Posner letter matching								
RT for PI	0.49	0.35	0.24	0.25	0.51	–	0.44	0.56
RT for NI	0.59	0.31	0.60	0.01	0.39	0.61	–	0.39
NI–PI	0.21	-0.04	0.22	0.00	0.78	0.22	–	0.78
General RT factor	0.53	0.29	0.39	0.12	0.49	0.52	–	0.48

RT, reaction time; NI, name identity; PI, physical identity.

the reaction time for the NI condition and the NI–PI difference in the Posner task, and the general factor from the reaction time tasks. For the reaction time to set size 1 in the Sternberg task and the reaction time to the PI condition in the Posner task, the best-fitting model required only shared environment and individual environment/error terms.

The final analysis was a computation of the genetic contribution of the correlation between psychometric intelligence scores and the general factor from the reaction time tests. These were 1.0 for RAPM, 0.86 for total LPS, 0.86 for the *g* factor, 0.97 for the fluid factor computed from the LPS, and 0.81 for the crystallized factor from the LPS. These estimates are for models that assume no common environment effect (non-significant in the models), and if this assumption were incorrect the estimates would fall to about 0.65. The authors suggest that the pattern of results fits a conjecture to the effect that more complex reaction time indices are more strongly related to psychometric ability test scores and are also more heritable. This new ability to point to a substantial source of variance shared by reaction times and psychometric intelligence is an important advance but, to exploit this lead more fully, there has to be an understanding of the processing nature of the reaction time tasks.

SLOPES: SLIPPERY PROBLEMS

The Hick, Sternberg, and Posner tasks have been adopted by individual differences researchers interested in the bases of psychometric intelligence because they appeared to offer theoretically tractable tasks, producing component scores that measured the efficiency of important stages of brain function. The data have many limitations and yield some surprises. There cannot be any doubt that there are significant correlations between reaction times, reaction time variabilities, and intercept scores on a variety of tasks that are, on the face of it, simpler than psychometric test scores. The correlations are modest, between 0.2 and 0.3, but sometimes getting towards 0.4 and above. Samples of subjects are often drawn from student populations, with a high mean and an attenuated distribution of mental ability. Studies are too few to decide which aspects of psychometric intelligence are best correlated with individual reaction time measures, although the lesson that adequate psychometric test batteries should be included is being learned (Stankov and Roberts 1997, 1999). However, the great disappointment is the lack of any special correlation with the component measures, which are typically slope or difference functions. The disappointment, though not always evinced in research papers, must be insisted upon, because, for at least the Hick, Sternberg, and Posner tasks, it was the slope-difference measures that attracted differential psychologists in the first place. Some commentators have found the lack of disappointment especially puzzling. In their bracing corrective to the slack use of the term mental speed and, in their view, its corresponding overemphasis, Stankov and Roberts (1997) worried that:

not a single investigator seems particularly perturbed by the fact that 'slope' measures (which originally spawned interest in this [the Hick reaction time] paradigm {see Roth 1964}) do not always show higher correlations with intelligence measures than do movement time, standard deviation measures or the like. This has led to a most curious state of affairs where intelligence has variously been shown to correlate most highly with median DT . . . , median MT . . . , slope of DT . . . , and intraindividual variability in DT. . . . How a basic process might be inferred from this series of seemingly diverse studies appears difficult to fathom. Yet, in the majority of empirical studies investigating the relationship between intelligence and choice response, this is precisely what is claimed when the results are finally interpreted. (p. 77)

To emphasize the assumptions and trust that differential psychologists have placed on cognitive tasks, here are descriptions of tasks in the study by McGue *et al.* (1984):

Posner Letter Identification . . . Dependent variables used in subsequent analyses were; the overall percentage correct, the mean response latencies (in ms) under physical (PI) and name (NI) identity conditions, and the difference between the mean response latencies in the name and physical identity conditions (NI–PI). NI–PI is thought to measure the added time needed to retrieve the name of the letter from memory (Hunt 1978), and is the primary measure of theoretical interest. (p. 241)

Sternberg Memory Search . . . The slope of the regression line measures the amount of time needed to scan an additional item in active memory and is the primary measure of theoretical interest. The intercept measures the speed of all additional processing (e.g., encoding, deciding, responding, etc.). (p. 242)

Shepard–Metzler Cube Rotation . . . The dependent variables used in subsequent analyses were the slope of the regression of median reaction time on angular displacement, a measure of rate of mental rotation; the intercept, a measure of speed of all remaining processing . . . (p. 242)

In each case the siren for differential psychologists has been the slope or difference variable, promising an estimate of the efficiency of a validated mental component, and in each case the correlation with the other indices, not theoretically split into components, has been as high or higher with psychometric tests.

Two aspects of the comment above demand attention. First, the promiscuity of correlations between supposed information processing measures and psychometric ability test scores raises the question of the generality of the phenomenon underlying the correlations. For example, Neubauer (1997; Neubauer and Bucik 1996) groups what he termed ECTs (elementary cognitive tasks; and what Hunt [1983, p. 143] termed 'elementary processes of information handling') under the common banner of mental speed, and then asks the question of whether mental speed is a unitary phenomenon and whether it relates to the general factor in mental test scores or to group or more specific factors.

The second matter is the problem of the slope-difference function and its failure to have substantial correlations with psychometric test scores. Matters concerning the Hick slope were discussed above, and problems associated with the stability of slope measures in the Sternberg memory scan paradigm have been noted (Valentine *et al.* 1984; Carter *et al.* 1986; Jensen 1987*b*; Roznowski and Smith 1993). Roznowski and Smith (1993) examined the stability of different indices from the Sternberg task using different contents (digits, letters, non-alphanumeric characters, and short words). The median reaction times showed high internal consistencies (usually at or above 0.9) but only moderately high stability over 1 week (0.51 to 0.74, the highest for digits). Correlations across content-types were high (usually > 0.8). Across the four content types the stability of the intercept ranged from 0.42 to 0.66. The only frankly unsatisfactory measure was the slope with stability coefficients of 0.05 (digits), 0.33 (letters), 0.21 (words), and 0.30 (non-alphanumeric characters).

Lohman's (1994, 1999) critique of the enterprise that searches for slope-based or difference-based components within cognitive tasks which will account for variance in psychometric ability tests addressed a number of the reaction time-type procedures discussed above. He was critical of efforts to seek individual differences in components of, for example: letter-matching using the name identity–physical identity reaction time differences in the Posner letter-matching task (Hunt *et al.* 1973); and the attempt to gauge speed of mental rotation in the Shepard and Metzler (1971) task using regression techniques to estimate the slope (Sternberg 1977*b*). Lohman's comments applied also to the Hick reaction time slope. He rejected the assumption that:

> We can decompose overall individual differences in performance on a task or ability factor into component scores that reflect individual differences in mental processes. . . .

> I claim, however, that these component scores do not decompose and therefore cannot explain individual differences in overall performance on such tasks. Rather, component scores salvage systematic individual variance from the error term. This may be a useful activity, but it does not help explain the main source of individual differences on the task. (p. 1)

Lohman (1994) charted the initial enthusiasm and later disenchantment with slope parameters in cognitive tasks; from the initial hope that slopes would offer pure processing components to the realization that slopes were unreliable and that the intercept and overall response time measures had the higher associations with psychometric test scores. Slope parameters, he explained (see also Lohman 1999), suffer the same difficulties as difference scores, which are known to be unreliable. He also raised the difficulty of assuming that subjects homogeneously apply the same process model to each task, and he offered examples from mental rotation tasks in which subjects approached the task in qualitatively different ways, invalidating the application of the model that produced the slope index. It was noted earlier that a substantial proportion of people fail to perform according to Hick's model in choice reaction time tasks. To these problems of unreliability and strategy shifting Lohman added the problem of individual differences in speed–accuracy trade-offs. He saw things as worse than that, however:

> even if we had subjects whose performance conformed to our model, who made no errors, who all adopted the same speed–accuracy tradeoff, and whose component scores could be estimated reliably, we would still find that component scores did not help us explain individual differences in overall task performance. (p. 4)

His reasoning is that, when a group of people undertake a series of items making up a test, the main sources of variance are person variance and item difficulty. Any slope variance is captured in the person by item/error variance component, which is typically small. He demonstrated that component scores do not decompose person variance in mental task performance and that:

> The intercept, which is the residual or wastebasket term in componential models, is actually the locus of individual difference variance that is consistent across trials, whereas component scores, which capture consistent variation in item difficulty, can only help explain residual individual difference variance. (p. 7)

VALIDATION OF COGNITIVE COMPONENTS

Because this is a text aimed at a problem within differential psychology—the bases of psychometric intelligence in terms of the brain's information processing structures and functions—it is tempting to remark purely on the psychometric nature, especially limitations, of cognitive tasks used to study intelligence. For example, cognitive components are often unreliable and supposedly independent components are in fact correlated, and vice versa. However, one must end by questioning the bases on which the constructs were founded. Therefore, in seeking the understanding of the correlations between reaction time and other variables it must be asked how much we know about the reaction time measures. A socially endearing, but scientifically dangerous, fault among differential psychologists is to believe the theoretical account printed on the wrapper when they buy off-the-shelf information processing tests from cognitive-experimental psychologists. Roznowski and Smith (1993) warned:

> A commonly held belief about many cognitive paradigms such as the memory search task is that responses to them are relatively content-free and are thus unlikely to be influenced greatly by individuals' background, experience, and

academic training. The idea that cognitive tasks are relatively independent of stimulus content arises from the view that task performance depends only on latency of response to a simple stimulus and thus, the underlying cognitive component or process of interest. A further assumption regarding reaction time scores is that information-processing abilities are enduring and reflect stable processes and attributes. It is important that researchers examine these propositions . . . (pp. 390–391)

Jenkinson (1983) reported significant correlations ranging from –0.30 to –0.43 between reaction times and intercept measures—but not the slope—from the Sternberg memory scan procedure and Raven's matrices and the Mill Hill vocabulary test. Some of the 11-year-old children's data did not show the expected slope in the Sternberg task and Jenkinson remarked that:

> it cannot be assumed that measures derived from information processing models based on group data are valid for individual subjects. These measures may have a different psychological meaning for individuals because of differences in strategies employed to cope with the demands of a task. Such strategies, inferred from differences in error rates and from deviations from predicted task models, may have a moderating effect on correlations obtained between speed, or other indicators of processing efficiency, and intelligence. (p. 105)

Her suggestion was to encourage researchers to embrace multivariate designs in which differences in strategies were considered. That is a helpful proposal, but a more serious possibility is that different people undertake the Sternberg task, and perhaps other reaction time-based tasks, by applying different sets of unknown cognitive processes.

CONCLUSION

This area of research is not without robust findings or substantial bodies of research, but the understanding achieved as a result of applying cognitive decomposition techniques to human ability differences is not impressive. The problem of isolating validated, interesting components from cognitive tasks has proved more difficult than was thought in the heydays of cognitive psychology's youth, and cognitive psychology has not produced the production line of components for differential psychologists simply to correlate with mental abilities:

> I do not think that cognitive psychology has had nearly the impact on measurement that a few brave souls prophesied it would have and that an even larger audience of less daring but equally optimistic folk expected it to have. Indeed, many of the early enthusiasts have abandoned the effort and quietly moved on to other topics. Those who were not involved from the beginning can little imagine the sense of excitement that pervaded the field in the early 1970s.

Cognitive psychology promised to rescue differential psychology from psychometrics and return it to the mainstream of psychological research. But this has not happened. (Lohman 1994, p. 1)

attempts to isolate component scores that decompose individual differences on homogeneous tasks into process measures cannot succeed, and so our efforts should be directed elsewhere. (p. 9)

Lohman's argument has force, but there is a broader point when we set his pessimistic comments in the context of there being many instances of significant associations between psychometric ability test scores and reaction times. The size of the effects is moderate, but is substantial enough to be of interest when one considers the difference in content between typical reaction time tests and psychometric tests. These potentially exciting results on their own leave the field in something of a no-man's land. The reaction time tests appear to lie somewhere between psychometric tests (which are not expected to reveal details of brain processing) and more basic aspects of brain function; yet there is hardly anywhere an account of the brain processing involved in any reaction time-based task that can live up to the epithet of 'elementary cognitive test' or 'information processing test' or 'speed of processing test'; all of these terms claim something that we do not yet know. Worst of all is the term 'mental speed' which tends to be stuck to any human cognitive outcome variable, in a spurious attempt at explanation, that has time or velocity as its unit of measurement. Many individual suggestions for possible confounding effects (top-down explanations) have been partially refuted; 'partially', because the confounding hypotheses are sometimes poorly formulated, and are based on constructs for which there is no agreed and valid test. The field cannot progress with researchers just refuting every conceivable confound. More must be done to understand the bases of individual differences in experimental–cognitive tests and reaction time-based procedures, and the bases of the cognitive test–psychometric test correlations. Nettelbeck (1998) suggested that the eventual decomposition of reaction time performance is likely to involve both low- and higher-level processing factors:

> I would confidently predict that Jensen's task [Hick reaction time] will be found to be influenced by higher-order cognitive processes . . . Although commonly referred to by those working in the field as 'elementary cognitive tasks' (ECTs), RT procedures are only elementary in the sense that they certainly present relatively low knowledge requirements for participants, compared to most items in traditional tests of cognitive abilities. They therefore have a long history as outcome variables exploited to reveal the nature of psychological functions. However, it is not the case that ECTs require only basic mental capacities and exclude the operation of more complex intellectual functions. (p. 238).

What we ended up with in this field is not what we expected. The tasks yielded associations with ability test scores, but the theoretically-derived components were either missing in action or bit players when it came to grabbing psychometric test variance. There can be no ducking this problem; it is one which has been around as long as the field has been active, and it was clearly stated by Hunt and MacLeod (1978):

> To apply sentence-verification [substitute Hick, Posner, or S. Sternberg task as appropriate] data to the study of individual differences, then, one must take one of two approaches. One way to proceed is to regard sentence verification itself as primitive, and to study the correlation between some summary statistic describing sentence verification, such as the mean reaction time over trials, and other measures of psychological traits. . . . This approach has the advantage of relying upon well-understood statistical procedures and of not depending on the truth of any particular theory. It has the disadvantage of being limited to regarding sentence verification as a primitive to be accepted rather than to be described. The analysis of averages discards any information contained in the relations between subsets of the data, in this case, in the differences between individual reaction times as a function of sentence complexity. (p. 133)

Throughout the modern decades of the information processing approach to human mental abilities researchers have noted this problem, and have sometimes seen in it more positive information. Sternberg and Gardner (1982) remarked that:

> A result that at first glance appears most peculiar has emerged from many of these [information processing] task analyses . . . The regression intercept, or global 'constant', often turns out to be as highly correlated or more highly correlated with scores from IQ tests than are the analysed parameters representing separated sources of variance. Since the constant includes speed of response, e.g. button pressing, one could interpret such results trivially as indicating that motor speed is an essential ingredient of intelligence. A more plausible interpretation, and, as it will turn out, one more consistent with the bulk of the data, is that there are certain constancies in information processing tasks that tend to be shared across wide variations in item types. We suggest that the search for the general component(s) and the search for the general factor are one and the same search—that whatever it is that leads to a unitary source of individual differences across subjects also leads to a unitary source of differences across stimulus types. (pp. 232–233)

Similarly, McGue *et al.* (1984) commented that:

> The results reported here support the existence of a general speed component underlying performance on most experimental cognitive tasks which is strongly related to psychometric measures of '*g*', and for which there are substantial genetic effects. (p. 256)

Finally, in agreement with both of the above, Neubauer's (1997) review distinguished between 'primary variables' from information processing tasks, meaning average reaction times and intraindividual variabilities, and 'secondary variables' such as the slope and difference measures that correspond to theoretical components. He concluded that primary variables have the highest associations with psychometric intelligence, predict across different types of mental ability, and have the higher heritabilities. Secondary variables, on the other hand, have more discriminant and convergent validity with different mental abilities. However, secondary variables rarely added independent variance after primary variables had been entered into a regression equation used to predict mental test scores.

To find, eventually, that indices from experimental tasks, originally designed to test distinct components, share much variance and that this conglomerate is successful in accounting for a moderate amount of psychometric ability test scores is interesting in itself. On reflection, though, it was not the intention of this field to end up with a factor analysis of tests of unknown processes (cognitive tests) to account for variance in scores derived from tests based on factor analyses and without known processes (psychometric tests). At worst, all we have is variance shared between two equally mysterious sets of human performance measures (see Chapter 5 for a similar conclusion). Neubauer (1997) interpreted the same state of affairs more optimistically:

> On the basis of the present state of knowledge, I would, therefore, conclude that a unitary process seems to be responsible for the relationship between psychometric intelligence and SIP [speed of information processing]. (p. 168)

Differential psychologists' intercourses with cognitive psychology have been somewhat fruitful in producing interesting results, but not yet understandings. Individual differences researchers have, with touching and pious hope, brought back cognitive tasks and processes like medieval pilgrims amassing the relics of holy persons encased in sealed caskets. Opening the casket rarely has revealed the relics expected, and often none at all. Nothing daunted, we have worshipped the casket.

7   Quick on the uptake

Inspection times: raking around in psychophysics

SUMMARY

In addition to cognitive psychology, and proceeding to an arguably lower level of reduction, differential psychologists have visited the domain of psychophysics to find correlates of psychometric intelligence test scores. Because this field of psychology isolates apparently elementary psychological functions, it has been attractive to discover whether some of these show individual differences that might explain part of the variance in psychometric intelligence. Some of the tasks investigated are thought to measure speed of information intake. The main difference between tasks in this chapter and those in the previous chapter, apart from the fact that they tend to arise from psychophysics rather than experimental/cognitive psychology, is that they do not involve speeded responses. The 'speed' of the tasks discussed below is an inferred speed of processing, based on evidence concerning subjects' coping with brief stimulus durations in simple decision-making tasks. Thus, the amount of stimulus information is manipulated by limiting the stimulus duration, and observing the effect of the subject's probability of achieving a correct response, rather than measuring speed as a part of the subject's response. The idea, then, is that the performance characteristics of some important aspect of brain function can be isolated and measured.

Examples of such tasks include visual inspection time, so-called auditory inspection time, other visual backward-masking approaches, and other auditory procedures. Each of these is explained from a theoretical point of view, their measurement characteristics are described, and their correlations with intelligence are summarized. Some integration across tasks is attempted, and conclusions are formulated about the contribution these tasks have made to understanding human psychometric intelligence differences.

Visual inspection time began as a theoretical account of how visual information was passed from iconic memory storage to decision-making processes in short-term memory. Many studies have shown that inspection time is correlated modestly (about 0.4) with measures of psychometric intelligence, especially performance IQ. There is a lively debate about the causal direction of the correlation; that is, whether inspection time differences are causal to intelligence or whether brighter people find strategies to perform better on inspection time tasks. In addition, having established a sizeable correlation between inspection time and psychometric intelligence tests scores, the theoretical account of inspection time is questioned. This, an argument that will be applied to other low-level tasks, exemplifies a general theme of the book, to wit, the degree to which supposedly low-level tasks really take us closer to valid aspects of brain function as opposed to being arbitrary task parameters that have no one-to-one relation with brain processes.

VISUAL INSPECTION TIME

Rationale

The idea of inspection time as a theoretical construct and as a measure of individual differences arose from two places. First, it has a source in theories of visual perception that hypothesize that visual information is sampled quantally rather than continuously. These types of theories state that information from the world comes through the visual system as a series of discrete frames, suggesting an analogy with movie cameras. Once this suggestion has been made there arise the questions of the rate at which these frames sample the world and the nature of any individual differences in the sampling rates. Second, inspection time theory has an origin in statistical models of decision-making processes. Once visual information has been sampled there is the question of how it is used to make decisions based on the stimulus attributes. Vickers *et al.* (1972) put these two concerns together in the theory of visual inspection times. Vickers sought an answer to the question of how much time it took an individual to sample visual information coming from the outside world. He viewed this so-called 'inspection time' as an information processing primitive.

An inspection time task was designed to provide a discrimination so distinct and easy that it might need only one 'inspection' of the stimulus. Given enough time to inspect the stimulus there should be errorless decision making. Although the theory of inspection time need not be associated with any one task, it makes an easier start in discussing inspection times to begin with a description of the typical type of task. The usual stimulus to be discriminated in the task has two parallel, vertical lines of markedly different lengths, joined at the top with a cross-bar (Fig. 7.1a). The subject's instruction is to state which of the two vertical lines, left or right, is the longer. A cue is given as a warning that the stimulus is due to occur at a specific time and location. The researcher records whether the subject's decision was right or wrong. No record of the subject's reaction time need be made. The subject is encouraged to be accurate and to respond at leisure. Seen without limitation of stimulus duration, the task is so easy that subjects do not make errors. Limitations in the subject's ability to make the discrimination with perfect accuracy are imposed using two procedures. First, the stimulus is immediately overwritten by a 'backward mask' figure (Breitmeyer 1984). One type of mask, typical of early studies on inspection times, is seen in Fig. 7.1b. More effective masks were introduced later (e.g. Simpson and Deary 1997). It is placed directly over the area which the stimulus occupied and, if effective, it prevents further processing of the stimulus after the latter's removal. Second, limiting the subject's decision-making accuracy is achieved by varying the duration of the stimulus from trial to trial.

a)   b)

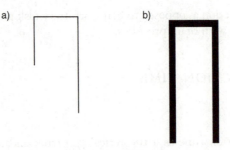

Fig. 7.1 A typical 'pi' stimulus (a) and mask (b) from the inspection time procedure. A cue warns the subject about an impeding stimulus. The stimulus or its mirror image is presented thereafter for a duration that can vary from a few milliseconds to a few hundred milliseconds. The mask replaces the stimulus immediately after stimulus offset. The subject indicates which of the two stimuli was presented, typically by stating the side on which the longer line appeared. There is no speeded response. The mask shown here is only one of various configurations used in different experiments. Stimuli, too, have varied across experiments, although this 'pi' figure is the most common. Tachistoscopes, computer monitors, and light-emitting diodes have been used to present the stimuli in different reports.

Each trial of the typical inspection time task runs as follows: (a) the subject sees a cue; (b) less than a second later the vertical-lines stimulus is presented for a controlled duration (taking a value, perhaps, between a few hundred milliseconds and a few milliseconds); (c) immediately after the stimulus has been removed a backward mask figure appears; and (d) in his or her own time the subject states which of the stimulus lines was longer. The response is recorded for correctness and the next trial begins. This is repeated so that the experimenter builds up a profile of the subject's responses to a number of different stimulus durations. The left–right position of the long line in the stimulus is varied randomly between trials.

When stimulus durations are very long, the position of the long line in the target stimulus is seen with ease and the subject responds correctly and with confidence. When durations are very brief, it seems that no stimulus has been seen preceding the mask, and the subject must be encouraged to guess. Intermediate durations induce the impression of having seen something, but there is uncertainty about the correctness of the response. Vickers *et al.* (1972) hypothesized that the stimulus, however brief, provided some information that could then be passed to a decision-making mechanism. This hypothetical mechanism had two counters of evidence, one for each response alternative. After a long-duration (easy) stimulus one of the two counters would be 'filled' beyond a threshold and the response would be made on that basis, and with subjective confidence. When the decision had to be made following a brief stimulus, none of the two counters would have enough evidence to pass the threshold on the basis of evidence from the stimulus. 'Evidence' might be sought in the mask, and the response would be made with low confidence. Evidence in any given trial was thought to be accumulated on the background of 'neural noise'.

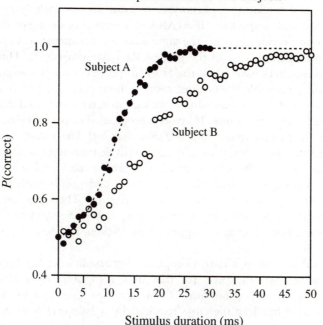

Fig. 7.2 The relationship between stimulus duration and the probability of a correct response in an inspection time (IT) experiment, using the 'pi' stimulus shown in Fig. 7.1. The stimulus duration varies between 0 and 50 ms. Data are shown for two observers, plotted separately. Each point on the diagram represents several hundred stimuli. The observers undertook tens of thousands of trials over a period of about 3 months. The data are extensions of those described in Deary *et al.* (1993*a*).

One prediction from this account of inspection time was that responses to even the briefest durations should exceed chance-level probability (0.5). Moreover, the psychometric function between stimulus duration and the probability of a correct response (from chance levels at 0.5 to perfectly correct responding) should be a cumulative normal ogive (an S-shaped curve); the top half of a phi-gamma function. The data on groups of subjects indicated that this was true. Figure 7.2 shows that the probability of a correct response does increase steadily, in the hypothesized manner, as the stimulus duration increases. The probability of correct response exceeds chance even at very brief durations and rises to almost perfect response at longer durations.

Some caution is necessary about terminology applied to the term 'inspection time'. The epithet is used to mean different things. It is used to cover the entire area of research, including the theory and measurement. It is used to mean the procedures and equipment involved in measurement. It is used to refer to the psychological construct underlying the measurement procedures. It is used to refer to individual differences discovered in the measurement procedures. There-fore, the error of conflating a phenotypic measure and an underlying construct is especially easy with inspection time. Also, it is tempting to accept that all proce-dures called 'inspection time' are the same sorts of phenomena; as we shall see, that is often questionable, a case of the jingle fallacy (see chapter 4). Throughout the literature, researchers have stuck the label 'inspection time' to several tasks that rather distantly resemble the original task, without checking criterion validity.

On the face of it, inspection time looks like an interesting candidate as a corre-late of mental ability test scores. It involves no speeded response. It has a theoretical background in psychophysics and decision making. The theory states that the measure captures individuals' limitations in a single parameter, and that parameter is important, that is, the rate at which we sample the visual world around us. The task is so simple to perform that children and people with mental handi-caps and dementia can perform the task to criterion. Therefore, inspection time measures might index differences in a valid, lower-level parameter of human nervous system functioning, as suggested by Vickers and Smith (1986):

> In the field of human information-processing research, it has been argued, an analogous measure of speed [to that of a computer's central processor] is provided by an inspection time (IT) index, first proposed by Vickers *et al.* (1972), and defined as the time required by a [subject] S to make a single observation or inspection of the sensory input on which a discrimination of relative magnitude is based.

> The IT paradigm was designed as a way of measuring performance under certain boundary conditions, in which effects of variations in decision rule, in sensory noise, threshold values and other parameters of the process became negligibly small, so that individual differences in performance could be ascribed with some confidence to differences in a single parameter, IT.

Correlations between inspection times and mental ability test scores

Evidence of a significant correlation, of modest effect size, between individual differences in inspection times and mental ability test scores has accumulated steadily since the first report by Nettelbeck and Lally (1976). The early reports, including Nettelbeck's and those of Brand (1979) and his students, had few subjects, often with a wide range of mental abilities, including normal and mentally handicapped people. Consequently, the early high correlations—up to 0.8 or 0.9—between inspection time and mental ability differences were overes-timates of the true strength of association and came with large confidence intervals. The correlations between inspection times and mental ability test scores are usually negative in direction—people with higher ability test scores have shorter inspection times because they can make accurate discriminations at briefer stim-ulus durations. However, the size only will be noted here and correlations will be given as positive decimals; a special mention will be made whenever a correlation occurs in the opposite direction. Nettelbeck (1982) recorded the interest shown by the international press in the possibility of an IQ test based on inspection time; an estimate reckoned to be uncontaminated by cultural factors. His opinion, after reviewing the few studies published at that time and publishing some new data, was that:

> The results of our studies . . . do not support the suggestion that such a speed factor could account for more than some small part of intelligence (p. 307).

In the same year as Nettelbeck's reassessment of the field, Brand and Deary (1982) published the first systematic review of the growing number of studies correlating inspection time alongside psychometric abilities. Of nine studies documented in their semi-quantitative review, they picked out five that had the following features: young adult subjects, a range of IQs around 100, an inspection time task involving the discrimination of two lines, and non-verbal/'culture fair' measures of mental ability. The median correlation was 0.8. Taking into account the extended IQ range of many of the samples corrected the coefficient down to about 0.7, but further allowance for the limitations of the measures' internal consistencies took it back up again to 0.85. In retrospect, it is clear that this unrealistically high estimate of the effect size was the result of extrapolating from small, unrepresentative samples. The next decade saw the correlation between inspection time and psychometric intelligence differences stabilize between Nettelbeck's (1982) pessimism and Brand and Deary's (1982) optimism.

During the 1980s several authors were sceptical about the existence and/or effect size of the correlation between inspection time and psychometric intelligence (Mackintosh 1981; Lubin and Fernandez 1986; Vernon 1986), with Howe (1988) writing that:

> When the methodological defects have been remedied and representative samples used, the magnitudes of the observed correlations [between inspection time and psychometric intelligence] reduce considerably, typically to around −0.3 or less . . . or to zero.

Two substantial reviews of the inspection time literature towards the end of the 1980s established its association with psychometric intelligence. The first was a semi-quantitative review by Nettelbeck (1987). At the empirical heart of this review were 16 studies that tested a total of 439 young adults without mental handicap. The uncorrected correlation between inspection time and psychometric intelligence was 0.35. There was attenuation of mental ability variance in many of the samples because they included students. Nettelbeck's estimate of the true effect size was an r of 0.5. Kranzler and Jensen (1989) were the first reviewers to apply formal meta-analytic techniques to the studies of inspection time and psychometric intelligence. They brought together 31 published and unpublished studies, comprising 1120 subjects without mental handicaps. The average correlations between inspection time and performance and verbal IQ were 0.45 and

0.18, respectively. They estimated the true effect size to be about 0.5, after disattenuation for the restricted ranges of the mental abilities of many samples.

By the 1990s the association between inspection time and psychometric intelligence was reckoned to have an effect size somewhere between 0.3 and 0.5 in the general population. That is sizeable enough to be of interest, but not large enough to feed the earlier desires for a psychophysical test that might replace psychometric tests of intelligence. Qualitative overviews of studies of inspection time and mental abilities published since then have confirmed this estimate (Deary 1996; Deary and Stough 1996), with Brand (1996) dissenting towards a higher value for the effect size.

Beyond establishing that there is a significant association between the psychophysical measure of visual information processing and psychometric test scores, the exact value of the effect size is not especially important. It is enough to state that inspection time is arguably the simplest psychological index that exceeds Hunt's (1980a) arbitrary 0.3 correlation barrier. Inspection time is not the basis for intelligence; it might be a partial basis for some facets of psychometric ability differences. The correlation between inspection time and psychometric intelligence differences is so well established that it leads on to more interesting questions, all of which are associated with explaining the association. The explanation of the association is the larger and more interesting task, involving several connected subtasks. To understand the association properly we must consider that all the correlation between inspection time and psychometric intelligence offers is a modest statistical connection between two complex and mysterious bits of human mental performance. As Nettelbeck (1987) stated:

> There is a reliable relationship between IT and IQ. This is despite the apparent disparity between the levels of processing presumed to be involved in IT tasks and mental ability tests so that, based solely on the content of these two types of mental measurement, there is no reason to predict IT–IQ correlation. If this assertion is accepted, then two further questions pertaining to the correlation can be posed; first, is the correlation sufficiently strong to be of theoretical significance; second, what does it mean? (p. 335)

Why does the inspection time–psychometric intelligence correlation occur, and what questions can we ask to find out? First, although we do not know the bases of human intelligence differences, there is a taxonomy of these differences. Therefore, it should be asked whether inspection time has especial correlations with different ability facets and levels. Second, because the assumption is that inspection time might offer a clue to the nature of human intelligence differences, it should be asked how well the nature of inspection time is understood and established as a basic mechanism of brain function. Third, there are questions about the direction of causation between inspection time and psychometric intelligence differences. The statistical mechanism of the cross-sectional correlation between inspection time and psychometric intelligence must be explored: do inspection time differences cause psychometric intelligence differences, or vice versa, or are they associated through some other variable or set of variables? Related to this is the question of whether there is any evidence that one variable causes differences in the other during human childhood development or mental decline in old age. Fourth, there are questions about mechanism beyond the mere statistical: can a truly mechanistic/reductionistic account of the association between inspection time and psychometric intelligence be discovered at the level of physiological processes that link the two variables? Many of these questions were raised in abstract form in Chapter 4. In the field of information processing models of psychometric intelligence, inspection time makes a good case study because it has accrued more reports than other candidate processes. However, given that even the large number of inspection time studies will prove too few to make much of a start at answering these important questions, there can be little hope for most other measures of information processing.

What is the meaning and mechanism of the inspection time–ability test score correlation?

Factors of ability and inspection time

After establishing the correlation between inspection time and psychometric intelligence a first question must be the detail of exactly which aspects of human psychometric intelligence differences relate to the psychophysical measure. As seen in Chapter 1, the taxonomy of human mental ability differences contains hierarchical layers that extend from very specific packages of ability variance, through group factors, to very general variance. If it is accepted that this taxonomy provides separable and sometimes near-orthogonal sources of variance with respect to human mental abilities then it is essential to go beyond merely stating that inspection time has a significant correlation with psychometric intelligence differences. The regions of the hierarchy that correlate best with inspection time should be found. This search must be undertaken while remembering that the taxonomy is an empirical achievement based upon humans' performances on standard mental tests. If it were to be found that inspection time had a stronger correlation with a particular facet of psychometric intelligence it would still remain to be shown that either inspection time or the facet were isomorphic with any validated processing parameters in the brain. There's a rather common error that can creep into such studies. That is, to find a correlation between an information processing measure and some but not all facets of psychometric intelligence, and then to infer the processes in the information processing measure using the psychometric factors as indicators. This forgets that the information processing measure was employed because its processes were supposedly understood and these were to be used to explain psychometric ability differences.

Nettelbeck (1987) found good evidence for a significant association between general and performance-type IQ measures and inspection times. The correlation with verbal ability was less certain. Kranzler and Jensen (1989) agreed. To secure this distinction, Nettelbeck (1987) called for a large-scale study of normal adults tested on a battery of mental tests with a known psychometric structure.

Two moderately sized studies examined the associations between inspection times and individual differences on the subtests in the Wechsler Adult Intelligence Scale-Revised (WAIS-R). They examined adults with a near-normal distribution of ability, a standard two-lines inspection time test (presented on computer-controlled light-emitting diodes to avoid the problems of computer monitor screens), and structural equation modelling to discover best fit models for the data. Deary (1993) studied 87 otherwise healthy people (aged 27–52 years) with diabetes on inspection time and nine subtests of the WAIS-R. The correlations between inspection time and all subtests, performance subtests, and verbal subtests were 0.24, 0.42, and 0.19, respectively. When inspection time and WAIS-R test scores were subjected to a joint principal components analysis, inspection time loaded 0.35 on the first unrotated principal component (general factor) and 0.04 and 0.66 on the verbal and performance rotated factors, respectively. The best-fit structural equation model was a confirmatory factor analytic model with two latent traits—one containing all verbal tests and one containing all performance tests—with a correlation of 0.66. Inspection time loaded only on the performance factor, with a parameter weight of 0.38.

Crawford *et al.* (1998) improved upon the above study by examining 134 healthy adults whose distribution of age and social class was well matched to that of the UK as a whole, and by including all 11 subtests of the WAIS-R. For comparison with Deary (1993), the correlations between inspection time and summed WAIS-R scaled scores were: full scale = 0.28, verbal = 0.18, and performance = 0.35. All were significant, and similar to those of Deary (1993). Structural equation modelling was used to test different models for the association between inspection time and the WAIS-R subtests. A nested factors approach was used, with a general factor and three orthogonal factors corresponding to the then-recognized subfactors of the WAIS-R, i.e. verbal, attention–concentration, and perceptual–organizational. Inspection time loaded significantly on both the general factor (0.19) and on the perceptual–organizational factor (0.39) (Fig. 7.3). It is important to note that the factors in this model are orthogonal. Therefore, the associations between inspection time and the general and perceptual–organizational factors in this model are independent. In the same study a hierarchical model was used to examine the data. As shown in Fig. 7.4, similar results are obtained, with inspection time loading 0.19 on the general factor and 0.41 on the residual component of the perceptual–organizational factor, i.e. that part of it which is not related to the general factor.

Fig. 7.3 Nested factors structural model of the associations among subtest scores of the Wechsler Adult Intelligence Scale-Revised (WAIS-R) and inspection times. Note that the general factor (g) of the WAIS-R is orthogonal to the verbal (V), attention–concentration (A/C), and perceptual–organizational (PO) factors. Inspection time loads –0.388 on the PO factor and –0.194 on the general factor. Redrawn from Crawford *et al.* (1998). Inf = Information; Voc = Vocabulary; Com = Comprehension; Sim = Similarities; DSp = Digit Span; Ari = Arithmetic; PC = Picture Completion; PA = Picture Arrangement; BD = Block Design; OA = Object Assembly; DSy = Digit Symbol; IT = Inspection Time.

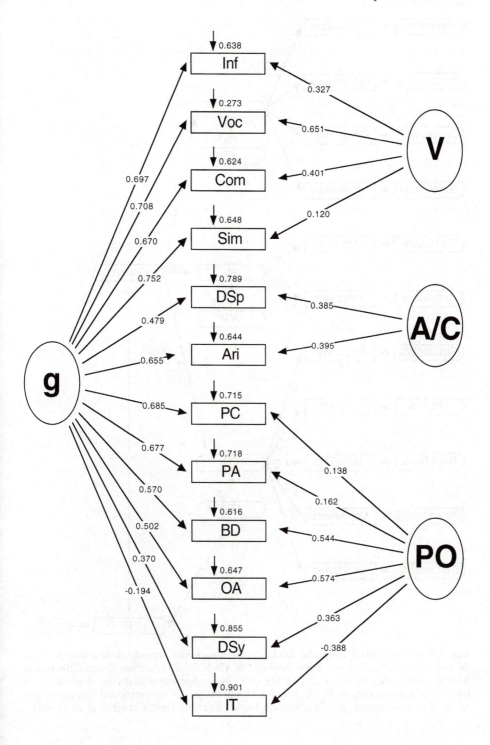

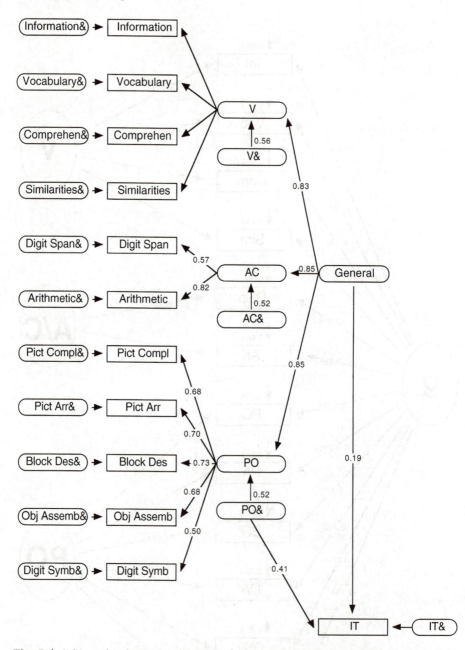

Fig. 7.4 A hierarchical structural model of the associations among subtest scores of the Wechlser Adult Intelligence Scale-Revised (WAIS-R) and inspection times. This model used the same data as the model in Fig. 7.3. Note that inspection time loads 0.19 on the general (g) factor of the WAIS-R and 0.41 on that part of the perceptual–organizational factor that is independent of the general factor. Redrawn from Crawford *et al.* (1998).

More support for the conclusion that inspection time is not associated espe-cially with *g* comes from evidence that it has a modest association (0.42) with a marker test of 'processing speed' from the Woodcock–Johnson Psycho-Educational battery-Revised (Burns *et al.*, 1999; $N = 64$). This battery's subtests were designed to give estimates of the group factors from Gf–Gc theory. Inspection time failed to correlate significantly with marker tests of short-term memory, visual processing, crystallized ability, and fluid ability. The authors, in agree-ment with Crawford *et al.* (1998), suggested that inspection time's loading on *g* is via its association with a group ability factor (in this instance of processing speed), and not fluid ability. These interesting findings await replication in studies that use more extensive batteries with several markers for each group-level factor.

More of these types of study are required, especially those that test beyond the WAIS-R. From a theoretical point of view, the WAIS-R battery leaves much to be desired. It grew as a clinically useful instrument rather than as a battery whose subscales were theoretically oriented. Nevertheless, the above two studies—with more representative samples of adults than have generally been employed in such studies heretofore, with adequate inspection time tasks, and with a hypothesis-test-ing structural equation modelling approach—allow some conclusions to be drawn, while at the same time conceding that larger-scale research is needed that uses IT in the setting of larger and better-defined mental test batteries (cf. Stankov and Roberts 1997; Roberts and Stankov, 1999). Inspection time's associations with this battery are not just those of general intelligence, although there is a modest asso-ciation with the general factor that requires explaining. Therefore, theories which posit the near-identity between general intelligence and inspection time (e.g. Anderson 1992; Brand 1996) are partly refuted by these results. The subtests of the WAIS-R that make up the perceptual–organizational factor—with which inspection time has the highest correlations in Deary (1993) and Crawford *et al.* (1998)—arguably involve speeded and spatial components and one may suggest that inspection time has a special affinity with this type of ability. Before finally concluding that the greatest interest in future research on inspection should be directed at group factors of intelligence, Crawford and colleagues offered a note of caution. The WAIS-R battery produces a general factor that is rather biased towards verbal components; another, broader battery might see inspection time as having a higher association with the general factor. This reminds us again that, in dealing with psychometric test factors, we are not dealing with natural kinds. Moreover, the tendency to appeal to psychometric tests to inquire after 'what inspection time is' reverses the causal inquiry; inspection time was employed as a theoretically sound measure to ask what psychometric intelligence is.

The direction of the correlation

If it is accepted that there is a significant correlation between inspection time and psychometric intelligence differences then, as a part of seeking the meaning of the correlation, we must inquire after its direction. There are three plausible

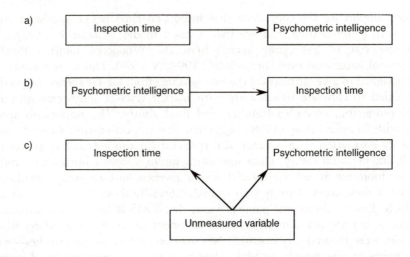

Fig. 7.5 Some possible reasons for the significant correlation found between inspection times and mental ability test scores. (a) Briefer inspection times might reflect some aspect of nervous system performance that is a partial basis for higher scores on mental ability tests. (b) Better performance on the inspection time task might result from having higher psychometric intelligence; for example, people with higher ability test scores might strive to find strategies that improve test performance on inspection time procedures. (c) The relation between inspection times and mental ability test scores might be the result of the shared influence of a third, unmeasured variable or set of variables. For example, people who score better on mental ability test scores and on inspection time tasks might, in general, be better motivated or have lower test anxiety. This type of 'third (or unmeasured) variable' hypothesis can address lower-level as well as higher-level constructs, or a mixture of both.

hypotheses. One, that inspection time is a valid index of elementary information processing efficiency and that it contributes some of the variance in certain facets of psychometric intelligence differences. Two, that inspection time is a complex mental task, like many others, that affords strategic (higher-level) opportunities for the person with high psychometric test scores to perform well. Three, there is some third and unmeasured variable that contributes to individual differences in both psychometric intelligence and inspection time performance; therefore, there is no direct link between the two measures. These possibilities are shown in Fig. 7.5. The arrows in the figures should not lead to the assumption that direct causation is implied. There may be a number of intervening—mediating—variables completing the causal chain between any of the constructs mentioned.

Hypothesizing that inspection time is a part cause of psychometric intelligence goes along with the assertion/belief that inspection time is in some sense fundamental, as was envisaged by Vickers *et al.* (1972). Table 7.1 lists a number of authors who have held this type of view, and offers their epithet for what inspection time is. In the table these authors are termed reductionist, because they assume that inspection time offers a lower-level construct to which psychometric intelligence differences may in part be reduced. These brief verbal descriptions of

Table 7.1 Comments on the nature of inspection time (IT) or the reasons for the IT–mental ability test score correlations

Author	Comment
Reductionist	
Vickers et al. (1972)	the average time needed to make one momentary inspection of the sensory input
Nettelbeck (1987)	an index of the *efficiency* of the activity associated with early central stages of perception rather than as speed of apprehension
Brand and Deary (1982)	speed of intake of the most elementary information
Anderson (1992)	The major differences in IT are probably caused by variations in the speed and efficiency of low-level processing mechanisms
Bates and Eysenck (1993a) Stough et al. (1994)	[speed of] processing of retinal signals into a short term store perceptual speed
Non-reductionist	
Irwin (1984)	It may be that more intelligent children were able to master the requirements of the task more quickly than the less intelligent, or to approach the task with less anxiety because of their general success at problem-solving, so that the slight correlations found stem from these effects
Mackintosh (1986)	[with regard to IQ-evoked potential correlations] one might want to attribute uniformity across trials to factors such as willingness to comply with instructions or ability to maintain concentration on a remarkably tedious task. . . . similar factors may underlie the correlation between IQ and both inspection times and reaction time
Howe (1988)	Even with very simple tasks that involve highly familiar materials it is more than likely that performance at them is affected by experience-induced differences in (for instance) motivation, confidence, and attentiveness, any of which, alone or in combination, could account for the observed correlations
Ceci (1990)	the more elaborately one represents a stimulus, the faster it can be recognised. If encoding were a straightforward measure of CNS efficiency, then why should knowledge-base effects such as these exist?

inspection time go beyond merely restating its operational characteristics to offering statements of belief about its underlying mechanisms. They are based partly upon the original research and rationale provided by Vickers. Below these comments in the table are some non-reductionists; some researchers who looked at the evidence for inspection time versus psychometric intelligence correlations and came up with a different view. They suggest that the correlation might be artefactual in the sense that quite high-level psychological constructs—not limitations in basic brain processes—are the key factors that bring about the association.

Possible confounding factors in the inspection time–psychometric intelligence correlation strategies

One way to explain the observed correlation between inspection times and psychometric intelligence in terms of higher-level processes is to hypothesize that bright subjects have briefer inspection times because they use cognitive strategies in the task. One such strategy, afforded by some versions of the inspection time task more than others, is to look for an apparent motion artefact between the inspection time stimulus and the mask that follows it. Contrary to the strategy hypothesis, the correlation between inspection time and psychometric intelligence is, if affected at all, lowered rather than caused by strategy use. That is, the usual correlation is found among non-strategy users and not among the users of strategies (Mackenzie and Bingham 1985; Mackenzie and Cumming 1986). In a large study Chaiken and Young (1993) found a correlation of 0.35 between inspection time and Cattell Culture Fair test scores. The correlation among the subgroup of strategy users was 0.21 (ns) and among the non-strategy users was 0.56 ($p < 0.01$). Others have found no effects of strategies on the correlation (Egan 1994). One study reported similar correlations between IQ-type test scores and inspection time estimates made with various inspection time procedures, some of which afforded strategies and some not (Stough *et al.*, in press). Simpson and Deary (1997) tested various hypotheses about inspection time performance generated by those who viewed the task as affected by higher cognitive processes. None was supported: they found no evidence that feedback encouraged the formation of strategies in the task; feedback did not aid performance on inspection time; and strategy users did not have superior inspection time performance. These and other results above support, by exclusion only, the view that more basic processes underlie inspection time performance.

No studies to date have suggested that the use of strategies accounts for the inspection time–psychometric intelligence association, although strategy theories are notoriously difficult to operationalize as testable hypotheses (Brand 1987). Moreover, there have been considerable improvements in masking procedures designed to eliminate stimulus–mask artefacts in the inspection time task (Knibb 1992; Evans and Nettelbeck 1993; Simpson and Deary 1997).

Motivation and personality

Howe (1990) suggested that a non-intellective variable such as a personality trait level might bring about inspection time's correlation with psychometric intelligence. This was tested by Stough *et al.* (1996) in 68 subjects. The subjects sat the Wechsler Adult Intelligence Scale, Raven's Advanced Progressive Matrices (RAPM), inspection time, the Eysenck Personality Questionnaire, and the Strelau Temperament Inventory. In accordance with other studies, they found a correlation of 0.44 between inspection time and performance IQ. Partial correlations, removing the effects of personality and temperament, were negligibly different from the raw correlations, leading the authors to conclude that these variables do not mediate between inspection time and ability test scores.

The hypothesis that a subject's level of motivation might affect performance on inspection time—and thus be a cause or confound in the correlation between inspection time and psychometric intelligence—was studied by Larson *et al.* (1994). They tested over 100 college students under conditions of incentive and no incentive during inspection time performance. In addition, effort expended on the task was assessed with physiological and self-report measures. They found no difference in the inspection time–psychometric intelligence correlation between groups who did and did not receive incentives to perform well. Subjects in the incentive condition were told that they would receive up to US$20 if they improved their scores over their first visit to the laboratory. The authors concluded that motivational differences were not responsible for individual differences in inspection time tests. They suggested two reasons for this: first, that subjects on the whole are well motivated in the laboratory; and second, that the inspection time task is so simple that additional motivation does not improve one's score anyway. They concluded that:

> The correlation between IQ and performance [on inspection time and other laboratory tasks] for experimentally motivated subjects is just as strong as it is for random groups. Clearly, then, the information processing/intelligence correlations found here and in previous studies cannot be attributed to motivation alone. Some other process such as some basic underlying aspect of intelligence is needed to account for the well documented IQ–Performance correlation. (pp. 35–36)

Generality of correlations (learning and novelty)

It is possible that the correlation between inspection time and cognitive test scores might be explained by the fact that brighter individuals perform better on any novel task, and simply learn more quickly the procedural requirements of a task. Evidence supporting such a hypothesis was provided by Nettelbeck and Vita (1992). They tested groups of 5–6-year-olds and 11–12-year-olds on Raven's Coloured Progressive Matrices and repeated estimations of inspection time. They found that initial correlations in the region of 0.5 eventually dropped to near-zero levels. However, they also found that, eventually, most subjects altered the way they performed the task; by the end most subjects were using post-stimulus apparent movement cues. It has already been mentioned that the presence of such cue use tends to decrease or eliminate the correlation between inspection time and psychometric intelligence. By contrast with Nettelbeck and Vita's (1992) results and those of Bors *et al.*, (1999), Chaiken (1993) found that the correlation between inspection time and Cattell Culture Fair scores was higher (0.50) at the second testing of inspection time than at the first (0.35). Chaiken concluded that the validity of inspection time increases with practice and the mechanism of this might be that practice on the task eliminates the use of the apparent movement strategy.

Chaiken's (1993) suggestions provide an important counterweight to the assumption that practice effects necessarily corrupt the inspection time measure with strategies/artefacts (cf. Mackintosh 1998). It is an open question whether the improvement of inspection time with practice represents: (a) a cleaning-up of the estimate by ridding performance of high-level factors (call them strategies) that initially induce suboptimal performance; or (b) a muddying of the index with accumulated artefacts (call them strategies) that allow the subject to 'improve' beyond their basic processing capabilities. Any study which examines changes in inspection time–mental test score correlations over time must, therefore, collect evidence about the factors causing the correlation at each testing occasion.

The psychophysiological basis of the correlation

Neither inspection time nor psychometric intelligence measurements are basic to the extent that we can point to the biological mechanisms that contribute to the individual differences in them. A rational way to proceed is to search for any biological correlates of these differences. It is not sufficient to examine the biological correlates of inspection time differences alone. If one discovered a correlate of inspection time there would be no guarantee that the variance shared with a biological construct was the same variance that it shared with psychometric intelligence. Indeed, it is quite conceivable that there could be a biological correlate of inspection time performance *and* that the individual differences that inspection time shared with psychometric intelligence were due to higher level factors. It is necessary, therefore, to ask whether there are biological correlates shared by both inspection time and psychometric intelligence. Chapter 9 presents evidence that individual differences in inspection time are correlated with the rise time of the P200 wave of the brain's electrical response to the inspection time stimulus. This provides a clue to the processes involved in producing individual differences in inspection time performance. Some evidence suggests that differences at this latency of the event-related potential are associated also with differences in psychometric intelligence. As related in Chapter 9, these studies are small and must be taken as only suggestive. They provide a model, though, for the way forward in this area. Finding a correlation between a putative information processing construct and psychometric intelligence should be followed up with a search for the more basic, shared correlates of both measures.

The above approach might be termed parallel reductionism. Another way to proceed is to discover factors which either enhance or reduce performance on both inspection time and psychometric intelligence. This method provides circumstantial evidence for the cause of the inspection time–psychometric intelligence association. For example, Stough and his colleagues have demonstrated, in a series of only modestly-powered studies, that smoking improves psychometric intelligence test scores (Stough *et al.* 1994), inspection time (Stough *et al.* 1995*b*), the decision time component of reaction times (Bates *et al.* 1994), and the string length measure of brain event-related potentials (Stough *et al.* 1995*a*). These authors suggested that cholinergic processes in the central nervous system are involved in information processing limitations common to each of these four levels of description. A study of Alzheimer's disease—in which there is a derangement of central cholinergic neurons—supported this notion. Fluid intelligence and inspection time were severely impaired in patients when compared with healthy controls (Deary *et al.* 1991*a*). However, in a study by Petrie and Deary (1989), smoking did not improve inspection time in normal subjects.

This experimentally-oriented research, though useful, can provide only circumstantial evidence in helping to understand the correlation between inspection time and psychometric intelligence. It may become informative about which neurotransmitter systems underpin performance on various psychometric and information processing tasks, but will leave important problems of interpretation. It is not clear whether factors that affect task performance are the same as those that produce individual differences in performance. For example, it might be the case that impairment of central cholinergic neurotransmitter mechanisms impairs inspection times and psychometric intelligence, but it is a further step to discover whether individual differences in cholinergic mechanisms are responsible for any part of the variance in psychometric intelligence. As a *reductio ad absurdum*, suppose that we gave subjects a strong sedative versus a placebo in a counterbalanced experiment. It would not surprise us to discover that many psychological tasks, psychometric intelligence test scores and inspection times included, were impaired while subjects were struggling to stay awake. We should not conclude definitively from that that level of consciousness was the key variable in producing the correlation between inspection time and psychometric intelligence (although it is a hypothesis that may be tested).

Another look at the psychophysics of inspection time

Part of the interest in inspection time as a correlate of psychometric intelligence lies in its apparent simplicity. Unlike psychometric tests, where different tests are needed for people of different ability levels, different ages, and in different clinical groups, the same inspection time test will measure reliably individual differences in anyone with good enough vision who can understand the simple instructions. There are no ceiling or floor effects. Yet, as the research on strategies and related matters has demonstrated, there are worries about the nature of the constructs being assessed by inspection time measures. Although some hypotheses about high-level constructs producing the inspection time–psychometric intelligence correlation have not been supported, there have been reassessments of the original account of the inspection time task that was offered by Vickers *et al.* (1972). This is an issue which psychologists interested in individual differences are destined to address again and again. In borrowing a task from another field of psychology, and intending to lean on it as a partial explanation for some molar aspect of behaviour, one is dependent on the construct validity of the borrowed task. In the case of inspection time there seemed good reason to accept the original account of the task, given its simplicity and the elaborate theoretical account in which the task was embedded.

The simple beauty of inspection time lay in its being a straightforward task that got directly to a benchmark limitation in human brain functioning. It seemed, to some, to meet Galton's (1890) criterion for a useful mental measurement:

> One of the most important objects of [human mental] measurement is hardly if at all alluded to here and should be emphasised. It is to obtain a general knowledge of the capacities of a man by sinking shafts, as it were, at a few critical points.

The unravelling of this closeted view of inspection time arose from at least four directions. First, although they have come to little, there were persistent suggestions that inspection time performance was importantly influenced by high-level psychological factors, as discussed above (Howe 1988; Mackintosh 1998). Second, when the original theoretical account of inspection time was addressed it was found wanting (e.g. Levy 1992). Third, suggestions followed that there might be more than one psychological parameter involved in inspection time performance differences (e.g. Chaiken 1993). Fourth, the realization dawned that inspection time belongs to a family of backward-masking techniques and should be discussed alongside them (Deary 1992, pp. 238–241; White 1993, 1996). And because the other techniques had theoretical conundrums, then so must inspection time. These enumerated points are now examined in more detail.

The first substantial critique of the psychophysical basis of inspection time was delivered by Levy (1992). He pointed out problems with the original theory of inspection time performance: that aspects of the theory were intuitive rather than explicit, that some of the theorizing was mathematically intractable, and that there were places in which alternative models had not been tested. Furthermore, he noted that much of the work on inspection time had been undertaken in the tradition of individual differences—where large numbers of subjects are paramount—rather than in psychophysics, where extensive testing of individual subjects is required fully to explore models of task performance. Levy (1992) demonstrated the danger of basing statistical models of performance on the basis of group data rather than the necessary single subject data. Research on, and critiques of, inspection time after Levy's review continued to reassess the basis of inspection time performance. Before discussing some of this research it should be made clear what this reassessment does not do. It does not necessarily call into question the basic nature of inspection time. Whereas research dealing with strategies, learning, motivation, personality, and so forth could have led to inspection time performance being accounted for at a high level—and thus losing much interest for differential psychologists—much of the reassessment of inspection time's theory is trying to find out the correct low-level limitations on inspection time functioning. Therefore, the interest in the correlation remains, and the desire is to find out the correct number and type of constructs involved in inspection time performance and in individual differences in inspection time.

White's (1993) examination of inspection time as a member of the family of backward-masking techniques led him to conclude that inspection time was a sensory rather than a cognitive phenomenon. That is, he rejected the notion that inspection time correlated with psychometric intelligence because both were cognitive tasks. White proposed that the correlation obtains either because inspection time reflects very general limitations in neuronal functioning that are reflected in many sensory and cognitive operations (the 'essential hypothesis'), or because people with high psychometric intelligence happen to be better motivated or use cues (the 'accidental' hypothesis). The accidental hypothesis was addressed above; it was found to have little substance, although it proved difficult to test definitively. In fact, until some form of White's essential hypothesis can be validated, the question of the accidental correlation must remain open. White (1996) continued his constructive critique of the inspection time oeuvre by warning more strongly that inspection time must not remain an etiolated psychophysical foster-child in a psychometric family. Instead, it should be integrated with mainstream backward-masking research. The effort to do this will be examined in the next subsection, but the urgent need for this research is underlined in a study by Bergen and Julez (1983), where a construct called 'inspection time' emerged from a different perceptual technique in apparent ignorance of the studies originating from Vickers' ideas. They asked subjects to find a vertical target line in a perceptual field of differently-oriented lines. They used backward masking, and found that the stimulus onset asynchrony needed to identify the target correctly was relatively short (about 60 ms) when the difference between target and other lines was 90° but was much longer (about 200 ms) when the lines had a difference of only 20°. Constructs like the inspection time and noise parameters first proposed by Vickers *et al.* (1972) emerged as explanations for subjects' performances on the task. These two 'inspection time' procedures call out for integration.

Before addressing some research that had broadened inspection time concepts into other tasks, we ask what is now known about inspection time that can address Levy's (1992) proper charge that the psychophysical research is wanting. Extensive, individual subject data were gathered on two observers by Deary *et al.* (1993*a*). Two observers completed 38,400 inspection time trials over 60 days of testing. The apparatus was an array of light-emitting diodes with millisecond accuracy. The data from both subjects—the stimulus duration versus the probability of a correct response—was well fitted by a cumulative normal ogive (Fig. 7.2). There was little support for the suggestion of Levy (1992) and Muise *et al.* (1991) that there were stimulus durations below which no information could be obtained from the stimulus and passed to decision-making mechanisms. However, the two subjects' data did reveal extra parameters in performance beyond the time of inspection. Their psychometric functions were non-stationary over time, and in different ways. One subject showed concurrent improvements and decrements at different stimulus durations at or below 10 ms. The other subject showed long-term improvements on that part of the psychometric curve lying midway between chance and perfect responding. These data tell us that there are temporal changes in inspection time task performance that have individual differences. At present these are largely ignored with regard to correlations between inspection time and psychometric intelligence. Any impact they might have on inspection time's correlation with mental ability measures might be small, but is unknown. Exceptions are the studies on the association between practice on the inspection time task and psychometric intelligence that were discussed above (Nettelbeck and Vita 1992; Chaiken 1993). However, these studies come to opposing conclusions and the subjects were not practised observers as one would see in a psychophysical study.

Expanding on the limited results of Deary *et al.* (1993*a*), Burns *et al.*'s (1998) studies suggested that there are durations below which no information may be extracted from a stimulus. This adds an extra parameter to inspection time performance, the sensory 'lag' as it was called by Muise and colleagues (1991). Despite this, however, Burns *et al.* used a number of different stimulus–mask configurations and concluded that inspection could validly be thought to assess speed of temporal resolution in the visual system. Moreover, they hypothesized that the correlation between psychometric intelligence and inspection time will be found across different backward-masking tasks, a topic addressed in the following section.

Visual information processing beyond inspection time

White's (1996) critique of the inspection time field included the plea for inspection time research to be integrated with other backward-masking research. This demand properly states that inspection time cannot stand alone outside other, related procedures in visual perception and must be understood along similar lines. In fact, there have been attempts to broaden visual research on inspection time.

Word recognition

Perhaps visual inspection time differences correlate more highly with performance than verbal scores in the Wechsler battery (Deary 1993; Crawford *et al.* 1998) because the stimuli used in the standard inspection time task are non-verbal. McGeorge *et al.* (1996) tested this hypothesis. They examined 123 adults aged between 18 and 77, whose sex, age, and social class distributions were close to those of the UK population. Subjects sat a full WAIS-R. Instead of inspection time, the authors measured the stimulus duration required by subjects to name correctly one out of every three words presented in a tachistoscope. Stimuli were six- or seven-lettered nouns of low-to-medium frequency and they were backward masked by rows of ampersands. The correlations between word recognition thresholds and the sum of verbal and performance subtests were 0.22 and 0.51, respectively. These correlations were significantly different. People with better psychometric ability test scores could name words correctly at lower stimulus durations. Moreover, a confirmatory factor analysis model demonstrated that:

> The pattern of correlations observed between the minimum time that a word must be presented in order for it to be identified correctly . . . and the various WAIS-R derived intelligence measures replicate the pattern reported for the correlations between IT and the WAIS-R measures (e.g., Deary 1993; Kranzler and Jensen 1989). . . . The three-factor model had zero paths between the threshold measure and the Verbal Ability and Attention factors . . . The Verbal Ability factor and the Attention factor play little role except through their correlations with the Performance factor. This is in spite of the verbal nature of the materials in the threshold task and the superficial appearance of a strong attentional requirement in the task . . . The aim of using words as the stimuli in the mental speed task was to test the prediction that the use of verbal materials would result in an advantage for subjects of high verbal ability. No such advantage was found . . . The fact that both types of materials result in a similar pattern of relationships to the standard psychometric measures of intelligence would appear to argue for what Anderson (1992) referred to as a low-level, domain-independent view of the role of mental speed in cognitive ability. (pp. 186–187)

A less successful attempt to broaden the method used to assess inspection time was made by Bowling and Mackenzie (1996) and Mackenzie *et al.* (1991). They reported effect sizes of about 0.4 (*N* = 60 students) between conventional two-lines inspection time and spatial relations and verbal reasoning tests from the Differential Aptitude Test. However, an attempt to sculpt a verbal inspection time task from the procedures involved in the Posner letter-matching task (see Chapter 6) produced an index that, although it had some significant associations with psychometric intelligence, did not correlate significantly with the standard two-lines inspection time test. Bowling and Mackenzie concluded that conventional inspection time correlates with *g* rather than a specific ability, in contrast with several studies that show a stronger association with performance-type measures. However, the 'verbal' test used in their study appeared to draw upon fluid intelligence to a considerable extent. They also found that inspection time had a negligible association with some reaction time measures alongside which they are typically portrayed as fellow 'speed-of-processing' measures.

Vickers' expanded judgement and FAST tasks

Vickers, who invented the inspection time theory and technique, devised other tasks to deliver the inspection time construct; that is, he created new tasks to measure people's limits in accumulating information as it arrives at the senses from the outside world. One of the reasons for moving on to new tasks was his concern about stimulus–mask interactions with the original inspection time task. The first task he reported was the expanded judgement task (Vickers *et al.* 1989). During each trial in this task the subject observed a series of horizontal lines on a computer screen. The lines were of different lengths and appeared one after the other on either side of a vertical dividing line in the centre of the screen (Fig. 7.6). The task of the subject was to decide whether, on average, the lines appearing on the left or right of the vertical line were longer. Based on the accumulator model, Vickers hypothesized that the principal limit to successful performance would be the rate at which people could sample the individual lines in the series. If the lines were flashed on the screen at too fast a rate for the subject, information would be lost, leading to missing data and incorrect answers. Although this test was little used by Vickers' team, and there was little evidence of its association with psychometric intelligence (it did correlate with inspection time, however), the importance of the task is the central idea. This idea is that the key ingredient of a task, the performance-limiting step, may be coated or packaged in very different surroundings and still measure the target construct. It is a powerful idea and holds potential for answering the charge, met by inspection time and other such tasks, that a task might be measuring performance parameters other than those that were intended.

Vickers (1995) completed more research with a related task, the Frequency Accrual Speed Test (FAST). In the FAST task the subject observes two adjacent light-emitting diodes or lights. In any one trial a series of flashes is seen, each with an identical duration. The subject's task is to state which of the lights, left or right, had more flashes. The actual ratio used is 17:13. The series of flashes is too long merely to be remembered by the subject, so Vickers hypothesized that the accumulator principal applies, whereby people are extracting information up to their limit of processing speed. The flash duration may be controlled, and when it is brief the idea is that subjects will be unable to sample all of the flashes. Thus, errors will emerge in deciding which side had more flashes. According to Vickers (1995) the FAST task was constructed to provide

Fig. 7.6 Four diagrams illustrating aspects of the 'expanded judgement task' devised by Vickers as an alternative procedure for assessing the processing limitation originally captured in the theoretical model of the inspection time task. The top panel shows how the stimulus display might appear to the subject at any one moment within a trial. The plot below shows the distribution that is used to generate the lines observed by the subject on the monitor; thus, overall within this trial, more and longer lines will appear on the right. The third diagram shows the first eight lines that might be generated from the distribution shown above. These lines are presented one at a time on the monitor and the subject must decide whether, overall, more has been seen on the right or left. The duration of lines between trials is controlled by the experimenter and this may vary to test the subject's ability to sample the incoming information. In the response panel (bottom of figure), subjects indicate whether more has been seen on the right or on the left, and they can then rate the confidence with which they made the judgement. Redrawn from Vickers *et al.* (1989).

MOMENTARY STIMULUS DISPLAY

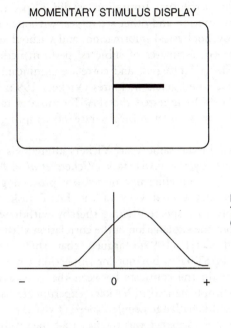

**DISTRIBUTION USED
TO GENERATE
OBSERVED LINES**

**SUCCESSIVE
OBSERVATIONS (1...8...n)
WITHIN A SINGLE TRIAL**

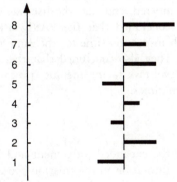

RESPONSE PANEL

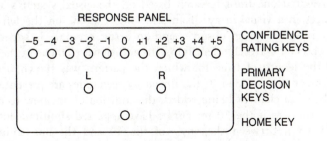

−5	−4	−3	−2	−1	0	+1	+2	+3	+4	+5
○	○	○	○	○	○	○	○	○	○	○

**CONFIDENCE
RATING KEYS**

L   R
○   ○

**PRIMARY
DECISION
KEYS**

○

HOME KEY

'an estimate of the speed or efficiency with which sensory input is sampled'. It was intended to index the same perceptual limitation as did inspection time without the problems of apparent motion and other strategies, without problems of non-stationarity, with more psychophysical information, and without indexing other processing parameters. Indeed, estimates of subjects' performances on the FAST task are reliable, not prone to strategies, and correlate significantly with inspection time and psychometric intelligence measures (Vickers 1995; Vickers and McDowell 1996). Vickers (1995) suggested that FAST estimates might be preferable to inspection time in assessing a subject's rate of sampling of the sensory input.

However, in a paper published in the same year, Vickers altered his opinion of the basic process being indexed by the FAST task (Vickers *et al.* 1995). He cited memory rather than the speed or efficiency of sensory processing as the limiting factor. Moreover, given his altered view of the FAST task, he also suggested that this revision apply to inspection time, thereby withdrawing his own theory of inspection time from the explanation of the correlation with psychometric intelligence. Deary and Caryl (1997*b*) argued that this theoretical realignment was correct for the FAST task, but not for inspection time. After a detailed description that made plain the contrasts between the two tasks, they concluded that the FAST task as implemented in Vickers' experiments had never presented stimuli at a rate that would challenge people's speed of visual processing. The obvious limitation to people's performance was the fact that they were seeing a long series of flashes that had to be remembered, and that the list was supra-span. Therefore, Deary and Caryl (1997*b*) concluded that the FAST task is a supra-span memory task that correlates with inspection time for the same reason that tasks of psychometric intelligence do. They also concluded that the theory of performance in the FAST task—a high-level task taxing memory processes in the main—had little relevance to inspection times.

Visual change detection

The essence of Vickers' idea in developing the expanded judgement and FAST tasks—to find another way of capturing the limitation in information processing free from the idiosyncrasies of the inspection time procedure—was adopted by Deary *et al.* (1997). Instead of developing a new test of visual information processing they adopted one from research based on the visual system's ability to notice differences in a visual array. If an array like the one on the left-hand panel in Fig. 7.7 is shown to an observer and an extra rectangle is added, the likelihood of the observer correctly identifying the additional element in the array is dependent on the length of time for which the pattern was shown prior to the additional element being added. If the initial 49 rectangles are presented too briefly prior to the extra element being added, the addition of one new rectangle is not noticed; it seems as if the 50 rectangles have appeared simultaneously. If sufficient time is given between the onset of the 49 and the one additional element, the new rectangle appears to 'pop out' and may be identified in an

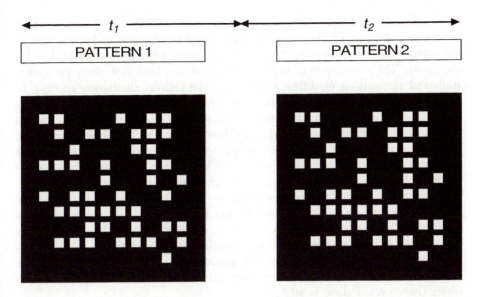

Fig. 7.7 An example of a stimulus from the visual change detection task. The pattern on the left is presented for some time (which takes one of a number of predetermined values) prior to a single rectangle being added to the display. In this case, counting from the bottom right, the extra square is five up and three along. Although it is difficult to spot when presented here, the subject clearly sees the extra square 'pop out' on the monitor when it is added. However, if Pattern 1 is displayed for a very brief duration (t_1) before adding the extra square, it is not seen. Pattern 2 (t_2) is displayed for an unlimited time until the subject responds by indicating which of the squares appeared in Pattern 2 but not Pattern 1. By varying the duration of Pattern 1 (t_1) prior to Pattern 2 (t_2) a psychometric function can be plotted for each subject, describing the association between stimulus duration and the probability of a correct response. Redrawn from Deary *et al.* (1997).

almost error free-way. When the duration (stimulus onset asynchrony) of the initial array is sufficiently long, and assuming that the observer has an unlimited opportunity to view the 50 rectangles once the additional element has been added, the function between the duration of the initial array and the probability of a correct response is monotonically increasing. Psychophysical data for the task were provided by Phillips and Singer (1974) and Royer and Gilmore (1985). The theoretical basis for the task was the action and interactions of on-centre and off-centre cells in the lateral geniculate nucleus. The fundamental idea is that there is a detectable difference in the evoked on-centre response between repeated and new elements of the array, such that the single new rectangle can be detected. Intra- and extracellular recordings of lateral geniculate nucleus cells in the visual system of cats showed that there were the expected differences in cellular discharges to repeated and new elements of a visual pattern (Singer and Phillips 1974).

Let us take stock to assess what the visual change detection task offers as an adjunct to inspection time. It is a psychophysical task in which performance may be described as a simple function of the duration of the initial array (within limits). It is based on a theory of the actions and interactions of known cells in the mammalian visual system. There are supporting neurophysiological data for the theory. The mechanism of success in the task has been described: the generation and recognition of difference between the cellular discharges relating to novel and non-novel elements of the array. Thus, the task represents an arguably basic aspect of information processing with some leads to mechanisms, although without any guarantee that individual differences in the task bear upon those same mechanisms. On a common-sense appraisal, the formal behavioural element of the task—the correctness of the response given a series of stimulus durations—is similar to inspection time. However, it lacks some of the aspects of inspection time that have made the latter problematic. There is no need for a backward mask, so stimulus–mask interactions do not occur. The target stimulus might appear anywhere in a relatively wide array, so attention must be spread across the whole field rather than on a much smaller area as is the case with inspection time. Because the chance level of responding is 2% in the visual change detection task, correct answers are more informative than in inspection time where chance responding is 50%.

Deary *et al.* (1997) argued that the principal shared aspect of inspection time and visual change detection was the need to make a correct decision based upon briefly presented visual information. They used a further task, called visual movement detection, which resembled visual change detection in all aspects except that the one of the elements of the initial array made a small lateral movement after the stimulus onset asynchrony. Their hypothesis was that a latent trait from these three tasks would correlate with psychometric intelligence. This hypothesis means that non-shared aspects of the tasks, such as specific strategies, are confined to the task-specific residual variance and are hypothesized not to be related to psychometric intelligence. So far, the idea was to take tasks that shared just the key ingredient of inspection time and to make them as different as possible in other aspects. However, it is not possible ever to rule out the possibility that some other, perhaps more general, aspect of each of the tasks might be shared and account for the correlation with psychometric intelligence. Therefore, it is necessary also to try to find a task that replicates many of the ingredients of the target task, but which lacks only that ingredient thought to be responsible for the correlation with psychometric intelligence. Deary *et al.* (1997) chose visual contrast sensitivity. This is a two-alternative forced choice task in which subjects chose which of two stimuli was a grating. The gratings had different levels of contrast and performance on the task was well described as a simple function of the contrast level. The important aspect of difference with inspection time and visual change detection was that this task had no stimulus duration limits; subjects were allowed to inspect the stimuli for as long as they wanted.

Table 7.2 shows the correlations obtained in the study (Deary *et al.* 1997). As indicated in other studies, inspection time correlates at lower levels with verbal rather than with non-verbal psychometric intelligence tasks. The visual change- and movement-detection tasks have similar patterns of correlation with psychometric intelligence. Contrast sensitivity has no significant correlations with psychometric intelligence, showing an especially disparate correlation with the non-verbal part of the Alice Heim 4 test. The three visual tasks with stimulus duration limitations have high inter-correlations, and none is significantly correlated with contrast sensitivity. A structural equation model of these associations is shown in Fig. 7.8. There is a correlation of 0.46 between the two latent, general factors, one loading highly on the three visual processing tests and one loading on all three psychometric tests. There is an additional loading (0.40) from the latent trait of the visual processing tests to the non-verbal section of the Alice Heim task. Contrast sensitivity does not appear in the model because it does not correlate significantly with any of the other measured variables. Thus whatever it is about inspection time that correlates with psychometric intelligence, it shares with visual change- and movement-detection but not with contrast sensitivity. One candidate for the key ingredient could be the need to make decisions based upon briefly presented information. Other possibilities can no doubt be suggested. However, this modestly-powered study does offer one way forward in picking out the meaning of the correlation between inspection time and psychometric intelligence, by exploring the latent characteristics of sensory processing tasks that mediate the correlation between the visual tasks and the factors extracted from psychometric tests.

AUDITORY INFORMATION PROCESSING

So-called auditory inspection time: rationale and results

It is reasonable to ask whether temporal limitations of processing information might be found in sensory systems other than vision, and whether individual differences in these limitations correlate significantly with visual inspection time differences and psychometric intelligence. There is little literature on attempts to construct information processing tasks in the auditory domain. Although such tasks were originally called auditory 'inspection time' tasks, this title was unwise, because it appears to assume that the limitation in processing is analogous to that tapped by visual inspection time tasks. In fact, the evidence for the association between visual and auditory 'inspection time' tests is still meagre, and it is wiser to address the tasks as auditory processing tasks.

Brand and Deary (1982) devised an 'auditory inspection time' task. Subjects listened to two consecutive square-wave tones, one of 770 Hz and one of 880 Hz. Their task was to state the order (high–low or low–high) of the two tones. White noise was used as a forward and backward mask. The duration of the tones to be compared was always identical, and was varied between 100 and 2.7 ms. Thus, the idea was to discover the stimulus duration that the subject required to make a correct (to some criterion) decision about relative pitch. The study was very small ($n = 13$) and correlations between auditory processing ability and the Mill Hill and Raven's Matrices tests were significant only when two

Table 7.2 Correlations ($n = 65$) among psychometric tests and visual processing tests from Deary et al. (1997)

	NART	AH4 verbal and numerical	AH4 non-verbal	Inspection time	Visual change detection	Visual movement detection
AH4 verbal and numerical	0.71***					
AH4 non-verbal	0.58***	0.67***				
Inspection time	0.28*	0.36**	0.45***			
Visual change detection	0.22	0.31*	0.52***	0.40***		
Visual movement detection	0.18	0.36**	0.49***	0.47***	0.64***	
Contrast sensitivity	0.11	0.22	0.04	0.01	0.05	0.10

NART, National Adult Reading Test; AH4, Alice Heim 4 test.
* $p < 0.05$; ** $p < 0.01$; *** $p < 0.001$.

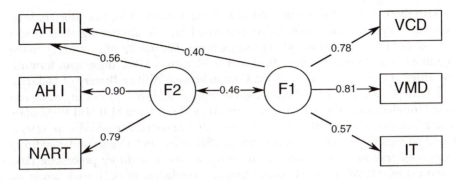

Fig. 7.8 Structural model of the associations between three psychometric ability test scores and three visual information processing tasks. The psychometric tests are: Alice Heim 4 Part I (AH I; verbal and numerical), Alice Heim 4 Part II (AH II; diagrammatic), and the National Adult Reading Test (NART). The visual processing tasks are visual change detection (VCD), visual movement detection (VMD), and inspection time (IT). Not shown here is a test of contrast sensitivity, which had no significant correlations with the other visual processing tasks or the psychometric intelligence test scores. F2 is a general latent trait from the three psychometric tests and F1 is a general latent trait from the three visual processing tasks. Note that associations between the visual processing tests and the psychometric tests occur at the level of the latent traits and not the manifest variables. Redrawn from Deary *et al.* (1997).

people with mental handicaps were included in the analyses. Some aspects of the auditory processing task were improved later. White noise proved an ineffective backward mask. Using pitch discrimination as the basis for the task was non-ideal, as many normal adults are unable, even at longer durations, to discriminate reliably between tones of markedly different pitch.

Irwin (1984) constructed an auditory task closely resembling Brand and Deary's (1982). Tones of 770 Hz and 880 Hz were played consecutively, one second apart, and the subjects—49 children—had to state which of the tones came first. Estimates of auditory processing threshold correlated at −0.23 and −0.32 with Raven's Matrices and the Mill Hill Vocabulary Scale, respectively. The children with better-ability test scores could make correct decisions on the basis of shorter stimulus durations. Problems of using pitch discrimination were evident. The mean of the group's auditory processing thresholds was 195 ms, the standard deviation was 340 ms, and the median was 16 ms. Thus, a substantial minority of people have undue problems in making even 'easy' pitch discriminations. Whereas Brand and Deary chose to omit those who did not achieve a predetermined pitch discrimination criterion, Irwin included all subjects. The former procedure takes the view that, if one allows into the analysis only those who can easily make the pitch discrimination at very long durations (in the same way that one would only allow people of good vision to proceed in a visual inspection time task), the duration of the stimulus must be the main ingredient of correct responding. The latter decision allows for the possibility that the ability to make pitch discriminations *per se* is related to speed of auditory processing and that this might also be related to psychometric intelligence (cf. Deary 1994*a*).

Nettelbeck *et al.* (1986) improved Brand and Deary's (1982) auditory task by devising a new masking sound that comprised rapidly alternating short bursts (15 ms) of both stimulus sounds and white noise. Testing 29 subjects, they found significant correlations between 0.33 and 0.38 with RAPM, digit span forward, and three out of nine subtests of the Comprehensive Ability Battery of Hakstian and Cattell. Deary *et al.* (1989*a*) used a similar auditory processing task and found correlations in the region of 0.3 with Alice Heim 5 and Mill Hill Vocabulary scores, but not with RAPM scores, in university students. Langsford *et al.* (1994) found no significant association between RAPM scores and a very similar auditory processing task in 78 students. Again, using a similar auditory processing task, Olsson *et al.* (1998) found a non-significant correlation of 0.21 with scores on RAPM. Deary *et al.* (1989*b*) reported a correlation of 0.39 between auditory information processing and university students' scores on the Alice Heim 6 test.

Whereas Nettelbeck *et al.* (1986) had included all subjects and used an adaptive staircase psychophysical procedure, Deary *et al.* (1989*a,b*) tended to pre-screen subjects and omit those with poor pitch discrimination. The idea behind this latter approach was to minimize variance in the sample due to pitch discrimination ability and to maximize variance due to temporal processing. The part played by pitch discrimination will be discussed further below. In a later study without omitting subjects on the basis of pitch discrimination screening, Deary (1994*b*) reported a correlation of just over 0.4 between auditory information processing and Mill Hill and Raven IQ scores in 108 13-year-old schoolchildren.

The six studies to date that have used similar auditory processing tasks (so-called auditory inspection time) are summarized in Table 7.3. Of the four studies with adults, only one (Nettelbeck *et al.* 1986) found an association between RAPM and auditory processing that was above 0.3. Two (Deary *et al.* 1989*a*; Langsford *et al.* 1994) are near to zero. Deary's studies with the Alice Heim test found correlations around 0.3. Of the four studies using adults, three are based wholly, and one substantially, on university students with a high mean and restricted range of ability scores. The two reports on schoolchildren (the same subjects 2 years apart) report correlations between 0.2 and 0.4. Thus, the present research is meagre and based on non-normal samples of the population.

For two reasons it is important to find out whether the ability to score well on the so-called auditory inspection time test depends on pitch discrimination ability. First, if pitch discrimination differences account for variance in the auditory task then speed of auditory processing might not be the sole construct in test scores as envisaged by inspection time theory. Second, there is a revival of Galton's suggestion that sensory discrimination correlates significantly with psychometric intelligence (Deary 1994*a*). The studies in Table 7.3 agree that, when subjects are not screened for the ability to perform the auditory processing tasks at the longer durations, the association between auditory processing and pitch discrimination is about 0.6. The correlation between auditory 'inspection time' and pitch discrimination falls considerably if the subjects included in the analyses are only those able to perform the auditory discrimination task at stimulus durations of around 200 ms. Table 7.3 shows that there is a trade-off. Being

Table 7.3 Summary of studies examining associations among tests of auditory discrimination and psychometric intelligence

Study	Ability test	Psychometric intelligence–AIT correlation (n)	AIT–pitch discrimination correlation	Psychometric intelligence–pitch discrimination correlation	% subjects omitted by pitch discrimination screening	AIT–VIT correlation	Comment
Nettelbeck et al. (1986)	RAPM	0.38 (29)	No pitch discrimination reported	–	–	0.39	Young adults, 40% graduates
Deary et al. (1989a)	RAPM Mill Hill Alice Heim 5	−0.05 (80) 0.27 (80) 0.31 (40)	No pitch discrimination reported	–	33	0.20, 0.24, 0.53 for three different VIT tests	Psychology students
Deary et al. (1989b)	Expt 1: Alice Heim 6	0.39 (34)	0.20	−0.08	42		Expt 1: psychology students
	Expt 2: RSPM Mill Hill	0.26 (53)	0.26	0.10	55	Not done	Expt 2: 11-year-old schoolchildren
Deary (1994b)	RSPM Mill Hill	0.41 (108) 0.42 (108)	0.60	0.34 0.29	None	Not done	13-year-old schoolchildren
Langsford et al. (1994)	RAPM Verbal reasoning	Near-zero (78) Near-zero (78)	0.55	−0.12 −0.06	17	0.19	Psychology students
Olsson et al. (1998)	RAPM	0.21 (63)	0.60	0.35	None	Not done	University students

AIT, auditory inspection time; VIT, visual inspection time; RAPM, Raven's Advanced Progressive Matrices; RSPM, Raven's Standard Progressive Matrices.

strict about pitch discrimination ability means omitting many subjects, perhaps over 50% when the testees are children. Being liberal about pitch discrimination means that the discrimination task becomes heavily suffused with pitch discrimination variance. The last comment on Table 7.3 is that there is very little evidence for a strong association between 'inspection time' in the visual modality and that in the auditory domain. There is no present warrant to assume that any known processing construct accounts for a substantial amount of shared variance.

Thus the effect size of the association between auditory processing and the major factors of mental ability in the normal population is unclear. It is unclear whether speeded auditory processing correlates significantly with speed of information processing in the visual modality. By using an auditory discrimination based on pitch difference, unless many subjects are omitted, the supposed duration-determined performance will be contaminated with pitch discrimination ability, which also might relate to psychometric intelligence. As can always be stated, some of these issues can be answered with more and better research. However, there is also a case for agreeing that a move away from the pitch continuum in auditory processing is required (Olsson *et al.* 1998). On the other hand, a large-scale study of auditory processing might involve a number of different stimulus durations and pitch differences and explore the landscape of decision-making performance that such permutations might offer.

Other auditory processing procedures and psychometric intelligence differences

Auditory recognition masking

Auditory processing tasks other than the so-called auditory inspection time tests have been used in studies of psychometric intelligence differences. Raz *et al.* (1983) found correlations above 0.5 between psychometric intelligence and an auditory task first devised by Massaro (1970, 1973). On performing the auditory task, the subject hears a single tone played for 20 ms, a variable interstimulus interval (ISI) follows, and finally a masking tone is heard. The tones differ by about 100 Hz and the judgement is whether the order was 'low–high' or 'high–low.' The measure of performance on the task is the ISI required by the subject to make a criterion level of correct responding. The two studies in the report involved small numbers of students. The authors interpreted their findings in terms of speed of information processing. In a follow-up study, the same researchers tested 36 students and found significant correlations, from 0.37 to 0.44, between a similar auditory backward masking task and scores on Cattell's Culture Fair Intelligence Test (Raz and Willerman 1985). In the auditory task, subjects heard a tone of either 870 or 770 Hz, followed by a silent ISI of between 0 and 480 ms, and finally a masking tone of 820 Hz. The target tones lasted for 10, 13, or 20 ms.

The repetition test

The 'repetition test' was devised by Tallal and Piercy (1973) to assess 'speed of auditory processing'. Subjects state which of four possible combinations (high–low, low–high, low–low, high–high) of two tones were played. The tones were markedly different in pitch (100 Hz versus 305 Hz). The tone duration and ISI were varied by Tallal and Piercy who discovered that people with developmental aphasia could not perceive 'auditory information at a normal rate' (p. 389). Saccuzzo *et al.* (1986) examined this auditory task in addition to visual processing, Scholastic Aptitude Test scores, and psychometric intelligence in 96 students. The mean of four correlations between two auditory processing measures and two visual inspection time variables was 0.21 ($p < 0.05$). Freshman-grade point average and scores on the repetition test (with the shorter ISI) correlated 0.23 and 0.25, although the correlations with two psychometric tests and high-school-grade point average were non-significant. They found that reaction time and visual and auditory processing measures loaded together with psychometric intelligence scores on a second-order factor, and emphasized the existence of task-specific as well as general mental speed variance in the experimental tests.

The Raz task

In what is hereinafter named the 'Raz task' subjects hear two tones, each lasting for 20 ms and separated by a silent gap of 850 ms. The tones differ in pitch and the subject is asked to state whether the higher of the tones came first or second. An adaptive psychophysical procedure is used to discover the pitch difference at which the subject can make decisions at a predetermined level of correctness. The tones begin by being 100 Hz apart, and some subjects can achieve the criterion when the difference descends to only 2 or 3 Hz. When Raz *et al.* (1987) first used the test they constructed stimuli with two different onset and offset ramp values, of 1 ms and 9 ms. In a small ($n = 25$) study of university students the two different versions of the RAZ task correlated at 0.47 and 0.54 (both $p < 0.05$) with Cattell's Culture Fair test scores. A second experiment replicated the first, with a correlation of 0.52. These authors then tested the hypothesis that psychometric intelligence might correlate significantly with any novel, non-entrenched task. They devised a signal detection task in which subjects had to listen to two consecutive observation periods, separated by a gap of 500 ms. In one of the periods there was a 1000 Hz tone burst of 20 ms duration. Signal detection thresholds were measured in three different conditions. There was no significant correlation between these thresholds and psychometric intelligence.

This paper was a small study, but its implications are powerful. After their earlier two papers (Raz *et al.* 1983; Raz and Willerman 1985) Raz and Willerman suggested that speed of auditory processing was the latent construct correlating with psychometric intelligence. The 1987 report saw them reorienting to the construct of 'fidelity of stimulus representation'. They suggested that the Raz task imposed few temporal processing constraints. Instead, it tapped differences in fine perceptual resolution. Moreover, because their signal detection task was also a difficult decision task but did not correlate significantly with psychometric intelligence, they concluded that general factors such as adaptation to the laboratory setting, motivation, and distractibility were not the constructs that caused the correlation between auditory processing and psychometric intelligence. Raz *et al.* (1987) thought that choosing definitively between the constructs of 'speed of processing' and 'fidelity of stimulus representation' was not possible using backward-masking techniques. However, they preferred the latter construct as the more basic factor in causing the correlation:

> The resolution of a system and its rate of information processing are intimately related. Under time constraints the system with lower need for external signal redundancy will respond faster than a noisy system, but this does not imply that the system actually processes information at a faster rate in terms of signal transmission velocity. Given the results of our experiments, the quality of signal representation rather than speed of processing may be the key feature of an intelligent brain. (p. 208)

Deary (1994*b*) argued in response that it was equally tenable to view the individual differences in pitch discrimination in the Raz task—involving stimuli of only 20 ms duration—as caused by more basic differences in some form of speed of processing, along the lines of the accumulator model of Vickers. He examined the associations among the Raz task, the auditory inspection time task, and the Seashore pitch discrimination task and their associations with psychometric intelligence. The subjects were just over 100 schoolchildren of average age 13.7 years (SD = 0.38 years). Deary argued that the tests varied along two dimensions of difficulty: temporal aspects and pitch discrimination aspects. All three auditory tasks required subjects to state the temporal order (high–low or low–high) of two consecutively played tones. The auditory 'inspection time' task used a constant large difference in frequency and varied stimulus duration. The Seashore pitch discrimination task varied pitch difference between the tone pairs and used a constant, long stimulus duration. The Raz task had a constant short stimulus duration and varied the pitch difference between the target tones.

The correlations among the three auditory processing tasks were high, from 0.60 to 0.75 (Table 7.4; Deary 1994*b*). Correlations between auditory 'inspection times' and the Raz task and psychometric intelligence were just over 0.4. Correlations between the Seashore pitch discrimination test and psychometric intelligence were around 0.3. The three auditory tasks were then separated in a two-factor solution, with auditory inspection time having a very high loading on one factor and the Seashore test loading highly on the other. The Raz test had intermediate loadings on both. A confirmatory factor analysis showed that the auditory 'inspection time'-dominated factor (speed of processing?) had higher associations with psychometric intelligence scores than the Seashore-dominated factor (pitch discrimination?). This solution was based on the hypothesis that the

Table 7.4 Correlations among psychometric intelligence and three auditory processing tests in 108 13-year-old schoolchildren (from Deary 1994*b*)

	Auditory inspection time score	Log of Raz test score	Seashore test score	Mill Hill Vocabulary IQ
Log of Raz test score	0.75**			
Seashore test score	0.60**	0.69**		
Mill Hill Vocabulary IQ	0.42**	0.40**	0.29*	
Raven's Progressive Matrices IQ	0.41**	0.44**	0.34**	0.39**

For correlations involving the Raz test, $n = 107$.
* $p < 0.01$; ** $p < 0.001$.

speed and pitch requirements of the three auditory processing tasks might be separated. However, by letting the data speak for themselves, a more economical solution to these data has been offered (Fig. 7.9; Deary 1999). In this model the three auditory tasks all have high loadings on a single latent trait. Scores from the three psychometric intelligence tests load on another, single latent trait. The correlation between the two latent traits is 0.64.

As ever, the difficulty lies in interpreting the correlation. The results tell us that there is something general from the three auditory processing tasks that correlates with something general from the three psychometric intelligence tasks. Therefore, one can rule out idiosyncratic aspects of either the auditory tests or the psychometric tests that lead to an artefactual correlation. This then leads to two quite distinct possibilities. First, that there is some fairly low-level aspect of sensory processing that underpins some of the variance in psychometric intelligence. Second, that the same high-level factors account for the correlation:

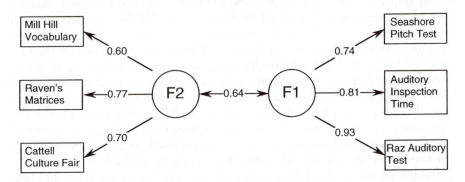

Fig. 7.9 Structural model of the associations between three psychometric ability test scores and three auditory information processing tasks. F2 is a latent trait from the three psychometric tests. F1 is a latent trait from the three auditory processing tests. Although the auditory processing tasks were designed to assess, with varying proportions, speed of processing and pitch discrimination, it is a general factor from the auditory tasks that correlated with the general factor from the psychometric test scores. Redrawn from Deary (1999).

maintenance of interest in the tasks, understanding of and willingness to go along with instructions, and so forth. This latter hypothesis is perhaps more tenable in a group of 13-year-old schoolchildren among whom such general factors might operate more strongly. Note, however, that the single latent trait model does not provide a good fit to the data used to provide the model in Fig. 7.9. It is ironic that the use of these psychometric and psychophysical tests in the 1990s, put through the analytic mangle of structural equation modelling, lead to the two widely opposed, though not exclusive, hypotheses that Spearman (1904) and Thorndike *et al.* (1909) contested 90 years earlier. Deary (1999), in agreement with Raz *et al.* (1987), concluded that tests at the psychophysical level show significant correlations with mental ability test scores, but that the understanding of such correlations must appeal to lower levels of reduction. Some progress in this reduction is discussed in Chapter 9 when the event-related potentials of auditory and visual processing tasks are examined.

Developments in so-called auditory inspection time

Olsson *et al.* (1998) reckoned that the problems with pitch discrimination as the basis for 'auditory inspection time' were sufficient to urge a move to a new sensory continuum. They cited the fact that pitch discrimination is correlated with both 'auditory inspection time' and psychometric intelligence. Thus the discrimination fails to meet Vickers' criterion of being an easy discrimination for which the only limitation is one of speed of processing. Researchers must omit a large minority of normal subjects to exclude people with pitch discrimination problems in auditory 'inspection time'. This limits severely the general application of auditory 'inspection time' as a tool for investigating the bases of psychometric intelligence. Olsson and colleagues used loudness instead of pitch discrimination as the sensory continuum for the basis of a new auditory 'inspection time' task. Among their 63 undergraduates they found the following correlations with RAPM: pitch discrimination = 0.35 ($p < 0.01$), loudness discrimination = 0.16 (ns), pitch-based auditory inspection time = 0.21 (ns), and loudness-based auditory inspection time = 0.36 ($p < 0.01$). Pitch discrimination had a high correlation with pitch-based auditory inspection time—there was no screening for pitch discrimination ability—and loudness discrimination but not loudness-based auditory inspection time. The study used a non-ideal subject pool and was too small for the key correlations to be significantly different. Nevertheless, the use of a sensory continuum that most people find easy to discriminate would be an advantage and more work on loudness as a continuum would be valuable.

Another continuum used as the basis for auditory 'inspection time' discriminations is spatial localization (Parker *et al.*, 1999). Again, these authors worried over the large number of subjects omitted from many studies of auditory inspection time because of poor pitch discrimination. In their novel task, subjects heard identical tones in their right and left ears. The tones differed only in phase. Using headphones, this produces a dichotic phantom and the impression is that of a single tone originating from the left or right of the midline, depending on the phase of the two tones. The actual tones were 450 Hz sine waves with a 40° phase shift. This target tone was varied in duration and was backward masked with a pair of tones delivered in-phase to both ears, which gives the impression of a single midline tone. Among a group of 67 students the correlation between spatial auditory inspection time and a modified Raven's Matrices test was 0.37 ($p < 0.01$). There was no significant association with a vocabulary test. In a second study among 41 students there was again a significant association between spatial localization-based auditory 'inspection time' and Raven scores. A standard visual inspection time test had a significant association with Raven scores in the same group, and the visual and auditory 'inspection time' tests correlated significantly ($r = 0.45$, $p < 0.01$).

The test of basic auditory capabilities

The test of basic auditory capabilities (TBAC) is a battery of auditory tests based upon a factor analysis of the dimensions of auditory abilities (Johnson *et al.* 1987). Each of the tasks within the battery is a forced-choice two-alternative discrimination test (in fact, the discrimination format is same–same–different versus same–different–same). Subjects hear a stimulus and must decide whether the next two stimuli follow the pattern same–different or different–same with respect to the first stimulus. The discrimination within each test is presented at about six levels of difficulty. The first task is based on pitch discrimination. The target tone is 1 kHz, 75 dB SPL, 250 ms, and the pitch difference of the 'different' tone ranges from 2 to 256 Hz. The second task is based on loudness discrimination, and the third on duration. The fourth test examines rhythm discrimination in a six-pulse sequence. The fifth test asks the listener to detect a present or missing fifth tone in a nine-tone sequence. The sixth test asks the listener to detect the temporal order of two tones of 550 Hz and 710 Hz. The tones are preceded and followed with 625 Hz tones. There is no gap between the tones, making this task similar to the original auditory inspection time test. The seventh test is similar to the sixth but the discrimination is based upon consonant–vowel complexes rather than simple tones. The eighth test involves discriminating nonsense syllables.

Watson (1991) found significant associations between scores on TBAC subtests and psychometric intelligence and academic aptitude. Among 52 undergraduates the mathematics score from the scholastic aptitude test (SAT) correlated significantly and between 0.30 and 0.42 with six of the eight TBAC tests. The exceptions were the discrimination of pulse trains (test 4) and the nonsense syllable test (test 8). The verbal score from the SAT had only one small significant association with the TBAC tests. Watson also examined 24 reading- or mathematics-disabled undergraduates. In this group the SAT and WAIS-R scores had significant correlations with the single-tone discrimination tasks (tasks 1–3) of the TBAC. Correlations were frequently greater than 0.5. Watson reckoned that, whereas the correlations between psychometric intelligence and the tonal pattern discrimination tasks of the TBAC might have a basis in working memory, the correlations with single-tone tasks require another explanation. For this she appealed to the ideas of Raz *et al.* (1987) who had speculated that the correlation between low-level auditory processing and intelligence might be caused by better signal representation and/or sensory resolution on the part of people with higher psychometric intelligence. In a later study Watson and Miller (1993) reported correlations between TBAC tests and Cattell Culture Fair IQ scores on 94 undergraduates, 24 of whom were learning disabled. Correlations ranged from 0.13 to 0.37 with a mean of 0.26. The non-significant correlations were with the pitch test (test 1) and the pulse train test (test 4), i.e. not the same pattern as in the previous studies. The highest correlation between non-syllable-based TBAC tests and psychometric intelligence was with tone duration discrimination (0.35).

Back to sensory discrimination?

In the modern era authors of reports on psychometric intelligence and auditory processing have expressed surprise that the results obtained appear to hark back to Spearman's (1904) original discovery of an association between sensory discrimination and higher mental abilities (e.g. Raz *et al.* 1987; Watson 1991; Deary 1994*a,b*). It is probably safe to conclude that Spearman got it right with respect to his empirical finding of a modest association, although he exaggerated the size of the effect (to unity) by overcorrecting. There might even be an association with tactile discrimination (Li *et al.* 1998). With regard to understanding the reason for such a correlation we have not come much further than Spearman. The studies described above do not form a large corpus, they test smallish numbers of subjects who are often undergraduates, they employ a range of tasks often without theoretical foundation, and they are rarely the subject of replication. Whereas it is possible to conclude that there is a correlation between simple-seeming auditory processing and psychometric intelligence, it would be premature to state which of the auditory continua produces the correlation. The pitch continuum produces correlations but the interplay between pitch discrimination and temporal factors has not been resolved. Loudness, spatial localization, and duration all exist as candidates for exploitation in correlational studies.

In addition to discovering which auditory processing tests correlate significantly with which psychometric intelligence tests, there is the question of which auditory processing tests correlate with each other. Deary (1999; reanalysing data from Deary 1994*b*) found that pitch-based auditory inspection time, Seashore pitch discrimination, and the Raz task were highly intercorrelated and extracted a single latent trait from the three. Data from the 94 undergraduates in Watson and Miller's (1993) study of the TBAC were reanalysed specially for this chapter. The first six TBAC tests, those based on tones, are highly interrelated, with correlations ranging from 0.35 to 0.65 with a mean of 0.48. Applying principal components analysis for data reduction reveals only one factor—the second eigenvalue is 0.76—accounting for 57.2% of the total variance. There is also some evidence of redundancy among auditory processing measures in the study of Olsson *et al.* (1998). This evidence points to the need for a validated structure of sensory processing tasks as well as psychometric tests. The name given to, say, each auditory processing test—pitch discrimination, duration discrimination, inspection time, and so forth—might lead falsely to an assumption that a specific process is being measured. It is potentially all the more convincing because the task's simplicity could betoken its tapping a single brain process. Just as proved necessary for psychometric tests, there must be a multivariate understanding of sensory processing tests. In addition, there must be attempts to understand them in more basic terms. This will be addressed with respect to physiological correlates and effects on auditory processing in Chapter 9.

CONCLUSION: DON'T QUOTE ME ON THIS . . .

It is still hard to shake off the surprise when one finds that apparently simple tasks have significant correlations with psychometric intelligence, and the visual inspection time task is the best example. However, a hard-headed outsider, while admitting that the correlation between visual inspection time and psychometric intelligence is interesting-looking, would be prone to ask some telling questions. A quarter of a century after the correlation between inspection time and psychometric intelligence differences was discovered, why have there been so few studies on representative population samples? Why has there been no study with a decent, factor-referenced battery of mental ability tests? Why are there still so many different methods of testing inspection time, some on computer monitor screens known to be suboptimal? Why has there been no decent study comparing differences on visual and auditory 'inspection time' tests? Why do people studying inspection time act, to a large extent, as if the rest of backward masking and perception research did not exist? The critic might proceed to ask: 'if inspection time is among the "simpler" tasks that correlate significantly with psychometric intelligence, and you still do not have a tractable account of its basic processing characteristics, what hope is there for giving a construct-validated account of more complex tasks, such as reaction time procedures?' 'The interest in R. J. Sternberg's components of intelligence seems to have ground to a halt', the critic continues, 'the studies of the Hick reaction time have remained uninformative and, if inspection time is the most-studied procedure/construct and has achieved so little, is there any realistic hope for the growth of this area?' Studies on inspection time are conducted by relatively few laboratories, with no large-scale, dedicated teams. The early years of intelligence saw the study of mechanisms of psychometric intelligence differences fade away after the successful studies of Spearman (1904) and Burt (1909–1910) and there is no guarantee against this happening once more. It begins to seem more likely that discovering the origins of individual differences in psychometric intelligence is not a mandatory task for research. It is not one of the research community's standing orders, unlike discovering the causes of cancers or the origins of the universe. With luck, the origins of psychometric intelligence differences might occur as a sideline to those who are investigating the biological bases of brain functions.

A more positive spin on the above findings would be to emphasize the robustness of the medium effect size that associates psychometric intelligence and visual inspection time, despite their very different levels of complexity. Note, however, that visual inspection time might correlate more strongly with a group factor of intelligence than with g (Deary and Crawford 1998). Moreover, there are many lines of fruitful investigation leading on from the correlation and inquiring about the mechanisms of the association. Several confounding variables, suggested as factors that might explain away the association, are refuted. Limited longitudinal research with the auditory 'inspection time' task suggests that sensory processing differences might be a partial cause of later psychometric intelligence differences rather than the reverse (Deary 1995a). Research into the development and ageing of cognitive abilities has put speed of information processing to the fore, and inspection time can take a seat at that empirical table (Chapter 8). Psychophysiological studies combining psychometric intelligence, inspection time, and event-related potentials are producing some replicated findings concerning the brain mechanisms underpinning ability test score and inspection time differences (Chapter 9). The retrenchment concerning the original theory of inspection time performance has produced more psychophysical research and a move away from a myopic concern with inspection time to a broader view of how perceptual constructs relate to psychometric intelligence differences. This refreshing change notwithstanding, inspection time remains unique in the field for its combination of (a) relatively high level of correlation with ability test scores, (b) task simplicity, and (c) promise of theoretical tractability. The field now possesses a number of visual and auditory processing tasks that correlate significantly with psychometric intelligence (Deary 1999). Future success of the field depends upon validating the theory behind the processing tasks, and building a mechanism for the association with mental ability test scores. There is no lasting credibility in pretending, by hand-waving (Deary [1995a] remonstrated with those who used rational argument to this end), that these jobs are anywhere near to being completed.

8 Wisdom from the ages

Slowing of speed of information processing is cognitive ageing!?

SUMMARY

Research into age-related changes in cognitive abilities proceeds largely independently of mainstream research into the information processing bases of human psychometric intelligence differences. Much research into ageing concerns problems of study design and the interpretation of results. Cross-sectional, longitudinal, and cross-sequential designs all contribute to an understanding of the typical and the range of changes that humans can expect from their cognitive functions with each subsequent decade. Among the more useful concepts are those of fluid and crystallized intelligence: put crudely, the former ages poorly and the latter well. Beyond merely describing the different age-related changes of different mental abilities, there is an interest in those factors that are associated with good and poor cognitive ageing. Some such factors are described. This much, though, is general background. The interest for this book is the suggestion that central to cognitive ageing is a slowing of some central nervous system speed of information processing. Evidence for this hypothesis comes from different approaches, but these are found wanting with regard to the specification of their underlying mechanisms. Sensory acuity is related to cognitive ageing, a finding that forces consideration beyond processing speed with regard to the causes of age-related cognitive decrements.

COGNITIVE AGEING: THE BASICS

Before discussing those theories of cognitive ageing that invoke some speed-of-information processing concepts, some of the basic findings in cognitive ageing are described. Studying the stability of psychometric intelligence can mean at least two things. It can mean the stability of individual differences; these were discussed in Chapter 1. Another meaning is the stability of mean levels of mental ability; whether, as a group, people score better or worse on mental ability tests as they grow older. This question quickly becomes rather complicated. There are likely to be different ageing patterns for different psychometric abilities, and people might well differ in their individual ageing patterns for the different abilities. The simplest place to begin is with the examination of some large cross-sectional studies.

Cross-sectional studies

The Wechsler Adult Intelligence Scale-Revised (WAIS-R) provides information on the different raw scores obtained by people of different chronological ages.

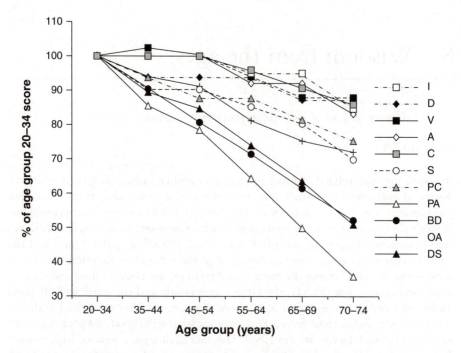

Fig. 8.1 The percentage of the score of 20–34-year-olds needed on the subtests of the Wechsler Adult Intelligence Scale-Revised to achieve a score that is the mean for the respective age group. Thus, from these cross-sectional data, people's scores mostly decline with age. Note the variability, however, in age-related changes for the different subtests. Information (I), comprehension (C), digit span (D), Arithmetic (A) and vocabulary (V), all verbal subtests, hold up well with age. On the other hand, digit symbol (DS), block design (BD), and picture arrangement (PA), all performance tests, decline more steeply. Similarities (S), picture completion (PC), and object assembly (OA), one verbal and two performance subtests, respectively, have intermediate ageing slopes.

Sattler (1982) calculated the raw scores that were needed by different age groups to achieve a scaled score of 10. These are shown in Fig. 8.1. The WAIS-R Performance subtests, in general, show steeper age-related declines than do the Verbal subtests. The only exception is the Similarities test. Picture Arrangement, Block Design, and Digit Symbol show especially steep ageing curves. These are timed tests. Four of the verbal tests decline very little, with performance in the oldest group averaging well over 80% of the young adults' mean. These tests that age well are Information, Vocabulary, Arithmetic, and Comprehension, mostly involving the recall of stored knowledge and strategies in an untimed setting. Sattler commented on these data as follows:

> Fluid intelligence, as measured by the Performance Scale tests, shows more of a decline with age than crystallized intelligence, as measured by the Verbal scales. (p. 785)

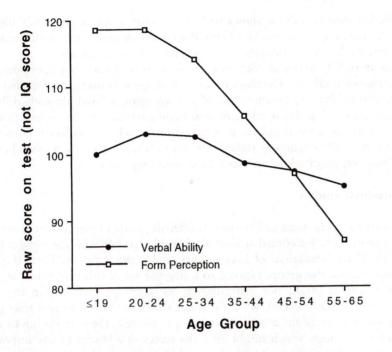

Fig. 8.2 Cross-sectional changes with age for form perception and verbal ability subtests of the General Aptitude Test battery. Each data point contains around 1000 to over 4000 subjects. Data taken from Avolio and Waldman (1994).

The ideas of fluid and crystallized intelligence were not evoked specifically to capture the differences between tests in cognitive ageing. Nevertheless, the mapping between these two concepts and cognitive ageing is rather good (Cattell 1998). Also, in one of the keynote papers on fluid and crystallized intelligences, Horn and Cattell (1966) remarked upon a tendency for primary abilities related to fluid intelligence to be negatively correlated with age, and for primaries associated with crystallized intelligence to be positively correlated with age. Their subjects were young adults, however, without much real 'ageing'.

More evidence along the same lines comes from the data collected between 1970 and 1984 by the US Employment Service, Department of Labor. Their data comprised test scores from the General Aptitude Test Battery (GATB) on over 25,000 people aged between 16 and 74 years (Avolio and Waldman 1994). The GATB contains nine subtests. The report's authors specifically identified certain of the subtests with crystallized ability—especially vocabulary—and some with fluid ability, such as form perception. They hypothesized that the latter are more likely to be negatively correlated with age. Avolio and Waldman gave full details of the age-related changes for all subtests. Subtests in the GATB were normed to means of 100 and standard deviations of 20. Figure 8.2 illustrates, for white subjects, the differential ageing of the Verbal Ability and Form Perception subtests. The numbers of subjects in each age group range from 968 to 4601.

The Verbal Ability subtest shows little mean change across the adult lifespan from the teens to 65 years. The Form Perception subtest shows a difference of 1.6 standard deviations between the youngest and oldest groups.

Cross-sectional studies are not ideal as methods of discovering age differences in psychological factors. The main reason is that age is perfectly confounded with cohort effects; that is, because each of the age groups lived through different social, medical, educational, and economic events, researchers are not in a position to state that the 20-year-olds in a cross-sectional study can expect to attain the same mental ability scores as today's 60-year-olds when they themselves become 60. Therefore, longitudinal methods have been employed.

Longitudinal studies

Studies that test the same individuals at different points in time have one obvious advantage over cross-sectional studies: they involve people with the same cultural histories. Three limitations of longitudinal studies are apparent. First, they tell us about a particular group, exposed to a singular set of cultural events, and the results might or might not generalize to other groups even within the same country and culture. Second, when the mean scores on a set of mental tests given to the same subjects for a second time are examined, there is the problem of practice on the tests which might alter the scores in addition to any improving or impairing effects of age. Third, there might be non-random dropout from the study such that subjects seen at waves after the first test might become increasingly non-representative of the original population. For example, if more able subjects tend to return for subsequent test waves, the conclusions about cognitive ageing might be unduly optimistic. Caveats aside for the moment, there are some impressive longitudinal studies of mental ability differences.

Some longitudinal studies are epic, involving follow-up epochs counted in decades. Some involve the mass ability testing that took place as a result of the two World Wars. Such was Owens' (1959, 1966) study, in which 129 male college freshmen (many engineers among them) sat the Army Alpha examination in 1919 at age 19 years. They were followed up in 1949–50 at age 50, and again in 1961–62 at age 61. Test scores between 19 and 50 years were characterized by stability of mean levels (Owens 1959). Changes from age 50 to age 61 were (in standard deviation units): verbal component = −0.03 (ns); numerical component = −0.20 ($p < 0.01$); reasoning component = 0.01 (ns). These results suggest much stability in these abilities up to age 61, but Owens discussed the problem of separating the changes in test scores that might be due to culture and those that might be considered intrinsic age changes. This separation was attempted via a quasi-experimental design in which the original cohort was compared with 101 freshmen from the same institution tested in 1961–62. When Owens (1966) compared the scores of the two groups of 19-year-olds (one from 1919 and one from 1961–62) he found what he called 'cultural' changes in six of the eight subtests of the Army Alpha. That is, the freshmen in 1961–62 had higher scores than those tested in 1919. This is a relatively early instance of the so-called

Flynn effect (Flynn 1987, 1999) in which absolute scores on mental tests have been rising with each subsequent generation. In fact, the possibility of such changes was recognized fairly early in the history of mental testing (Kuhlen 1940). Although psychologists today argue about whether the generational rises in mental ability test scores are intrinsic increases in people's mental abilities, perhaps due to better nutrition (Lynn 1990), or a cultural artefact, typically attributed to our becoming more familiar with test items (see Neisser 1998), Owens took the straightforward line that differences between the freshmen in 1919 and 1961–62 were due to cultural factors and should be controlled in order to assess the real changes attributable to age. That done, the following picture emerged (in standard deviation units): verbal ability increased by 0.37 (p < 0.01); numerical ability decreased by 0.18 (p < 0.05); and reasoning decreased by 0.61 (p < 0.01). Owen used Cattell's theory of fluid and crystallized intelligences to interpret these differential changes in cognitive ageing: fluid ability declines with age whereas crystallized ability holds and even increases in some cases.

A later generation, involved in World War II, was tested on a psychometric intelligence test battery and followed-up after a similar interval. Two hundred and sixty Canadian recruits in their 20s sat the Revised Examination 'M' and were tested again after a 40-year interval at an average age of 64.7 years (Schwartzman *et al.* 1987). The Revised Examination 'M' has concurrent validity coefficients of 0.8 with the Army Alpha and 0.72 with Raven's Matrices. It comprises eight subtests which are combined to give verbal, mechanical, and non-verbal scores. The subjects in this study had a wider social class range than those of Owens (1966). Verbal ability was almost identical in mean level across the 40-year gap between tests (ns), mechanical ability rose by about 0.14 standard deviation units (p < 0.01), and non-verbal ability fell by 0.85 units (p < 0.001). The authors found that extra time on the non-verbal sections of the test failed to hoist the scores to World War II levels and concluded that:

> Most of the loss was incurred on the Non-verbal section of the test in the regular timed condition and persisted in the double time extension. Performance speed, therefore, did not appear to be a major factor contributing to the deficit. These results are consistent with previous reports of age-related decrement in the cognitive functions which have been identified as components of 'fluid' intelligence. (p. 252)

In agreement with other studies Schwartzman and colleagues found that vocabulary was especially well preserved with age and that spatial problem solving showed the largest decline. These results persisted when the study rose to over 300 subjects, although only verbal and non-verbal scores were reported (Pushkar Gold *et al.* 1995). The apparent stability of mean levels of verbal ability came about because vocabulary actually increased with age and verbal analogies and arithmetic decreased slightly. In accordance with studies discussed previously, these authors appealed to the ideas of fluid and crystallized intelligence to describe the differences in age-related changes they found. It might be the case that each

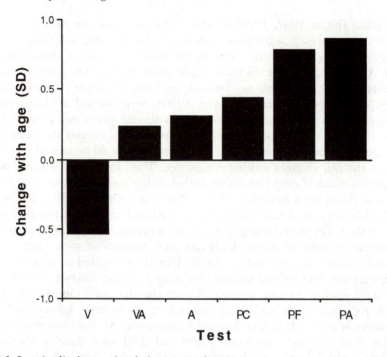

Fig. 8.3 Longitudinal age-related changes in ability test scores from the Concordia study of Canadian World War II veterans tested in their mid-20s and then 40 years later. The tests are: vocabulary (V), verbal analogies (VA), arithmetic (A), picture completion (PC), paper formboard (PF), and picture anomalies (PA). Changes are shown in units of standard deviation: changes below zero are improvements with age; changes greater than zero are declines with age. Data taken from Pushkar Gold *et al.* (1995).

subtest demands a ratio of fluid and crystallized intelligence for completion, because the data from Pushkar Gold and colleagues do not suggest that psychometric tests form an easy dichotomy of fluid (age-declining) and crystallized (age-retaining) tests that is isomorphic with the verbal and non-verbal components; nor do they claim such a thing. Figure 8.3 was drawn from the data in Table 2 of their study and suggests a continuum of tests with respect to their liability to change with age.

A cross-sequential study

The cross-sequential design for studying cognitive ageing includes both cross-sectional and longitudinal aspects and adds the ability to examine cohort effects also. The best-known cross-sequential study of cognitive ageing is the Seattle Longitudinal Study. This has run since 1956 when K. W. Schaie began it as his PhD study. Subjects were members of an HMO (Health Maintenance Organization), aged in years from the 20s to the 80s, broadly representative of US social classes, although underrepresented at the lower end. The design is best

Table 8.1 Design of the Seattle Longitudinal Study

Study waves

1956	1963	1970	1977	1984	1991
S1T1	S1T2	S1T3	S1T4	S1T5	S1T6
(N = 500)	(N = 303)	(N = 162)	(N = 130)	(N = 92)	(N = 71)
	S2T2	S2T3	S2T4	S2T5	S2T6
	(N = 997)	(N = 420)	(N = 337)	(N = 204)	(N = 161)
		S3T3	S3T4	S3T5	S3T6
		(N = 705)	(N = 340)	(N = 225)	(N = 175)
			S4T4	S4T5	S4T6
			(N = 612)	(N = 294)	(N = 201)
				S5T5	S5T6
				(N = 628)	(N = 428)
					S6T6
					(N = 690)

S, sample; T, time of measurement.

understood by referring to Table 8.1. Five hundred subjects were tested on measures of Thurstone's primary mental abilities in 1956. This gives a cross-sectional study of cognitive ageing. They were then followed up every 7 years, providing a longitudinal study. Also, every 7 years, a new cohort was recruited. Therefore, by comparing the diagonal cells in Table 8.1 we can discover whether there are changes in the scores of people meeting the test for the first time, of the same age, but born at different times. This allows measurement of the cohort effect. Additional mental tests, life history data, medical information, and satellite studies have been added since the study's inception. The study is a remarkable and massive achievement and, even though it has generated dozens of reports, there are some excellent summaries of the main findings (Schaie 1989, 1994, 1996). These have been used in collating the following information.

Cross-sectional cognitive data (Schaie 1994) show peaks in youth and accelerating age-related declines for inductive reasoning and spatial orientation. Word fluency shows a steady decline from youth to old age. Verbal meaning and number ability peak in middle adulthood, and verbal meaning shows the greater tendency to decline with old age. These involved single tests for each primary mental ability. In later waves of the Seattle Longitudinal Study multiple markers were included for each ability domain. Using these, arguably better, data there were linear declines from age 25 to age 81 on inductive reasoning, verbal memory, perceptual speed, and spatial orientation. Numerical and verbal ability peaked in early middle age and remained fairly stable until the late-70s.

Summarizing many data, 7-year longitudinal findings using single tests for each primary mental ability indicated stability or some gains in the five primary mental abilities (as conceived by Thurstone) until the 40s, stability until 50–60, and declines on all abilities after age 60. When multiple markers for each test were employed only perceptual speed showed a constant decline from the 20s to the 80s. Most tests showed small improvements up to the 50s and modest though different declines thereafter. The age-related changes in the longitudinal results are confounded with practice effects on the test and perhaps selective attrition. These effects might falsely create or exaggerate the gains after young adulthood and might underestimate declines with age. Schaie (1994) concluded from these data using ideas developed below:

> Much of the late life decline, however, must be attributed to slowing of processing and response speed. When age changes in perceptual speed are [statistically] removed from the other abilities, their magnitude of age decrement is significantly reduced. (p. 308.)

This adumbrates a principal theme of this chapter. Data discussed in later sections insist that there is strong empirical support for the idea that speed of processing might be a source of much of the age-related cognitive decline.

Finally, strong cohort effects were found (Schaie 1994, 1996). These were different for different abilities. When multiple markers were used for mental ability domains there were linear rises in scores across cohorts for inductive reasoning and verbal memory. The last cohort was scoring over one standard deviation higher than the earliest cohort. Other ability domains showed smaller cohort effects, with some described as concave, where cohort scores rose up to the 1920s, plateaued until the 1950s, and then fell.

Concluding from these illustrations sampled from a large body of literature, it is impermissible to talk about monolithic age changes in psychometric intelligence. Fluid abilities, spatial ability, and perceptual speed decline more with age than do crystallized abilities, especially vocabulary. These ability terms are employed merely to corral certain surface characteristics of psychometric tests. A useful pair of parallel constructs is Baltes' (1987) concepts of the 'mechanics' and 'pragmatics' of intelligence. Figure 8.4 shows that Baltes aligns fluid ability with the mechanics of intelligent functioning, indexed by problem solving and memory tasks, and underpinned by the integrity of the central nervous system's basic information processing. Baltes and Horn envisaged fluid ability differences and changes based in the brain's level of efficiency of basic processing mechanisms (Horn and Hofer 1992; Lindenberger and Baltes 1994*a*).

COGNITIVE AGEING: DETERMINANTS OF DIFFERENT TRAJECTORIES

Longitudinal studies show differences in the ageing trajectories of different psychometric tasks. To complicate matters further, there are interindividual differences in the trajectories of individual mental abilities. Some people retain their mental abilities better than others. This matter has attracted more interest in recent years because of the larger absolute number and proportion of people living to

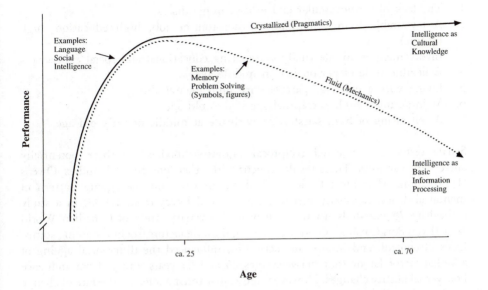

Fig. 8.4 Cartoon of suggested age-related changes in fluid (mechanics) and crystallized (pragmatics) aspects of mental ability. Redrawn from Baltes (1987).

older ages, the burden of care issuing from the larger numbers of people with dementias and cognitive decrements that fall short of frank dementia, and the desire to discover the determinants of cognitive ageing in order to ameliorate its untoward effects on quality of life (Deary 1995*b*; Writing Committee 1996). The most extreme expression of the important influence of cognitive functioning on quality of life is the association between cognitive ability level in old age and mortality; people with higher ability levels live longer (Korten *et al.* 1999).

Research literature on the determinants of differential cognitive ageing is oddly scattered. Relevant studies are almost equally liable to be found in medical, epidemiological, gerontological, and psychometric journals. Studies concerned with pathological cognitive ageing states such as the dementias and those addressing variations within 'healthy cognitive ageing' meet in the grey area of age-associated cognitive impairment (Deary 1995*b*). Established or likely risk factors for Alzheimer's dementia include old age, Down's syndrome, family history, APOE gene status, female sex, head injury, hypertension, and myocardial infarction (Writing Committee 1996). Some of these overlap with the risk factors for non-dementia cognitive decline differences. For example, age, head injury, and hypertension were significant risk factors for cognitive decline in a longitudinal population study of non-demented old people (Luukinen *et al.* 1999).

Schaie's (1994, 1996) cumulative work from the Seattle Longitudinal Study produced a number of putative protective factors with respect to cognitive ageing:

1.   The lack of cardiovascular and other chronic diseases
2.   A favourable living environment (non-routine job, high education, high income)
3.   Involvement in intellectually stimulating educational and social experiences
4.   A flexible style of personality in middle age
5.   Living with a marriage partner with high mental ability
6.   Maintaining a high perceptual speed into old age
7.   A self-rating of high satisfaction with life at middle or early old age.

Schaie tested and rejected reciprocal causation models for these potentially antecedent variables. These results concur with other longitudinal studies. Owens (1966) found that lifestyle factors had an influence on the ageing pattern of mental abilities, especially verbal ability, as did Deary *et al.* (1998) in a study of healthy 75 year-olds. In the Concordia University study of Canadian World War II veterans (Pushkar Gold *et al.* 1995), lifestyle factors (socio-economic status, locus of control, and intellectual activities) influenced the differential ageing of a verbal factor latent trait between ages 25 and 65 years, but did not influence non-verbal ability changes. However, age at first testing affected the rate of change over time, with older people at first testing declining faster. These data were reanalysed by Hultsch *et al.* (1999) who confirmed that socio-economic status affected change in verbal intelligence over time; however, there was no such effect of health or intellectual activities, contrary to the analyses conducted by Pushkar Gold *et al.* (1995). Hultsch *et al.* (1999) reported data from the Victoria Longitudinal Study that provided evidence for the protective effect of intellectual engagement against cognitive decline. Taking part in social activities, too, appears to protect against cognitive decline (Bassuk *et al.* 1999).

   Initial ability level itself might have an influence on the rate of change of ability as people grow older. The idea that 'age is kinder to the initially more able' has a long history (Foster and Taylor 1920), and a review of relevant studies is provided by Deary *et al.* (1998). Cross-sectional studies show little indication of differential decline in mental abilities by initial ability level. There is no such effect in analyses of the WAIS standardization sample (Birren and Morrison 1961) or in other large studies (Orsini *et al.* 1986; Rabbitt 1993). However, Avolio and Waldman (1994) found small but significant interactions between age and job experience for four of the nine subtests of the GATB. Job experience might act as a surrogate for ability, but could also relate to other social and/or medical factors. From the few longitudinal studies that are directly relevant, the strongest interpretation of the evidence is that there might be some small lessening in the rate of decline with age in high-ability people, especially for verbal abilities (Riegel and Riegel 1972; Deary *et al.* 1998). Among other problems in deciding this issue are the statistical problems of regression to mean scores over time (Baltes *et al.* 1972) and the fact that many of the imputed protective factors are highly intercorrelated, making it difficult to tease out the key causal variables for healthy cognitive ageing. This is summarized well in the conclusions from the Concordia study of Canadian World War II veterans:

The results of the study provide some support for an interactive model by rein-forcing the hypothesis that more intellectual, capable, better educated, and socioeconomically advantaged individuals are more likely to develop an engaged lifestyle, which, in turn, helps retain cognitive competence in later life . . . in response to the question of whether the rate of cognitive decline varies with initial level of intelligence, the answer tentatively appears to be yes for verbal intelligence but no for nonverbal intelligence (Pushkar Gold *et al.* 1995, p. 301)

MECHANISMS OF COGNITIVE AGEING: SPEED OF INFORMATION PROCESSING APPROACHES

Important aspects of people's mental abilities decline with old age; some abilities decline more than others, some people decline faster than others, and some of the factors—demographic, social, psychometric, medical, and biological—that might influence the rate of change of cognitive ability with age are known. What are the mechanisms of cognitive ageing and differential cognitive ageing? Are there findings and constructs to explain the life changes in mental abilities? Might any such mech-anisms throw light upon the bases of mental ability differences in other circumstances?

To say that fluid general intelligence declines more with age than does crys-tallized general intelligence is a descriptive statement, not an explanatory account. From what was said in Chapter 1, this is a fact that needs explaining, because psychometric abilities are not necessarily, or even probably, isomorphic with brain processes, whatever level of description is chosen. In Chapter 9 there are the beginnings of a possible biological account of differential cognitive ageing, but in what follows the focus is on some remarkable findings from cognitive ageing that have taken an information processing approach that lies somewhere between psychometrics and biology in the reductionistic ladder.

Cognitive abilities do not age independently

Asked simply: do those cognitive abilities that decline with age all decline together? And is this because some single general processing system is declining? On the other hand, do the results suggest that there are independent rates of decline for different mental abilities; is there a number of independent brain mechanisms with their own, uncorrelated, rates of decline? Rabbitt (1992) reviewed relevant data and made two broad conclusions. First, that memory does not decline independently of changes in performance-type psychometric intelli-gence ability, so that memory changes are not entirely the result of specific memory processes changing with increasing age. Second, he concluded that cogni-tive decline common to different psychometric abilities might be caused partly by the slowing of information processing in older people:

[S]uch age changes as are detectable are well detected by a single, very brief, performance IQ test that assesses only a restricted range of activities . . . A series of laboratory studies suggested that individual differences in performance both on a variety of tests of immediate and short term memory for simple material, and of memory for propositions in text, may all reflect a general change in information processing rate with advancing age. (Rabbitt 1992, p. 477)

Hultsch *et al.* (1999) found moderate to high loadings for a number of different abilities (speed-based, memory, comprehension, and verbal) on a single latent factor of cognitive change in subjects in the Victoria Longitudinal Study.

Salthouse (1996a; see also Salthouse and Czaja 2000) asked similar questions of the cognitive ageing data and came to similar conclusions. He posed the question of the number of processes that must be invoked to account for cognitive ageing and referred to data showing that many psychometric tasks are sensitive to the effects of ageing, and that tasks share much age-related variance. For example, he showed that, in a large group of people aged from 18 to 94 years, a test of learning and memory (paired associates) shared 68.8% of its age-related variance with a test of inductive reasoning. His review of 13 studies involving 855 pairs of cognitive variables (including tasks from memory and spatial reasoning to reaction time tests) found that, on average, psychometric tasks shared about 50% of age-related variance. It is important to comprehend fully what this result means. First, it does not mean that the tasks shared 50% of their overall variance. It means that 50% of the variance that overlapped with chronological age was shared between tasks. Second, this amount of shared, age-related variance was found between tasks that were supposedly indexing quite distinct cognitive functions. A similar result was reported by Cockburn and Smith (1991) who found that, among older people, scores on Raven's Progressive Matrices (a test of fluid intelligence) accounted for 32.8% of the variance on a test of everyday memory. After entering Raven scores in a regression model, chronological age accounted for only 5.5% of the variance in memory scores.

Another way to express such shared age-related variance is to extract a common factor from a variety of cognitive tasks and find out whether chronological age relates strongly to the common factor and whether age effects are strong for any non-common variance. Salthouse *et al.* (1996) collected data on a variety of neuropsychological tests from over 250 adults aged from 18 to 94 years. The tests were selected to include putative tests of frontal, parietal, and temporal lobe function and thus included the Wisconsin Card Sorting Test, tests of memory and learning, spatial ability tests, and others. The variables shared a mean of 58% of age-related variance. Salthouse (1996*a*) reanalysed these data, and other data sets comprising other cognitive tests, using structural equation modelling. The results of all of his reanalyses point to the same conclusion. A common factor can be extracted from the battery of tests and chronological age is strongly associated with this factor. The structural equation model of Salthouse's reanalysis of Salthouse *et al.* (1996) is shown in Fig. 8.5. All tests have significant and moderately large loadings on the common factor, on which age loads −0.77. Thereafter, Salthouse's method is to test for the significance of additional pathways that lead directly from age to the cognitive test in question and to retain those

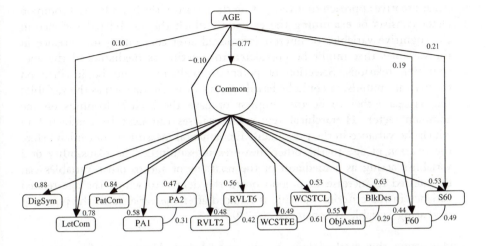

Fig. 8.5 Structural model demonstrating the effects of age on a battery of cognitive abilities. Note that the influence of age is largely on the general (common) factor extracted from the battery of tests. Significant effects of age on specific tests, beyond those effects which are mediated by the general factor, are limited to four relatively small contributions. The tests are: digit symbol from the Wechsler Adult Intelligence Scale-Revised (WAIS-R) (DigSym), letter comparison (LetCom), pattern comparison (PatCom), trials 1 and 2 in paired associates memory (PA1 and PA2), trials 2 and 6 in the Rey Auditory Verbal Learning Test (RVLT2 and RVLT6), per cent perseverative errors and conceptual level responses in the Wisconsin Card Sorting Test (WCSTPE and WCSTCL), WAIS-R object assembly and block design score (ObjAssm and BlkDes), and numbers of words produced beginning with F and S in 60 s (F60 and S60). Redrawn from Salthouse (1996*a*).

with significant parameter estimates. The figure shows that only four tests out of 13 had significant, specific ageing effects and that these were all small.

In addition to providing multiple analyses of large data sets to support the foregoing conclusion—that some age-related cognitive decline is general as well as specific—Salthouse's (1996*a*) data also show that age-related variance can be found in people's first contact with a cognitive task rather than their improvement with practice. Also, where mental tasks involve stimuli of different durations, the age-related variance may be found even among the shortest durations of a task.

Here is an interesting and counter-intuitive finding; that much of the age-related variance in cognitive test performances is general rather than test-specific. As with many other findings in human intelligence differences, this is an important finding that does not explain very much. Rather, it calls out for explanation and, as seen in earlier chapters of the book, the levels of explanation spread across the range from psychometric through experimental and psychophysical to biological, as discussed by Salthouse and Czaja (2000). It is not immediately clear how to proceed and discover the nature of the age-related general ability variance. Salthouse (1996*a*) discussed one way forward:

An alternative approach to investigating the nature of the hypothesised common factor consists of examining the extent to which the age-related variance in the cognitive variables of interest is reduced after controlling for variance in the variables that might be postulated to function as mediators of the age-cognition relations. Selection of potential mediators could be justified on theoretical grounds, or could be based on empirical criteria such as the variables that appear either to be the simplest or have the highest loadings on the common factor. Hierarchical regression analyses can next be conducted in which the variance in the presumably fundamental measure is controlled before the relation of age to the other measures is examined. The plausibility of a variable's acting as a mediator of the relations of age to other variables can be inferred to increase in proportion to the degree to which the age-related variance in the criterion variable is reduced after the variance in the potential mediating variable is controlled. (p. 294)

Studies using this methodology are discussed below. However, a few notes on the comparability between this research area and that of the task of finding information processing bases for differences in age-homogeneous young adults should be mentioned. The two areas have gathered much data on the psychometric structure of their phenomena. Both seek to account for the psychometric findings in terms of more basic variables. Both enterprises depend on the validity that can be mustered for the mediating/explanatory variables. Any such variable carries the explanatory weight and, if its invocation is to be construed as progress, then the information processing essence of the variable must be apparent. The most used variables tend to be those that are measures of working memory or speed of processing (Salthouse 1996*a,b*). Before assessing the studies that have used Salthouse's mediating variables methodology, do some of the favourite mediating variables—measures of processing speed—age at different rates?

Information processing tasks do not develop and age independently

Evidence from experimental tasks of reaction times conducted in young and old people suggests that cognitive ageing consists partly in the slowing of general processes. Cerella (1985) asked whether, with respect to speeded processing tasks, a separate explanatory account was required for the slowing of each task with increased age. Surprisingly, he found that a very simple formula could be used to express the relationship between young people's reaction times and those of old people on a number of disparate tasks, involving putatively different processes and very different reaction times: old people's reaction time = 1.35 young people's reaction time. A single factor could explain up to 90% or more of the variance in older people's data, although the slope of such a regression line might be steeper for those over age 60 years than for those under 60. Therefore, one possibility for explaining cognitive ageing is that there is a slowing of some very general speed of processing. Although Cerella did suggest a universal slowing, he also allowed that comparisons of old and young people's reaction times might require different intercepts and slopes depending on the amounts of sensorimotor and computational demands within a task.

The method of plotting the young people's reaction times for different cognitive tasks on the x-axis of a graph and older people's on the y-axis is called a Brinley plot (1965). The general finding has been that, despite the tasks thus plotted tapping different putative cognitive processes and involving vastly different absolute reaction times, the points for almost all tasks fall on or near to a straight line. Controversy has continued since the conception of the Brinley plot and the provocative idea deduced from it—that a single general slowing might characterize many of the cognitive performance decrements seen in multifarious cognitive tasks as people grow older. For example, Fisk *et al.* (1992) argued that Brinley plots masked considerable heterogeneity in cognitive slowing across different tasks; large (over 90%) proportions of the variance between young and old people might appear to be explained by a single slowing factor even when such a model is incorrect. Rabbitt (1996) has shown that Brinley plot analysis will account for large amounts of variance even when the ratios affecting each test are quite different.

Salthouse (1996*b*) gathered evidence to test his hypothesis that:

Age-related slowing is a broad phenomenon and not simply attributable to specific and independent processing deficits. (p. 407)

Although admitting their controversial nature, he alluded to the impressive data expressed in Brinley (1965) plots, which he called the 'analysis of systematic relations'. He showed that there is much shared, age-related variance among different speeded tasks, including paper-and-pencil tasks and reaction time-type measures. Even tasks with different regression lines showed much shared variance. However, Salthouse used Brinley-type plots principally to point to tasks with specific age-related influences. His main effort was put into two methods of statistical control to demonstrate how many speeded tasks showed an overlap in their age-related variance. The regression procedure is illustrated in Fig. 8.6. In this model, age is related to two measures of speed of processing, one being denoted the criterion variable and one the controlled variable. The criterion variable is related to age; thus, typically, age brings with it a slowing of cognitive processing. In Fig. 8.6(a) the variance shared between age and the criterion variable is b + d. Then ask the question: how many age-related influences must be specified to describe the slowing of cognitive task performance with age? Salthouse's answer was to bring in another speed of processing variable—denoted the controlled variable—and to discover what proportion of the age-related variance is shared between the criterion and the controlled tasks. This is captured by the expression b/(b + d) in the figure. Assume that this has been done for countless criterion and controlled variables. At one extreme it might transpire that both the criterion and the controlled variable have substantial age-related variance but that these did not overlap (Fig. 8.6(b)). The implication here is that there is independent slowing of the processes involved in the two tasks and that there must be some unique age-related slowing mechanisms. At the other extreme there might be complete overlap in the age-related variance of the two tasks (Fig. 8.6(c)). One implication here might be that there is a general slowing with age in a few or even one general process with influences over many or most cognitive tasks. As an example, Salthouse (1994*a*) tested 910 adult subjects of different ages. Digit symbol (DS) was the criterion speed-of-processing task and a composite of letter and pattern comparison tasks was used as the controlled speed-of-processing variable. The variance shared between age and DS performance was 28.9%. However, after controlling for perceptual speed, DS added only 0.8% additional age-related variance. Therefore, over 97% of age-related variance was shared between DS and the perceptual speed composite. This illustrative result is closer to Fig. 8.6(c) than to either of the other models. Salthouse (1996*b*) reviewed many sets of individual studies using the same procedures and found proportions of shared variances almost always over 50% for individual tests. Means of over 60% occurred when studies using highly disparate measures of processing speed were employed, e.g. vocal, written, and reaction time speed measures (Salthouse 1996*c*). He not unusually found shared variances between single measures of over 70, 80, and 90%.

Beyond regression procedures Salthouse (1996*b,c*) employed structural equation modelling techniques to estimate the relative amount of general and specific age-variance among mental tests. In this approach he posited a latent trait (call it processing speed) that had loadings on all of the manifest (measured) processing speed measures. In this model the measured, speeded performances are dependent variables and the latent speed measure is an independent variable. Age is entered to the model as an independent variable affecting the general, latent speed of processing trait. Following the usual path-analytic methodology, the general, age-related speed of processing influence on each test is the square of the product of the influence of age on the latent trait and the influence of the latent trait on the individual measure. In addition to this, pathways can be stipulated that run directly from age to the measured, speed of processing variables. These pathways represent unique effects of ageing on speed of processing in measured variables that are not due to the common speed of processing variable. In a review of four sets of data Salthouse (1996*c*) found the influence of the age-related general speed variance to be larger than the specific variance for all variables. In addition, the direct influences of age on manifest variables (i.e. the imputed unique age-related speed factors) had path coefficients that were significantly greater than zero in only 19 out of 53 cases.

Fig. 8.6 Diagram to illustrate Salthouse's regression method of examining the effects of age on cognitive function. Criterion and controlled variables are psychometric and/or information processing tests that have significant correlations with age. (a) Some of the age-related variance in the controlled variable is shared with the criterion variable: e, f, and g are sources of variance unique to the controlled, criterion, and age variables, respectively; b is variance shared by all three measures; a, c, and d are sources of variance shared by two of the variables but not the other variable. (b) The criterion and controlled variables both correlate significantly with age but do not share age-related variance. (c) All of the age-related variance in the criterion and controlled variables is shared.

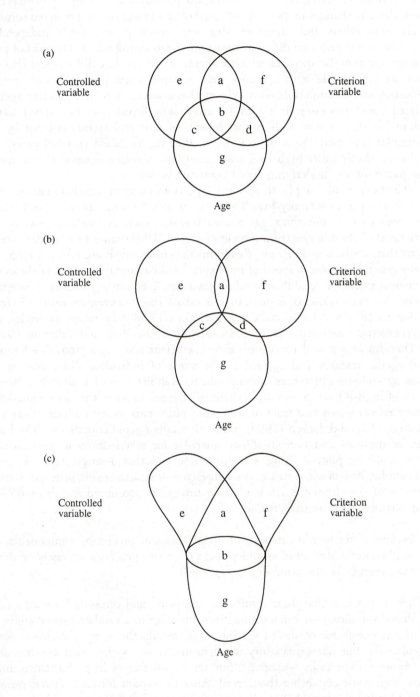

In summary, Salthouse (1996*b*) amassed an impressive body of evidence to show that age changes in measures of speed of processing can be predicted substantially from others and, therefore, that one cannot posit entirely independent age-related influences on different measures of processing speed. He did not posit a single process the speed of which controls all others, but did suggest that the data are compatible with a theory that contains a few processes with general influence, and incompatible with a theory that assumes many independent ageing-related speed processes. It might be asked how broad any such speed factors might be; that is how well is the domain of temporal factors covered by the particular test used? Second, it is noted that the so-called speed-of-processing tasks are mostly quite high-level tasks with long absolute reaction times, and so the nature of any underlying speed construct is not clear.

The above results apply to speeded aspects of cognitive ageing, not to accuracy in tasks or to memory loss. There might well be some specific speed-related processes that do not show age-related slowing, such as lexical access. At the other end of the age spectrum a review by Kail (1991) came to a similar conclusions that, across a wide range of experimental tasks involving speeded reactions, some general increase in speed of processing could account for much of the developmental change in childhood and adolescence. Even among infants, 'perceptual speed' has been adduced as one possible causal link between measures of recognition memory and cross-modal transfer taken 12 months of age or under, and psychometric intelligence at 11 years (McCall 1994; Rose and Feldman 1995).

The idea of a global processing time coefficient was taken from development and ageing research and applied to the study of individual differences, rather than age-related differences, among adults. Rabbitt (1996) found that Brinley plots of high-IQ versus low-IQ individuals tended to show the same remarkably linear associations across tasks as seen when old versus young reaction times were plotted. Hale and Jansen (1994) found that, among undergraduates, the latencies of the top- and bottom-ability quartiles for seven different reaction time tests could be plotted along a straight line and that a single function could account for 99% of the variance. A single factor—extracted using principal components analysis—from the seven reaction time tests accounted for about 65% of the variance. They remarked that:

> Because different tasks may involve very different processing components, the implication is that all of an individual's cognitive processes are faster or slower than average to the same degree. (p. 388)

Whereas it is true that these results are impressive and certainly indicate sources of shared variance, they cannot unequivocally point to a validated speed construct as the source factor of shared variance. The results throw up a dramatic set of regularities, but not explanatory mechanisms. It so happens that the measured outcome of their tasks was speed, but the causal factors in performance might have been constructs other than speed. Also, to account for such shared variance it need not be assumed that all of the cognitive processes were subject to the same slowing coefficients (see below and Fisher and Glaser 1996). However, concurrence with Hale and Jansen is permissible on two points. First, they remarked that a cognitive account of the seven tasks they used would emphasize qualitative differences among the tasks in terms of processing, but would be silent on the quantitative aspects of differential performance. As such, the cognitive description would fail to account for the large amount of shared variance. Second, they commented that such shared variance compels an explanation at the biological level. While agreeing with this—people are compelled to run each task on the same nervous system and some general biological aspects of the central nervous system could be a candidate source of variance for processing differences—it is important to note the complexity of many of their tasks. The reaction times range from about 500 ms to about 1700 ms. Therefore, how much further down an explanatory chain does this travel than Spearman when he sought a biological account of g?

Thus, in the field of developmental psychology, and especially in the area of cognitive ageing, there are some of the strongest theories of psychometric intelligence and speed of information processing. We now examine some specific data sets to clarify the theory, methods of testing, statistical tools, and limitations of such findings. Although it will become more complex, a simple statement of the research might go as follows: some psychometric abilities decline with age; behind much of the decline in many such abilities might lie a slowing of some general speed of information processing; therefore, if psychometric test scores are controlled for differences in the speed of information processing, the age-related variance in the tests should fall markedly.

Can age-related variance in psychometric abilities be attributed to slowing of information processing?

This question was asked and answered most comprehensively in a theoretical and review article by Salthouse (1996*b*) which will be used heavily hereafter to illustrate this research programme. He stated his general idea as follows:

> The fundamental assumption in the theory is that a major factor contributing to age-related differences in memory and other aspects of cognitive functioning is a reduction with increased age in the speed with which many cognitive operations can be executed. (p. 403)

Two mechanisms—a limited time mechanism and a simultaneity mechanism—were the key constructs invoked to account for the relation between speed of processing and cognitive ageing. Salthouse employed the assembly line as his metaphor for the limited time mechanism; cognitive operations must be carried out within specific time windows. This idea of time quanta in perception and thinking is popular at present (Poppel 1994). He used juggling as a descriptive metaphor for the simultaneity mechanism; individual cognitive operations must perforce be coordinated to complete a task successfully. Salthouse (1985) had already shown that a wide range of speed measures had significant and moderately sized associations with age. With respect to using speed measures as mediating variables between age and cognitive test scores he considered three issues. First, simple tasks should be employed; thus speed rather than knowledge would be the factor affecting performance. Second, the speed task should not merely capture sensory and motor—input and output, respectively—processes, but should reflect relevant cognitive operations. Third, multiple measures of constructs should be employed to minimize specific variance and to emphasize common, construct-related variance.

To understand this research programme it is invaluable to know how speed of processing has been operationalized, because the measures of speed of processing bear the explanatory weight of the enterprise. Salthouse's (1996*b*) review discussed studies that used combinations of the following tasks as putative measures of speed of processing: the digit symbol task from the Wechsler Adult Intelligence Scale; letter and pattern comparison tasks where subjects must write 's' or 'd' between a pair of letters or patterns to indicate whether they are the same or different; copying of digits; speed of drawing lines in specified locations; and two reaction time-type versions based on the digit symbol task, one based on matching a code to a digit and one based on looking for physical identity in the stimuli.

In Salthouse's (1996*b*) review his second hypothesis was that:

> Processing speed functions as an important mediator of the relations between age and measures of cognitive functioning. (p. 417)

Table 8.2 offers data relevant to this, compiled by Kail and Salthouse (1994). In each instance in the table the cognitive performance measure is Raven's Matrices, a non-verbal cognitive test involving a logical pattern completion. In the studies mentioned—they included children, young adults, and old people— age accounted for 15–37% of the variance in matrix-reasoning scores. When the effect of processing speed was removed the attenuation in age-related variance dropped by 70–93%. The implication is that ageing of cognitive functions consists largely in the slowing of processing speed; that is, processing speed might be seen as a mediator between age and cognitive performance. Salthouse (1996*b*, p. 419) reported the results of this statistical control procedure when individual and composite cognitive tasks were measured. Across many sets of data, age initially accounted for an average of 16.2% of the variance in single cognitive test performance. After controlling for processing speed this reduced by 78%. By using composite cognitive measures the mean age-related variance was 25.2%, which reduced to 4.3% after controlling for processing speed differences, an attenuation of over 80%. These effects are not caused because the cognitive tasks are speeded. Salthouse reported similar effects for decision accuracy as well as decision speed. Moreover, he reported attenuations in the age-related variance of memory tasks of 78% and 85% when reaction time and paper-and-pencil measures, respectively, of processing speed were used in statistical control analyses. Processing speed's mediation of age effects on mental ability test scores occurs, then, for a

Table 8.2 Percentage of age-related variance in Raven's Progressive Matrices performance before and after controlling for individual differences in speed of processing (from Kail and Salthouse 1994)

Study	Subjects' ages	% variance for age alone	% variance for age after controlling for processing speed	Attenuation of age-related variance after controlling for processing speed
Paper-and-pencil tests				
Salthouse (1993, Exp. 1)	20–80	32.2	5.6	82.6
Babcock (1992)	21–83	21.2	3.5	83.5
Computer-administered tests				
Kail and Park (1992)	8–20	27.4	1.8	93.4
Salthouse (1993, Exp. 2)	20, 62			
Successive presentation		34.7	6.2	82.1
Simultaneous presentation		22.8	2.1	90.8
Salthouse (1993, Exp. 3)	20, 61	37.5	11.1	70.4
Salthouse (1994a, Exp. 1)	18–84	14.9	1.5	89.9

wide range of mental tests including memory tests, for tests that are timed and untimed, and the result is obtained using a number of different speed-of-processing measures.

Nettelbeck and Rabbitt (1992) showed that lower-level tasks measuring speed of processing, such as inspection time (Chapter 7) and four-choice reaction time (Chapter 8), could account arguably for some of the age-related variance in cognitive performance of people aged 54–85 years, although such measures of cognitive slowing were less effective in accounting for changes in learning with rehearsal (Nettelbeck *et al.* 1996). The data supported Salthouse's hypothesis by demonstrating that the correlations between age and performance IQ-type psychometric measures became non-significant after controlling for processing speed differences, and they concluded that:

> decline in information-processing speed is a major factor in age-related decline in general cognitive activities. (p. 203)

These data contain some notable features. Nettelbeck and Rabbitt included psychometric (a coding test akin to the WAIS digit symbol test), cognitive-experimental (reaction time) and psychophysical (inspection time) measures of processing speed. The performance IQ subtests—block design (BD), picture arrangement (PA), and picture completion (PC)—were recorded untimed and timed. Full data on these tests were available for 98 subjects and were reanalysed by the present author. The following hypothesis was tested using structural equation modelling: a latent 'processing speed' trait, extracted from the three speed measures (inspection time, reaction time, and coding), would act as a mediator between age and a latent trait extracted from the three performance IQ subtests. Such a model fits the data well, and is shown in Fig. 8.7(a). The latent trait F2 is strongly associated with the three psychometric tests and represents a general factor from these three performance tests from the WAIS. The latent trait F1 has strong associations with each of the three processing speed measures and strongly affects F2 (path coefficient of 0.941). Age affects F1 (path coefficient 0.442) which mediates its effect on F2. A Wald test was included to discover whether any of the included paths could be removed to achieve a more economical model. In fact, all paths in the diagram contributed significantly to the fit of the model. A Lagrange multiplier test was included to discover whether some paths had been omitted that might have significant contributions to make. This indicated that paths between inspection time and the latent trait F2, and between block design and age, would be the only non-included paths that would be significant. Therefore, the mediating effect of a latent 'processing speed' trait, extracted from three quite different tasks, almost completely mediates the age effect on some performance IQ tests, showing powerful support for Salthouse's hypothesis. The additional fillip to Salthouse's theory is the reductionistic range of speed-of-processing measures employed in this study.

Another feature of the model in Fig. 8.7(a) is the coefficient of 0.941 between the two latent traits. Such a strong association, and the fact that one of the tasks

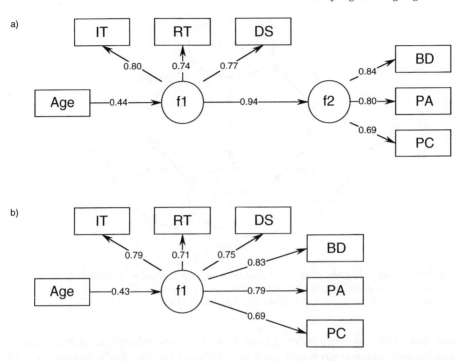

Fig. 8.7 Mediating structural equation models of age on psychometric ability test scores and tests of information processing. Tests are: inspection time (IT), reaction time (RT), digit symbol (DS), block design (BD), picture arrangement (PA), and picture completion (PC). The last four tests are performance subtests from the Wechsler Adult Intelligence Scale. In model (a) a latent trait extracted from three putative information processing tests mediates the influence of age on psychometric intelligence, represented by a general factor extracted from three tests. In model (b) age influences a general factor extracted from all of the tests, with no distinction made between information processing and psychometric tests. Some additional paths that were significant are not included here but are described in the text. The models were based on a reanalysis of the data from Nettelbeck and Rabbitt (1992), which the authors kindly made available.

contributing to latent trait F1 is a psychometric test, similar to the digit symbol test from the performance IQ section of the WAIS, invite the hypothesis that a more economical model would include only one latent trait, underlying all six psychometric and processing speed tests. This model is shown in Fig. 8.7(b). The model states simply that age affects a latent trait underlying all six tasks and that no task-specific effects are needed. It fits the data very well, with only one additional path—between age and block design—suggested by the Lagrange multiplier test. A competitive test of the two models favours the more economical (chi square difference = 2.56, d.f. difference = 1). Therefore, there is support in these data for a very simple—and ultimately quite unhelpful, from a reductionist viewpoint—model that states that all six tests share age-related variance

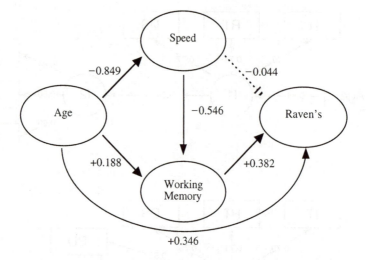

Fig. 8.8 Structural model of the associations among age, speed of information processing, working memory, and scores on Raven's progressive matrices. The dotted line represents a non-significant path. Redrawn from Fry and Hale (1996).

and that none can be considered more basic than any other; age, in effect, alters psychological performance very generally. Others have, in similar fashion, treated speed as just one aspect of psychometric ability rather than a variable at some more fundamental level (Lindenberger and Baltes 1994*b*). Ultimately, choosing between these two models will not be done by statistics, but by validating the tests of processing speed as true indicators of important brain functions.

Salthouse's (e.g. 1996*b*) ideas about the causal primacy of processing speed were tested by Fry and Hale (1996) in a group of over 200 subjects aged 7–19 years. Four reaction time tasks were used to estimate processing speed differences; there were four working memory tasks, and Raven's Matrices were included. One of the hypotheses tested with structural equation modelling was that:

> much of cognitive development may represent a cascade wherein age-related changes in processing speed lead to changes in working memory that, in turn, lead to changes in fluid intelligence. (p. 237)

The well-fitting model shown in Fig. 8.8 shows that this notion was supported by the data. However, it is difficult to accept that the hypothesis can be supported to the exclusion of others. The tasks used to estimate processing speed have relatively long latencies, frequently greater than one second, and it is difficult conceptually or statistically to separate working memory from psychometric intelligence (Kyllonen and Crystal 1990; Chapter 5). Moreover, a reanalysis of Table 1 in Fry and Hale's paper (conducted by this author), which has the correlations among age, speed, memory, and Raven's, reveals a single factor that accounts for well over 70% of the variance among the tests. Without a longitudinal study, without better validation for the constructs of speed and working memory, and without testing more economical hypotheses—such as stating that all of the variables are a reflection of some more basic latent variable—William of Occam's razor suggests that this paper progresses little beyond Spearman's *g*.

Thus far, slowing of psychometric-based and reaction-time-based speed of processing goes along with cognitive ageing, but the direction of causation has not been addressed, and ageing might cause slowing of processing speed or vice versa. Salthouse (1996*b*) considered a statistical method for asking this question; namely, what happens to the age-related variance in speed of processing measures when they are controlled for other variables and vice versa. These statistical operations are not symmetrical and it is interesting to inquire which measure can 'absorb' most of the age-related variance. Thus, Salthouse ran many exercises in which speed of processing's age-related variance is controlled for other variables and in which the other variables' age-related variances are controlled for speed of processing. The answer is that speed of processing retains more age-related variance than working memory, inhibition, pattern memory, serial learning, pattern comparison, vigilance, and hand–eye coordination. One wonders, though, whether this type of analysis takes the process of theory building much further. None of the psychometric tests involved has a tractable theoretical basis. What seems to be rediscovered is the nature of those (high-level) tasks that decline most with age.

One less imperfect way of addressing the causal position of speed of processing in cognitive ageing (in addition to discovering a construct-validated test of speed of processing) is to set up a longitudinal design including processing speed and other cognitive tests and to analyse a cross-lagged panel design with structural equation modelling techniques. Deary (1995*a*) used this type of design to ask whether so-called auditory inspection time differences were a cause or a consequence of psychometric intelligence differences. The problems with divining the contribution of pitch discrimination and speed of processing in this auditory test were discussed in Chapter 7. Therefore, this auditory processing task is offered merely as an example of a task that is at least arguably at a lower level than a standard psychometric test or a reaction time task. Over 100 12-year-old children were tested on auditory inspection time, Raven's Progressive Matrices, and the Mill Hill Vocabulary test. They were retested at age 14 years. The cross-lagged panel of correlations for these data are shown in Fig. 8.9. There are contemporaneous correlations of just under 0.3 and just over 0.4 between auditory processing and both Raven and Mill Hill scores. The stability coefficients for the tests are high, with auditory processing showing particularly high stability (0.83). The cross-lagged correlations show the influence of auditory processing on psychometric test scores across the 2-year gap and vice versa. However, although the relative size of these correlations used to be accepted as an indicator of causal influence—the larger cross-lagged association was taken to indicate the principal causal direction—such inferences are incorrect when stability coefficients are not identical (Rogosa 1980). Deary used structural equation modelling to test competitively three hypotheses of the associations between auditory information processing and psychometric intelligence. These were: (1) that changes

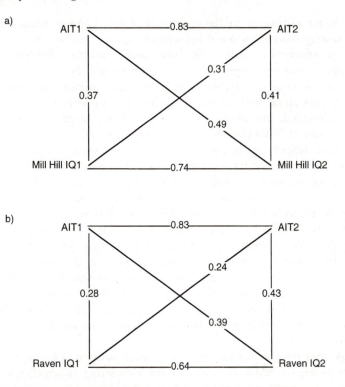

Fig. 8.9 Cross-lagged panel of correlations between psychometric ability test scores (Mill Hill Vocabulary and Raven's Progressive Matrices) and auditory information processing (AIT, or 'auditory inspection time'). Redrawn from Deary (1995*a*).

in both were caused by some other factor; (2) that auditory processing partly causes psychometric intelligence differences; and (3) that psychometric intelligence differences partly cause auditory processing differences. These hypotheses are shown in Fig. 8.10. The best-fitting models are shown in Fig. 8.11. For both Raven and Mill Hill scores there is some cross-lagged influence from auditory processing scores. However, these models did not require paths from the psychometric tests at age 12 to the auditory processing measures at age 14. These data provide some tentative evidence that information processing measures are partly causal to psychometric intelligence differences in childhood. This type of design could be applied to studies of processing efficiency in cognitive ageing, although it might be improved by having multiple indicators of each construct and by testing on more than two occasions.

What is this speed of information processing?

The next step after finding that so-called processing speed is a mediator between age and cognitive ability test scores is to identify the nature of the processing speed construct or constructs. Salthouse (1996*b*) noted that:

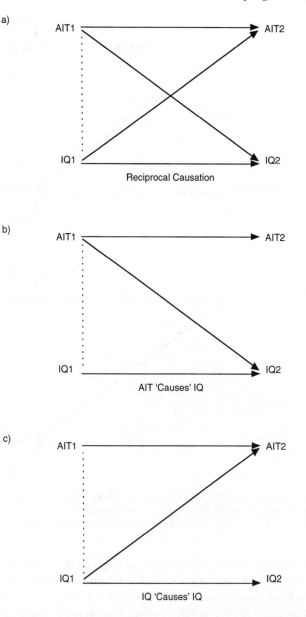

Fig. 8.10 Three hypotheses tested using the data represented by the correlations in Fig. 8.9. In model (a) it is assumed that some third variable influences both mental ability test scores and auditory information processing. In model (b) it is assumed that auditory information processing at time 1 influences mental ability test scores at time 2, but not the reverse. In model (c) it is assumed that mental ability test scores at time 1 influence later auditory information processing but not the reverse. Redrawn from Deary (1995*a*).

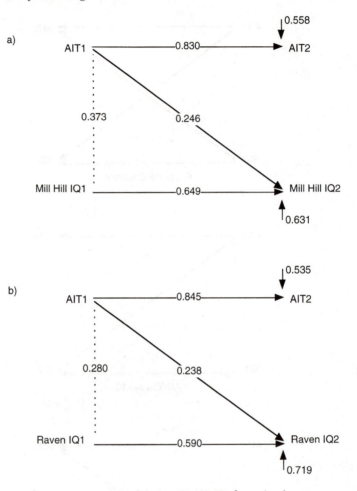

Fig. 8.11 Best-fitting structural models (see Fig. 8.10) from the data represented in Fig. 8.9. There are significant paths from auditory information processing at time 1 to psychometric test scores at time 2 but not the reverse. Redrawn from Deary (1995*a*).

in several studies, the proportional attenuation of the age-related variance was greater with speed measures from tasks involving perceptual or cognitive operations, such as substitution, transformation, or comparison, than with tasks merely requiring copying or line drawing responses . . . the speed most relevant to the mediation of adult age differences in cognition therefore appears to reflect the duration of cognitive operations rather than simply the speed of sensory and motor processes. (p. 420)

Perhaps, however, this gazing into the nature of psychometric tests is not a sure way to tease out basic processing mechanisms. To equate motor speed with copying and sensory speed with time to compare letters and lines, as Salthouse does, is to ask too much detail from these blunt instruments. In fairness, one must support Salthouse's assertion that, when compared with competitor theories of cognitive ageing including those based on constructs such as processing resources and attention/inhibition, the key variable in the processing speed theory has been relatively well operationalized and many relevant data have been collated.

The data gathered by researchers in cognitive ageing are impressive in their extent and importance. There is much shared age-related variance among psychometric and so-called information processing tasks and between these two aspects of human individual difference measurement. What the researchers are calling measures of information processing are able to capture much of the age-related variance in psychometric tests of higher-level cognitive abilities. Near the start of this book it was stated that psychometric tests can map individual differences but cannot explain them. Therefore, there is appeal to other variables to carry this explanatory burden. The tests used as mediating variables (indicators of 'speed of processing') in cognitive ageing studies fall into two groups. There are the more psychometric ('paper and pencil') tests and the more experimental (based on reaction time procedures) tests. Often, the digit symbol test from the WAIS battery was used as a measure of speed of processing. It is certainly quite a simple test to perform; given no time limit almost everyone who understood the instructions would complete the task without error. The score is based on speed of performance. However, in an area where researchers are far from understanding the bases of individual differences in, say inspection times and reaction times, digit symbol cannot be remotely entertained as an explanatory variable. It does not measure any basic speed of processing that can be tied to fundamental brain mechanisms. It is a psychometric test and, without much more validating evidence, it cannot by fiat become an information processing variable, with the implications for tractability that such a label conveys. Even when multiple tests are combined to offer latent trait versions of the speed of processing measure, the individual tests are relatively complex and the nature of the shared variance cannot be identified any more clearly than the general factor from a battery of mental tests. Many of these data, it might be stated reluctantly, take the field not much further than stating that general mental ability accounts for much of the variance in general mental ability. More research in age-related cognitive change must be done with better validated measures of information processing. Nettelbeck and Rabbitt's (1992) use of inspection time as a mediating variable between age and cognitive test scores marks an improvement on most other studies in the field.

Thus, again, there is a return to resolving to find better measures of information processing; tests that will map tractably on to human brain processes (Salthouse and Czaja 2000). And, again, it must be recalled that until there is a model of brain processing, the use of only psychometric and cognitive/experimental variables can induce a false sense of understanding. Fisher and Glaser (1996) used a handy terminology in the terms 'molar' to refer to measurable, overt aspects of behaviour and 'latent' to denote the information processing mechanisms not yet identified. They recognized that research on cognitive ageing often debates whether there is a small number of general processes that slow with age or a large number of specific processes that slow independently. They argued that not too much can be decided on this issue using psychometric or experimental data that are divorced from—floating at an unknown distance above—actual brain processes. They showed that even when impressive amounts of variance are accounted for by a general factor, subprocesses might slow at very different rates. Vice versa, they showed that, if psychometric tasks actually aged at different rates with little shared variance, there might still be identical slowing of the underlying information processing mechanisms. In one instance they clearly demonstrated this using a path model of cognitive functioning in which two processes run in parallel and in which both must be completed before one progresses to the next stage.

Fisher and Glaser (1996) identified the key issue in explaining molar slowing as the stipulation of latent processes. This is a task that cannot proceed until there is an explicit, testable model of cognitive functioning. Citing a number of possible cognitive architectures—PERT networks, associative networks, connectionist networks, and queuing networks—they discussed some implications of PERT architecture as a basis for some cognitive operations. Performance on the task runs from 'source' to 'sink'. Assumptions of the network are that no processes may begin until all predecessors are complete, and that all processes begin as soon as they can. The response time is the duration of the longest of the paths. Similar molar slowing might arise from the same slowing function being applied to each arc (process) or from their having unique slowing quotients. They suggested that the hypothesis that old people's cognitive functions are less than young people's because of some general slowing might be true if it were known that cognitive tasks were arranged as PERT networks with only a limited range of types of process, that the groups being compared (e.g. young versus old, high ability versus low ability, child versus adult) had the same task structure, and that latent slowing functions were common and multiplicative. The conclusion from their largely theoretical paper is clear. There must be a neural model of task performance to make firm conclusions. Perhaps in innocence, perhaps disingenuously, they ask that:

> In order to avoid logically incorrect inferences, it is necessary to specify the general characteristics of the latent model that governs performance in each task. In particular, it is necessary as a minimum to identify for each task that type of architecture, the limits on resources, and the possible dependencies that exist among the various process durations. (p. 462)

Salthouse (1996b), the principal advocate of speed of processing as a key element in cognitive ageing, warned similarly:

> Prediction of the specific consequences of a processing-speed limitation requires a detailed understanding of, or a willingness to make many assumptions about, the processes involved in a particular task. (p. 406)

With these warnings in mind it is instructive to reflect upon Salthouse's (1996b) guidelines for assessing speed of processing, as listed above. He advocated the use of simple tasks to ensure that speed is the determining factor in test performance. What is simple? Digit symbol appears simple compared to composing a Mozart symphony, or to some of the harder problems in Raven's Matrices. However, it looks more complex than, say, simple reaction time, inspection time, P300 of the event related potential, and nerve conduction velocity. The processes that govern different people's performances on the test, and the resulting individual differences, are unknown. With regard to the timing of neural operations each item takes a long time. It is not known whether the task structure is similar among different people. Digit symbol does not look promising as a tool for reductionism. The simplicity of a task is relative, but to account for variance in a psychometric task in terms of digit symbol arguably does not take us further down the explanatory ladder of intelligence differences.

Salthouse's second recommendation for speed of processing measures was that any measure should not merely tap sensory or motor processes. The task should include all relevant cognitive operations. This might be a misguided attempt to ensure comprehensiveness over comprehensibility. If a so-called speed measure accounts for much of the age-related variance in cognitive test performance, one has learned only as much as one understands of the brain processing involved in the speed task. If the task or tasks used are of unknown task structure then all that can be concluded is that variance in one set of complex tasks (measured by the number of correct answers) can be accounted for by variance in another set of complex tasks (measured by speed of completion). Rather than comprehensibility, one could argue that it would be better to argue for specificity. Thus, if one knew that one of the processing parameters of the brain was captured by, say, an event-related response measure, one could estimate this in people and discover whether it accounted for some of the age-related variance. One by one, brain processing parameters could be explored to discover which of them altered with age and accounted for cognitive test changes with age. Several clean-informative packets of variance like this would be more informative than one big dirty-obscure packet.

Salthouse's third suggestion about speed and other cognitive measures was that multiple measures of a construct should be used to emphasize the common variance. This type of argument was used in visual information processing tasks, allowing only the common variance among the tasks to be associated with psychometric intelligence (Deary *et al.* 1997). Once again, this type of approach is only as good as the understanding of the processing involved in the individual tasks. With the visual processing measures every attempt was made to collect visual processing tasks that differed in aspects except the need for processing under stimulus presentation time constraints. In addition, a task was included that appeared to share many aspects of the speed-of-processing tasks except the need for discrimination under time-limited conditions. This imperfect study was an attempt to create a latent construct that was as comprehensible as possible, using low-level tasks. The tasks used to construct latent speed trait in Salthouse's review don't appear to offer such tractability. They are psychometric or reaction time-based tasks with, compared to inspection time, long completion times per item.

What is the latent construct that is produced from such a distillation? It's impossible to say. Certainly the tasks are all speeded, but they all involve unknown melanges of as-yet-obscure cognitive processes. At worst, their common variance might be viewed as the same beast as the first unrotated component from a battery of psychometric tests (Spearman's *g*). That is, one might have merely 'explained' cognitive test scores in their own terms. To avoid such scientific pleonasms there must be a better understanding of the speed measures employed. This is not something that escaped Salthouse (1996*b*), who commented that:

> One-to-one relations between a particular hypothetical process and a behavioral variable are extremely rare. (p. 416)

Having made so much of the necessity of knowing the nature of speed-of-processing tasks—in the sense of understanding the component processes that combine to generate performance and performance differences on tasks—it may be asked if there are clues to be gained from the ways the principal investigators hypothesize. Often, the metaphor of the digital computer is used. Therefore, when Salthouse (1996*b*) discussed the possibility of there being more than one source of age-related processing speed he commented:

> Several different types of speed affect the performance of a computer, including the processor clock rate; the speed of specialized mathematical and graphics co-processors; hard disc access time; input rate from devices such as keyboards, scanners, or modems; and output rate to devices such as display monitors, printers, plotters, or modems. Nevertheless, knowledge of a small number of speed 'factors' allows performance on an extremely large number of tasks to be predicted quite accurately. (p. 416)

The metaphor makes the point clearly—and is remarkably similar to Anderson's (1992) computational model of human intelligence differences—but does not take us much further in discovering the way that such concepts might map on to the brain's biology.

Such appeals to computer metaphors are popular among those who work within a theoretical framework that posits a small number of sources, or even a single source, of speed of information processing. In Kail's (1991) review of reaction times in children and adolescents, in which he concluded that the developmental results were consistent with an increasing general speed of processing, one of the three mechanistic hypotheses he entertained ran as follows:

> If two computers have identical software but one machine has a slower cycle time (i.e. the time for the central processor to execute a single instruction), that machine will execute all processes more slowly by an amount that depends on the total number of instructions to be executed. The human analog to cycle time might be the time to scan productions (i.e. condition–action instructions) in working memory, or it might refer to the time to execute the action side

of a production ... In either case, a developmental decrease in the human cognitive cycle time would be associated with decreased time to complete cognitive operations. (p. 499)

Kail and Salthouse (1994) suggested a similar metaphor if one accepts 'processing speed as a cognitive primitive':

> processing speed may be analogous to the operating speed of the central processing unit (CPU) of a microcomputer. The speed is, for all practical purposes, fixed for a given CPU, and, consequently, is simply considered to be part of the architecture of the computer in which it is installed. Differences between CPUs in the rate of processing are explained at a lower level of analysis, in terms of the complexities of the electronic circuitry (e.g., more transistors in a faster CPU).

A useful list of possible neural sites for the origins of molar processing speed differences followed this metaphor. At a relatively high, and still metaphorical, level Kail and Salthouse discussed processing speed as a measure of the speed of activation through neural networks. They discussed the basic speed of recognition–act cycles of activity within working memory. These are used principally to show that current cognitive theories (or metaphors) can cope with general speed factors affecting much of cognitive performance. They then considered the possible mechanisms within neural structures proper that might account for age-related speeding up (during childhood) and slowing down (during old-age) of processing speed. Candidate processes were plucked from different levels of neuronal functioning: changes in myelination, changes in numbers of neural connections, weakened inhibitory circuits, changes in various neurotransmitter–receptor systems. These are similar speculations to those that emerge from work relating brain size to intelligence (see Chapter 9). Myelination of neurons has been suggested elsewhere as a basis for integrating various aspects of human ability differences (Miller 1994). In so far as the white matter abnormalities (leukoaraiosis) in brain imaging studies represent problems of demyelination, there is evidence that individual differences in leukoaraiosis correlate significantly with performance IQ and especially with speed of processing (as tested by psychometric tests and the Sternberg memory scanning task) (de Groot *et al.* 2000; Junque *et al.* 1990).

Beyond processing speed

The empirical and review-collating work of Salthouse has alerted researchers to the fact that mental abilities do not age independently; there is considerable shared ageing among tests of psychometric intelligence and memory. Furthermore, tests of so-called processing speed mediate large proportions of age-related variance. A reanalysis of a data set of Nettelbeck and Rabbitt (1992) suggested the possibility that tests of processing speed might be considered not as mediators, but as merely another facet of a very general effect of age on the human brain functions.

This evidence might be looked upon in another way. Suspend disbelief for the moment and accept the construct validity of processing speed measures. It might then be accepted that processing speed is a construct that accounts for much of the brain's age-related changes that lead to poorer performances on psychometric intelligence tests and aspects of tests of memory. This might be a clue to a specific mechanism within cognitive ageing. However, this would still fall short of our having a mechanistic understanding of cognitive ageing without research which had shown that, in longitudinal studies, alterations in processing speed were causally prior to cognitive ageing (Sliwinski and Buschke 1999; Deary 1995*a*). Even if these proved positive, the field would still be guilty of having failed to ask whether there are other aspects of brain functioning that are associated with cognitive ageing. Even if true, the association between slowed processing speed might be only one aspect of measurable brain processing that correlates with cognitive ageing. By documenting those aspects of brain processing that do and do not co-occur with age-related cognitive change, the field grows closer to an understanding of mechanism. And it is here that evidence is addressed that calls into question an especially privileged role for processing speed within cognitive ageing.

The setting for this evidence is the Berlin Aging Study (BASE), which examined people aged 70–100 years (Lindenberger and Baltes 1994*b*). Over 150 people in the study undertook 14 cognitive tests (grouped into five composite abilities: speed, reasoning, memory, knowledge, and fluency), and tests of visual and auditory functioning. The auditory tests were thresholds at different frequencies and the visual tests included near and far vision. Structural equation modelling was used to test the hypothesis that the effects of age on the five domains of cognitive functioning could be mediated by sensory abilities. Thus vision and hearing were interposed between age and a general factor extracted from all five psychometric ability groupings (Fig. 8.12). The resulting model fitted the data well, allowing Lindenberger and Baltes to conclude that:

> a structural model that represents age differences in intellectual functioning as an indirect (mediated) consequence of age differences in sensory functioning was completely consistent with the data. (p. 345)

Further, the interaction between vision and hearing was 'absorbed' by age differences, although the paths from age via vision to intellectual function are stronger than for hearing. Beyond these senses, balance and gait were also rather strongly associated with psychometric intelligence. When speed was moved to the position of mediating variable between age and psychometric intelligence, sensory functioning was the more successful mediating variable. A similar set of analyses with a larger sample ($N = 516$) found that sensorimotor functions (balance–gait, hearing, and vision) entirely mediated the association between age and intelligence (Lindenberger and Baltes 1997). Sociobiographical factors influenced intelligence but were not involved in ageing effects.

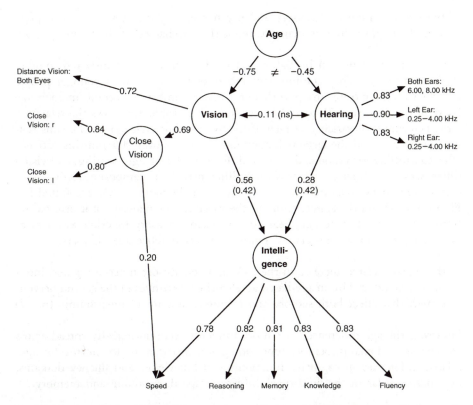

Fig. 8.12 Structural model showing measures of vision and hearing as mediating variables between age and mental ability test scores. Note that the influence of the sensory measures is relatively distinct and is largely mediated via the general factor extracted from the five domains of psychometric ability. Redrawn from Lindenberger and Baltes (1994*b*). The 0.42 values in parentheses occur when vision and hearing are constrained to be equal.

These remarkable results demand an explanation, and Lindenberger and Baltes (1994) considered three. First, they doubted whether the cognitive demands of the sensory tests were responsible for the associations, although this is reminiscent of Thorndike *et al.*'s (1909) response to Spearman's (1904) discovery of a correlation between sensory discrimination and imputed intelligence in children. The Berlin ageing study includes people with dementia (21% met the criteria according to the Diagnostic and Statistical Manual for Mental Disorders Version III-R; American Psychiatric Association 1994) and people, presumably, with cognitive decrements short of frank dementia. Therefore, the possibility that there are age-related individual differences in the ability to carry out even quite simple test instructions should be borne in mind. Another possible explanation was that sensory deterioration was responsible for decreased stimulation, leading to lower levels of cognitive functioning with age. Last, and perhaps most likely, was the 'common cause' hypothesis that:

Both sets of measures (sensory and psychometric ability tests) are an expression of the physiological architecture, or the 'mechanics' of the brain. (p. 339)

A follow-up investigation by Baltes and Lindenberger (1997) answered some of these reservations. They combined members of the BASE with younger people to achieve a composite group with fairly equal numbers of people in each age band all the way from 25 to 103 years (N = 315). Table 8.3 shows the relatively large percentage of variance of each of the five psychometric ability domains that was due to age, and the large reduction (an average of over 90%) in this variance after controlling for vision and hearing differences. Using age, hearing, and vision differences as predictors of individual differences in a composite ability score comprising all five cognitive domains, 71.5% of the variance was accounted for. Figure 8.13 shows the apportioning of the variance, the majority of it originating from sources common to age, hearing, and vision. Sensory function was a more powerful predictor of age-related cognitive function above age 70 years:

this age-associated increase in the link between sensory functioning and intelligence is induced by an age-based acceleration of changes in the central nervous system that affect both sensory and cognitive systems of functioning. (p. 17)

However, the age differences in sensory influence were not equally spread across the cognitive domains. Sensory functioning was disparate in accounting for age-related differences in cognitive functioning in knowledge and fluency domains, but more similar in the fluid-type abilities of speed, reasoning and memory:

The high degree of predictive overlap between age and sensory functioning for fluid abilities in both age groups is consistent with the notion that mechanisms associated with chronological age are the driving force behind the sensory–cognitive link across the entire age range considered in this study. From this perspective, the increase in the strength of the connection between sensory and intellectual functioning with advancing age is due to an acceleration of negative age-based changes in both domains during the last decades of the life span. (p. 17)

In agreement with the main complaint of this chapter, Baltes and Lindenberger (1997) called for a componential account of the sensory and cognitive tasks so that there might be a better understanding of these results. They suggested that sensory tasks might offer a better opportunity for decomposition to processing 'primitives' than might cognitive tests. And their view of these primitives was that the majority must:

operate at a relatively global, rather than modular or domain-specific level. (p. 20)

Important questions arise from these data. Do young people of lower IQ have similar brains in some ways to older people of higher IQ; that is, are there brain

Table 8.3 Reductions in age-related variance in various mental ability test scores after controlling for audition and vision (Lindenberger and Baltes 1997)

	Perceptual speed	Reasoning	Memory	Knowledge	Fluency	Vision	Hearing
% variance due to age (linear + quadratic)	71.5	64.1	52.8	45.0	40.4		
Control for vision	19.0	15.5	15.8	12.1	8.5		
Control for hearing	9.1	7.2	4.6	4.4	5.8		
Control for vision and hearing	4.6	3.4	2.7	1.8	2.3		
Control for perceptual speed		4.3	1.2	1.5	0.4	9.0	16.5

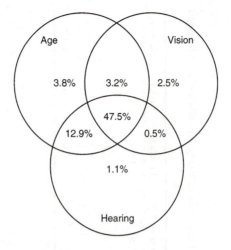

Fig. 8.13 Venn diagram showing the variance contributions to mental ability test scores of age and tests of vision and hearing. See Fig. 8.6 for an explanation of the procedure. Data from Baltes and Lindenberger (1997).

parameters that relate to absolute level of fluid ability? How broadly should researchers look for variables that can account for age-related cognitive ability variance and how informative would they be about mechanisms of cognitive ageing? Now that sensory function has been added to speed of processing, the field must consider what might underlie Baltes and Lindenberger's (1997) 'common cause'. Other brain parameters could be considered, and even beyond that. What would be concluded if indicators, say, of respiratory function that are known to deteriorate with age (such as the forced expiratory volume in one second, FEV1) also accounted for age-related cognitive variance (Anstey and Smith 1999)?

CONCLUSION

Studies of cognitive ageing have lived, until recently, outside the mainstream of information processing research on human psychometric intelligence. This can no longer be justified, because the research on ageing is about the single best corpus of research in the field. The data showing that there are shared, age-related influences on diverse cognitive abilities are monumental and definitive. Thus, any theory of changes in cognitive functions with age must be able to explain this shared variance. There are similar impressive data for shared ageing effects on more experimental tasks based on a number of reaction time procedures. The data showing that age-related variance in high-level psychometric tests can be accounted for largely by putative tests of processing speed are again monumental and definitive. The methods used in ageing research might be applicable to individual differences among age-homogeneous young adults. Problems and caveats of the methods were outlined. However, the one fundamental limitation in the entire oeuvre is the operationalization of speed of processing. All too often what should be some basic limitation in processing takes the form of a psychometric task and, even when the task is apparently more simple, it is far from basic in terms of being understood as limitations in nervous system functioning. The information processing data described in this chapter form a large and impressive set of regularities. The extent to which the explanatory vanguard has proceeded below the psychometric level is debatable. The information needs to be understood, the area of cognitive ageing is remarkably healthy in its scientific activity and its usefulness, but we must not skirt the central problem. There is a lack of tractable measures of the brain's information processing capabilities that will bridge behaviour and biology with an explanation. Salthouse (1996*b*) wrote that:

Speed may function as a bridging construct between behavioral and neurophysiological research. Because time is an objective and absolute dimension rather than a norm-reference scale, as is the case with most behavioral measures, it is inherently meaningful in all disciplines and thus has the potential to function as a Rosetta stone in linking concepts from different disciplines. (p. 425)

Still, one asks, speed of what?

9 Wetware

Reaching for the brain: raking around in biological sciences

SUMMARY

The 'biology of human intelligence differences' is not a coordinated field of study. It is a collection of pragmatic stabs at uncovering correlations between putative brain parameters and mental ability test differences. The brain parameters are rarely arrived at via detailed theory; rather they have been alighted on by convenience and common sense. Five main strands of research are surveyed and discussed critically. These cover associations between mental ability test differences and brain size, nerve conduction velocity, event-related potentials (ERPs) and electroencephalography, functional brain scanning and molecular genetics. In no area is there a large effect size that combines with a clear mechanistic story. Some approaches have more promise than others. Searching for and explaining molecular genetic associations with ability differences has barely begun, although perhaps finding the associations is more likely to succeed than explaining them in the medium term. Studying the brain's metabolic changes in people of different ability levels is also a just-started enterprise, and one that seems certain to yield empirical differences that will need further work to understand. Surprisingly, bigger brains do covary with higher psychometric intelligence; no-one knows why as yet. Studies of nerve conduction velocity and mental ability differences have yet to lift the effect size much beyond zero. Nerve conduction velocity is not the basis for reaction time differences. Studies of the brain's ERPs have allowed a thousand methodological differences to bloom, providing a challenge to those wishing to extract pattern from noise; an attempt is made around a number of promising ERP-related themes and some replicated findings. On the one hand, therefore, this area of research is lively, with some associations being produced and replicated; on the other hand, there is much conceptual work to be done in understanding any brain difference–ability difference correlations.

INTRODUCTION

if (as many factorists affirm) it is unfair, in our present state of ignorance, to import physiological considerations into the picture, and if we are consequently to take our factors as describing, not hypothetical characteristics of the individual nervous system, but only observable characteristics of the individual mind, then certainly we had better refrain altogether from referring to such factors as concrete entities: to speak of 'factors in the mind' as if they existed in the same way as, but in addition to, the physical organs and tissues of the body and their properties, is assuredly both indefensible and misleading. (Burt 1940, p. 218)

Perhaps equally infused with Burt's urge to get down to the roots of ability differences in brain biology, researchers frequently correlate biological variables with psychometric intelligence scores. Much of the work is atheoretical and non-programmatic; that is, little of it builds towards theory or arises from it, and there are few large bodies of complementary research. The research presented here comes from the study of electroencephalography, evoked potentials, functional brain scanning, magnetic resonance imaging (MRI) scanning, nerve conduction speed, and brain size. There is an intention to integrate biological findings with information presented in other chapters. For example, some research has associated the P200 wave of the brain's evoked potential to inspection time performance and to individual differences in psychometric intelligence. The P300 of the evoked potential has been related to both reaction time and intelligence. Within the psychopharmacological tradition, cholinergic receptors have been manipulated with drugs to affect intelligence test scores, reaction times, and inspection times. Some studies of intelligence test scores and functional brain scanning have spawned 'neural efficiency' theories of intelligence.

The areas of study not included here are those in which the data appear not immediately understandable in terms of brain function. Thus, readers may wish to visit Jensen and Sinha's (1993) review of the correlations of mental ability differences with body size, mostly-pre-MRI-based measures of head and brain size, myopia, eye pigmentation, blood group types, serum uric acid, and a host of other variables. In addition to a surprising gallimaufry of ability difference–bodily difference correlations, there are in their review some useful explanations and warnings about the validity of results and the meanings of correlations that presage some of the strictures issued in Chapter 4.

Also not included below are studies in which a single report, though interesting, seems theoretically to lead nowhere obvious, or has not been replicated. The job of this book is to try to get at the information processing limitations in human brains that correlate with and perhaps explain some variance in human mental ability, and some judgement must be made about the explanatory value of any measure reported in the literature. For example, one study of over 40 schoolchildren reported a moderate-sized correlation between the pH of the brain and scores on the Wechsler Intelligence Scale for Children (WISC)-III (the full-scale and verbal scores but not the performance scale; Rae *et al.* 1996). The introduction to the article contains one reference that makes no argument for a mechanistic basis on which to seek and run the correlation. The discussion throws up possibilities for the mechanism of association via constructs such as ERP amplitude and synaptic neuroreceptor modulation, both of which might reflect information processing, but neither of which has a replicated strong association with mental ability test scores. A later study did not replicate this correlation, but it used a subject sample with different ages and proportions of the sexes, people with epilepsy versus healthy controls, different mental tests, and different brain areas to measure the pH of the brain (Anderson *et al.* 1998). Likewise, the finding, using proton magnetic resonance spectroscopy, that the brain's concentrations of compounds containing *N*-acetylaspartate (lower levels are associated with brain injury and cognitive decrements) and choline (elevated in brain injury) are correlated at or above 0.4 with Wechsler performance IQ in healthy adults awaits replication (Jung *et al.* 1999*a,b*). The report of an association between the blood concentration of the carotenoid antioxidants and cognitive performance is another potentially interesting one-off study associating markers of neuronal integrity and psychometric intelligence (Berr *et al.* 1998). Speculation on such inconclusive and underdeveloped lines of investigation is not a good use of the reader's or the author's time.

The field must wait until such studies gather more evidence before judging them worthy of more consideration. In the meantime there are some areas of investigation that have already collected a mass of evidence that qualifies them for inclusion here. The nature of the brain variables studied in relation to human ability differences makes for some interesting contrasts. In the cases of brain size and nerve conduction velocity the measures themselves have an accessible meaning; the quantities they assess are straightforward. On the other hand, if they do evince convincing correlations with psychometric intelligence, the explanatory gap between a big brain (or high nerve conduction velocities) and a high Wechsler Adult Intelligence Scale-Revised (WAIS-R) score is vertigo-inducing. Event-related potentials and electroencephalography appear closer to a measurement of the brain's function during thought, offering what seems like explanatory proximity to mental test score differences. The same might be said also for functional brain scanning procedures such as positron and photon emission tomography and functional MRI. Finally, one of the interesting possibilities in this field is offered by the long trail of investigation that will begin with any replicated associations between gene loci differences and mental ability differences.

MENTAL ABILITY AND BRAIN SIZE

Quite how a bigger brain could have some influence in attaining higher psychometric ability test scores, or perhaps even the reverse, is not clear. The absence of an explanatory construct to join these two distal variables notwithstanding, there is an interest in the association going back to antiquity. In Chapter 2, Huarte's sixteenth-century disquisition on human mental abilities discussed brain size as a correlate of high ability, but also insisted on the importance of the brain's quality and integrity of connections. He further noted that the size of the head, using a metaphor based on oranges, might not be a good indicator of brain size or quality. Fuller, in 1648, wrote equivocally about mental ability and brain size:

> Generally nature hangs out a sign of simplicity in the face of a fool; and there is enough in his countenance for a hue and cry to take him on suspicion: or else it is

stamped on the figure of his body; their heads sometimes so little, that there is no room for wit, sometimes so long, that there is no wit for so much room. (p. 75)

A digression on head size

Until *in vivo* imaging of the body's internal organs became possible, scientists wishing to measure the size of the inaccessible brain used what appeared to be the next best thing, the size of the head. On occasion, they would also use the skull of a deceased person and fill it with packing materials to gauge the brain's volume, and proceed to associate this with some proxy for mental ability level. These efforts were criticized and, arguably, lampooned by Gould (1981), who implied motives in addition to scientific curiosity in some researchers. Gould's allegations of bias were refuted (Michael 1988; Rushton 1997) and summaries of this research are available from Jensen and Sinha (1993), Rushton and Ankney (1996) and Vernon *et al.* (2000).

Pearson (1906–1907), at the beginning of the twentieth century, and almost concurrently with Spearman's (1904) discovery of *g* and Binet's (1905) invention of a psychometric ability test, stated:

(a) that there is a slight correlation between size of head and general intelligence,
(b) that this correlation is not sensibly increased by allowing for the size of the body relative to the size of the head,
(c) that the correlation is so small that it would be absolutely idle to endeavour to predict the intellectual ability of an individual from his or her head measurements. On the other hand, if a population were divided into those with large and those with small heads, we should expect to find a very slight balance of average intelligence in the former group. (p. 105)

Pearson studied data from 4638 schoolchildren and 1011 Cambridge graduates (data from Galton 1888). Teachers' estimates stood for the intelligence of children and degree classes were used to rank the graduates. A combined ranking of children and graduates used a 7-point scale from,

(α) Specially able: a mind especially bright and quick both in perception and reasoning about not only customary but novel facts. Able and accustomed to reason rightly about things on pure self-initiative.

to,

(η) Very dull. A mind capable of holding only the simplest facts, and incapable of grasping or reasoning about the relationship between facts; the very dull group covers but extends somewhat further up than the mentally defective. (p. 107)

Pearson's scale of intelligence was based on the idea of 'mentaces'. The median individual was set at zero and each standard deviation was 100 mentaces removed.

Genius he reckoned to be somewhere greater than +300 mentaces (nowadays, using a standard deviation of 15, an IQ of >145). The correlations between degree class and length and breadth of head for the 1011 Cambridge graduates were 0.111 and 0.097, respectively. The correlations between teachers' estimates of intelligence and length and breadth of the head were 0.139 and 0.109 for boys (N = 2298 and 2299, respectively) and 0.084 and 0.113 for girls (N = 2188 and 2165). Pearson appreciated the small amount of intelligence variance accounted for by head size:

> Thus, at a maximum, size of head might account for 12 to 20 mentaces out of the 350 which separate the mean of the specially able group from the mean of the very dull group. The millimetre which separates the head measurements of the slow boy from that of the intelligent corresponding to 2 mentaces—or if supposed additive for several measurements, to 6 to 10 at most—is of no effectiveness or value for purposes of prediction compared with the other causes which lead to an average difference of 120 mentaces. (p. 121)

> ... head measurements are not of real service as intelligence tests. ... We cannot measure agricultural labourers and men of science and point triumphantly to great differences in head volumes as marking widely separate intellectual grades. (p. 122).

Pearson rubbed in the point by discovering that hair colour was just as strong a predictor of intelligence as was head size:

> If you wish to take anthropometric measures into account—and they are not worth much—hair and eye colour will be as valuable as head measurements, and you need not produce the callipers in order to observe them! (p. 128)

Pearson concluded that there was little association between external physical and psychical aspects of man. He did not discuss the reason for the slight, but significant, association between head size and estimated intelligence. There were probably two reasons: the small size of the association, and the other, less interesting variables which had just as strong correlations with estimated intelligence.

Ninety years later Rushton and Ankney (1996) reviewed the association between head and brain size and psychometric intelligence. For external head size in children and adolescents, they found 13 studies containing 17 samples (including Pearson's) reported between 1906 and 1993 with a total N of 45,056. The range of correlations was 0.08 to 0.35; larger heads were associated with higher test scores in all studies. The weighted (for size of sample) mean correlation coefficient was 0.20 and the unweighted mean correlation was 0.21. Thus, head size in children and adolescents might account for about 4% of the variance in psychometric test scores. Between 1906 and 1994 there were 13 studies of the association between external head size and mental ability in adults. They recounted 15 samples with a total N of 6437. The range of correlations was 0.02 to 0.30; again, correlations always indicated that, overall, larger heads were associated with higher ability test scores. The weighted and unweighted correlations were 0.15. An updated review by Vernon *et al.* (2000) confirmed these effect sizes. These results are not distinctly different from Pearson's and there is no reason to differ from his assessment of the uselessness of external head size in assessing human mental ability.

Stott (1983) discussed problems related to some of the older studies of head size and intelligence. Among these were the findings that the small correlations between head size and psychometric intelligence or intelligence estimates would disappear when height was controlled, raters were not blind to the other measurements being made, and null results might not be published. Any or all of these effects might conjure small significant correlations out of nothing. Stott implied that apparent correlations between mental ability and head size were accepted uncritically by those who wished to promulgate a biologically-based theory of mental ability differences; he phrased the charge as no stronger than unconscious bias. He further charged that a proper perusal of the original publications did not afford acceptance of the association. Rushton and Ankney (1996) were more equivocal than Stott (1983) about the need to control for body size in studying head size–mental ability associations—and what questions are being asked when one does and does not make such a correction—but a final message must be that confounding variables can be especially devastating when effect sizes are small. The tone of Stott's review is not an uncommon one in this field of research; his search for factors that explain away any association between head size and psychometric intelligence takes him to broader areas of the practice of science and the agendas of those engaged in uncovering the bases of human ability differences (cf. Gould 1981). However, the threnody-writers, having fulfilled their obligation to science in terms of rooting out sources of potentially confounding variance, have a continuing obligation to notify the mourners of the corpse's revival, if such an event were to occur.

Brain size and psychometric intelligence

Head size is a poor proxy variable for brain size and, now that there is a coalescing bulk of studies relating brain size to psychometric intelligence, the correlations with head size—or the even more archaic studies involving post-mortem samples—are of mere historical interest. Year zero in this field of research was 1991, when Willerman *et al.* studied *in vivo* brain size and mental ability test scores. Forty students, 20 with IQs of 130 or greater (WAIS-R short form) and 20 with IQs of 103 or less, underwent magnetic resonance imaging of the brain. Inter-rater agreement for total brain volume was 0.99. Body size was controlled, and the sexes were analysed separately. All subjects were deemed middle class. The separated groups design is non-ideal for estimating a correlation between variables and, although there was a correlation of 0.51 between brain size and IQ, 0.35 was considered a more likely value in the general population. Bigger brains went with higher psychometric intelligence test scores.

Andreasen *et al.* (1993) reported the following correlations between total, MRI-estimated intracranial volumes and WAIS-R test scores in 67 normal adults: verbal

IQ = 0.37; performance IQ = 0.27; and full-scale IQ = 0.38. The corresponding correlations with cerebral grey matter volumes were 0.31, 0.32, and 0.35, although white matter and cerebrospinal fluid volumes gave non-significant correlations. Height was partialled from all correlations. There were similar correlations when, instead of total volumes, the volumes of the left and right cortices were considered. Examining specific areas, volume differences from the temporal lobes, the hippocampus, and the cerebellum gave similar correlations. There were no significant associations with caudate or lateral ventricle volumes. There were some male–female differences in the effect sizes of specific correlations, but the numbers were too small to have confidence in the robustness of such differences. These specific results add some discriminant and convergent validity; significant ability test score correlations were found with those areas subserving higher cognitive functions. The significant association with cerebellar volume provides the only modest surprise. The same research group replicated the associations between total brain size and WAIS-R full-scale IQ (r = 0.38) and cerebellar volume and ability test scores in a separate sample of 62 healthy adults (Paradiso *et al.* 1997). The effect sizes for cerebellum were smaller, between 0.19 and 0.27, and appeared to be important in their own right, the associations being corrected for total brain size. A later and larger study by the same team failed to replicate a significant ability test–cerebellar volume association (Flashman *et al.* 1998). Andreasen *et al.* (1993) commented that:

> Head size in human beings is influenced by brain growth; it is largely determined by the second year of life, when the skull sutures close, and is nearly complete by the sixth year. . . . one might infer that the factors that influence head and brain growth and intelligence are in operation quite early. This study does not point to what these factors might be.

In what might be taken as a replication of these results Raz *et al.* (1993) reported a significant correlation of 0.43 between MRI-estimated total volume of the cerebral hemispheres and scores on Cattell's Culture Fair Intelligence Test. The subjects were 29 healthy people (17 men) aged between 17 and 78 years. The mean age was 43.8 years and the age standard deviation was 21.5 years. There was no significant association with the hippocampal formation volume, by contrast with Andreasen *et al.*'s (1993) results. Controlling for age, head size, and sex rendered all correlations between brain size and mental ability test scores non-significant. Indeed, controlling for age alone rendered the association between ability test scores and brain volume non-significant. There was a significant association between leftward asymmetry of the brain and cognitive test scores that was independent of age, and this association attracted much of the hypothesis-forming energy in the paper. The small number of subjects combined with the large number of brain outcome measures provided a fertile seedbed for the sprouting of Type I and II statistical errors. The large age range of the subjects poses the question of whether the causes of any correlation between age and brain size are different from those that subserve any correlation between psychometric intelligence differences and brain size in an age-homogeneous sample. Bigler *et al.* (1995) provided some circumstantial evidence for such a view by demonstrating near-identical slopes for the age-related decline in brain volume (estimated by MRI) and the decline in WAIS-R performance subtest scores (sum of scaled scores). The brain volume and WAIS-R data were not gathered from the same subjects.

Intracranial volume correlated 0.69 with scores on the National Adult Reading Test in 34 normal adults aged between 19 and 49 years (Harvey *et al.* 1994). However, this study also contained a group of 26 bipolar (manic-depressive) patients with a premorbid IQ nine points lower than the controls (means of 109 versus 118); the two groups did not differ on 15 MRI-estimated brain volume indices. MRI-estimated brain size and Multidimensional Aptitude Battery test scores correlated 0.39 (full-scale IQ), 0.44 (verbal IQ), and 0.28 (performance IQ, non-significant) in an age- and sex-homogeneous group of 40 women aged between 20 and 40 years (Wickett *et al.* 1994). Similar results were obtained when left and right hemisphere volumes were assessed separately. Controlling for body size altered the correlations very little. There were no significant associations between head perimeter and ability test scores. There were no significant associations between brain size and the scores of two spatial ability tests. Brain size and head perimeter correlated only just above 0.2.

Egan and colleagues (1994, 1995) studied 40 soldiers (38 male) in their early 20s, and found uncorrected correlations (controlling for height and weight) between total brain volume and WAIS-R IQs as follows: full-scale = 0.32, verbal = 0.24, and performance = 0.24. The latter two are non-significant. The largest uncorrected correlation was a negative association between total brain volume and delayed logical memory (−0.40). When corrected for range attenuation the respective correlations are 0.40, 0.33, and 0.48. There were no significant associations between total brain volume and other memory tests or trail making, but the association with word fluency was 0.32 ($p < 0.025$). Grey matter volumes did not correlate significantly with ability test scores. White matter volume correlated significantly ($r = 0.27$) with WAIS-R full-scale IQ.

Grey matter volume did, however, correlate significantly ($r = 0.39$, after controlling for age and sex) with IQ in 69 children aged between 5 and 17 years (Reiss *et al.* 1996). The correlation with whole brain volume was 0.45. Both cortical and subcortical grey matter volumes contributed to the correlation, although the prefrontal grey matter volume within the cerebral cortices was the most important region contributing to the correlation with IQ scores. The frontal and temporal regions and total brain size, although not occipital, parietal, or cerebellar volumes, correlated significantly (between 0.25 and 0.28) with ability test scores on 90 young, healthy adults tested on the WAIS-R (Flashman *et al.* 1998). Examining WAIS-R subscales, there were similar associations with performance but not verbal IQs. There were no specific brain area associations with verbal versus performance IQ. Performance subtests, especially, had correlations with diffuse parts of the cerebral cortex.

Rushton and Ankney's (1996) semi-quantitative review of the associations between brain size and psychometric intelligence contained eight studies of normal (non-clinical) adults (total $N = 381$); seven employed magnetic resonance imaging and one used computerized axial tomography (an X-ray technique). Six of the studies administered psychometric ability tests, one recorded educational level, and one noted occupational status. The range of correlations between brain size and mental ability test scores (or proxies in the form of education or occupation) was 0.33 to 0.69, with larger brains associated with higher test scores. The *N*-weighted mean correlation was 0.42 and the unweighted mean correlation was 0.44. In Vernon *et al.*'s (2000) updated review the respective effect sizes were 0.40 and 0.38 for non-clinical samples. Similar results were found in a large twin sample (Pennington *et al.*, 2000). In examining the details of these studies and those newer studies that have added to this corpus, as discussed above, there is a significant residue association between total brain volume and mental ability test scores. Subtracting somewhat is a small study of 10 monozygotic co-twin pairs in whom there were near-zero correlations between WAIS-R IQ scores and forebrain volume, cortical surface area, corpus callosum area, and head circumference (Tramo *et al.* 1998). There are too few studies to specify a type of ability that has especially high associations and, as for brain areas, the frontal and temporal lobe volumes, perhaps, have the highest associations.

Rushton and Ankney (1996) began the process of reflecting on such an association. Their computed effect size is moderately large, with the shared variance being at least 16%. It is 'at least' this because the measurements (brain size and IQ) are typically uncorrected for any unreliability or restriction in the samples' ranges. On the other hand, some newer studies have more modest effects, and one must bear in mind that reports with smaller effect sizes or negative results may be more likely to go unpublished and thus incorrectly inflate the publicly apparent effect size. Examination of the correlation has proceeded by asking more detailed questions about the areas of the brain that have the strongest associations with ability test scores and by positing the constructs that might provide part of the mechanism of association. Some of the suggested constructs are listed in Table 9.1. There is much variety: some notions pertain to whole brain indices, some to multicellular organizational units within the cortex of the cerebral hemispheres, some to cell number, some to intercellular factors, some to intracellular factors, and some to development. At worst, one looks at the variety and vagueness and wonders how much these guesses better the sixteenth century speculations of Huarte (Chapter 2). However, they are better based on evidence and the onus is on those following up the reasonably well-established brain size–mental ability correlation to better formulate and rigorously test some of these ideas. It is important to keep in mind, however, that subsequent effort is not being thrown at the problem of what makes some people better at ability test scores, it is attempting to explain a small minority of the variance in such differences. Empirically testing some of the hypothesis has begun. For example, Anderson (1995) failed to find any significant association between ability differences in 41 rats and measures of the dendritic arborization in their parietal lobes. Comparability with humans is obviously limited, although a variety of mental tests in these rats showed a general factor accounting for 29% of the variance in mental test performances. Another novel approach to following up brain size–mental ability associations has been to compare the brains of exceptional persons with normal controls. Reflecting his unusually insightful visuospatial

Table 9.1 Suggestions for constructs to account for the correlation between brain size and psychometric ability test scores

Author	Suggested mechanisms of association
Willerman *et al.* (1991)	'larger size might reflect more cortical columns available for analyzing high-noise or low-redundancy signals, thus enabling more efficient information processing pertinent to IQ test performance.' 'a greater number of stem cells, an increased number of mitotic divisions producing more descendant neurons, or different rates of neuronal death.'
Andreasen *et al.* (1993)	'aspects of brain structure that reflect "quality" rather than "quantity" of brain tissue: complexity of circuitry, dendritic expansion, number of synapses, thickness of myelin, metabolic efficiency, or efficiency of neurotransmitter production, release, and reuptake. Factors such as these would facilitate the speed and efficiency of information transfer within the brain as well as expand its capacity, so that multiple tasks of multiple kinds could be performed simultaneously.' 'The greater volume of grey matter can be postulated to reflect a greater number of nerve cell bodies and dendritic expansion; a greater number of neuronal connections presumably enhances the efficiency of computational processing in the brain.'
Raz *et al.* (1993)	'leftward volume asymmetry may reflect either a greater number of processing elements or more extensive connectivity in the left hemisphere. Gross hemispheric asymmetries are likely to arise from differences in the number of neurons rather than from altered dendritic arborization or cell packing density ... the volume advantage is likely to reflect the excess of processing modules (cortical columns).'
Wickett *et al.* (1994)	'The brain size–IQ correlation of $r = 0.395$ clearly indicates that either there are many more variables to be introduced in an attempt to explain intelligence, or that the measure of brain size is itself only a proxy, and an imperfect one, to some aspect of the brain (e.g. neuronal quantity or myelinization) that is relevant to cognitive ability.'
Egan *et al.* (1994)	'it at [sic] seems plausible that small differences in brain volume translate into millions of excess neurones for some individuals, accounting for their higher IQ.'

cognition, Einstein's brain had unusual morphology in the posterior parietal lobes, although his brain was not large, overall (Witelson *et al.* 1999). Assuming that anything at all can be gleaned from a single brain, this report encourages a search for brain size–morphology associations with specific mental abilities with less emphasis on general mental ability.

NERVE CONDUCTION VELOCITY

The motivation to find some simple measure of speed of nervous function is not a driving principle in this volume. If it were, then among the simpler routes would be to seek an account of psychometric intelligence in the speed with which nervous impulses pass along axons and dendrites. The techniques for assessing peripheral nerve conduction velocity are well established, and the reduced velocity with which the peripheral nerves transmit an externally induced nervous impulse in some clinical conditions is well known. Wickett and Vernon's (1994) thinking behind examining individual differences in nerve conduction velocity and mental ability differences was as follows:

> It is logical, given the relationship between RT [reaction time] and IQ, to ponder what the neural substrate of this speed factor might be. The simplest, and clearest, explanation is that the speed at which the neuron fires is the key neural underpinning.

The research did not begin auspiciously. Barrett *et al.* (1990) did not find a significant association between nerve conduction velocity and scores on Raven's Advanced Progressive Matrices in 44 people. They did, however, find an association with variability in nerve conduction velocity. A limitation in this study was less-than-sufficient stimulation of the peripheral nerves in order to induce an impulse. In a study of 200 male students Reed and Jensen (1991) found no significant association between nerve conduction velocity and scores on Raven's Matrices. However, they did not appropriately and equally warm the arms of their subjects. The conduction velocity of the limbs is affected by temperature and Reed and Jensen instead controlled for temperature statistically.

In two studies that included over 170 students, Vernon and Mori (1992) assessed mental ability differences (Multidimensional Aptitude Battery, MAB), reaction times, and upper limb nerve conduction velocity without the aforementioned limitations in methodology. In the first study the MAB subtests, 12 reaction time measures and various nerve conduction velocity measures were separately factored to deliver general measures of each. The general psychometric intelligence measure correlated –0.44 with general reaction time and 0.42 with the nerve conduction velocity measure. General reaction time correlated –0.28 with nerve conduction velocity. In the second study only three reaction time tests were used and there was a single measure of nerve conduction velocity, and the respective correlations were –0.45, 0.48, and –0.18. These are all in the expected direction, such that higher mental ability test scores go with faster reaction times and increased velocity of nervous conduction. However, when nerve conduction velocity was partialled from the reaction time–psychometric intelligence correlation, the correlation remained almost the same in both studies. Therefore, although there might be some association between nerve conduction velocity and psychometric intelligence, it is not the basis for the correlation between ability test score differences and reaction times (at least for the rather complex reaction times employed by Vernon and Mori). Neural modelling studies by Anderson (1994) concurred in suggesting that nerve conduction velocity parameter changes did not replicate the pattern of results expected from human reaction time studies.

Wickett and Vernon (1994) used the same methodology and tried to replicate Vernon and Mori's (1992) findings in 38 young women. The correlations were all non-significant: ability test scores versus reaction times = −0.24, and nerve conduction velocity correlations with psychometric intelligence were near to zero, as were reaction time correlations with nerve conduction velocity. A re-examination of the data from Vernon and Mori unearthed the possibility that nerve conduction velocity was related to mental ability differences in men but not in women. Tan (1996) concurred and even suggested a reverse association in women. In two reports on a group of over 300 Dutch twins, correlations of −0.02 and 0.15 ($p < 0.05$) were obtained between peripheral nerve conduction velocity and psychometric intelligence (Rijsdijk *et al.* 1995; Rijsdijk and Boomsma 1997). The latter, small but significant association was entirely mediated by genetic factors, which offers an interesting lead in unpicking the causes of this association if it is deemed to be of sufficient importance. Vernon *et al.* (2000) reviewed the literature on psychometric intelligence and nerve conduction velocity. In 12 samples, with a total N of 922, the unweighted and n-weighted mean *r*'s were 0.17 and 0.15. Separating the samples into men (N = 368) and women (N = 166) resulted in effect sizes of 0.33 (n-weighted = 0.22) and 0.00 (n-weighted = 0.05), respectively.

Reed and Jensen (1992) examined conduction velocity and Raven's Advanced Progressive Matrices scores in 147 males. Their thinking was that such an association might obtain because of differences in 'brain design', conduction velocity, and/or cortical speed of synaptic transmission. Conduction velocity was assessed in the brain. Pattern reversal visual-evoked potentials, using checkerboard stimuli, were used to find latencies of the negative peak at 70 ms and the positive peak at 100 ms. Fore-to-aft head size was measured and the combination of velocities and head size was used to achieve measures of 'brain nerve conduction velocities'. The validity of such velocity measures is moot; however, the associations between Raven's and conduction velocities based upon the N70 and P100 latencies were 0.18 and 0.26, respectively, with higher test scores and faster conduction going together. Correlations between the actual latency scores for N70 and P100 and matrices scores were only slightly lower and in the same direction.

Reed and Jensen (1993*a*) went on to examine somatosensory evoked potentials and Raven's Matrices in 205 male college and university students. Somatosensory evoked potentials are brief latencies observed after stimulation of a peripheral nerve (in this case the median nerve at the wrist). Negative troughs at means of about

13 and 19 ms after stimulation, respectively, are measured over the cervical verte-
brae and somatosensory cortex, and originate in the upper spinal cord/medulla and
thalamus. P22, recorded at the same site as N19, originates in the somatosensory
cortex. Arguing from their previous study of brain nerve conduction velocity and
psychometric intelligence, Reed and Jensen suggested that the difference between
P22 and N19 represents the time for impulses to travel from the thalamus to the
parietal cortex and that this time difference might correlate with ability differences. Subjects' physical sizes and temperatures were used as covariates. The only
significant association was between P22–N19 latency difference and ability test
scores ($r = -0.217$), although the correlation between matrices scores and P22
latency was marginally significant (-0.156); higher ability test scorers had shorter
latency differences, although the effect is not large and is in the midst of other,
non-significant outcome variables, so a Type I error cannot be ruled out. Reed and
Jensen's suggestion was that central but not peripheral nerve conduction velocities
contribute to ability test score differences. However, in this and another study of
the differences in conduction velocity in the visual system, Reed and Jensen
(1993*a,b*) found near-zero correlations between central nervous system conduction
velocities and reaction times, although each had significant associations with ability test scores. Reed and Jensen (1993*b*) concluded and then speculated that:

> there are two independent processes affecting information-processing sped [sic],
> one RT linked and one cortical NCV linked. . . . Increased cortical NCV
> (reflected by increased thalamocortical NCV) would carry information faster
> along the cortical nerve fibers and therefore increase information-processing
> speed and, consequently, level of intelligence, and vice versa. Decreased total
> cortical nerve path length (between visual cortex and motor cortex), required
> for a correct RT decision (for example), might also increase information
> processing speed, and vice versa. (p. 449)

Quite a lot needs to be said about that short passage. There are few studies in
this field and the methods used for visual pathway length estimation have yet
to be validated. The effect sizes obtained account for small amounts of variance
(well below 10%). These comments do not contradict anything stated by the
researchers, they just act as a reminder that small packets of variance, if any, are
being picked off. It is a concern that the authors so quickly invoke two separate
brain constructs to account for processing speed differences. Again, these might
be defensible in that they merely follow the results but they do little more. The
mentioning of the construct 'information-processing speed' needs special attention
in the above paragraph. We should ask: what explanatory work does it do, and
how could it be measured independently of the physiological and psychometric
measures whose correlation it has been summoned to bridge? In other words, is
'information-processing speed' as used here (a) a theoretical soup stone (Navon
1984), (b) a sensible higher-level description of what happens at a molar level
in the brain, governed by a number of neural parameters, or (c) an independent
explanatory construct or emergent property?

In summary, as Vernon *et al.* (2000) concluded, "the evidence for an NCV-IQ correlation is weak and mixed . . . the *pattern* of the relationships between them does not appear to follow predictions."

THE BRAIN'S ELECTRICAL RESPONSES

The brain is a computer, albeit one built out of neural and glial tissues ('wetware') rather than hardware. Still, differences in the power of personal computers typically reflect hardware differences among them, e.g. in clock rate. On similar logic, some writers have suggested that individual differences in brain power might depend on differences in basic biological computing machinery on which higher-level mental abilities are instantiated. One long-standing idea (Chalke and Ertl 1965) has been that variation in intelligence might reflect measurable individual differences in speed or reliability of nerve transmission in the central nervous system (CNS). But the brain is a complicated organ, and any simple analogy between brain power and CPU power may be misleading, even though this metaphor recurs frequently in intelligence research (Chapter 8). If, instead, we liken brains to competing sports cars, it becomes obvious that differences in speed might reflect not only engine capacity or performance but differences in the operators' skills in using their engine's capabilities, tactical decisions (to conserve fuel, to push through a rare opening, etc.), or knowledge (of risks and demands of a specific part of the course). On this analogy, differences in measures of the performance of the biological machinery in the brains of bright and less intelligent people might reflect differences in the way the basic machinery was employed that were consequences of differences in intelligence, rather than factors causing these differences. This latter theme is picked up again in the discussion on functional brain scanning later in the chapter.

Can the study of differences in brain activity in people with high and low intelligence distinguish between such possibilities and show whether biological variation underpins normal variability in intelligence? The most readily available non-intrusive indices of brain operation (Posner and Raichle 1994) are brain event-related potentials (ERPs, termed averaged evoked potentials, AEPs, in early literature) and the familiar EEG (electroencephalogram) record.

ERPs are tiny potential changes at the surface of the scalp (changes of only a few microvolts buried in electroencephalographic activity of much greater magnitude) that are time-locked to stimuli or responses. They reflect electrical activity in the underlying brain associated with stimulus analysis, decision making, and initiation of the responses (Rugg and Coles 1995). They can yield information about activation and timing of the kinds of cognitive processes that psychologists represent in black-box diagrams, in addition to (and relatively independently of) the information from response measures such as reaction times. A typical ERP waveform displays a series of irregular peaks and troughs, and some of these can be linked to particular cognitive processes. For instance, the widely-studied P3 or P300 peak (a positive wave around 300 ms after stimulus onset) is elicited particularly by rare, significant variants of an otherwise monotonously repeated stimulus; it is thought to reflect identification of these 'oddball' stimuli and updating of working memory to note their occurrence. Since even people with dementia notice these stimuli, latency of this peak can provide a measure of the latency of an aspect of brain functioning in patients for whom a task requiring active decision making and response would be impossible (Polich *et al.* 1986). The N400 component (a negative wave around 400 ms after stimulus onset) is elicited by words which are incongruous in the context of a preceding sentence frame, e.g. by the last word in 'He took his tea with milk and Sarajevo'. For psycholinguists, variation in the amplitude of the N400 can provide a sensitive electrophysiological index of the semantic priming between related words (Kutas and van Petten 1994). For clinicians, it can provide evidence, for example, of the reduced and delayed semantic priming effects in patients with language difficulties arising from Alzheimer's type dementia (Iragui *et al.* 1996). Thus ERPs (and their magnetic equivalents—MEPs) offer a window on the progress of even complex mental operations over the half-second or second before any response occurs (Posner and Raichle 1994).

An ongoing EEG, discovered by Berger in the 1920s (Gloor 1994), is composed of rhythmic activity across a number of frequency bands, and changes in distribution of activity among these bands have been linked to alertness and mental effort. In deep sleep, slow delta and theta rhythms dominate; in awake but relaxed subjects faster alpha and beta activity is observed; and mental effort or attention to the visual world leads to displacement of the alpha by the faster beta rhythms giving a desynchronized, low-voltage EEG. Even faster gamma rhythms are important in linking the electrical responses of cells that are responding to the same stimulus object, but knowledge of these comes chiefly from physiological studies of animals, and they have not been examined in connection with human mental ability differences (Jefferys *et al.* 1996). Variation in distribution of electroencephalography activity across the scalp can be linked to the demands of specific tasks, while analyses of coherence (similarity of activity at different frequencies) and phase differences in the EEG at different points on the scalp have thrown light on differentiation of functioning in different parts of the brain, for example during cognitive development (Thatcher *et al.* 1987). But frequency analysis of the EEG requires sampling over a second or two, and so spontaneous electroencephalography provides a coarse-grained time resolution more comparable to functional magnetic resonance imaging than to the fine-grained picture of stimulus processing that is provided by ERPs (Posner and Raichle 1994).

Efforts to use these psychophysiological measures to understand normal variation in psychometric intelligence have a lengthy history (Barrett and Eysenck 1992*a,b*; Deary and Caryl 1993, 1997*a*). Early workers thought that ERPs might eventually provide a 'culture-fair test of intellectual potential' (Crawford 1974). The recent consensus view (Neisser *et al.* 1996) is that some aspects of EEG and ERP measures do show moderate correlations with psychometric intelligence (although some claimed that there are no meaningful correlations once studies including brain-damaged subjects have been excluded, e.g. Howe 1988). ERP measures certainly do not provide a physiological substitute for psychometric tests: rather, they provide indirect evidence about the underlying cognitive processes that might be likened to the indirect evidence about enemy plans and strategies available to wireless intelligence officers in the Second World War.

Several different kinds of ERP measure have been linked to psychometric intelligence differences: differences in the latency of ERP components (individual peaks or troughs of the ERP); differences in the frequency content or overall 'complexity' of the waveform; differences in overall amplitude of the waveform that reflect task conditions or the predictability of stimuli; and differences in the shape of specific parts of the waveform. These links provide support for a variety of ideas about underlying mechanisms, from global differences in the speed or reliability of the CNS, through variability in the way different people allocate processing power between predictable and unpredictable stimuli, to more specific differences in performance of particular stages of stimulus processing. Whereas the hope that ERPs would provide a direct, culture-free measure of intelligence now seems naïve and unrealizable, a more realistic goal is to apply ERPs to understand brain function in tasks that are of psychometric interest, with an increased understanding of 'biological' underpinnings of psychometric intelligence differences as a likely side-benefit. It is worth emphasizing that, although writers such as Eysenck (1982) have equated 'biological' intelligence with the heritable element of intelligence, there are no grounds for believing that biological measures such as ERPs or EEGs provide a direct route to this. After all, the variation in semantic priming which is revealed by ERP measures such as N400 amplitude is more likely to reflect variation in acquired knowledge of the meanings of words than variation in inherited linguistic ability, while studies of heritability of EEG measures demonstrate that individual differences in these measures reflect shared environment as well as shared genotype (e.g. Ibatoullina *et al.* 1994).

Event-related potential latencies

As Chalke and Ertl (1965) expected, 'smarter' people's brains apparently do run faster: one of the most consistent correlates of high intelligence has been shorter latency of particular components of the ERP waveform (Deary and Caryl 1993). The studies reviewed here illustrate this negative correlation across a variety of methodologies, with demanding ERP tasks or no task at all, and using a variety of participants; but the review also points to some of the issues that make it difficult to extrapolate from ERP latencies to the (hypothetical) more basic differences in speed of some aspect of central nervous system performance.

Gasser *et al.* (1988) presented 10–13-year-old children with simple visual flash stimuli; no decision task was required, and they observed rank correlations up to –0.30 between latency of ERP components and WISC verbal IQ and correlations up to –0.55 with another ability measure (Prufsystem für Schul- und Bildungsberatung, PSB). The widely used oddball task is a little more demanding: participants must identify occasional rare variants in a stream of identical common tones that differ substantially from the oddballs, and these oddballs trigger a

P300 component in participants' ERPs. O'Donnell *et al.* (1990) compared healthy controls and people with dementia aged around 65 years in active (counting) and passive (ignoring) versions of the task. Correlations of up to –0.76 (median –0.50) were found between P300 latency and subtests of the WAIS-R and Wechsler Memory Scale in the control group performing the active task, although their correlations were substantially smaller (median –0.18) in the passive task. McGarry-Roberts *et al.* (1992) analysed the ERPs of young adults performing a range of tasks from simple RT to more demanding memory scanning and decision tasks. Correlations between P300 latency and full-scale IQ varied between tasks and ranged up to –0.38, while the correlation of –0.36 between the *g*-factors extracted from P300 latencies and from the intelligence-test battery was stronger than that for the *g*-factor from RT. Burns *et al.* (2000) also found substantial negative correlations between ERP latencies and measures of fluid and crystallised intelligence. Thus, modern studies partly confirm the negative relationship claimed in Ertl's pioneering work.

As not all studies have revealed a significant negative relationship, are there 'right' and 'wrong' ways to look for it? Does it show up more clearly with demanding or undemanding tasks, and with short- or long-latency ERP components? Using simple click stimuli, Widaman *et al.* (1993) found only weak negative relationships between psychometric ability test scores and latencies of the mid-latency ERP components (around 100–200 ms). Zúrron and Díaz (1998) found no mental ability-related differences in early (up to 10 ms) or mid-latency ERP components using simple auditory stimuli, but found a correlation of –0.45 for the later P300 component in an active version of the oddball task, but not in the passive version of this task. McGarry-Roberts *et al.* (1992) found substantial negative correlations between P300 latency and ability test scores in complex decision tasks, but not in elementary reaction time tasks. O'Donnell *et al.* (1990) found that the strongest correlations among non-demented participants were in the active version of their oddball task—but among demented participants the correlation was stronger in the passive version.

Shucard and Horn (1972) discovered that correlations with psychometric intelligence depended on task conditions: their ERP latency correlations were highest when subjects relaxed and were given no task to perform with the ERP stimuli, and lowest when task involvement was high. Such important early results are difficult to link to more recent work: as in most early studies, Schucard and Horn adopted the practice of labelling ERP components sequentially rather than in terms of latency and polarity, and used Ertl's bipolar electrode placement rather than the monopolar placement used in most modern work, creating two problems in interpreting the results. First, early peaks or troughs may be missing in some ERPs (e.g. Gasser *et al.* 1988) and some components may have more than one peak; therefore, strictly applied, sequential labelling can assign the same identity to peaks (or troughs) that represent different (functional) ERP components in different subjects. This happened in early studies of intelligence (Prescott 1975), confounding the within-component and between-component latency differences in their results. Second, Ertl's bipolar electrodes (Ertl and Schafer 1969) measured potential difference between two active neighbouring sites on the scalp, whereas the monopolar placements usual today compare activity between an active site on the scalp and an inactive site such as the linked earlobes. (As a nautical analogy, contrast the estimates of the size of the sea's swell obtained by sighting from bow to stern of a rowing boat, and by sighting from the boat to a stationary mark on the nearby sea-wall.) Ertl's placement emphasized the (high-frequency) local variation in the broad (low-frequency) waves of electrical activity that are revealed by monopolar placements (Regan 1989). These two features make most early studies of correlations between latency and intelligence very difficult to interpret or to relate to more recent work.

Neural adaptability: dependence on task conditions

The above-mentioned variation across task conditions hints that ERP latency–psychometric intelligence correlations may not reflect differences in the basic speed of all brain operations in bright and dull subjects, but rather differences in the way in which they use their brains in particular circumstances. Thus ERP–ability correlations may reflect the state-consequences of ability differences rather than their trait-causes. Schafer's (1982, 1985) work linked variation in the overall amplitude of the ERP under different conditions to hypothetical differences in a construct termed 'neural adaptability'. Schafer believed that higher-ability subjects would allocate processing power away from predictable, unimportant stimuli while lower-ability subjects would distribute their stimulus processing effort more evenly. He found that, compared with lower-ability people, higher-ability people showed greater amplitude decrements to predictable but irregular click stimuli (compared to equally irregular but unpredictable stimuli), and that higher-ability people habituated faster than lower-ability people to loud repeated stimuli. Although Schafer's measures of 'neural adaptability' based on the amplitude of the overall ERP showed substantial correlations with psychometric intelligence (e.g. 0.66 with Wechsler full-scale IQ, and correlations with subtest scores that reflected each subtest's *g*-loading; Schafer 1985), his results have stimulated little further investigation, presumably because the direction of causation here is apparently from intelligence to the differences in allocation of processing power—electrophysiology here reveals consequences of differences in intelligence, rather than tapping into their causes.

Elementary cognitive tasks, event-related potentials and psychometric intelligence

The stimuli or tasks used in many ERP studies of intelligence impose trivial or zero processing loads on most subjects and so are far removed from the demands of the typical intelligence test. There is little reason to expect strong relationships between IQ test performance and the speed of processing of simple visual or auditory stimuli by relaxed subjects—but experimenters have looked for one anyway, rather as a person might begin to look for their car keys under a street-light where searching was easy, rather than in the dark nearer the car where they had dropped them (Chapter 4). A few studies have used ERP tasks which, although still repetitive and less demanding than psychometric ability test items, can with greater justification to be linked to ability test scores. For example, several research groups have studied the inspection time task, which demands discrimination of simple visual stimuli under conditions of different stimulus durations (Chapter 7). ERPs in this task should reveal processing differences that might link to psychometric ability test scores, as the differences in inspection time threshold that are consequences of these differences in processing do correlate significantly, around −0.4 with some ability test scores. Recent ERP studies identify a region relatively early in the ERP, between 100 and 200 ms after stimulus onset, ending with the P200 component, as the primary region of interest in this task.

The P200 component of the ERP has not been studied extensively, but can be linked to early phases of stimulus identification. The N100–P200 (or N1–P2) wavefront has been identified by Chapman *et al.* (1981) as the point at which the 'sensory event' of sensory decision theory occurs. Lindholm and Koriath (1985) identified a process starting around 150 ms and peaking at P200 that was responsible for the preliminary identification and classification of stimuli, and for starting the decision process involved in responding to them. Therefore, individual differences (e.g. in efficiency) in this early stage of stimulus processing might account for differences in inspection time threshold. In observers performing inspection time tasks, Zhang *et al.* (1989) found individual differences in the rise-time of the N1–P2 wavefront; it was steeper in subjects with high ability test scores. This difference was confirmed by Caryl (1994) and Morris and Alcorn (1995), using different but related tasks and measures of the ERP. Representative correlations of the various ERP-based measures with psychometric intelligence test scores ranged from 0.34 to 0.52, disregarding sign, which depends on whether slope or rise-time is used as the index.

Similar differences in the N1–P2 wavefront were linked to individual differences in inspection time, correlations ranging from 0.34 to 0.59, again disregarding the sign (Fig. 9.1). The higher ability test-scoring participants used here showed only modest correlations between inspection time and ability test scores, so these correlations with psychometric intelligence were not mere consequences of correlations with inspection time. There were other signs of independence of the relationships to inspection time and psychometric test scores: weaker correlations with ability test scores were observed with brief inspection stimuli than with longer-duration unmasked stimuli in the same tasks (Zhang *et al.* 1989; Caryl 1994; Morris and Alcorn 1995). This suggests that processing differences normally linked to psychometric intelligence may be reduced when observers are forced to speed up stimulus analysis because of the backward mask. Attention certainly affects the ERP in this latency range. In an experimental condition in which observers did not need to attend to inspection time stimuli, the correlation between N1–P2 rise time and inspection time was reduced (Zhang *et al.* 1989). So ERP techniques have shown that higher psychometric intelligence is accompanied by differences in just those early stages of stimulus processing that might be important for the rapid discrimination required by the inspection time

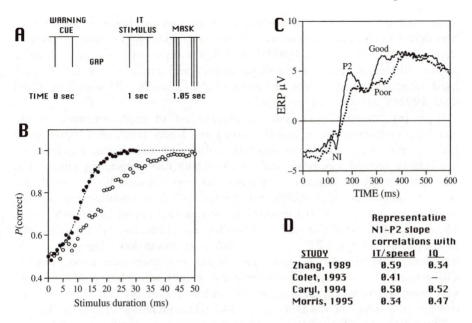

A

WARNING
CUE

IT
STIMULUS   MASK

GAP

TIME 0 sec   1 sec   1.05 sec

B

P(correct)

Stimulus duration (ms)

C

ERP µV

Good

P2

Poor

N1

TIME (ms)

D

Representative
N1–P2 slope
correlations with

STUDY	IT/speed	IQ
Zhang, 1989	0.59	0.34
Colet, 1993	0.41	–
Caryl, 1994	0.50	0.52
Morris, 1995	0.34	0.47

Fig. 9.1 Studies of triangulating psychometric test scores, psychophysical measures, and psychophysiological indices. (A) A cartoon of a typical inspection time task trial, with a cue, stimulus, and backward mask (see Fig. 7.1). (B) The association between stimulus duration (ms) in the inspection time task and the probability of a correct response (see Fig. 7.2). (C) Event-related potentials (ERPs) averaged across groups who were deemed good and poor on the basis of their performance on the inspection time task. ERPs were collected in response to inspection time stimuli; that is, subjects were performing the inspection time task while the ERPs were being collected. Note the difference between the groups in the excursion of the ERP waveform from N1 to P2. (D) Representative correlations between measures of the N1–P2 slope (not always collected concurrently with inspection time performance, and sometimes including auditory oddball stimuli) and measures of inspection time (or other speed of processing measure) and with psychometric intelligence test scores. Redrawn from Deary and Caryl (1997*a*).

task. However, the differences revealed are in speed of transition between different stages of the ERP, rather than simple differences in processing speed or ERP latency as would be expected on the CPU clock rate analogy.

ERP slope differences in the N1–P2 region are important in contexts other than with the standard pi-figure of the visual inspection time task. Morris and Alcorn (1985) found comparable differences using backward-masked letters as stimuli, while Colet *et al.* (1993) reported differences (linked to visual inspection time) in the N1–P2 wavefront of auditory ERPs from a conventional oddball task. However, in an auditory processing task, originally designed to capture processing limitations analogous to those of visual inspection time, the N1–P2 wavefront was not steeper, although it did occur later in the subjects who had a low auditory processing threshold (Caryl *et al.* 1995), while in other tasks, other early waveform differences are linked to intelligence or task performance.

Some evidence shows that people scoring higher on psychometric ability tests have better pitch discrimination as well as shorter auditory processing thresholds (Raz *et al.* 1987; Deary *et al.* 1989*b*). The ERPs of those with good pitch discrimination differed in terms of the shape (latency and amplitude) of the P2 peak itself, rather than in the slope or timing of the earlier N1–P2 wavefront (Caryl *et al.* 1995; Caryl and Harper 1996).

High psychometric intelligence is also linked to faster responses on the Sternberg memory-scanning task (Neubauer and Knorr 1998; see Chapter 6). In ERPs to the target stimuli in this task, subgroups with higher psychometric intelligence showed a negative shift in the whole ERP, beginning around 165 ms, with consequent negative correlations between full-scale IQ and amplitude of later components (e.g. P400) that reached –0.60 in visually-presented and –0.67 in auditorily-presented versions of the task (Pelosi and Blumhardt 1992). The onset (165 ms) of this shift in the ERP waveforms corresponds fairly well to the timing of the ERP differences linked to inspection times; but in the inspection time task, people with higher ability test scores have a more positive ERP around P2, whereas in the Sternberg task, bright people have a more negative ERP from P2 onwards, indicating that differences in N1–P2 slope are only relevant in a subset of the elementary tasks that correlate with intelligence.

These various ERP studies confirm that psychometric intelligence differences can modulate the relatively early stages of stimulus processing in ways that are relevant to performance in some demanding tasks. As this influence can be detected even where stimuli impose no special processing demands, this makes it less likely that it indicates, for example, that bright people employ a different strategy to do the task, prompting the tenable hypothesis that it reflects biologically-based differences in information-processing potential in people who differ in psychometric intelligence.

Event-related potential amplitudes

Various differences in the amplitude of ERP components, in a range of ERP tasks, have been linked empirically to psychometric intelligence (e.g. Josiassen *et al.* 1988). The results do not tell a consistent story. Alcorn and Morris (1996) found positive correlations between scores on Raven's Matrices and P300 amplitude in adults performing an inspection time task. In an oddball task, Lubar *et al.* (1990) and Segalowitz *et al.* (1992) reported greater P300 amplitude in higher-ability child subjects. In contrast, negative correlations were found by McGarry-Roberts *et al.* (1992) between full-scale IQ and P300 amplitude across a range of decision tasks in 18–25-year olds. Gasser *et al.* (1988) found negative correlations between intelligence and amplitude of several components in ERPs to simple flashes in children. Robaey *et al.* (1995) also reported negative relationships in children between psychometric intelligence and the amplitude of several ERP components from a variety of decision tasks; the strength of the effect varied depending on the measure of psychometric intelligence (verbal IQ, performance IQ, or Piagetian) and whether it was corrected for age. Differences in P300 amplitude may reflect the effort invested or the person's confidence in the identification of a stimulus (Caryl and Harper 1996). The precise explanations for these discrepancies in results remain to be clarified, but since higher-ability people can show higher-amplitude ERPs in some studies and lower amplitude in others, measures of ERP amplitude do not offer a straightforward biological correlate of psychometric intelligence.

Event-related potential complexity and psychometric intelligence

Early studies suggested that ERP traces of lower-ability subjects were simple, smooth curves, whereas the traces of higher-ability subjects were more complex and irregular (Ertl and Schafer 1969; Perry and Childers 1969). The first attempts to quantify this used power in different frequency bands (Fourier analysis) or simple 'map-wheel' line-length measures. Frequency bands reappear in work by Robinson (1993), who argued that individual differences can be represented best by filtering the complex ERP waveform into three separate frequency bands. Measures akin to map-wheel indices were used by the Hendricksons who suggested that the ERP differences reflected reliability in the CNS (A. E. Hendrickson 1982; D. E. Hendrickson 1982). They proposed 'string-length' and variance measures to quantify complexity of the averaged ERP waveform and variability of individual records. They showed that intelligence had substantial positive correlations with string length (e.g. 0.72 in a large sample of schoolchildren), and negative correlations with the variance measure. There is still very little support for the details of the complex nerve pulse-train and biochemical mechanisms put forward by A. E. Hendrickson (1982), and there is mixed support for their more focused empirical claims concerning string-length measures of the ERP and psychometric intelligence (Barrett and Eysenck 1994; Burns *et al.* 1996). From 1981 to 1996 a significant positive string-length correlation was found in six published studies. Nine studies over this period failed to find the hypothesized positive relationship; three of these reported a correlation that was significant in the direction opposite to the hypothesis. The unsuccessful studies include some in which great efforts were made to replicate the Hendricksons' procedures (Barrett and Eysenck 1994), as well as those with substantial differences in technique.

Several factors may underlie this variation in results. The Hendricksons used auditory stimuli and resting subjects while others employed a wider range of stimuli or used situations in which the subjects could not relax. Differences in ERP amplitude may occur when subjects differ in intelligence and these will tend to increase string length. Some researchers have scaled ('normalized') their ERPs so that the string measure was uncontaminated by amplitude differences and thus supposedly reflected complexity only. The Hendricksons used unscaled ERPs so that their values would include the effects of amplitude differences. In several studies a strong contribution to overall string length has been identified as arising from that part of the ERP around N1, or the N1–P2 wavefront. In such cases the string-length measure might be a surrogate for N1–P2 amplitude. Attention affects the ERP waveform around N1; thus Bates and Eysenck (1993*b*) proposed that string length might provide a capacity index when ERPs are taken at rest, but an efficiency index when ERPs are recorded to an attended task. Psychometric intelligence scores do correlate highly with the difference in string length between 'attend' and 'ignore' runs in an auditory oddball task (Bates *et al.* 1995*b*). This indicates a need to regulate the attentional state of participants in future string-length studies; the original procedure, with its lack of task demands, leaves this state poorly defined. Moreover, it confirms the view, now familiar, that ERP measures are unlikely to yield the simple, monotonic, indicators of biological intelligence hoped for by pioneers such as Ertl.

The Hendricksons' variance measure, which reflected variability of individual ERPs around their mean, received less theoretical emphasis, but overall this measure has received more consistent support (Barrett and Eysenck 1994). There is some other evidence linking psychometric intelligence to lower within- and between-subject variability in ERPs (Segalowitz *et al.* 1992; Caryl 1994; Caryl *et al.* 1995) as would be expected if higher psychometric intelligence scores depended on greater reliability of operations in the CNS. However, variability as indexed by these measures might reflect a different admixture of stimulus-related and -unrelated mental activity on each trial, rather than the error-dependent variation in the stimulus-related component of the response suggested by the concept of lower reliability of brain function.

Electroencephalographic measures

Some of the ideas discussed in connection with work on ERPs and psychometric intelligence find echoes in work on the EEG; for example, the idea that higher-ability subjects' brains run faster. In addition, EEG studies raise issues that have not been addressed in the previous discussion; for example the degree of coupling between activity in different, well-separated parts of the brain and the distribution across the scalp (and underlying brain) of those components of the rhythmic activity displayed in the EEG that correlate well with intelligence.

The EEG comprises a mixture of faster and slower rhythms, conventionally divided into four frequency bands: beta, alpha, theta, and delta. Some EEG studies have focused on peak or mean frequency of brain rhythms in the alpha band (8–12 Hz), and support the equating of psychometric intelligence differences with speed of the brain's electrical activity, by showing positive correlations between alpha frequency and verbal intelligence in normal individuals (Juolasmaa *et al.* 1986; Anokhin and Vogel 1996). There are also parallels in EEG work to the context-to-context variability observed in the relationship between ERP laten-cies and psychometric intelligence: Gasser *et al.* (1983) found that positive correlations between alpha frequency and intelligence were present in mentally retarded children but not in controls. In the same study, EEG measures of power, particularly in the theta band, correlated with psychometric intelligence, and these correlations were present in both control and mentally retarded groups.

In subjects who are engaged in stimulus processing rather than completely relaxed, variation in the alpha band of the EEG reflects the demands of the processing task as well as, perhaps, the ability level of the subject. Giannitrapani (1969) found changes in EEG mean frequency, comparing thinking to resting conditions, and the magnitude of the change observed correlated with full-scale IQ and performance IQ. Higher-ability subjects showed smaller increases in EEG frequency when required to perform mental activity. More precise measures of event-related desynchronization (ERD)—the blocking or desynchronization of activity in the alpha band due to the demands of the task—at different points on the scalp have been used to map the demands of a simple sentence-verification task on different parts of the brain, and examine the way in which these interact with psychometric intelligence (Neubauer *et al.* 1995). Lower-ability subjects showed a progressive desynchronization (i.e. blocking of alpha activity, indicating cortical activation) from the first (prestimulus) to the final (sentence verification and response) stages of the task. Higher-ability subjects showed less blocking (i.e. lower activation), particularly in the interval before the final response, and a different pattern of development of activation across the scalp. Whereas lower-ability subjects showed progressively greater activation as the trial progressed, spreading from the posterior scalp forwards into the frontal cortex, higher-ability subjects showed progressive deactivation of the frontal cortex as the posterior cortex became activated over the course of each trial. These compensating changes in the activation of frontal and posterior parts of the cortex in individuals with higher ability explains their lower overall activation. The study emphasizes that EEG measures can provide information about the localization of the differences in brain function among subjects of different ability test scores.

Although, conventionally, the EEG is broken into four broad frequency bands, some studies adopt 2-Hz-wide bands to give a more detailed picture of variation among individuals or groups at different EEG frequencies (e.g. Giannitrapani 1985; Martin-Loeches *et al.* 1993). Giannitrapani (1985) analysed the relation between EEG power in each narrow-frequency band (at eight electrode locations, under various task conditions, and at rest) and mental abilities of 11–13-year olds (including full-scale IQ, verbal IQ, and performance IQ, and the separate scores on the various WISC subtests). The tables and plots of significant correlations show that such high-resolution analysis may reveal findings that conventional analyses would miss. For instance, activity in the 13 Hz band was correlated with verbal IQ (in the resting condition after prior mental activity), whereas in the adjacent 11 Hz band (the dominant alpha frequency band) correlations were minimal. Significant correlations with psychometric intelligence were more frequent in the resting samples taken after a spell of mental activity than in equivalent resting samples taken before the mental tasks were carried out. EEG power at specific frequencies (such as the 11 and 13 Hz bands) at particular sites could be related to verbal, performance, and full-scale IQ, and in many cases to scores in particular WISC subtests. For example, comprehension scores were correlated, in the 13 Hz band, with EEG power in a left fronto-temporal and central group of sites, whereas block design scores were correlated with power in more posterior central, parietal, and left occipital sites.

Giannitrapani's analyses also revealed correlations between psychometric intelligence and measures of the coupling of EEG activity at different sites. These can provide useful information about changes in the strength of relationship between brain electrical activity in distant parts of the brain, e.g. as the brain develops in early school-age children (Thatcher *et al.* 1987). Coupling of EEG activity between sites is indexed by measures of phase and coherence in the frequency domain, or by their time-domain *alter egos*. Coherence measures the extent to which EEG activity at one site mirrors activity at another, with maximal similarity at a delay indexed by the phase measure. Thatcher's results from 5–16-year olds indicate that higher coherence between different electrode sites is associated with lower psychometric intelligence, implying that greater differentiation of brain activity goes with higher ability (Thatcher *et al.* 1983). In this sample, between-hemisphere relationships were stronger predictors of intelligence than within-hemisphere relationships, and the asymmetry of EEG amplitude between the hemispheres was a further predictor of intelligence.

Such EEG studies are inevitably hard to summarize concisely because of the number of electrode sites, the range of different frequencies, and the variety of within-site and between-site indices used. Although some of the results are easy to rationalize (e.g. that block design, a visual task, is related to EEG activity at posterior-occipital sites, and comprehension, a verbal task, to activity at left fronto-temporal sites), in other cases it is not obvious why EEG activity at rest should be related to performance on the particular subtest. But Thatcher's developmental work emphasizes that the changes in capacity during early childhood are associated with changes in activity and interrelationships among parts of the brain that can be tracked by EEG measures. Detailed understanding of the way in which variation in its biological computing machinery is related to variation in psychometric intelligence must ultimately depend on better understanding of these relationships in all their complexity. There is a clear contrast with simplistic interpretations of electrophysiological evidence, such as the view that intelligence equates to faster information transmission.

THE BRAIN'S METABOLIC ACTIVITY

Surprising as it might seem, for Spearman (1927) mental abilities were modular. Different mental tasks were completed by different special abilities, located in different parts of the brain. The reason that individual differences in these tasks tended positively to covary was that the individual specific abilities were all 'engines' fired by a general 'mental energy'. The level of mental energy was characteristic for any one person and it provided a limit on test performance (to the degree that the test required *g* versus a specific ability). Other such metaphors come to mind: however pristine one's set of vinyl records in a collection of different composers' classical symphonies, the record deck they are played upon will impose signal quality limitations to all. But Spearman chose an energy metaphor and, crudely, the person scoring better on an ability test literally was 'brighter' because more Spearmanian mental energy had arrived at the brain site to fire the engine solving the problem. Centuries before, Huarte's (1575) hypothesis was that thinking drew metabolic energy to the brain, and he based intra- and interindividual ability differences on temperature differences in the brain. In fact, his theory was more general; that any active organ demanded extra energy. Spearman's and Huarte's thoughts were guesses based on little evidence. But the two key ideas—that active thought results in increased metabolism in specific areas of the brain, and that individual differences in ability are correlated with amount of metabolism—are among those addressed nowadays with functional brain scanning methods.

Functional brain-scanning techniques are commonly applied in clinical and cognitive studies. On the one hand, disease groups may be compared with controls to discover any different patterns of brain metabolism during rest or cognitive activity. On the other hand, studies within the field of cognitive neuroscience have found a new way of applying the subtraction-type technique previously applied to reaction times (Chapter 6). Two cognitive tasks may be performed by the same person and the difference between the brain's activity during the two tasks may, if one accepts the rationale, reveal the cerebral localization of the process(es) specific to the more complex task. Studies of individual differences that utilize functional brain-scanning techniques are relatively rare; and they tend to have too few subjects and too many outcome variables, with the consequent risks of Type I and II statistical errors. Of the studies that have entered the literature there are at least three types. First, there are studies that examine the amount of metabolic activity in different brain regions and correlate these values with performance on cognitive tasks. Second, some studies use a repeated measures design and examine the brain activity during different types of ability test items, attempting to discover the cerebral localization of the cognitive activity involved in their solution. Third, other studies examine the localization of cerebral metabolic activity of different groups during cognitive performance, e.g. young versus old. Because there are so few studies to date, the following should be seen as illustrative of types of research. There can be no definitive conclusions on these few, small studies concerning the biological bases of human psychometric intelligence differences save, perhaps, to point to some techniques that will increase in their informativeness in due course.

Correlating metabolic and performance differences

Some studies of people whose brains have undergone degeneration suggest that higher ability is positively associated with greater metabolism, whereas studies of healthy young adults suggest the opposite. Chase *et al.* (1984) studied regional brain metabolism and cognitive performance in a group of 22 older people, 17 of whom had Alzheimer's-type dementia. Subjects' brains were studied after a period of rest, not during cognitive activity. Positron emission tomography (PET) was used and the radioactive tracer was fluoro-deoxyglucose (FDG) labelled with the 18 isotope of fluorine. This compound, like glucose, is taken into cells in proportion to their metabolism. The PET scanner is able to detect and localize gamma rays which are emitted in proportion to the amount of FDG taken into each area of the brain. The most actively metabolizing areas of the brain emit the greatest signals. Performance differences on the WAIS correlated significantly and positively with metabolic activity in the brain; people with better scores on the WAIS tended to have more actively metabolizing brains. Moreover, there were more numerous, significant correlations between performance and verbal IQ scores and metabolic activity in the right and left hemispheres, respectively. As one of the first of this new type of study of human ability differences, Chase and colleagues' conclusion heralded the possibilities:

> The WAIS was not devised to map human cognitive processes and can hardly be considered an adequate tool for such applications. Nevertheless, the present results support its use as a limited test of cortical function: the high inter-correlation of its subtests and the relative consistency of their cortical mapping patterns suggest that most WAIS subtests focus on the evaluation of either of two general skills (language or visuospatial cognition) and on either of two areas of the cerebral cortex (left temporoparietal and right posteroparietal). The ultimate ability of man to localize with precision his own highest mental faculties has long been debated. Evolving cerebral imaging techniques, combined with more sophisticated psychometric instruments, may eventually provide a more definitive answer to this question than was previously thought possible. (p. 1247)

Because subjects in the study by Chase *et al.* (1984) were tested at rest and the majority had undergone the cerebral degeneration associated with Alzheimer's disease, the results might merely reflect an association between the amount of active neural tissue and ability test scores. A similar finding was reported by Berent *et al.* (1988) who studied resting brain activity and WAIS score differences in 15 people with Huntingdon's disease. Again, this might reflect the degree of damage to the brain and have little relevance to understanding the association between psychometric ability test scores and normal brain physiology (Haier 1993).

Haier *et al.* (1988) reported, by contrast, strong negative correlations between scores on Raven's Advanced Matrices and cerebral metabolic activity—assessed by PET using FDG uptake—in eight normal males. These subjects performed the Raven task during tracer uptake, therefore the metabolic activity measured was that which occurred during psychometric ability test performance. There was little evidence of localization; significant associations (often well above 0.7 in effect size) were found widely throughout the cerebral cortex. A reanalysis of these data revealed that the most significant negative associations were found in the temporal lobes, although areas 18 and 19 of the occipital cortex and the superior frontal area also showed significant associations despite the small sample size (Haier 1993). Performing verbal fluency during FDG uptake resulted in negative correlations between test scores and relative cerebral metabolism in the frontal, temporal, and parietal areas of the cerebral cortex (Parks *et al.* 1988). The correlations were above 0.5, but there were only 16 subjects. Berent *et al.*

(1988) tended to find negative associations between ability test scores and FDG-based PET-estimated metabolism. Few associations were significant, and the metabolic data, though agreeing with those of Haier (1993) in being negative in sign, were measured at rest.

The binding construct used for these studies is 'efficiency' such that, in normal brains, the more able people are said to have more efficient brains. The locus of this efficiency is not spelled out, and Haier (1993) suggested explanatory loci from neural pruning to cognitive strategy differences during cognitive tasks. Despite Haier's urging that PET studies become a priority for intelligence researchers, this has largely failed to materialize. Partly, it is because of the cost and other burdens of conducting the studies. But perhaps the main factor has been the redirection of cognitive psychologists toward functional magnetic resonance imaging of the brain. This technique, unlike PET scanning, involves no ionising radiation exposure to the subject, making it ethically more acceptable for studies of humans, especially healthy subjects. Therefore, unless more studies based on PET are forthcoming, the field will be left with an inadequate corpus, insufficient for drawing conclusions or developing theory.

Localizing 'intelligent' brain activity using brain scanning

A different approach from the 'intelligence correlates (positively or negatively) with metabolic intensity' principle is to examine the brain areas that are active during psychometric intelligence-type tasks. This might lead to the identification of neural circuits involved in ability test performance and thus suggest possible loci for the sources of individual differences. (In addition, differences in the pattern of brain activation between groups of different ability levels might be revealed.) An example of this type of study was an examination of the brain activation patterns induced by actively performing the paced auditory serial addition task (PASAT; Deary *et al.* 1994). The PASAT, a counting task that makes heavy demands on working memory, has strong associations with psychometric intelligence test scores (Deary *et al.* 1991*b*). Brain activity was examined using single photon emission tomography (SPET) to detect the uptake of 99mTC-exametazine. Uptake of this tracer is closely linked to cerebral blood flow, which is linked to metabolism. The 20 subjects' brains were scanned twice following tracer injection. On one occasion subjects rested during tracer uptake and on the other they performed the PASAT task. The difference in tracer uptake was assessed between the conditions. Performing the PASAT task was associated with decreased tracer uptake in the right anterior cingulate and left posterior cingulate areas. The authors argued that this implicates the involvement of Posner's 'anterior attention system' in performing a task with an association to psychometric ability test scores (Posner and Petersen 1990). Some limited analyses of individual differences were undertaken. These suggested that those subjects with the greatest reduction in posterior cingulate function had the poorest PASAT performance. However, these subjects also had the highest anxiety scores during the PASAT test, implicating mood state as a potential confound of any ability–brain metabolism associations.

Until this point, the brain-scanning methods mentioned (PET and SPET) involved radioactive tracer compounds which are injected into a subject's bloodstream and thereafter taken into bodily tissues, including brain. Magnetic resonance imaging involves no tracer substance and depends instead on the magnetic properties of molecules within the brain (Ebmeier 1998). Also, the duration of mental activity over which the scanning takes place is different. For some PET scanning studies the tracer uptake was based upon an epoch of about 30 minutes. Therefore, studies such as those described by Haier (1993) involved patterns of imputed brain metabolism over a period of half an hour. On the other hand, SPET tracer uptake was based on an epoch of about 4 minutes, explaining in part why Deary *et al.* (1994) used the PASAT task, which takes a few minutes' time to complete. Functional magnetic resonance imaging (fMRI) has the ability to examine shorter epochs of mental activity. The block-type study, of which an example is presented next, allows the examination of separate periods of about 30 seconds, although event-related techniques can analyse responses within much briefer periods. Menon and Kim (1999) and D'Esposito *et al.* (1999) provide useful critical reviews of the opportunities that fMRI offers to psychologists, especially concerning its temporal limits.

fMRI was used to investigate the activity of brain areas while seven graduate students performed items adapted from Raven's Matrices tests (Prabhakaran *et al.* 1997). Three types of problem were constructed. Two were 'active' problem types: one type could be solved using visuospatial analyses ('figural') and the other was rule-based ('analytic'). The third type required only matching ('match') a shape in the problem to one answer option, and was the 'control' task that is assumed to control for things other than the active thinking elements of the cognitive test. Of course, the notion of a control task is as moot as any other proposition in the subtractive method in cognitive psychology. Many cognitively oriented brain-scanning studies employ a control-versus-active-test design and report the difference between the active and control tasks as brain activation–deactivation patterns. There must be sensible scepticism about what that difference represents. For example, subjects might be in a different mood state during the activation task and the difference scan pattern might partly reflect that (Deary *et al.* 1994). Prabhakaran *et al.* (1997) examined brain activity in epochs of 30 seconds, and there were six epochs per type of matrix problem. One test item was displayed during an epoch, and subjects attempted to solve it. One answer option was highlighted in the last 5 seconds of the epoch and subjects indicated whether or not it was the correct answer. The authors systematically subtracted one brain activity pattern from others and hypothesized that the brain activity pattern differences represented brain processing as follows:

- Analytic/match difference: all cortical areas beyond perceptuo-motor demands
- Figural/match difference: cortical areas for figural matching
- Analytic/figural difference: cortical areas for analytic reasoning.

When the brain activity patterns of analytic and figural items were compared with match (i.e. control) items the latter were associated with less activation. For analytic over match items there were areas of increased activation in the prefrontal, frontal, parietal, temporal, and occipital cortical regions. For figural over match items the areas of increased activation were fewer and more localized to the right hemisphere, except for parietal cortex. Anterior cingulate activity was increased during figural problems. When brain activation patterns were compared for the figural and analytic items it was the latter that were associated with greater activation, and the differences were relatively widely spread through the cerebral cortex. Overall, analytic reasoning items had more left- than right-sided activity and more anterior than posterior, with figural items showing a reversed pattern. The authors commented as follows:

> Thus, fluid reasoning during RPM performance activated not only areas associated with rehearsing and storing domain-specific information, but also areas associated with the executive or self-initiated control of working memory systems . . . .

> The present study suggests that strong links between working memory and fluid reasoning occur because the tasks measuring those processes are, in fact, measuring common neural systems.

> Second, the present findings indicate why performance on the Raven's Progressive matrices predicts performance so well for so many other tasks. Namely, performance on the Raven's Progressive Matrices reflects the status of numerous, perhaps almost all, working memory systems. (pp. 59–60)

Psychometric ability test scores and fMRI brain scanning were conjoined also in a study by Seidman *et al.* (1998) who examined only a small (7 to 12) number of subjects with high mean ability levels. The basic task that subjects performed while their brain activation was scanned was termed 'auditory vigilance': subjects indicated each time in a stream of letters that a 'q' was followed by an 'a'. The comparison task was a more demanding version ('working memory-loaded') in which three letters had to intervene between the q and the a. This more difficult auditory vigilance task correlated over 0.7 with an IQ estimate based on a brief form of the WAIS-R. The harder task was associated with greater brain activation compared with the baseline task in sections of the following areas:

- Superior, middle, and inferior frontal gyri and medial prefrontal cortex
- Precentral cortex
- Parietal-occipital cortex
- Temporal lobe and insula
- Anterior and posterior cingulate
- Thalamus
- Superior colliculus

The harder task was associated with significantly less activation than the baseline task in sections of the following brain areas:

- Right superior frontal gyrus, left inferior frontal gyrus, left medial prefrontal cortex
- Right superior temporal gyrus and right hippocampus
- Anterior cingulate

The authors thoroughly reviewed the areas activated by the working memory-loaded task and found many agreements with previous studies. Although the sample was only seven-strong and all of high ability, the authors examined associations between baseline–hard task fMRI signal change and psychometric intelligence scores. There were negative correlations above 0.4 in right inferior parietal cortex, right insula, and right inferior frontal gyrus, and positive correlations greater than 0.4 with signal change in left inferior frontal gyrus and left middle frontal gyrus. Bearing in mind that the authors found a high correlation between their working memory task and IQ scores, they commented that their preliminary results were:

> consistent with previous hypotheses suggesting that widespread, distributed networks are responsible for effortful attention and working memory and that these networks are largely independent of input modality. (p. 516)

Localization of brain activity during cognitive performance: age-group and task differences

The power and potential of brain-scanning techniques to unpick the sources of individual differences is well illustrated by a PET study involving 41 healthy people aged 18–80 years who performed the Wisconsin Card Sorting Test (WCST) and Raven's Progressive Matrices (RPM) during tracer uptake (Esposito *et al.* 1999). There were sensorimotor control tasks for the Wisconsin and Raven tasks; therefore, subjects were scanned four times in all. Although scores on both the Wisconsin and Raven tasks were negatively associated with age, global cerebral blood flow was not. In agreement with Seidman *et al.* (1998) there were brain areas of activation and deactivation during cognitive activity. Thus, both the Wisconsin and Raven tasks activated the following areas in younger subjects: dorsolateral prefrontal cortex (typically activated during working memory tasks), inferior parietal lobule, anterior cingulate, and inferolateral and occipital cortex. In younger subjects, both tasks were associated with deactivation in the following areas: mesial polar regions of the prefrontal cortex, perisylvian areas of the superior and inferior temporal lobe and posterior cingulate. There were also task-specific areas of activation and deactivation. In older subjects, for the Raven task, there was less activation and deactivation of correspondingly activated and deactivated regions of younger brains during task performance. These patterns persisted after partialling out age-related performance on the task. Thus:

> there was a failure to produce a focussed neural response by engaging task appropriate neural activity patterns and inhibiting inappropriate ones; the

neural activity patterns during the RPM and the RPMc [the control task] (and perhaps the cognitive operations employed during them) became more alike in the older cohort. (p. 973)

During the Wisconsin task, in addition to this type of pattern, there was evidence of older subjects' recruiting alternative neural paths during the task. There were complex interactions between task and age with respect to activation and deactivation of brain areas during task performance. During the Wisconsin and Raven tasks there was activation of the dorso-lateral prefrontal cortex (DLPFC). However, as age increased, this area became deactivated during the Wisconsin task, whereas there continued to be activation during the Raven task. A different pattern was seen in the polar prefrontal cortex; here, there was a lessening of the suppression (deactivation) of the area seen in younger subjects. The authors concluded that:

Across-task differences appear to reflect the more circumscribed dependence of the WCST on working memory and prefrontal cortical systems, and of RPM in visuospatial processing systems, computational problem solving and postrolandic regions. This hypothesis is suggested by the observation that, for example, the DLPFC and the inferior parietal lobule showed significantly greater age-related decreases in activation during the WCST than the RPM, and these areas have been linked specifically to working memory and to the WCST . . . On the other hand, the inferolateral temporal cortex, which has been related more to visual processing . . . than to working memory *per se*, showed significantly greater age-related decline in function during RPM than WCST, and RPM is more highly dependent on visual processing and more sensitive to damage in this area than in prefrontal cortex. (p. 974)

The authors proceeded with an exploratory analysis that linked dispersed brain areas of activation or deactivation into putative neural networks, and related these to task performance and ageing. With regard to mechanisms of age-related change they invoked constructs of capacity limitation and inhibition, which are the main rivals to speed of processing as candidate constructs in the ageing and cognitive performance literature (see Chapter 8, and Baltes *et al.* 1999). This is grounded upon the dopamine system which they envisage as providing a function in sorting signal from noise, their idea being that ageing involves in part a poorer signal to noise ratio. They recommended more experimental pharmacological manipulations of the dopamine system in the further investigation of these findings, and others have suggested that dopamine pathways in the CNS have a role in the processing of information (Rammsayer 1997).

Among the larger studies using fMRI technology applied to ability test score differences, the report by Esposito *et al.* (1999) had little power, but the interest in the study is the range of possibilities it heralded for the biological examination of individual differences. In addition to age-related variability in regional activation–deactivation differences in separate tasks, there might be studies that examined the effects of psychometric intelligence level. This would be informative about possible strategy differences in performing mental tasks. Moreover, the ability statistically to link dispersed brain areas moves the field away from measuring the size of a lump of, say, frontal lobe, to assessing integrated functional units in the brain. The report also points to the necessity for constructs at the psychological level to bring together the findings; it is not just a case of linking behaviour directly to biology, because system-level constructs aid the process of comprehension and integrate data from different levels. And the report makes it clear that brain-scanning data can usefully be complemented with other biological techniques, such as pharmacological studies of information processing.

Promises and limitations of functional brain scanning in individual differences research

The avenues of psychological investigation opened by functional brain scanning are hardly yet appreciated. The limits of existing techniques have yet to be found, and new investigate methods appear with frequency (for example, optical methods were described by Gratton and Fabiani 1998). As psychologists, including those interested in the origins of psychometric intelligence differences, jump on the brain-scanning bandwagon—which is rolling just as quickly and perhaps as near-sightedly as the molecular genetic bandwagon—it is useful to reflect on what this approach can and cannot offer.

Still bound by the subtractive method

Many studies of cognitive function in an fMRI setting are based upon the subtractive method. Thus, the panoply of equipment and personnel serving these expensive and burdensome studies is founded on the quality of the tasks and their control tasks. Whatever may be revealed in the brain-activation and -deactivation patterns is being revealed about the difference between two mental tasks. Chapter 6 discussed some of the difficulties in such cognitive dissection; the components of mental function presumed to lie in the differences between the active and control tasks will require independent validation before being acceptable.

Differences in processing efficiency and/or strategies

Brain-scanning studies might not reveal individual differences in the way that differential psychologists would find most convenient. It would be handy if, during cognitive performance, different subjects implemented the same processing sequences. There would follow a search for individual differences in the efficiency of these processes, and these efficiency differences might be basic to psychometric intelligence differences. However, studies using fMRI and allied technology might, instead, be better suited to revealing how different types of subjects recruit different neural networks in any given task, as the study by Esposito *et al.* (1999) demonstrated in young–old comparisons. If it is shown that different brains have different activation–deactivation patterns during cognitive test performance, then construct-formation based on these data need not omit 'information processing efficiency' from its hypothesizing. However, attention must be given to qualitative differences in the recruitment of integrated neuronal systems. This is a modern restatement of Hunt's (1980*a*) view that strategy differences in cognitive task performance were a problem for models that assumed a universal model of task performance based on tractable stages of information processing.

Psychological constructs still needed

In the above studies using brain scanning there was frequent recourse to higher-level constructs such as working memory, fluid intelligence, and 'mental efficiency'. The presence of these terms raises at least two points concerning how much work they do. First, although working memory is at times used as an explanatory construct for fluid intelligence differences, it is not clear whether these two constructs are at the same or different levels of description (Kyllonen and Christal 1990). Working memory has received more experimental-cognitive and brain-scanning attention, whereas fluid intelligence has been raised by psychometricians. The family backgrounds of these tasks should not conceal the fact that they are both assessed using mental tests. Second, there is a danger in appealing to constructs, such as 'mental efficiency', that appear useful but run the risk of merely redescribing the data. They have the patina of theoretical progression without the solid metal. These considerations warn that behaviour–biology connections do not deliver understandings, and that an explanatory bridging effort with validated system-level constructs is required. There is an irony in reading reports that relate brain-scanning variables to psychological variables and that appeal to psychological constructs to 'understand' the biological changes. Reductionism was meant to go the other way. This puts brain-scanning studies in a similar position to molecular genetic research because the latter, too, appeals to psychological constructs to bridge the explanatory gap between gene and phenotypic differences. Plomin and Crabbe (in press) have termed this survival of the usefulness of psychological constructs 'behavioural genomics'.

Direction of correlation

If a differently sized brain or a genetically different brain were proven to afford better scores on mental tests, there would be little worry about the direction of causation, even though the meaning of any such association might remain obscure; it is unlikely, but not inconceivable in the case of brain size, that higher psychometric intelligence would cause a bigger or genetically different brain. With fMRI studies there should be no such assumption. Differences in brain activation–deactivation might be caused by basic design differences that put limits on mental abilities, but the converse might also hold. Thus, differences in mental abilities might put limits on the types of responses the brain can make in the face of mental work. A simple and powerful example is that people with high ability on psychometric tests might just throw a lot of mental effort at every task, and the construct that joined any fMRI–ability test score correlation might be just this conscious effort. Such a hypothesis has been found wanting in reaction time and inspection time research (Chapters 6 and 7, respectively). Another version of a mental effort hypothesis is that differences in brain activation–deactivation patterns might arise because, when presented with the same test material in a brain scanner, people with low mental ability have to work harder. Thus, people with different levels of ability might simply be doing different things during the mental tasks, which are picked up by the scanning method. Such an hypothesis was tested by Larson *et al.* (1995) in a PET study. Confusingly, and in contrast to previous studies, however, the lower-ability subjects showed less cortical glucose use. Nevertheless, the following question must be kept in mind: are brain scanning (or ERP) correlations with mental ability test scores informative about basic, trait-like competence limitations, or are they epiphenomena of state-like, current performance?

Does brain scanning reveal what is important to individual differences?

Functional brain-scanning techniques at least allow the possibility of visualizing brain systems involving many distal areas, possibly involving many neurotransmitter systems. Structural brain imaging is limited to potentially non-functionally-related, though contiguous, volumes of brain. Although some correlations have arisen from this latter approach, explanations need alternative methods of analysis. Psychopharmacological studies enable blockade and enhancement of different neurotransmitter systems, but functional scanning can improve on this by indicating functionally linked brain regions driven by different transmitter–receptor systems. Using the 'windows on the mind' metaphor, each of these biological methods is limited, and functional brain scanning assumes that whatever happens in brain processing is 'visible' through its window, say, of brain activation–deactivation. If the locus of individual differences in mental abilities lies elsewhere it will pass unnoticed by these techniques.

There is still novelty in watching *in vivo* brain function in response to cognitive tests. As novelty wears off there will be a shedding of the limitations of small numbers of subjects and lack of theory that blight many functional brain studies. If newer brain-scanning techniques were applied with sufficient rigour and volume to the problem of psychometric intelligence differences it is hard to envisage that such effort would reveal nothing, but at present the data are crude and few; not the bases for extensive theory-building. Even at this early stage there has been a refinement away from unelaborated expectations about higher-ability brains being overall more or less energetic, to a partial appreciation of the parameters that may be considered, and the problems of interpretation encountered, when comparing different brains' metabolic responses to cognitive tests.

MOLECULAR GENETICS: FROM GENETIC DIFFERENCES THROUGH BRAIN DIFFERENCES TO BEHAVIOURAL DIFFERENCES?

The most exciting way in which genetic research is moving beyond the nature–nurture question is to begin to harness the power of molecular genetics to identify specific genes responsible for the substantial influence of genetics on intelligence. (Plomin and Petrill 1997, p. 66)

There is significant heritability of individual differences in mental ability test scores, whether at the level of general ability or group factors (Chapter 1). A key challenge for researchers interested in the mechanisms of human mental ability differences is the identification of the genes that contribute to these differences. The study of molecular genetic associations of ability test differences, like the study of ageing and psychometric intelligence differences (Chapter 8), is mind-broadening. The central question is still the origins of mental ability differences in, say, the normal young adult. But, because of the sources drawn upon in the field of genetics, additional important questions appear, such as: are the processes underlying ability differences the same in all age groups; are clinical studies applicable to the healthy population; are there different processes at work at different regions of the ability distribution; are the brain mechanisms the same for types of ability difference, such as spatial and verbal abilities, and memory? For example, there are studies of genetic associations with cognitive decline in old people and in medical conditions, and of genetic differences in young gifted children, and it is debatable whether the brain mechanisms that such associations signal are relevant to ability differences in the 70-kg, middle-class, healthy, 25-year-old man or woman.

The technology of molecular genetics means that regions of human DNA can be tested for differences and that these differences can be associated statistically with phenotypic characteristics, such as illnesses and behavioural dispositions. Some cognitively-related, early successes in this field have involved linking DNA variations to Huntingdon's disease, familial Alzheimer's disease, and language difficulties (McGuffin and Martin 1999). Significant heritability of mental ability differences merely informs us about the likelihood of there being individual differences in regions of DNA across the human genome that are associated with individual differences in mental ability test scores. That is, somewhere in the 3.3 billion DNA base pairs, adding to about 70,000 genes, some of which code for the 11,060 known human proteins affecting the 85 billion neurons in a brain (Wahlsten 1999), there is an unknown number of variable regions that might have functional effects of unknown size via unguessably-complex mechanisms that eventually contribute some variance to performances on mental tests. Managing the search for those regions of variability that are correlated with mental ability differences and then charting mechanisms (functional genomics; Plomin and Crabbe, in press) for each of the associations are the barely-begun tasks for this field of research.

Molecular genetic studies promise to find the starting lines of possibly long and tortuous, and sometimes untraceable, routes between phenotypic differences (such as ability test scores) and actual differences in human DNA. The discovery of any replicated, significant association between psychometric intelligence differences and a particular region of DNA can be the beginning of a search for the genetically-mediated brain mechanisms of ability differences. The possibilities of this type of research are arguably among the better biological routes to understanding some variance in psychometric intelligence, but some cautions must be stated at the beginning. First, studies of molecular genetic associations of human phenotypes that are affected by multiple genes are fraught with initial positive reports that are then not replicated; examples include schizophrenia, depression, and personality traits (e.g. Deary *et al.* 1999; McGuffin and Martin 1999). Second, the best guess at present is that an association between any one DNA region and mental ability differences is likely to account for small amounts of variance (Plomin and Petrill 1997). Third, and to repeat for emphasis, the mechanistic route from DNA via brain mechanisms to measured ability test differences is likely to be long and difficult and often impossible to chart.

To balance these examples of dour pessimism the opportunities of molecular genetic studies are considerable. The increasingly detailed characterization of the human genome means that it is now possible to perform a detailed, though non-comprehensive, 'sweep' using DNA markers spaced along human chromosomes to search for associations between DNA variations and mental ability differences. No theory of intelligence, beyond the current knowledge about the psychometric structure of test scores, is needed or generally employed; if positive associations emerge from the sweep they can be studied for replication in additional samples to check whether they are mere Type I errors. In a second approach, allelic variations in some gene that has a theoretical association with ability differences can be studied to discover whether, indeed, the expected correlation occurs. An example is the weight of evidence linking serotonin function in the brain to mood, anxiety, and neuroticism differences that then led to the seeking of serotonin system-affecting genes with these same phenotypic differences. Although a clear remit existed in this latter approach, the studies have still suffered from failures to replicate (Deary *et al.* 1999). The first type of approach—the gene sweep—is like fishing with a trawl net; everything thrown up in the process must be examined individually. The second type of approach may be compared to fishing with a rod and a line and special fly; a specific gene is examined because of some forethought which concluded that genotype and phenotype should be related.

This section of this chapter, then, has two stories to tell. The first story (the sweep) concerns the progress, prospects, and problems of the broad sweep for links between DNA and mental ability differences. The second story (a thread to the minotaur's cave?) describes what a mechanistic account of mental ability differences might involve once a specific (gene product–mental ability difference) association has been identified and replicated.

The sweep

In searching for genes that contribute to mental ability differences in the normal range, a common guess is that many genes will each contribute different, and small, effects. Recall that the total effect will amount only to the heritability and that the rest is environmental and still to be accounted for. These genes are known as quantitative trait loci (QTLs); multiple regions of variable DNA that contribute to individual differences in a measurable phenotypic trait. Plomin and Petrill (1997) described the avenues of search for QTLs using linkage and allelic association techniques. Linkage is better suited to large effects of QTLs and can detect an association between behavioural differences and a marker that covers a relatively large section of a chromosome. Allelic association can detect much smaller QTL effects, but requires a DNA marker that is either the QTL itself or a DNA marker very close to it. Allelic association requires a prior guess at an actual gene that might be associated with a trait, a so-called candidate gene. Therefore, one may sweep the human complement of DNA with some hundreds of markers to detect larger effect sizes, but allelic association techniques are needed to detect smaller effects. Metaphorically, one might compare this with a search for a given star in the night sky. To examine the whole, clear night sky for Venus takes a few broad, non-specific looks at different, large areas, whereas detecting a large number of dim stars will take thousands of looks with a powerful telescope targeted at specific regions of the sky. Using the former approach, to seek a big signal, one does not need much prior knowledge and looking some distance from the object will provide a hit; using the latter approach one needs prior information about where to look and only actually hitting the signal source or being very near to it will be of any use.

What are the implications of the assumption that in psychometric intelligence many genes will contribute to the variance and that each will have a small effect? Perhaps the possession of no one allele will be necessary for a higher ability test score. Therefore, an allelic association technique has been employed. This technique depends on a region of DNA showing variability in a population. Given this, one can examine whether specific types of this variability are associated with different levels of mental ability. Imagine an implausibly convenient case in which there were just two different forms of a region of DNA and that we were able to test for these using samples of people's DNA. Thousands of people are tested and it is found that people with one form (form a, say) of the DNA region have significantly higher mental ability test scores than those with form b. In fact, a percentage of variance can be assigned to the effect; the variable region accounts for, say, 2% of the variance in the ability test scores. The next question is: what does this region of DNA do? Sometimes in allelic association a significant effect does not mean that that region of DNA *per se* has any function; it might just be very close to another region of DNA that is functional. Sometimes the region of DNA being tested is a functional region. In the case of nervous system-relevant polymorphisms there are regions of DNA that code for messenger RNA relevant to the serotonin transporter gene, to the dopamine gene, and to the apolipoprotein E gene, among others. The convenient and implausible example can be extended further. It might transpire that the variable DNA region that was linked to ability test scores codes for a protein that influences the myelination of neurons, or the efficiency of transmitter release or reuptake, or the efficiency of neuronal repair, or some such. At that point there begins the process of tracing through the labyrinth that leads from gene differences to phenotype.

Wahlsten (1999) provided some good examples of the false starts in this field of research and underlined some of the cautions raised above. Type I errors were a major concern as a result of the large numbers of DNA markers used to scan animal genomes; very stringent α levels, such as 0.0001, have been recommended in order to keep the false positives low. A further problem arises after discovering a significant and replicated allelic association:

> A 1% recombination frequency corresponds to a distance along the chromosome of about 1 centiMorgan (cM), that in mice contains about 2 Mb of DNA and about 65 genes. A review of 22 QTLs believed to be important for alcohol and drug sensitivity . . . found that the interval in most cases was more than 15 cM. If the QTL can be localised within a 15 cM interval, it could be any one of about 1000 genes. (p. 605)

These problems are of scale rather than of principle. However, the failures to replicate, for example, the much-trumpeted association between the personality trait of novelty seeking and the long 7 repeat allele of the *DRD4* gene exemplify the former point well (Wahlsten 1999).

The IQ QTL project

The first thing to do, then, is to find some likely-seeming regions of DNA—candidate genes likely to influence brain function, that is—in which there are differences. This was the first approach taken by the IQ Quantitative Trait Loci Project (Plomin *et al.* 1994*a*, 1995). Plomin *et al.* compared the frequencies of different alleles of DNA markers that were 'in or near genes of neurological relevance' (1995, p. 34). For added power they did not examine frequencies of alleles in the whole normal ability test score range. They examined the top and bottom 5% of test scorers (mean IQs of 130 and 82, with Ns of 24 and 18) and then examined any positive associations on even more extreme samples (mean IQs of 142 and 59, Ns of 27 and 17). These samples had the power to detect only those effects contributing 2% or more of the population variance in mental ability differences. In an original study of 60 DNA markers that were likely to be brain-function related, nine showed significant allele associations with ability test scores. None held up in the replication sample, although two approached significance: CTGB33 and the human leukocyte antigen marker HLA-A(B). The authors evinced interest in these specific results because the first of these is expressed in brain and the latter points to a region where various interesting candidate genes reside. However, neither association was replicated in a study of high- and lower-ability old people tested on the National Adult Reading Test (Jacomb *et al.* 1999). A follow-up study (Plomin *et al.* 1995) added a further 40 likely DNA markers. Three—alcohol dehydrogenase 5 (ADH5), EST00083 (cDNA sequence from hippocampal library), and nerve growth factor, beta polypeptide (NGFB)—

showed significant allelic association with ability test score level in the original sample. The only one that replicated in the next sample, EST00083, was problematic as it later emerged as a marker for mitochondrial rather than genomic DNA (Skuder *et al.* 1995). The authors were wary of suggesting that mitochondrial DNA, which is passed on by maternal transmission, might be associated with mental ability.

These early, largely non-replicated findings from the IQ QTL project emphasize the possibilities as well as the problems in this area. Clearly, much replication is needed before researchers begin a search for the mechanisms of the associations. With the increasing number of DNA markers available there will be more Type I errors. The relatively small sample sizes will need massively to be increased to avoid these and also to avoid Type II errors as a result of insufficient power. Plomin *et al.* (1995) added to these points their intention to examine high versus average ability test score groups, a sensible move because genes that link to very low IQ might not generalize to the normal range. This research group has also examined allelic association in specific as well as general cognitive abilities (Petrill *et al.* 1996). They examined the eight DNA markers that had appeared to show the most significant allelic association with general mental ability in the previous studies. They used regression techniques to discover whether there were genetic effects on specific cognitive abilities after overall Wechsler IQ was removed. The analysis has the problems of the DNA markers being preselected for possible associations with general ability (which might in fact have made it more difficult to find associations with specific abilities), and there being too many outcomes and too few subjects. Nevertheless, there were significant associations, after removing effects for general ability, between ADH5 and spatial and memory abilities, dystrophia myotonica marker and verbal ability, and NGFB and spatial ability. This is very preliminary evidence for there being genetic effects on general and specific cognitive abilities, supporting a nested/hierarchical view of their organization (Chapter 1).

Members of the IQ QTL project considered, on reflection, that the above, earlier phases of the project had not revealed any replicated associations (Chorney *et al.* 1998). The IQ QTL project moved towards a more systematic sweep of human DNA, by using over 3000 DNA markers spaced along the human genome. This brings them within half a million base pairs of any possible QTL. The systematic search began on the long arm of chromosome 6 (Chorney *et al.* 1998). They employed 37 DNA markers, an extreme groups design with respect to cognitive abilities, and multiple replication samples to guard against Type 1 errors. The first test samples were two groups of 51 children aged 6 to 16 years with mean IQs of 136 and 103 (SDs 9.3 and 5.6), respectively. This marked a move away from genes that might just affect the lower end of the ability test score distribution. Mental abilities were tested using the WISC-R. There were high ($N = 52$) and average ability ($N = 51$) replication samples also. Of the 37 DNA markers only one showed a significant allelic association with mental ability test scores. This was the insulin-like growth factor-2 receptor (IGF2R) gene. The most common allele (Allele 4) was present in 66% of the high-ability group and in 81% of the low-ability group (p = 0.021). In the replication sample the respective percentages were 63 and 78 (p = 0.024). Additional analyses revealed that allele 5 was more common in the high-ability groups. Combining the two samples and Bonferroni correcting for the 37 markers tested resulted in an eventual p value of 0.009.

The IGF2R gene accounted for only 2% of the variance in general ability. Allele 5 was associated with high ability, but only 46% of high-ability subjects had one of these alleles. This underscores the likelihood that, if multiple genes are found to be associated with ability, none might be necessary for high ability and all might have small effects. Chorney *et al.* (1998) discussed the IGF2R gene's function as coding for a receptor for an insulin-like compound among other substances. They also discussed other sites near to this DNA region that might be the beginnings of the mechanism that links this allele difference with mental ability differences, but much of the discussion was taken up with caveats and warnings against overinterpretation of such results.

The tenor of the publications in this area is a confidence in the results that lie ahead; significant allelic associations with mental ability differences will happen, they imply. However, there is a range of opinions on the likely progress, from optimism (Plomin 1999) to pessimism (Flint 1999). The field moves rapidly, and automation and novel techniques ease the burden of individual genotyping. The IQ QTL project, having doubled its sample sizes, used pooled DNA from different ability groups, obviating the need for individual genotyping in the early stages of the search for genes linked to cognitive ability (Daniels *et al.* 1998). This method ruled out major allelic associations between general mental ability and loci on chromosome 22 (Hill *et al.* 1999). It found and replicated, though, three QTLs on chromosome 4 that were associated with cognitive ability (*D4S2943, MSX1, D4S1607*; P. J. Fisher *et al.* 1999). These DNA pooling results were confirmed by individual genotyping. Assuming associations do replicate, they can only account for as much of the variance in mental ability differences as is heritable (say, 50% plus or minus 20%). Achieving anything like that 50% (or whatever) is bounded by the number of contributing genes that have an above-minimum detectable effect size. And the results will only move beyond mysterious associations when some mechanisms are understood. According to some, though, the molecular genetic approach to mental ability differences can hardly fail:

> if you are looking for a place to invest your intellectual capital and have a high tolerance for risk, then the search for QTLs for complex behavioral traits and diseases can be recommended as a long-term buy—but beware of the near-term volatile oscillations in your investment. (Gottesman 1997, p. 1523)

Molecular genetic research on cognitive ability differences might tie cognitive phenotypes to bits of human biochemical variation—not to unvalidated cognitive/experimental/psychophysical constructs—in the form of DNA differences. But it can only do so much, and the difficulties of unscrambling mechanisms pose many problems, and Flint (1999) suggested that:

> Some investigators hope to isolate the genes that determine variation in IQ using methods of genetic linkage and association ... but the non-specific nature of the genetic effects may render genetic dissection very difficult, if not impossible.

It is understanding these mechanisms that this book addresses—and this is the next story. The forbidding task of tying together a story for any one DNA–mental ability link—i.e. moving from correlation to mechanism—is now exemplified using an early success in the field of molecular genetic research as applied to decrements in cognitive ability: the connection between a polymorphism in the apolipoprotein E gene and cognitive decline (MacLullich *et al.* 1998). This example is chosen because of the large literature already published on this gene. Other avenues await more research; for example, the finding that overexpression of the N-methyl-D-aspartate (NMDA) 2B synaptic receptor in the forebrains of transgenic mice improves their cognitive performance makes the NMDA system an interesting site for investigation in humans (Tang *et al.* 1999). In general, transgenic and genetic 'knockout' mice may offer clues to genetic sites related to cognitive variations in humans.

A thread to and from the minotaur's cave?

After some of the general principles of molecular genetic research, and some tentative associations between DNA differences and behaviour differences, should come a detailed, specific example. That is, it would be a mistake to view any allelic association as an end of the QTL story. The interesting work lies in building the explanatory bridge from association to mechanism. The example of cognitive function and the ε4 allele of the apolipoprotein E gene is discussed next as an example of 'functional genomics' (Plomin and Crabbe, in press).

To date, few genetic polymorphisms or mutations have been identified that associate replicably with variations in psychometric intelligence, especially in the normal range. The genetic differences that have been identified include those underlying common causes of mental retardation, such as Fragile X syndrome (Nelson 1998). An association was identified and replicated between a region on chromosome 6 and reading disability (Cardon *et al.* 1994; S. E. Fisher *et al.* 1999). The ε4 allele of the apolipoprotein E gene has an association with Alzheimer's disease and with milder cognitive impairments in ageing human populations (MacLullich *et al.* 1998). It is in a different category from other associations because of the large numbers of replication studies. The published studies suggest that the possession of ε4 is associated with relatively stronger decrements on tests of declarative memory, and that this is linked with relatively greater damage to brain structures which are thought to play a fundamental role in declarative memory. In this section the studies linking cognitive function with ε4 are summarized, and neuropathological mechanisms that might mediate these links are described.

Physiology of apoE

Apolipoprotein E (apoE) plays a key role in central and peripheral lipid metabolism (Poirier 1994). Several apolipoproteins are involved in the peripheral regulation and metabolism of lipids, but apoE is the main apolipoprotein in the brain, and thus apoE function is of particular importance in the CNS (Mahley *et al.* 1996). ApoE is involved in scavenging of lipids following cell damage, and in the re-distribution of lipids during neuronal membrane repair, reactive synaptogenesis, and neuronal sprouting (Poirier 1994; Cotman 1999, p. 595). The importance of apoE in these processes has been demonstrated in many studies. For example, aged mice deficient of apoE (through gene knockout) show synaptic loss and disrupted dendritic cytoskeletons (Masliah *et al.* 1995).

ApoE is coded for by the gene *APOE* on the long arm of chromosome 19. In humans there are three common alleles, designated ε2, ε3, and ε4, with population frequencies of 7%, 78%, and 15%, respectively (Roses 1996). These alleles code for three different isoforms of the protein ApoE, designated Apoe2, Apoe3, and Apoe4.

Alzheimer's disease and ε4

The association of ε4 with late-onset Alzheimer's disease (AD) was discovered in 1993 (Corder *et al.* 1993), and the finding has been replicated many times (Roses 1996). The association is only partial: the lifetime risk of AD in carriers of one or more ε4 alleles is estimated at 29% versus 9% in individuals with no ε4 alleles (Seshadri *et al.* 1995). Homozygosity for ε4 carries a greater risk than heterozygosity (Roses 1996). As well as AD, ε4 may be associated with several other disorders affecting the CNS, for example vascular dementia (Katzman *et al.* 1997) and cerebrovascular disease (Terry *et al.* 1996; Bronge *et al.* 1999). In some reports ε4 has also been linked with a reduced age of onset for schizophrenia (Arnold *et al.* 1997), bipolar (manic-depressive) illness (Bellivier *et al.* 1997), and fronto-temporal dementia (Minthon *et al.* 1997).

Although there is generalized brain atrophy in AD, certain brain regions are affected earlier and show more severe atrophy over time. As determined by brain imaging, the hippocampus is one of the most severely affected regions in AD (Killiany *et al.* 1993; Jack *et al.* 1997). Much evidence supports the key role of the hippocampus (amongst other brain regions) in declarative memory (Lezak 1995, p. 27; Tulving and Markowitsch 1997). In AD the early decrements in performance on tests of declarative memory tend to parallel the hippocampal atrophy seen on structural brain imaging (Smith *et al.* 1999). In general terms the hippocampus is particularly vulnerable to various brain insults such as ischaemia, and shows relatively greater neuronal loss with ageing (Seckl and Olsson 1995). Relative deficits in the brain's response to injury may therefore affect the hippocampus more severely. In AD, MRI studies demonstrate that patients carrying the ε4 allele show a greater degree of hippocampal atrophy and worse performance on tests of declarative memory compared with AD patients with ε2 or ε3 (Lehtovirta *et al.* 1995; Smith *et al.* 1998). AD patients with ε4 may also show greater reductions in regional cerebral blood flow versus ε2 or ε3 carriers (Lehtovirta *et al.* 1998).

Cognitive function and brain imaging: the impact of ageing and ε4

A striking feature of cognitive ageing is the very wide range of changes that are observed (Chapter 8). Individuals with the rare, dominantly-inherited mutations in the presenilin genes may develop AD in midlife or at an even earlier stage (Kamino *et al.* 1996; Sherrington *et al.* 1996), whilst others may exhibit very little decline in cognitive ability with ageing (Starr *et al.* 1997). The mechanisms underlying these differences are unclear, although genetic differences are likely to be important (Pedersen *et al.* 1992; Plomin *et al.* 1994*b*). These genetic differences may act through pathological processes that affect brain function and hence cognitive function. For example, type II diabetes mellitus, which affects 10–20% of over-60s in industrialized countries (Beck-Nielsen and Groop 1994), is commoner with increasing age, has a high heritability, and is associated with cognitive impairment (Strachan *et al.* 1997). However, no genes that contribute both to the risk of type II diabetes and to the risk of age-related cognitive impairment have yet been identified.

Since the discovery of the association between ε4 and risk of AD, several studies have demonstrated that carriage of ε4 is also associated with greater susceptibility to less severe forms of cognitive impairment. Given the wide variety of sample sizes and tests used it is not clear whether particular cognitive functions are affected more than others, although declarative memory appears to be affected in the majority of studies in which it has been measured. Feskens *et al.* (1994) prospectively studied the impact of APOE genotype on cognitive function in a sample of men aged 70–89 using the mini-mental state examination (MMSE; Folstein *et al.* 1975). Baseline MMSE scores were lower in ε4 carriers. At 3-year follow-up the highest decline in MMSE scores was seen in ε4 homozygotes, and ε4 heterozygotes also showed significantly greater decline than men with no ε4 alleles. In a large community sample of non-demented women aged 65 and over, Yaffe *et al.* (1997) found that carriage of ε4 was associated with significant decline in performance on 6-year follow-up on the MMSE, and the digit–symbol subtest of the WAIS-R. Performance on Trails B was not assessed at baseline, but was incorporated at 2 years, with retesting 4 years later; carriage of ε4 was associated with worse performance at baseline and with greater decline. No other tests were administered.

Berr *et al.* (1996), in a study of 1174 non-demented individuals aged 59–71, found that carriage of ε4 was associated with worse performance on the MMSE, trail-making B and the finger-tapping test (a test of psychomotor rapidity). Significant differences were not found on standard tests of immediate and delayed verbal memory (Auditory–Verbal Learning Test), perceptual processing (Benton Facial Recognition Test), logical reasoning (RPM), visual memory (Benton Visual Retention Test), auditory attention (PASAT), and verbal fluency. Schmidt *et al.* (1996), by contrast, found that, in 214 randomly selected individuals aged 50–75 without general or neuropsychiatric disease, ε4 carriers performed significantly worse than non-carriers when assessed for learning and memory abilities, while there were no differences in test results of conceptualization, attention, speed of mental processing, and visuopractical skills. MRI in this study showed no differences in white-matter lesions (a marker of cerebrovascular disease), or in volumetric analyses of hippocampus or parahippocampal regions. Other brain regions were not assessed.

In a sample of non-demented elderly individuals, Bondi *et al.* (1995) found worse performance on the California Verbal Learning Test in ε4 carriers (*N* = 17) versus non-carriers (*N* = 35). Helkala *et al.* (1995, 1996) and Hyman *et al.* (1996) reported similar findings using different tests of word list learning. The studies by Helkala *et al.* included several other tests, which did not reveal significant differences. Reed *et al.* (1994) examined 20 healthy dizygotic twins who were discordant for ε4 and found that ε4 carriers showed worse performance on the Benton Visual Retention Test (a test of short-term memory) and on overall performance on the Iowa Battery (Eslinger *et al.* 1985). Smith *et al.* (1998) studied 157 patients with AD, 35 patients with mild cognitive impairment (MCI), and 341 normal controls. Carriage of ε4 was associated with deficits in a verbal delayed recall task in the AD and MCI groups, but not in the healthy controls.

Some studies have examined the impact of APOE polymorphisms on structural and functional brain imaging. In an MRI study of 10 non-demented twin pairs, carriage of ε4 correlated with smaller hippocampal volumes but not with any of a battery of neuropsychological tests (Plassman *et al.* 1997). Using PET scanning, Reiman *et al.* (1998) found reduced glucose metabolism in the posterior cingulate cortex in 11 cognitively normal, healthy ε4 carriers aged 50–62 compared with 22 controls. MRI scanning in the same groups found trends for reduced hippocampal volume in ε4 carriers; hippocampal volumes correlated with reduced performance on a long-term memory test. A previous study from the same group (Reiman *et al.* 1996) demonstrated reduced glucose metabolism in the posterior cingulate cortex, and particular areas in the parietal, temporal, and prefrontal regions that show reduced glucose metabolism in AD. Kuller *et al.* (1998), in a sample of 3469 men and women, found that ε4 was significantly associated with higher ventricular volume (a measure of brain atrophy), white-matter lesions, and also with worse performance on a modified version of the MMSE (Teng and Chui 1987).

These studies demonstrate that carriage of ε4 is associated with decrements in cognitive function in old people without AD. It is unclear whether particular cognitive functions are affected preferentially, as the studies differ in the tests used, the age groups, and the sample sizes. However, at present it appears that, when declarative memory is measured, it commonly shows deficits. The limited number of published imaging studies in non-demented old people have shown that ε4 is associated with brain atrophy, perhaps preferentially affecting temporal lobe structures such as the hippocampus, and also with alterations in brain glucose metabolism. Thus, ε4 carriers may develop dementia, but of those who do not, there is a tendency to show cognitive deficits and changes in brain structure and function with ageing as opposed to non-carriers.

Brain injury, cognitive function, and ε4

Ageing is associated with an increasing incidence of adverse effects on the brain. Differences in the effectiveness of repair mechanisms may thus become more apparent with ageing. Another circumstance in which these differences might become more apparent is after various forms of brain injury.

Head trauma is a risk factor for AD, conferring a relative risk of 1.82 (Mortimer *et al*. 1991). Given the key role of apolipoprotein E in the mechanisms of brain repair, several studies have examined the interaction between the presence of different APOE genotypes and the impact of brain injury (Nicoll 1996). Mayeux *et al*. (1995) reported that, in 236 community-dwelling individuals with a history of head injury, carriage of ε4 was associated with a tenfold increase in the risk for the later development of AD. Individuals with no ε4 alleles showed no increased risk. Boxing can lead to a syndrome known as dementia pugilistica, which shares similarities with AD both behaviourally and neuropathologically. Jordan *et al*. (1997) studied the impact of APOE status on cognitive function in a group of boxers. They found that in 'high-exposure' boxers (those with 12 or more professional bouts), carriage of ε4 was associated with a significantly greater degree of cognitive impairment on a 10-point clinical rating scale ($p = 0.04$).

Adverse brain outcome following head injury also appears to be associated with carriage of ε4 (Teasdale *et al*. 1997). APOE genotyping was performed on 89 patients admitted with head injury, and outcome assessed at 6 months, with adverse outcome defined as death, vegetative state, or severe disability. Patients with ε4 ($N = 30$) were twice as likely as non-carriers to suffer an adverse outcome ($p = 0.006$). Similar findings were reported by Friedman *et al*. (1999). A similar association has been observed in another form of brain injury, intracerebral haemorrhage (Alberts *et al*. 1995), where carriage of ε4 was associated with a higher mortality rate and a worse functional outcome in survivors. Coronary artery bypass grafting (CABG) is associated with cognitive impairment (Newman *et al*. 1995); possible mechanisms of brain injury in this context include episodes of low blood pressure and microemboli. Tardiff *et al*. (1994) found that ε4 was associated with poorer performance on tests of immediate and delayed declarative memory following CABG.

The studies relating APOE alleles with AD, age-related cognitive decline, and outcome following various forms of brain injury provide convincing evidence for robust statistical associations between this gene and variations in cognitive ability. A small number of studies have included structural and functional imaging and these tend to show that, as well as affecting performance on cognitive tests, ε4 is associated with atrophy of the hippocampus and with changes in brain metabolism. We now review some of the studies in animals and humans which have examined possible mechanisms underlying these associations.

Molecular and cellular mechanisms

As with cognitive changes with ageing, there is a wide range of changes in the brain with ageing, from the molecular to the macroscopic levels. These changes are difficult to chart accurately for several reasons, not least because they are superimposed on a high degree of pre-existing biological variability (Woodruff-Pak 1997, p. 89). In addition, ageing-related changes occur throughout the lifespan. For example, although atherosclerosis is commonly seen as a disease of middle age and beyond, the first arterial pathological changes can be seen in a proportion of infants and young children (Napoli *et al.* 1997). The effects of genetic differences on brain structure and function probably occur at every stage during the lifespan, and some changes may only occur under certain environmental circumstances, as in the case of traumatic brain injury described above.

Neuropathologically, AD is characterized by the accumulation of β-amyloid protein in β-pleated sheet structures (these form the core of senile plaques), neurofibrillary tangles, and amyloid angiopathy (Blennow and Cowburn 1996; Hachinski and Munoz 1997). These features have been linked with several mechanisms of neurotoxicity and neuronal loss (Yankner 1996; Mark *et al.* 1997). However, these features are not specific to AD, and can be observed in the brains of individuals without dementia, but to a lesser degree (Arkin 1998, p. 220). Some studies show that amyloid accumulation and neurofibrillary tangles can be observed in relatively young individuals without dementia (Mann *et al.* 1990), again demonstrating the long time-scales over which ageing-associated changes may occur.

Apoe4, the protein isoform coded for by ε4, promotes increased aggregation of single molecules of β-amyloid into β-pleated sheets relative to Apoe3 or Apoe2 (LaDu *et al.* 1994; Smith 1996, p. 468). Apoe4 may also be associated with relatively greater formation of neurofibrillary tangles (Smith 1996). Notably, a recent study of the brains of younger people ($N = 44$, mean age of 38) found that carriage of ε4 was associated with the presence of early neurofibrillary changes (Ghebremedhin *et al.* 1998). Apoe4 may also be directly toxic to neurons (Tolar *et al.* 1997). Because of the key role of Apoe in membrane repair, isoform differences in effectiveness may have particular relevance to neurons with long projections (and hence larger membranes), such as the cholinergic projections from the nucleus basalis of Meynert to the hippocampus. Cholinergic neurons are known to be particularly severely affected in AD (Smith 1996, p. 467).

Apoe4 is also probably associated with less effective responses to brain injury and less effective synaptic remodelling (Smith 1996, p. 467). Nathan *et al.* (1994) found that Apoe4 inhibited neurite outgrowth in cultured chicken hippocampal cells. Sun *et al.* (1998) reported significantly greater neurite outgrowth in cultured mice hippocampal cells in the presence of astrocytes expressing Apoe3 compared with astrocytes expressing Apoe4. Another study examined the effects of ischaemic injury in the brains of transgenic mice with either ε3 or ε4 using a model of experimental occlusion of the middle cerebral artery (Sheng *et al.* 1998). In this study, 60 minutes of occlusion caused larger infarct size (measured 24 hours after occlusion) and more severe paralysis in mice expressing Apoe4 versus mice expressing Apoe3.

Carriage of ε4 is associated with worse outcome in various forms of brain injury in humans, although the mechanisms underlying the associations are unclear. One hypothesis implicates β-amyloid protein. As stated above, accumulation of β-amyloid and its aggregation into β-pleated sheets is a key feature of the neuropathology of AD, and β-amyloid accumulation is thought to have adverse effects on neuron survival. In a key study, Nicoll *et al.* (1995) found that carriage of ε4 was strongly linked with increased deposition of β-amyloid in victims of traumatic brain injury. Of 90 patients who had died within 2 weeks of a head injury, 23 showed β-amyloid deposition. The frequency of ε4 in this group was 0.52 in comparison to an ε4 frequency of 0.16 in the group with no β-amyloid deposition, a highly significant difference ($p < 0.00001$). Notably, ε4 homozygotes showed 100% rate of β-amyloid deposition and patients with the genotypes ε2/2 or ε2/3 showed no β-amyloid deposition. It is suggested elsewhere that apoE3 might protect neurons from damage caused by β-amyloid, thus reducing cognitive deterioration (Raber *et al.*, 2000).

As well as possible direct effects upon neurons, and promoting the accumulation of β-amyloid, and the development of neurofibrillary tangles and amyloid angiopathy, ε4 may impact upon cognitive ageing through other mechanisms. Carriers of ε4 have elevated plasma cholesterol (Kamboh *et al.* 1993). Elevated cholesterol is associated with cerebrovascular disease, which is an important cause of age-related cognitive decline. ε4 has been specifically associated with narrowing of the carotid artery (Terry *et al.* 1996), which has been linked with cognitive impairment in the elderly (Yamauchi *et al.* 1996).

ApoE summary

The research on APOE, cognitive function, and brain structure and function has opened up new perspectives on the biology of human psychometric intelligence differences. Most research on the role of genetic differences in influencing ability levels is based on measuring associations. The work on APOE is different in that the gene, its polymorphisms, and protein products are characterized, and the roles of apolipoprotein E in the brain are beginning to be understood. Thus the mechanisms leading from genetic differences to mental ability differences can begin to be explored at different levels of analysis. The ways ahead will doubtless involve cataloguing the key brain proteins and their genes, and looking for polymorphisms in humans. However, with 70,000 to 80,000 genes the task will not be easy.

The APOE story has also highlighted many of the methodological and conceptual difficulties that afflict research enterprises combining the work of different disciplines. Medical researchers often take the neuropsychological approach, sometimes glibly assuming that different tests test not only distinct cognitive abilities but also distinct geographical regions of the brain. These assumptions are largely derived from work with animals and humans with experimentally or traumatically induced, relatively discrete lesions. Linkage among construct, test, and region is often strong under these special circumstances. However, in more diffuse and perhaps less severe processes, such as that seen in early AD, and also in looking at cognitive abilities in the normal range in healthy people, these linkages are likely to be less strong. Evidence challenging these assumptions emerges from several sources. Carroll's (1993) synthesis of factor analytic studies of human mental abilities refers to hundreds of studies that show that virtually all cognitive tests correlate, including tests of 'declarative memory', and thus, particularly in the normal range, performance on virtually any test of cognitive ability is strongly influenced by *g*. Functional neuroimaging studies have demonstrated that although functionally distinct modules can be identified, most tests will require the proper functioning of several neurobiological modules. For example, learning and delayed recall of word lists requires (at least) the hippocampal formation, attentional mechanisms thought to be localized in the cingulate cortex, and 'executive' functions thought to be localized in various regions of the frontal lobes. Processes affecting any of these regions might affect performance on neuropsychological tests of 'declarative memory'. In APOE research, although carriers tend to perform relatively worse on tests of declarative memory, clearly a diverse range of cognitive abilities is affected, as shown by Yaffe *et al.*'s finding linking declining performance on the digit–symbol substitution test with carriage of ε4 (Yaffe *et al.* 1997), and Berr *et al.*'s (1996) finding linking ε4 with worse performance on trail-making B and the finger-tapping test.

Another lesson from the APOE literature arises from the studies on head injury. This work shows that the effect sizes of genetic polymorphisms need not be fixed, but that they may change according to changing environmental circumstances. This observation is relevant to the study of the impact of variations in the prenatal and early environment on brain development and the possible associated effects on cognitive abilities. As psychometric intelligence remains fairly stable from late childhood until old age (Deary *et al.* 2000), it might be at the extremes of life where genetic–environmental interactions have their largest effects.

CONCLUSION

The story of Apoe differences and cognitive and other bodily system functions, e.g. cardiovascular status, presents some hard lessons for those interested in individual differences in mental abilities. Thousand of papers have been generated in a short time, directed at a single risk factor which is not large in effect, and the story is still far from being fully told. It is sensible to ask whether one can imagine such a coordinated and sustained research effort issuing from the finding that a given gene shows association with mental ability in the normal range. The history of high-technology studies and mental ability differences is one of too few studies, often conducted as offshoots of other research concerns. As the examples of brain size, brain scanning, and event-related potentials show, there are few large-scale, long-term programmes of research in the biology of mental ability differences, the IQ QTL and some twin studies being exceptions.

Table 9.2 (adapted from Caryl *et al.* 1999) compiles a very brief summary of the correlations with, and comprehensions of, human psychometric intelligence

Table 9.2 A summary assessment of some biological/information processing approaches to psychometric intelligence differences (adapted from Caryl *et al.* 1999)

Measure	Correlation with psychometric intelligence (effect size)	Criterion of assessment		Comment
		Theoretical tractability	Cause or consequence of ability test score differences	
Brain size	Around 0.4	Poor: several proposed, vague constructs	Probably cause	
Nerve conduction velocity	0.2 at most, probably less	Good: simple biological measure	Probably cause	Too few studies to date
ERP string length	Contradictory	Poor[a]	Ambiguous[b]	One of many ERP measures
Hick reaction time	< 0.25 for single parameters	Poor: not well understood[c]	Ambiguous[d]	R^2 improves when parameters combined
Inspection time	Around 0.4	Problematic	Probably cause, but disputed	

[a] Parameters that govern the variance in this measure are speculative.

[b] Could be a response characteristic secondary to intelligence level (i.e. could be consequence or cause).

[c] 'Rate of gain of information' has not proved a robust correlate of IQ-type test scores.

[d] Slope differences could be caused by learning differences.

differences that are offered by biological approaches in competition with the best that reaction times (Chapter 6) and psychophysics (Chapter 7) have produced. For those inclined to optimism and hope, there are moderate effect sizes, some evidence of tractability and some indications that causes rather than consequences of human ability differences are being uncovered. In no case, however, does a decent effect size combine with theoretical tractability of the biological/ information processing measure and unambiguity of causal direction. Brain size and inspection time perhaps achieve the best aggregate impressions. It is perhaps neither very convincing to the reader, nor good science, but it is tempting to say that the hope lies mainly in the less-put-to-the-test approaches of functional brain scanning and molecular genetics.

10 Den Finger in die Wunde legen

Avoiding 'cargo cult science' and 'the glass bead game'

Chapter 4 was the real discussion chapter, and readers might want to review it after the foregoing empirical accounts in Chapters 5–9. What follows is a postlegomenon (metalegomenon?); some discursive, *fin de travail* reflections on the field's successes, faults, dangers, and future.

REASONS TO BE CHEERFUL

After reading a draft of Chapter 6 an esteemed European colleague, an expert in the field, said that the tone of my account was to:

> Place your fingers into some of the most important wounds of this approach to human intelligence. Do you say this in English like that: *'Den Finger in die Wunde legen'*?

That might appear to be gratuitous self-harm to the cause of seeking processing accounts of human mental ability differences. There are articulate critics from outside mental ability research prepared to shoulder this job. But the aim throughout these essay-critiques was to demarcate the strong empirical findings from the correlational flotsam and jetsam, the theoretically well-conceived from the flimflam. There is no point in dodging the main problem facing this field: that we do not have a validated cognitive or biological architecture of human information processing that can be the basis for more theoretically oriented research. Two other headlines from the foregoing accounts need emphasizing: (1) finding the normative structure of human mental abilities is not the same as finding the sources of differences in those abilities (although the two tasks might overlap); and (2) a correlation between psychometric test scores and putative indices of brain processing needs explaining, as they do not usually tell us anything in themselves.

There are already some empirical data to build upon. Chapter 1 saw a growing agreement about the psychometric structure of human ability differences. This structure is a reminder that explaining human ability is not the same as explaining Spearman's *g*. Ability differences come in variously general packages and, to the extent that any or all of these covariance packets prove to be valid constructs, their differences need explaining in terms of brain functions. Mental ability differences have fair to good predictive validity, are quite highly stable over human adult life (although the reasons for change are a research priority too), and are interestingly heritable to different levels across the lifespan. Heritability patterns for different types and generalities of ability support the search for the basis of both general and more specific mental factors.

Quite understandably, people since antiquity have been curious about the origins of human ability differences and this occurred long before the invention of psychometric ability tests (Chapter 2). The ways that some early guesses about the nature of ability differences were framed have resonances with some present-day ideas. Frankly, that is probably because many of today's accounts have progressed little with respect to understanding the relevant brain–function constructs that hold the relevant individual differences. Huarte's (1575) book requires reviving in the minds of researchers; Spearman's impressive contributions have been worshipped as the progenitors of our research field to the exclusion of a true and far-seeing original. Spearman's agenda, shared with other members of the 'London School' of psychology, was to understand rather than merely to measure human ability differences. In a rich mix of empiricism and rational thought he threw up hypotheses about the origins of mental ability differences that ranged across cognitive, psychophysical, and physiological constructs (Chapters 2 and 3). The modest and significant associations he and others found between mental ability differences and sensory discrimination have been revived and replicated, newly waiting for an explanation (Chapters 7 and 8).

Various clever forays have been made on the integrity of psychometric ability test items, employing statistical, information processing, and artificial intelligence approaches (Chapter 5). Although these have failed at all times to cleave test items into mental components, there have been other benefits. The manipulation of test item difficulty has proved possible, along understood lines. More important, this type of research has directed mental ability researchers to relevant constructs more usually wielded by cognitive scientists and neuropsychologists. Thus, the concepts of working memory and g are known to be too closely related for their respective champions not to join forces and learn about each other's methods and findings. And ideas concerning frontal lobe function—incorporating goal management and other functions— must become a facet of thinking about the origins of human ability differences.

No-one can be in doubt that there are strong-enough, surprising, and interesting associations between some reaction time indices and visual and auditory processing measures (Chapters 6–8). We know less about the meaning of these than we thought we did when the 'reasons' were deemed to be 'mental speed', 'information processing speed', 'processing efficiency differences', or whatever. As discussed in Chapter 4, in Dennett's (1995) parlance, these pseudo-explanatory epithets are mere 'skyhooks'; that is, apparently explanatory terms that lack grounding to validated constructs and offer an illusory lift into causal space. More useful, better-grounded constructs are termed 'cranes'. But the realization that these secure findings link human performance across apparent boundaries of reduction makes them nourishing fodder for more explanatory research. More research is needed along the lines of studies that link psychometric and cognitive and psychophysical variables with the brain's event-related electrical potentials, gene differences, brain metabolism, and brain size (Chapter 9).

There are many well-operationalized mental tasks, but few have theoretical tractability. That is, the supposedly basic task parameters rarely have validity in terms of even lower-level processes themselves, and rarely or never can they be construed in terms of what is happening in the brain. This leads on to the problem that Spearman met, namely preparedness; one cannot succeed in understanding the information processing bases of intelligence until the relevant information processing variables have been isolated and operationalized. If that has not occurred, then the programme cannot progress.

The way forward for this sensible research question—what are the origins of mental ability differences—is not a theoretical breakthrough and not a catch-all model of intelligence (Deary and Stough 1997). It is simply more good, normal science that pays attention to the basics, such as:

- coordinated and agreed operationalization of mental ability and information processing variables
- testing the same subjects on multiple psychometric and information processing measures
- testing subjects on processing tests at multiple levels of reduction
- recruiting subject samples of adequate size and representativeness
- recruiting subject samples with adequate ability variance
- replicating findings, building to meta-analyses
- holding back on theory that goes too far ahead of the data
- holding back on cheap epithets to describe what a task measures when one does not know
- being sceptical about the validity of tests and constructs borrowed from other areas of scientific inquiry
- not being too keen to move to the 'next big thing' when there are perfectly strong associations to be explained from present methods (human imagination places a premium on fashion, truth does not)
- knowing historical precedents, and not re-inventing the wheel
- not confusing metaphor and simile with reality.

Following these prosaic recommendations, there follow some reminders of what might happen if some current bad research habits persist.

INTELLIGENCE AND CARGO CULT SCIENCE

Indigenous people of Oceania (South Sea islanders) were intermittently exposed to Western presence, especially the occasional appearance of abundant goods, or cargo. Understandably unclear about the origins of these unpredictable bounties, so-called cargo cults developed, in which rituals were enacted to bring wanted goods. Although they existed before World War II, the influx of allied Western transport and cargo at that time saw the development of new cargo cults. In Irian Jaya (New Guinea) in 1942 local armies were formed with imitation equipment in the hope that real equipment would be produced. John Frum cult members on Tanna (Vanuatu) constructed aeroplane runways and buildings to house cargo and waited for the air freight to arrive. Some descriptions have cult members in fake air traffic control towers controlling non-existent air traffic, and some in fake aeroplanes, but the cargo did not return.

These are fascinating human phenomena and, for the present purpose, anthropological and historical accuracy is not essential. Cargo cults are raised here because the 1965 Nobel Laureate in Physics, Richard Feynman (citation: for fundamental work in quantum electrodynamics, with deep-ploughing consequences for the physics of elementary particles), gave a celebrated address in 1974 at Caltech in which he talked about 'cargo cult science'. It was printed as an essay later (Feynman 1985). He continued the above account as follows:

> So they've arranged to make things like runways, to put fires along the sides of the runways, to make a wooden hut for a man to sit in, with two wooden pieces on his head for headphones and bars sticking out like antennas—he's the controller—and they wait for the airplanes to land. They're doing everything right. The form is perfect. It looks exactly the way it looked before. But it doesn't work. No airplanes land. So I call these things cargo cult science, because they follow all the apparent precepts and forms of scientific investigation, but they're missing something essential, because the planes don't land.

Feynman proceeded to identify the essential ingredient that is missing in cargo cult science:

> It's a kind of scientific integrity, a principle of scientific thought that corresponds to a kind of utter honesty—a kind of leaning over backwards. For example, if you're doing an experiment, you should report everything that you think might make it invalid—not only what you think is right about it: other causes that could possibly explain your results; and things you thought of that you've eliminated by some other experiment, and how they worked—to make sure the other fellow can tell they have been eliminated.

> Details that could throw doubt on your interpretation must be given, if you know them. You must do the best you can—if you know anything at all wrong, or possibly wrong—to explain it. If you make a theory, for example, and advertise it, or put it out, then you must also put down all the facts that disagree with it, as well as those that agree with it. There is also a more subtle problem. When you have put a lot of ideas together to make an elaborate theory, you want to make sure, when explaining what it fits, that those things it fits are not just the things that gave you the idea for the theory; but that the finished theory makes something else come out right, in addition.

This is not dissimilar to Popper's (1972) view of science as conjectures and refutations, although it is expressed in lay terms. The rigorous self-scrutiny that

Feynman judged to be the signature of science, perhaps constipating if taken to extremes, makes a good measuring stick for the science of mental ability differences and influenced the ethos of this book. A recurring theme, a mantra even, of this book is that correlation needs establishing and then explaining. There can be a tendency to foreclosure in intelligence research, a feeling that one should 'declare victory and withdraw' by finding a correlation and acting as if an explanation is immanent in the Pearson's *r*. But there are examples of bending-over-backwards too. Attempts to rule out strategic, motivational, and other 'top-down' explanations for the correlations between reaction and inspection times and psychometric intelligence differences are examples of researchers trying to rule out counter-explanations provided by confounding variables (Chapters 6 and 7). Therefore, not addressing potential confounders as alternative explanatory variables is, in Feynman's sense, cargo cult science within psychometric intelligence research and must be avoided.

There might be an opposite extreme, a kind of 'crying wolf' science, that could be equally conducive to blocking progress in discovering the bases of mental ability differences. In the chapters on reaction times and inspection times there were several suggestions for explaining the correlations that were found, including strategies, motivation, attention, concentration, personality, learning, adaptation to novelty, and so forth. The problem is that some of these hypotheses are poorly formulated and based on constructs that are poorly operationalized. Personal experience in our laboratories indicates that the process of operationalizing every possible counter-explanation to an information-processing-efficiency-based account of inspection time–psychometric intelligence correlations could have taken all our efforts and produced little (Egan and Deary 1992, 1993; Egan 1994; Simpson and Deary 1997). A judgement must be made about which suggestions are scientifically sensible and testable, and which are lazily formulated diverting tactics.

There is another way in which the psychology of psychometric intelligence differences must avoid cargo cult science, not an aspect of the metaphor developed by Feynman. There is a poignancy about research that uses reaction times like those of Hick and S. Sternberg; procedures that were supposed to deliver freight in the form of an information processing ingredient that was going to account for some worth-bothering-about slice of human mental ability test score variance. The freight, in the form of correlations between slope parameters and psychometric intelligence, did not return after initial, fleeting appearances (Chapter 6), but the research using these procedures continued anyway. Attention turned instead to the packaging (the mean reaction times, the intercepts, the variabilities) that was to be opened to reveal the processing treasure, and researchers are now eking out a living from that. Feynman was urging that science involves taking the job of criticism seriously, not just going through the motions and ignoring the flak. This second metaphorical use of cargo cultism in science urges that one be clear about why one is continuing with a line of research when the original rationale for the procedure promised a result that did not replicate. Another example involves nerve conduction velocity (Chapter 9), which seemed interesting to look at with respect to intelligence because it might account for some of the association between reaction times and ability differences. That it did not do so forced a rethink of the idea of an integrated vision of 'speed of information processing' that crossed levels of description from physiology to psychology.

One last example of cargo cult wishful thinking (or self-deception) is the continued, widespread use of the term 'elementary cognitive tasks' to refer to some reaction time and other procedures whose variables correlate with psychometric intelligence. They are anything but elementary in any respectable scientific sense, and corralling them with the same group noun/phrase forces them closer in the imagination than the reality that the correlations attest.

Cargo cult relics may often be found in elementary psychology textbooks. These are prime sites for finding abandoned theories of all types, such as personality theories long-disowned by empirical research. As stated in Chapter 5, R. J. Sternberg's components of analogical reasoning appear regularly in textbook accounts, despite their ceasing to attract current empirical interest. Another type of Feynmanian cargo cult science is supposedly explanatory work that turns out to be mere redescriptions of the data. This was suspected of some of the psychometric approaches to information processing components in Chapter 5.

INTELLIGENCE AND THE GLASS BEAD GAME

Scientists try to find the elements which nature comprises and their interactions. If science involves imagination, it does not also offer the freedom to say anything. The limits are the way the world is. If psychology is a science it does not offer the freedom to invent the lineaments and functions of mind anew when we tire of previous findings. Here are Howe's (1997) objections to Anderson's (1992) evidence-based theory of intelligence and its development:

> The outcome is ingenious but cumbersome. A key problem, in my view, is that no attempt to develop a theory which builds on the approach originating with Spearman and improves and elaborates it in order to bring it into line with recent changes in knowledge can be entirely successful. Anderson might been wiser to build a new approach from scratch, unhindered by the preconceptions and faulty assumptions of what has remained essentially a faculty theory of intelligence. In terms of Sternberg's categories of intellectual functioning, Anderson could have been advised to engage in less adapting to the environment and more shaping of it.

Howe was urging Anderson to abandon perhaps the most replicated result in psychology—*g*—and criticizing him for updating it to fit with more modern results from information processing and cognitive psychology. The critique is off the mark in associating Spearman with faculty psychology. Spearman's (1927) critique of faculty psychology is withering. In any case, what ill-advised advice—to berate a young researcher from standing on the shoulders of a sound empirical finding. This form of intellectual arrogance, which advocates ignoring replicated empirical findings in favour of starting from scratch, is reminiscent of the intellectual matters dealt with in Wilbur's (1957) poem *Mind*:

Mind in its purest play is like some bat
That beats about in caverns all alone,
Contriving by a kind of senseless wit
Not to conclude against a wall of stone.

It has no need to falter or explore;
Darkly it knows what obstacles are there,
And so may weave and flitter, dip and soar
In perfect courses through the blackest air.

And has this simile a like perfection?
The mind is like a bat. Precisely. Save
That in the very happiest intellection
A graceful error may correct the cave.

The last stanza affords two interpretations, according to whether the walls of the cave represent the mental representation of the cave in the mind or the true state of the world. In the first interpretation, breaking through commonly held assumptions can be a source of discovery and creativity. In the second interpretation we have the dubious freedom to deny or ignore truths about the world in our thinking about its state. This more cynical interpretation is captured in another of Wilbur's (1957) poems, *Epistemology*:

We milk the cow of the world, and as we do
We whisper in her ear, 'You are not true.'

If Howe (1997) was criticizing Anderson for conducting normal science—building sensibly from known facts—what was he advocating? Something closer to the 'glass bead game' than to scientific psychology. In *The glass bead game* (1943) by Hesse (1946 Nobel Laureate in Literature with the citation: for his inspired writing which, while growing in boldness and penetration, exemplifies the classical humanitarian ideals and high qualities of style), the Benedictine Father Jacobus says to Joseph Knecht, a glass bead game player and future Magister Ludi:

You could at least do with a few simpler foundations, with a science of man, for example, a real doctrine and real knowledge about the human race. You do not know man, do not understand him in his bestiality and as the image of God. All you know is the Castilian, a special product, a caste, a rare experiment in breeding. (p. 188)

The competition involved working out sketches for Games based on three or four prescribed main themes. Stress was placed on new, bold, and original associations of themes, impeccable logic, and beautiful calligraphy. Moreover, this was the sole occasion when competitors were permitted to overstep the bounds of the canon. That is, they could employ new symbols not yet admitted to the official code and vocabulary of hieroglyphs. This made the competition—which in any case was the most exciting annual event in Waldzell except for the great public ceremonial games—a contest among the most promising advocates of new Game symbols, and the very highest distinction for a winner in this competition consisted in the recognition of his proposed additions to the grammar and vocabulary of the Game and their acceptance into the Game Archives and the Game language. This was a very rare distinction indeed; usually the winner had to be content only with the ceremonial performance of his game as the best candidate's Game of the year. Once, some twenty-five years ago, the great Thomas von der Trave, the present Magister Ludi, had been awarded this honor with his new abbreviations for the alchemical significance of the signs of the zodiac . . . (pp. 195–196)

In the first extract the monk criticizes Knecht for the lack of a basis in the science of man. In the second extract we get some idea of the criteria by which the glass bead game players were judged. Tragically, this sounds all too like the development of theories of intelligence, with a push towards elaborate theorizing, new constructs pebble-dashed with jargon, laying aside known empirical findings, and playing to the crowd rather than the cognoscenti.

In another scientific discipline, or perhaps elsewhere in psychology, a monograph such as the present one might cast the known facts in the field as a novel theoretical account. That such an undertaking would be premature folly I am utterly convinced. I have refused to invent a premature and fanciful periodic table of cognitive and/or biological components dripping with parameters from which issue individual differences in human ability. The cognito-genuflective act of writing down the name of a process, drawing a box around it, and connecting it with an arrow to another box will not deliver a science of intelligence differences. Nor will arbitrarily dividing up and naming the resulting shards of complex behaviour, such as the actions involved in solving a mental test item. I feel no rush to shower the reader with neo-Guilfordian, Sternbergian, Andersonian, Gardnerian, and so forth, components/facets/processes, even as a set of harmless novelty pastime items, let alone a heaven of false gods, until science delivers.

One is reminded, in considering the state of research in information processing approaches to intelligence differences, of the earliest exploring geographers' attempts to describe the earth's polar regions. Islands, continental coastlines, and gruesome monsters were conjured into existence by acts of will, yet never verified. From meagre sightings, great ranges of mountains were brought into being, but never seen again. Fluid polar seas were hypothesized, but remained frozen. From an aesthetic point of view—judging from enjoyment rather than truth—the fanciful accounts make better reading. On the other hand, the sober accounts of those who added small bits of secure knowledge but who refused to speculate are more dull. Real discovery came about because the instruments of travel, navigation, and scientific measurement became more refined, allowing people to visit the disputed sights and describe them with veracity. The strength with which this conviction is held is all the more so because it has to disagree with my recently rediscovered hero:

As for such who want invention, the common wealth should not consent that they make bookes, nor suffer them to be printed, because they do nought else save heap up matters alreadie delivered, and sentences of grave authors, returning to repeat the selfe things, stealing one from hence, and taking another from thence; and there is no man, but after such a fashion may make a booke. (Huarte 1595, p. 67)

Writing this account of some of the research into the bases of human cognitive ability differences seems, in retrospect, like spring-cleaning. Like other colleagues around the world, I was familiar with much of the material in the book already, 'living' with it, day in, day out. After forcing myself to look at the field afresh, it became clear that there were articles of furniture that were broken or unfinished and needed to be thrown out. There were other useful bits that needed further DIY work to make them serviceable. Others needed some form of specialist to make them useful. Some rooms, relatively little used, were opened up and found to be ideal for modern living.

The ultimate judgement on each area of research within the information processing approach to psychometric intelligence differences must not be whether a given line of inquiry has yet delivered a mechanistic account. Instead, we should estimate the viability of the approach based upon the robustness (not necessarily the effect size) of the association, and the apparent tractability of the information processing procedure and its correlation with ability test scores. Like the managers of a mine, we need to estimate, with imperfect information, whether it is worth committing time and person-power to the excavation of any given seam.

INTELLIGENCE AND HUNTER-GATHERER SCIENCE

Much of the research presented in Chapters 5–7, and 9, may be characterized as a scientific subsistence living; foraging at the margins of other disciplines, awaiting the crumbs from cognitive and neuroscience tables, finding a variable here and there that might just, or just not, correlate significantly with psychometric intelligence differences, compiling a post-hoc rationale for the experiment, renaming the rationale a theory, and moving on. Few of the lines of inquiry are well developed, and investigators tend to move on when a given task has offered up what limited promise it contained. Successful science, exemplified by the account of apolipoprotein E in Chapter 9, is a more concerted, large-scale effort; an agricultural rather than a hunter-gatherer pursuit. Perhaps that can change. The IQ QTL project (Chapter 9) is a coordinated research effort to find genes whose differences covary with mental ability differences. Psychologists play leading roles alongside molecular geneticists. Whether this will prove to be a model for future research on individual differences, or the exception that tests the rule that the origins of ability differences will remain a scrappy and marginalized effort, is hard to judge. Another way to conceive this limitation of research on the causes of mental ability differences is to view it as a pastime for people who have real jobs elsewhere. Detterman (1979) attributed the lack of coordination in the research programme to the researchers mostly having primary identifications in other areas of psychology:

> while this diversity might be viewed as a strength, in actuality it produces a multifaceted science with no two researchers concentrating on the same facet. This has left us with a hodge-podge of findings which we are unable to integrate into a common theoretical approach. (p. 298)

Chabris (1998) described a future in which, although the science of mental ability differences gets a glimpse of the promised land of explanatory-variable-milk-and-honey (with associated technology), they never get to eat or drink:

> The great irony is that this [the exit from the scientific scene of leading psychometricians] is occurring just as the field of behavioral genetics has begun to thrive as never before. One of its most striking successes has been to document, through the convergence of numerous family and twin studies, the heritability of intelligence. Now researchers have been able to identify a specific gene whose variations are associated with differences in intelligence. This is a crucial step in building a complete theory of intelligence that can explain individual differences in biological as well as psychological terms. But the new generation of cognitive scientists, who focus on characteristics of the mind and brain that are common to everyone, are not too interested in differences among people, while the psychometricians, who stand to be vindicated, have been side-lined on their own playing field. (p. 40)

Chabris's view was that, poised with a validated descriptive model for psychometric intelligence and massive confirmatory evidence concerning the heritability of mental ability differences, differential psychologists will find their progress halted because they are not fashionable. Chorney *et al.* (1998) stated that *g* had a key role in cognitive neuroscience. The dearth of brain-scanning studies addressing individual differences in mental abilities, at a time when thousands of cognitive studies are reported, and the lack of mention of mental ability differences in cognitive neuroscience texts suggest that the role is one of potential rather than achievement.

If individual differences do become fashionable, Chabris's (1998) sidelining metaphor might take a different hue. The measurement of mental ability differences is almost too easy: Raven's matrices that were developed in the 1930s and 1940s are almost unchanged; some of Binet's original items are still there in today's tests. If the ground on which the hunter-gatherers of differential psychology forage looks likely to provide a living beyond subsistence, they will discover that cognitive agriculturalists will find it all too easy to borrow and apply the venerable tests. Differential psychology will certainly have a role in better defining the pheno-type and perhaps improving the hierarchical model of ability differences, but the reductionistic work will demand cooperatives with cognitive and biological neuroscientists in which differential psychologists might find themselves the junior partners.

A VALEDICTORY MESSAGE TO THE NEW MILLENNIAL PROPHETS—OR A TALE OF TWO STERNBERGS (A TRAGEDY)

From Huarte, through Hobbes, Wolff, Spearman, the cognitive revolution (see Chapter 3), and to the end of the twentieth century (e.g. Matarazzo, 1992, was particularly optimistic) there have been bouts of enthusiasm that human mental ability differences will be explained by some new way of construing the elements of mind. Perhaps these possibilities look better from afar than close up and within the research area. Nettelbeck (1998), in my view, was correct in the following assessment:

> optimism about ECTs [so-called elementary cognitive tests] as replacements for current psychometric tests of cognitive abilities is not warranted. Reflecting on the future of psychological testing and assessment during the first two decades of the twenty-first century, Matarazzo (1992) has predicted the practical application of what he termed 'biological indices of brain function and structure' (p. 1012), by which he meant parameters of performance drawn from the electroencephalogram (EEG), from RT [reaction time] and from IT [inspection time]. Having considered the literature on these topics during the previous decade or so, Matarazzo was convinced that such measures have the potential to serve in the relatively near future as practical measures of intelligence. I disagree with this assessment. Such measures are not biological; they are psychological. Even EEG, which many psychologists regard as essentially physiological, may be influenced by personal factors including motivation and mood (Callaway 1975). For another thing, although ECTs provide useful tools for the advancement of theoretical explanations about the psychological nature of intelligence, they are insufficiently reliable to permit accurate assessment of individual differences in cognitive abilities . . . (p. 238)

I share Nettelbeck's reservations.

The split between cognitive-experimental and differential psychology is arguably the most persistent malaise hindering the advance of our understanding individual differences in psychometric intelligence. Differential psychology can measure intelligence differences with reliability and validity, but an alliance with experimental psychology and neuroscience is needed before the cognitive and biological sources of mental ability (general and more specific) differences can be understood. Spearman (1904) knew that mental tests divorced from mainstream experimental psychology would impoverish his correlational (differential) psychology. Cognitive-experimental and differential psychology have been affianced more than once: in 1957 (Cronbach), in 1964 (McNemar), in 1978 (Carroll; Glaser and Pellegrino; Snow; Sternberg), in 1995 (Eysenck), and in 1996 (Kyllonen). Now, at the end of 1999, Gustafsson is still urging this marriage:

> During the past couple of decades, research conducted along experimental lines has contributed greatly to our understanding of the nature of G, both in terms

of low-level reductionistic models and in terms of higher level cognitive models. There is, however, still a long way to go until the major individual-differences constructs have been adequately accounted for in theoretical terms. It would seem, however, that an approach combining experimental methodology with multivariate modeling techniques may prove useful in researchers' future attempts to achieve such an understanding. (p. 287)

Glaser and Pellegrino (1978) summed up the 1978 cognitive–differential symposium—the one whose authors are described at the end of Chapter 3—in *Intelligence* as follows:

> Hopefully, new concepts of individual differences that emphasize the cognitive processes of human performance will foster the development of educational possibilities that increase individual accomplishments.
>
> Twenty-two years ago, Cronbach reported that 'constructs originating in differentiating psychology' are now being tied to experimental variables. As a result, the whole theoretical picture in such an area as human abilities is changing' (p. 682). Presumably, with the momentum displayed by this symposium, we can now move faster. (p. 318).

Rather neatly, at the time of closing the writing of this book, it is now another 22 years on. The evidence presented in the previous chapters demonstrates empirical advances, but it would be overstating things to say that the marriage of cognitive and differential psychology had been productively consummated over the last two decades. However, even Hunt, one of the more pessimistic of the 1978 symposiasts (Hunt and MacLeod 1978), saw progress as he reviewed the cognitive–differential association in 1999:

> There is a psychometric dimension of Gf, performance along this dimension is closely associated with working memory capacity and the ability to control attention, and these functions are largely mediated by forebrain structures. Those who feel that psychology simply recycles old issues should rethink their position. None of these propositions could be made with so much confidence 50 years ago. (p. 13)

The next quote from Hunt (1999) illustrates that the hopes of the 1978 symposiasts, and those other well-meaning folk down the century who have cheered from the sidelines, willing on the successful union of experimental and differential psychology's joint contribution to human mental ability differences, are yet to be realized:

> People do clearly vary in that statistical abstraction, Gf. They also vary in visual–spatial reasoning and in a number of other important aspects of intellectual competence. Some of this variation is clearly tied to information-

processing capacity . . . We need to know the biological mechanisms by which this is achieved. (p. 24)

That last comment captures the biggest change in the field since the late-1970s, i.e. the increasing emphasis on new biological techniques and constructs as adjuncts to, or substitutes for, cognitive-level constructs. The hopes in the late-1970s rested to a large extent in the approaches exemplified by two Sternbergs: the one (R. J.) offering atomic elements from psychometric test items (see Chapter 5), the other (S.) producing processing variables from clever reaction time manipulations (see Chapter 6). Neither of these was the high road to, as Hunt (1999) put it,

the biological goal of finding the power of the mind in the brain. (p. 25)

A good and important scientific question—such as the underpinnings of mental ability differences—does not become a bad one because the field has moved slowly. A combination of enough persistent, good science and the availability of the necessary investigative tools and theoretical constructs is the prerequisite for advancement. Neisser (1979) realized this:

> Some day soon, psychologist *P* may claim that intelligence is really *X*, a particular amalgam of cognitive components and strategies. How will *P* support this claim when it is challenged? There are really only two ways. First, *P* will probably report that there's a high correlation between scores on *X* and scores on tests. Unfortunately, such a correlation cannot prove that *X* is *intelligence* unless we have already accepted Boring's doctrine about what the tests test. Second, *P* may simply try to persuade us. Look, says *P*, there are these good reasons to identify *X* with intelligence . . . its success will depend critically on what we include in the concept to begin with. (p. 218)

> In some cases . . . different intelligent activities may be based on the same underlying processes. Cognitive research may indeed be successful in identifying those processes, and thus account for some of the observable correlations among attributes of intelligence. Such research is certainly worth pursuing. We must be wary, however, of believing that it will enable us to define intelligence itself. Otherwise we may find ourselves acting out a new version of Boring's scenario in the year 2000, when someone defines intelligence as what the models model. I hope we don't because it isn't. (p. 226)

These comments were taken from another symposium in the early days of the journal *Intelligence*, in 1979, which looked forward to the prospects for mental testing in the year 2000.

With only 19 days to go to AD 2000 at the time of writing this epilogue, and with no sign of the information processing cavalry riding across the gardens outside my office to bring the reductionistic account of psychometric intelligence differences that some of the contributors back in 1979 expected, it seems proper to recollect the reticence of some contributors (Resnick 1979), and to learn the art of scientific patience. Indeed, Sternberg (1979), in a cynical moment quipped:

Intelligence Tests in the Year 2000? They're here! (p. 292)

True to an extent, but the hierarchical model of ability differences had not then been fully appreciated (Chapter 1). Turnbull (1979, p. 276) delineated 'neural efficiency' (meaning event-related potentials) and 'information processing' (meaning R. J. Sternbergian components) approaches and wished them more success than we have since seen; but there are still interesting cognitive and biological leads in the study of ability differences. Horn (1979) thought that, from 1979 to 2000:

Reaction time recordings will become more common and important in future measures of human abilities . . . Scoring procedures and function models based on ideas about processing time will become increasingly prominent in our theories about intellect and in our practical devices for diagnosing problems and indicating strengths of intellectual capacities. (p. 233)

Increasing computerization of mental testing has meant that Horn was partly correct. However, as a view of how influential cognitive models might be in accounting for psychometric intelligence differences in 2000 it is quaint and unrealized,

As cognitive theorists work to relate such processes to the abilities of intelligence, there should be notable movement toward describing the interrelationship among processes and thus improved description of the architectonic structure of intelligence. This influential push from cognitive psychology will encourage the development of multiple-process models of intelligence. (Horn 1979, p. 236)

the year 2000 should see us making notable advances in identifying just what it is that we mean when we talk about adult intelligence being the quintessence of intelligence. (p. 237)

Horn was unique, though, in foreseeing that auditory and visual processing (Chapter 7) might re-enter the reckoning of mental ability differences.

In summing up that symposium back in 1979, and in guessing forward to 2000, the then-and-now editor of *Intelligence* (Detterman 1979) called the science of human intelligence differences 'a job half done' (p. 295) and called for 'an integrated science of the study of intellectual ability' (p. 306). If his estimate of half-done was correct, then it is more, but not much more, than half-done still. The integration has not fully happened, but it must; a science of mental ability differences without cognitive scientists and neuroscientists as partners does not seem feasible. Compared with the organizational leviathans of cognitive science and neuroscience, the study of the origins of human ability differences is largely a collection of near-independent cottage industries. It must have seemed a distant future to be writing about the year 2000 in the late-1970s. If we compare what has happened in that time in structural and functional brain scanning and in molecular genetics then we see, in addition to potentially very useful tools for use in our investigations, how modestly the science of understanding the bases of psychometric intelligence differences has progressed. Snow (1980) was overoptimistic in his millennial predictions:

> an information processing account of intelligence seems destined to become a monument in the next 20 years, if it cannot already be counted as such now. (p. 185)

The 'monument' metaphor is a gift to destructive critics: folly?, war memorial?, celebration of a false idol? That monument is still only part-built, and may never be completed. The scientific tools needed to finish the job are still being manufactured. There is a pace to scientific progress that will and imagination cannot force, as Nichols and Newsome (1999) related,

> Exciting new findings have emerged in recent decades concerning the neural underpinnings of cognitive functions such as perception, learning, memory, attention, decision-making, language and motor planning . . . With very few exceptions, however, our understanding of these phenomena remains rudimentary. We can identify particular locations within the brain where neural activity is modulated in concert with particular external or internal stimuli. In some cases we can even artificially manipulate neural activity in a specific brain structure (using electrical or pharmacological techniques) and cause predictable changes in behaviour. But we encounter substantial difficulties in understanding how modulations in neural activity at one point in the nervous system are actually produced by synaptic interactions between neural systems. Thus our current state of knowledge is some what akin to looking out of the window of an airplane at night. We can see patches of light from cities and towns scattered across the landscape, we know that roads, railways and telephone wires connect those cities, but we gain little sense of the social, political and economic interactions within and between cities that define a functioning society. (p. 38)

The purpose in writing this account was not to review the various literature (that has been done elsewhere), not to provide an interim, *Annual Review*-type update of the field (something that has a limited currency). Rather, it was hoped that it would be useful to challenge assumptions, pore over constructs, engage in self-criticism, and worry about scientific continuity in the research area. It was written with the research area's Diaspora in mind. It was intended to be frank and, where appropriate, frankly pessimistic. The idea was to afford the solid achievements of psychometric intelligence researchers more definition. The tone was intended to meet the Scottish stereotype of dourness: stern and unrelenting but not, it is hoped, dull.

References

Abelson, A. R. (1911). The measurement of mental ability of backward children. *British Journal of Psychology, 4*, 268–314.

Ackerman, P. L. (1988). Determinants of individual differences during skill acquisition: cognitive abilities and information processing perspectives. *Journal of Experimental Psychology: General, 117*, 288–318.

Ackerman, P. L. and Schneider, W. (1985). Individual differences in automatic and controlled information processing. In R. Dillon (Ed.), *Individual differences in cognition*, vol. 2. New York: Academic.

Alarcon, M., Plomin, R., Fulker, D. W., Corely, R., and DeFries, J. C. (1998). Multivariate path analysis of specific cognitive abilities data. *Behavior Genetics, 28*, 255–264.

Alberts, M. J., Graffagnino, C., McClenny, C., Strittmatter, W., Saunders, A. M., and Roses, A. D. (1995). ApoE genotype and survival from intracerebral haemorrhage. *Lancet, 346*, 575.

Alcorn, M. R. and Morris, G. L. (1996). P300 correlates of inspection time. *Personality and Individual Differences, 20*, 619–627.

Alderton, D. L., Goldman, S. R., and Pellegrino, J. W. (1985). Individual differences in process outcomes for analogy and classification solution. *Intelligence, 9*, 69–85.

American Psychiatric Association. (1994). *Diagnostic and Statistical Manual of Mental Disorders*, Fourth Edition. Washington, DC: American Psychiatric Association.

Anderson, B. (1994). Speed of neuron conduction is not the basis of the IQ–RT correlation: results from a simple neural model. *Intelligence, 19*, 317–323.

Anderson, B. (1995). Dendrites and cognition: a negative pilot study in the rat. *Intelligence, 20*, 291–308.

Anderson, B., Elgavish, G. A., Chu, W.-J., Simor, T., Martin, R. C., Hugg, J. W., *et al.* (1998). Temporal lobe pHi and IQ: no consistent correlation. *Intelligence, 26*, 75–79.

Anderson, M. (1992). *Intelligence and development: a cognitive theory*. Oxford, UK: Blackwell.

Andreasen, N., Flaum, M., Swayze, V., O'Leary, D. S., Alliger, R., Cohen, G., *et al.* (1993). Intelligence and brain structure in normal individuals. *American Journal of Psychiatry, 150*, 130–134.

Anokhin, A. and Vogel, F. (1996). EEG alpha rhythm frequency and intelligence in normal adults. *Intelligence, 23*, 1–14.

Anstey, K. J. and Smith, G. A. (1999). Interrelationships among biological markers of aging, health, activity, acculturation, and cognitive performance in late adulthood. *Psychology and Aging, 14*, 605–618.

Arkin, R. (1998). *The biology of aging* (2nd ed.). Sinauer: Sunderland.

Arnold, S. E., Joo, E., Martinoli, M.-G., Roy, N., Trojanowski, J. Q., Gur, R. E., *et al.* (1997). Apolipoprotein E genotype in schizophrenia: frequency, age of onset, and neuropathologic features. *NeuroReport, 8*, 1523–1526.

Austin, E. J. and Deary, I. J. (1999). Effects of repeated hypoglycaemia on cognitive function: a psychometrically validated re-analysis of the Diabetes Control and Complications Trial data. *Diabetes Care, 22*, 1273–1277.

Avolio, B. J. and Waldman, D. A. (1994). Variations in cognitive, perceptual, and psychometric abilities across the working life span: examining the effects of race, sex, experience, education, and occupational type. *Psychology and Aging, 9*, 430–442.

Babcock, R. L. (1992). Analysis of adult age differences on the Raven's Advanced Progressive Matrices Test. PhD dissertation, Georgia Institute of Technology.

Bachelder, B. L. and Denny, M. R. (1977). A theory of intelligence: 1. Span and the complexity of stimulus control. *Intelligence, 1*, 127–150.

Baddeley, A. D. (1986). *Working memory*. Oxford: Clarendon.

Baddeley, A. (1992*a*). Working memory. *Science, 255*, 556–559.

Baddeley, A. (1992*b*). Working memory: the interface between memory and cognition. *Journal of Cognitive Neuroscience, 4*, 281–288.

Baddeley, A. and Gathercole, S. (1999). Individual differences in learning and memory: psychometrics and the single case. In P. L. Ackerman, P. C. Kyllonen, and R. D. Roberts (Eds.), *Learning and individual differences: process, trait, and content determinants* (pp. 33–54). Washington, DC: American Psychological Association.

Baker, L. A., Vernon, P. A., and Ho, H. Z. (1991). The genetic correlation between intelligence and speed of information processing. *Behavior Genetics, 21*, 351–368.

Baltes, P. B. (1987). Theoretical propositions of life-span developmental psychology: on the dynamics between growth and decline. *Developmental Psychology, 23*, 611–626.

Baltes, P. B. and Lindenberger, U. (1997). Evidence of a powerful connection between sensory and cognitive functions across the adult life span: a new window to the study of cognitive aging. *Psychology and Aging, 12*, 12–31.

Baltes, P. B., Nesselroade, J. R., Schaie, K. W., and Labouvie, E. W. (1972). On the dilemma of regression effects in examining ability-level-related differentials in ontogenic patterns of intelligence. *Developmental Psychology, 6*, 78–84.

Baltes, P. B., Staudinger, U. M., and Lindenberger, U. (1999). Lifespan psychology: theory and application to intellectual functioning. *Annual Review of Psychology, 50*, 471–507.

Barrett, P. T. and Eysenck, H. J. (1992*a*). Brain-evoked potentials and intelligence: the Hendrickson paradigm. *Intelligence, 16*, 361–381.

Barrett, P. T. and Eysenck, H. J. (1992*b*). Brain electrical potentials and intelligence. In A. Gale and H. J. Eysenck (Eds.), *Handbook of individual differences: biological perspectives*. New York: Wiley.

Barrett, P. T. and Eysenck, H. J. (1994). The relationship between evoked potential component amplitude, latency, contour length, variability, zero-crossings and psychometric intelligence. *Personality and Individual Differences*, *16*, 3–32.

Barrett, P., Eysenck, H. J., and Lucking, S. (1986). Reaction time and intelligence: a replicated study. *Intelligence*, *10*, 9–40.

Barrett, P. T., Daum, I., and Eysenck, H. J. (1990). Sensory nerve conduction velocity and intelligence: a methodological study. *Journal of Psychophysiology*, *4*, 1–13.

Bassuk, S. S., Glass, T. A., and Berkman, L. F. (1999). Social disengagement and incident cognitive decline in community-dwelling elderly persons. *Annals of Internal Medicine*, *131*, 165–173.

Bates, T. C. and Eysenck, H. J. (1993*a*). Intelligence, inspection time, and decision time. *Intelligence*, *17*, 523–531.

Bates, T. and Eysenck, H. J. (1993*b*). String length, attention and intelligence-focussed attention reverses the string length IQ relationship. *Personality and Individual Differences*, *15*, 363–371.

Bates, T. and Stough, C. (1998). Improved reaction time method, information processing speed, and intelligence. *Intelligence*, *26*, 53–62.

Bates, T., Pellett, O., Stough, C., and Mangan, G. L. (1994). The effects of smoking on simple and choice reaction time. *Psychopharmacology*, *114*, 365–378.

Bates, T., Mangan, G., Stough, C., and Corballis, P. (1995*a*). Smoking, processing speed, and attention in a choice–reaction time task. *Psychopharmacology*, *120*, 209–212.

Bates, T., Stough, C., Mangan, G., and Pellett, O. (1995*b*). Intelligence and complexity of the averaged evoked potential: an attentional theory. *Intelligence*, *20*, 27–39.

Beauducel, A. and Brocke, B. (1993). Intelligence and speed of information processing: further results and questions on Hick's paradigm and beyond. *Personality and Individual Differences*, *15*, 627–636.

Beck, L. F. (1933). The role of speed in intelligence. *Psychological Bulletin*, *30*, 169–178.

Beck-Nielsen, H. and Groop, L. C. (1994). Metabolic and genetic characterisation of prediabetic states. *Journal of Clinical Investigation*, *94*, 1714–1721.

Beeton, I. (1861). *The Book of Household Management*. London: Cape.

Beh, H. C., Roberts, R. D., and Prichard-Levy, A. (1994). The relationship between intelligence and choice reaction time within the framework of an extended model of Hick's law: a preliminary report. *Personality and Individual Differences*, *16*, 891–897.

Bellivier, F., Laplanche, J. L., Schurhoff, F., Feingold, J., Jouvent, R., Launay, J. M., *et al.* (1997). Apolipoprotein E gene polymorphism in early and late onset bipolar patients. *Neuroscience Letters*, *233*, 45–48.

Benton, D. and Roberts, G. (1988). Effect of vitamin and mineral supplementation on intelligence of a sample of schoolchildren. *Lancet*, *i*, 140–143.

Berent, S., Giordani, B., Lehtinen, S., Markel, D., Penney, J. B., Buchtel, H. A., *et al.* (1988). Positron emission tomographic scan investigations of

Huntingdon's disease: cerebral metabolic correlates of cognitive function. *Annals of Neurology*, *232*, 541–546.

Bergen, J. and Julez, B. (1983). Rapid discrimination of visual patterns. *IEEE Transactions on Systems, Man and Cybernetics*, *SMC-13*, 857–863.

Bernstein, D. A., Roy, E. J., Srull, T. K., and Wickens, C. D. (1988). *Psychology*. Boston: Houghton Mifflin.

Berr, C., Dufouil, C., Brousseau, T., Richard, F., Amouyel, P., Marceteau, E., *et al.* (1996). Early effect of ApoE-epsilon4 allele on cognitive results in a group of highly performing subjects: the EVA study. *Neuroscience Letters*, *218*, 9–12.

Berr, C., Richard, M. J., Roussel, A. M., and Bonithon-Kopp, C. (1998). Systemic oxidative stress and cognitive performance in the population-based EVA study. *Free Radical Biology and Medicine*, *24*, 1202–1208.

Bickley, P. G., Keith, T. Z., and Wolfle, L. M. (1995). The three-stratum theory of cognitive abilities: test of the structure of intelligence across the life span. *Intelligence*, *20*, 309–328.

Bigler, E. D., Johnson, S. C., Jackson, C., and Blatter, D. D. (1995). Aging, brain size and IQ. *Intelligence*, *21*, 109–119.

Binet, A. (1905). New methods for the diagnosis of the intellectual level of subnormals. *L'Annee Psychologique*, *12*, 191–244. (Translated in 1916 by E. S. Kite in *The development of intelligence in children*. Vineland, NJ: Publications of the Training School at Vineland.)

Birren, J. E. and Morrison, D. F. (1961). An analysis of the WAIS subtests in relation to age and education. *Journal of Gerontology*, *16*, 363–369.

Blank, G. (1934). Brauchbarkeit optischer reactionsmessungen. *Ind. Psychotechnology*, *11*, 140–150.

Blennow, K. and Cowburn, R. F. (1996). The neurochemistry of Alzheimer's disease. *Acta Neurologica Scandinavica, Suppl.* *168*, 77–86.

Blum, L. (1978). *Pseudoscience and mental ability*. London: Monthly Review Press.

Bondi, M. W., Salmon, D. P., Monsch, A. U., Galasko, D., Butters, N., Klauber, M. R., *et al.* (1995). Episodic memory changes are associated with the APOE-e4 allele in nondemented older adults. *Neurology*, *45*, 2203–2206.

Boring, E. G. (1923). Intelligence as the tests test it. *New Republic*, *35*, 35–37.

Boring, E. G. (1950). *A history of experimental psychology*. New York: Appleton Century Crofts.

Bors, D. A., MacLeod, C. M., and Forrin, B. (1993). Eliminating the IT–IQ correlation by eliminating an experimental confound. *Intelligence*, *17*, 475–500.

Bors, D. A., Stokes, T. L., Forrin, B., and Hodder, S. L. (1999). Inspection time and intelligence: practice, strategies, and attention. *Intelligence*, *27*, 111–129.

Bouchard, T. J. (1998). Genetic and environmental influences on adult intelligence and special mental abilities. *Human Biology*, *70*, 257–279.

Bouchard, T. J., Lykken, D. T., McGue, M., Segal, N. L., and Tellegen, A. (1990). Sources of human psychological differences: the Minnesota study of twins reared apart. *Science*, *250*, 223–228.

Bowling, A. C. and Mackenzie, B. D. (1996). The relationship between speed of information processing and cognitive ability. *Personality and Individual Differences, 20*, 775–800.

Brand, C. R. (1979). General intelligence and mental speed: their relationship and development. In J. P. Das and N. O'Connor (Eds.), *Intelligence and learning* (pp. 589–593). New York: Plenum.

Brand, C. R. (1987). A rejoinder to Pellegrino. In S. Modgil and C. Modgil (Eds.), *Arthur Jensen: consensus and controversy*. Brighton, UK: Falmer.

Brand, C. R. (1996). *The g factor*. Chichester, UK: Wiley. (This book was withdrawn by the publisher shortly after publication, making it difficult to obtain.)

Brand, C. and Deary, I. J. (1982). Intelligence and 'inspection time'. In H. J. Eysenck (Ed.), *A model for intelligence* (pp. 133–148). Berlin: Springer-Verlag.

Breitmeyer, B. (1984). *Visual masking: an integrated approach*. Oxford: Oxford University Press.

Brinley, J. F. (1965). Cognitive sets, speed and accuracy of performance in the elderly. In A. T. Welford and J. E. Birren (Eds.), *Behavior, aging, and the nervous system* (pp. 114–149). Springfield, IL: Charles C. Thomas.

Brody, N. (1992). *Intelligence* (2nd ed.). New York: Academic.

Bronge, L., Fernaeus, S. E., Blomberg, M., Ingelson, M., Lannfelt, L., Isberg, B., *et al.* (1999). White matter lesions in Alzheimer disease patients are influenced by apolipoprotein E genotype. *Dementia and Geriatric Cognitive Disorders, 10*, 89–96.

Brooks, D. N., Aughton, M. E., Bond, M. R., Jones, P., and Rizvi, S. (1980). Cognitive sequelae in relationship to early indices of severity of brain damage after severe blunt head injury. *Journal of Neurology, Neurosurgery, and Psychiatry, 43*, 529–534.

Brozek, J. and Evans, R. B. (Eds.). (1979). *R. I. Watson's selected papers on the history of psychology*. Hanover, NH: University Press of New England.

Buckhalt, J. A. (1991). Reaction time measures of processing speed: are they yielding new information about intelligence? *Personality and Individual Differences, 12*, 683–688.

Burns, N. R., Nettelbeck. T., and Cooper, C. J. (1996). The string measure of the event-related potential, IQ and inspection time. *Personality and Individual Differences, 21*, 563–572.

Burns, N. R., Nettelbeck, T., and White, M. (1998). Testing the interpretation of inspection time as a measure of speed of sensory processing. *Personality and Individual Differences, 24*, 25–39.

Burns, N. R., Nettelbeck. T., and Cooper, C. J. (1999). Inspection time correlates with general speed of processing but not with fluid ability. *Intelligence, 27*, 37–44.

Burns, N. R., Nettlebeck, T., and Cooper, C. J. (2000). Event-related potential correlates of some human cognitive ability constructs. *Personality and Individual Differences, 29*, 157–168.

Burt, C. (1909–1910). Experimental tests of general intelligence. *British Journal of Psychology, 3*, 94–177.

Burt, C. (1940). *The factors of the mind*. London: University of London Press.

Cairns, R. B. and Ornstein, P. E. (1979). Developmental psychology. In E. Hearst (Ed.), *The first century of experimental psychology*. London: LEA.

Cardon, L. R., Smith, S. D., Fulker, D. W., Kimberling, W. J., Pennington, B. F., and DeFries, J. C. (1994). Quantitative trait locus for reading disability on chromosome 6. *Science, 266*, 276–279.

Carey, N. (1914–1915). Factors in the mental processes of schoolchildren. *British Journal of Psychology, 7*, 453–490.

Carey, N. (1915–1917). Factors in the mental processes of schoolchildren: II. On the nature of specific mental factors. *British Journal of Psychology, 8*, 70–92.

Carpenter, P. A., Just, M. A., and Reichle, E. D. (2000). Working memory and executive function: evidence from neuroimaging. *Current Opinion in Neurobiology, 10*, 195–199.

Carpenter, P. A., Just, M. A., and Shell, P. (1990). What one intelligence test measures: a theoretical account of processing in the Raven's Progressive Matrices Test. *Psychological Review, 97*, 404–431.

Carpintero, H. (1995). http://www.ucm.es/info/Psyap/hispania/helio.htm

Carretta, T. R. and Ree, M. J. (1995). Near identity of cognitive structure in sex and ethnic groups. *Personality and Individual Differences, 19*, 149–155.

Carroll, J. B. (1978). How shall we study individual differences in cognitive abilities?—Methodological and theoretical problems. *Intelligence, 2*, 87–115.

Carroll, J. B. (1982). The measurement of intelligence. In R. J. Sternberg (Ed.), *Handbook of human intelligence*. Cambridge: Viking Press.

Carroll, J. B. (1993). *Human cognitive abilities: a survey of factor analytic studies*. Cambridge, UK: Cambridge University Press.

Carroll, J. B. (1995). Reflections on Stephen Jay Gould's *The Mismeasure of Man* (1981): a retrospective review. *Intelligence, 21*, 121–134.

Carroll, J. B. (1997). Psychometrics, intelligence, and public perception. *Intelligence, 24*, 25–52.

Carroll, J. B. and Maxwell, S. E. (1979). Individual differences in cognitive abilities. *Annual Review of Psychology, 30*, 603–640.

Carter, R. C., Krause, M., and Harbeson, M. M. (1986). Beware the reliability of slope scores for individuals. *Human Factors, 28*, 673–683.

Caryl, P. G. (1994). Event-related potentials correlate with inspection time and intelligence. *Intelligence, 18*, 15–46.

Caryl, P. G. and Harper, A. (1996). Event related potentials (ERPs) in elementary cognitive tasks reflect task difficulty and task threshold. *Intelligence, 22*, 1–22.

Caryl, P. G., Golding, S. J. J., and Hall, B. J. D. (1995). Interrelationships among auditory and visual cognitive tasks: an event-related potential (ERP) study. *Intelligence, 21*, 297–326.

Caryl, P. G., Deary, I. J., Jensen, A. R., Neubauer, A. C., and Vickers, D. (1999). Information processing approaches to intelligence: progress and prospects. In I. Mervielde, I. Deary, F. de Fruyt, and F. Ostendorf (Eds.), *Personality psychology in Europe*, vol. 7. Tilburg: Tilburg University Press.

Cattell, R. B. (1998). Where is intelligence? Some answers from the triadic theory. In J. J. McArdle and R. W. Woodcock (Eds), *Human cognitive abilities in theory and practice*. Mahwah, NJ: Lawrence Erlhaum Associates.

Ceci, S. J. (1990). On the relation between microlevel processing efficiency and macrolevel measures of intelligence: some arguments against current reductionism. *Intelligence*, *14*, 141–150.

Cerella, J. (1985). Information processing rates in the elderly. *Psychological Bulletin*, *98*, 67–83.

Chabris, C. F. (1998). IQ since '*The bell curve.*' *Commentary*, *106*, 33–40.

Chaiken, S. R. (1993). Two models for an inspection time paradigm: processing distraction and processing speed versus processing speed and asymptotic strength. *Intelligence*, *17*, 257–283.

Chaiken, S. R. and Young, R. K. (1993). Inspection time and intelligence: attempts to eliminate the apparent movement strategy. *American Journal of Psychology*, *106*, 191–210.

Chalke, F. and Ertl, J. (1965). Evoked potentials and intelligence. *Life Sciences*, *4*, 1319–1322.

Chapman, C. R., Chen, A. C. N., Colpitts, Y. M., and Martin, R. W. (1981). Sensory decision theory describes evoked potentials in pain discrimination. *Psychophysiology*, *18*, 114–120.

Chase, T. N., Fedio, P., Foster, N. L., Brooks, R., Di Chiro, G., and Mansi, L. (1984). Wechsler Adult Intelligence Scale performance: cortical localisation by fluorodeoxyglucoseF18-positron emission tomography. *Archives of Neurology*, *41*, 1244–1247.

Chorney, M. J., Chorney, K., Seese, N., Owen, M. J., Daniels, J., McGuffin, P., *et al.* (1998). A quantitative trait locus associated with cognitive ability in children. *Psychological Science*, *9*, 159–166.

Clark, H. H. and Chase, W. G. (1972). On the process of comparing sentences against pictures. *Cognitive Psychology*, *3*, 472–517.

Cockburn, J. and Smith, P. T. (1991). The relative influence of intelligence and age on everyday memory. *Journal of Gerontology: Psychological Sciences*, *46*, P31–P36.

Colet, A. V. I., Piera, P. J. F. I., and Pueyo, A. A. (1993). Initial stages of information processing and inspection time: electrophysiological correlates. *Personality and Individual Differences*, *14*, 733–738.

Cooper, C. (1999). *Intelligence and abilities*. London: Sage.

Corder, E. H., Saunders, A. M., Strittmatter, W. J., Schmechel, D. E., Gaskell, P. C., Small, G. W., *et al.* (1993). Gene dose of apolipoprotein E type 4 allele and the risk of Alzheimer's disease in late onset families. *Science*, *261*, 921–923.

Cotman, C. W. (1999). Axon sprouting and regeneration. In G. J. Siegel, B. W. Agranoff, and M. E. Uhler (Eds.), *Basic neurochemistry: molecular, cellular, and medical aspects* (6th ed.). Philadelphia: Lippincott-Raven.

Craik, K. (1943). *The nature of explanation*. Cambridge: Cambridge University Press.

Crawford, C. B. (1974). A canonical correlation analysis of cortical evoked response and intelligence test data. *Canadian Journal of Psychology*, *28*, 319–332.

Crawford, J. R., Allan, K. M., Stephen, D. W., Parker, D. M., and Besson, J. A. O. (1989). The Wechsler Adult Intelligence Scale-Revised (WAIS-R): factor structure in a U.K. sample. *Personality and Individual Differences, 10*, 1209–1212.

Crawford, J. R., Deary, I. J., Allan, K. M., and Gustafsson, J.-E. (1998). Evaluating competing models of the relationship between inspection time and psychometric intelligence. *Intelligence, 26*, 27–42.

Cronbach, L. J. (1957). The two disciplines of scientific psychology. *American Psychologist, 12*, 671–684.

Daniels, J., McGuffin, P., Owen, M. J., and Plomin, R. (1998). Molecular genetic studies of cognitive ability. *Human Biology, 70*, 281–296.

David, A. S. (1992). Frontal lobology—psychiatry's new pseudoscience. *British Journal of Psychiatry, 161*, 244–248.

Dawson, M. R. W. (1998). *Understanding cognitive science.* Oxford: Blackwell.

de Groot, J. C., de Leeuw, F. E., Oudkerk, M., van Gijn, J., Hofman, A., Jolles, J., and Breteler, M. M. B. (2000). Cerebral white matter lesions and cognitive function: The Rotterdam Study. *Annals of Neurology, 47*, 145–151.

Deary, I. J. (1986). Inspection time: discovery or rediscovery? *Personality and Individual Differences, 7*, 625–631.

Deary, I. J. (1992). Auditory inspection time and intelligence. Unpublished PhD thesis, University of Edinburgh.

Deary, I. J. (1993). Inspection time and WAIS-R IQ subtypes: a confirmatory factor analysis study. *Intelligence, 17*, 223–236.

Deary, I. J. (1994a). Sensory discrimination and intelligence: postmortem or resurrection? *American Journal of Psychology, 107*, 95–115.

Deary, I. J. (1994b). Intelligence and auditory discrimination: separating processing speed and fidelity of stimulus representation. *Intelligence, 18*, 189–213.

Deary, I. J. (1995a). Auditory inspection time and intelligence: what is the direction of causation? *Developmental Psychology, 31*, 237–250.

Deary, I. J. (1995b). Age-associated memory impairment: a suitable case for treatment? *Ageing and Society, 15*, 393–406.

Deary, I. J. (1996). Reductionism and intelligence: the case of inspection time. *Journal of Biosocial Science, 28*, 405–423.

Deary, I. J. (1997). Intelligence and information processing. In H. Nyborg (Ed.), *The scientific study of human nature* (pp. 282–310). New York: Pergamon.

Deary, I. J. (1998). The effects of diabetes on cognitive function. *Diabetes Annual, 11*, 97–118.

Deary, I. J. (1999). Intelligence and visual and auditory information processing. In P. L. Ackerman, P. C. Kyllonen, and R. D. Roberts (Eds.), *Learning and individual differences: process, trait, and content determinants* (pp. 111–133). Washington, DC: American Psychological Association.

Deary, I. J. and Caryl, P. G. (1993). Intelligence, EEG, and evoked potentials (pp. 259–315). In P. A. Vernon (Ed.), *Biological approaches to the study of human intelligence.* Norwood, NJ: Ablex.

Deary, I. J. and Caryl, P. G. (1997a). Neuroscience and human intelligence differences. *Trends in Neurosciences, 20*, 365–371.

Deary, I. J. and Caryl, P. G. (1997*b*). Not so F.A.S.T., Dr Vickers! *Intelligence*, *24*, 397–404.

Deary, I. J. and Crawford, J. R. (1998). A triarchic theory of Jensenism: persistent, conservative reductionism. *Intelligence*, *26*, 273–282.

Deary, I. J. and Stough, C. (1996). Intelligence and inspection time: achievements, prospects and problems. *American Psychologist*, *51*, 599–608.

Deary, I. J., and Stough, C. (1997). Looking down on human intelligence. *American Psychologist*, *52*, 1148–1150.

Deary, I. J., Caryl, P. G., Egan, V., and Wight, D. (1989*a*). Visual and auditory inspection times: their interrelationship and correlations with IQ in high ability subjects. *Personality and Individual Differences*, *10*, 525–533.

Deary, I. J., Head, B., and Egan, V. (1989*b*). Auditory inspection time, intelligence and pitch discrimination. *Intelligence*, *13*, 135–147.

Deary, I. J., Hunter, R., Langan, S. J., and Goodwin, G. M. (1991*a*) Inspection time, psychometric intelligence and clinical estimates of cognitive ability in pre-senile Alzheimer's disease and Korsakoff's psychosis. *Brain*, *114*, 2543–2554.

Deary, I. J., Langan, S. J., Hepburn, D., and Frier, B. M. (1991*b*). Which abilities does the PASAT test? *Personality and Individual Differences*, *12*, 983–987.

Deary, I. J., Langan, S. J., Graham, K. S., Hepburn, D., and Frier, B. M. (1992). Recurrent severe hypoglycaemia, intelligence, and speed of information processing. *Intelligence*, *16*, 337–359.

Deary, I. J., Caryl, P. G., and Gibson, G. J. (1993*a*). Nonstationarity and the measurement of psychophysical response in a visual inspection-time task. *Perception*, *22*, 1245–1256.

Deary, I. J., Hepburn, D. A., MacLeod, K. M., and Frier, B. M. (1993*b*). Partitioning the symptoms of hypoglycaemia using multi-sample confirmatory factor analyses. *Diabetologia*, *36*, 771–777.

Deary, I. J., Ebmeier, K. P., MacLeod, K. M., Dougall, N., Hepburn, D. A., Frier, B. M., *et al.* (1994). PASAT performance and the pattern of uptake of 99mTc-exametazine in brain estimated with single photon emission tomography. *Biological Psychology*, *38*, 1–18.

Deary, I. J., McCrimmon, R. J., and Bradshaw, J. (1997). Visual information processing and intelligence. *Intelligence*, *24*, 461–479.

Deary, I. J., MacLennan, W. J. and Starr, J. M. (1998). Is age kinder to the initially more able. Differential ageing of verbal ability in the HOPE study. *Intelligence*, *26*, 357–375.

Deary, I. J., Battersby, S., Whiteman, M. C., Connor, J. M., Fowkes, F. G. R., and Harmar, A. (1999). Neuroticism and polymorphisms in the serotonin transporter gene. *Psychological Medicine*, *29*, 735–739.

Deary, I. J., Caryl, P. G., and Austin, E. J. (in press). Measuring versus understanding human intelligence. *Psychology, Public policy and Law*.

Deary, I. J., Whalley, L. J., Lemmon, H., Starr, J. S. and Crawford, J. R. (2000). The stability of individual differences in mental ability from childhood to old age: follow-up of the 1932 Scottish Mental Survey. *Intelligence*, *28*, 49–55.

Deeg, D. J. H., Hofman, A., and van Zonneveld, J. (1990). The association between change in cognitive function and longevity in Dutch elderly. *American Journal of Epidemiology*, *132*, 973–982.

Dennett, D. C. (1995). *Darwin's dangerous idea: evolution and the meanings of life*. London: Allen Lane.

D'Esposito, M., Zarahn, E., and Aguirre, G. K. (1999). Event-related functional MRI: implications for cognitive psychology. *Psychological Bulletin*, *125*, 155–164.

Detterman, D. K. (1977). Is intelligence necessary? *Intelligence*, *1*, 1–3.

Detterman, D. K. (1979). A job half done: the road to intelligence testing in the year 2000. *Intelligence*, *3*, 295–306.

Detterman, D. K. (1982). Does 'g' exist? *Intelligence*, *6*, 99–108.

Detterman, D. K. (1986). Human intelligence is a complex system of separate processes. In R. J. Sternberg and D. K. Detterman (Eds.), *What is intelligence? contemporary viewpoints on its nature and measurement* (pp. 57–61). Norwood, NJ: Ablex.

Devlin, B., Daniels, M., and Roeder, K. (1997). The heritability of IQ. *Nature*, *388*, 468–471.

Diascro, M. N. and Brody, N. (1994). Odd-man-out and intelligence. *Intelligence*, *19*, 79–92.

Duncan, J., Emslie, H., and Williams, P. (1996). Intelligence and the frontal lobe: the organisation of goal-directed behavior. *Cognitive Psychology*, *30*, 257–303.

Ebmeier, K. P. (1998). Neuroimaging. In E. C. Johnstone, C. P. L. Freeman, and A. K. Zealley (Eds.), *Companion to psychiatric studies* (6th ed.). Edinburgh: Churchill Livingstone.

Eckberg, D. L. (1979). *Intelligence and race*. New York: Praeger.

Egan, V. (1994). Intelligence, inspection time and cognitive strategies. *British Journal of Psychology*, *85*, 305–316.

Egan, V. and Deary, I. J. (1992). Are specific inspection time strategies prevented by concurrent tasks? *Intelligence*, *16*, 151–167.

Egan, V. and Deary, I. J. (1993). Does perceptual intake speed reflect intelligent use of feedback in an inspection time task? The effect of restricted feedback. *Journal of General Psychology*, *120*, 123–137.

Egan, V., Chiswick, A., Santosh, C., Naidu, K., Rimmington, J. E., and Best, J. J. K. (1994). Size isn't everything: a study of brain volume, intelligence and auditory evoked potentials. *Personality and Individual Differences*, *17*, 357–367.

Egan, V., Wickett, J. C., and Vernon, P. A. (1995). Brain size and intelligence: erratum, addendum and correction. *Personality and Individual Differences*, *19*, 113–115.

Eichorn, D. H., Hunt, J. V., and Honzik, M. P. (1981). Experience, personality, and IQ: adolescence to middle age. In D. H. Eichorn, J. A. Clausen, N. Haan, M. P. Honzik, and P. H. Mussen (Eds.), *Present and past in middle life*. New York: Academic Press.

Embretson, S. E. (1995). The role of working memory capacity and general control processes in intelligence. *Intelligence*, *20*, 169–189.

Ertl, J. P. and Schafer, E. W. P. (1969). Brain response correlates of psychometric intelligence. *Nature*, *223*, 421–422.

Eslinger, P. J., Damasio, A. R., Benton, A. L., and Van Allen, M. (1985). Neuropsychologic detection of abnormal mental decline in older persons. *Journal of the American Medical Association*, *253*, 670–674.

Esposito, G., Kirkby, B. S., Van Horn, J. D., Ellmore, T. M., and Berman, K. F. (1999). Context-dependent, neural system-specific neurophysiological concomitants of ageing: mapping PET correlates during cognitive activation. *Brain*, *122*, 963–979.

Estes, W. K. (1974). Learning theory and intelligence. *American Psychologist*, *29*, 740–749.

Evans, G. and Nettelbeck, T. (1993). Inspection time: a flash mask to reduce apparent movement effects. *Personality and Individual Differences*, *15*, 91–94.

Eysenck, H. J. (1939). Primary mental abilities. *British Journal of Educational Psychology*, *9*, 270–275.

Eysenck, H. J. (1967). Intelligence assessment: a theoretical and experimental approach. *British Journal of Educational Psychology*, *37*, 81–97.

Eysenck, H. J. (1982). *A model for intelligence*. Berlin: Springer Verlag.

Eysenck, H. J. (1995). Can we study intelligence using the experimental method? *Intelligence*, *20*, 217–228.

Fancher, R. E. (1985*a*). *The intelligence men: makers of the IQ controversy*. New York: Norton.

Fancher, R. E. (1985*b*). Spearman's original computation of *g*: a model for Burt? *British Journal of Psychology*, *76*, 341–352.

Feskens, E. J. M., Havekes, L. M., Kalmijn, S., de Knijff, P., Launer, L. J., and Kromhout, D. (1994) Apolipoprotein e4 allele and cognitive decline in elderly men. *British Medical Journal*, *309*, 1202–1206.

Feynman, R. (1985). *Surely you're joking Mr Feynman*. New York: Norton.

Finkel, D., Pedersen, N. L., McClearn, G. E., Plomin, R., and Berg, S. (1996). Cross-sequential analysis of genetic influences on cognitive ability in the Swedish adoption/twin study of aging. *Aging, Neuropsychology and Cognition*, *3*, 84–99.

Fisher, D. L. and Glaser, R. A. (1996). Molar and latent models of cognitive slowing: implications for aging, dementia, depression, development, and intelligence. *Psychonomic Bulletin and Review*, *3*, 458–480.

Fisher, P. J., Turic, D., Williams, N. M., McGuffin, P., Asherson, P., Ball, D., et al. (1999). DNA pooling identifies QTLs on chromosome 4 for general cognitive ability in children. *Human Molecular Genetics*, *8*, 915–922.

Fisher, S. E., Marlow, A. J., Lamb, J., Maestrini, E., Williams, D. F., Richardson, A. J., et al. (1999). A quantitative trait locus on chromosome 6p influences different aspects of developmental dyslexia. *American Journal of Human Genetics*, *64*, 146–156.

Fisk, A. D., Fisher, D. L., and Rogers, W. A. (1992). General slowing alone cannot explain age-related search effects: reply to Cerella (1991). *Journal of Experimental Psychology: General*, *121*, 73–78.

Flashman, L. A., Andreasen, N. C., Flaum, M., and Swayze, V. W. (1998). Intelligence and regional brain volumes in normal controls. *Intelligence, 25,* 149–160.

Flint, J. (1999). The genetic basis of cognition. *Brain, 122,* 2015–2031.

Flynn, J. R. (1987). Massive IQ gains in 14 nations: what IQ tests really measure. *Psychological Bulletin, 95,* 29–51.

Flynn, J. R. (1999). Searching for justice: the discovery of IQ gains over time. *American Psychologist, 54,* 5–20.

Fodor, J. A. (1983). *The modularity of mind.* Cambridge, MA: MIT Press.

Folstein, M. F., Folstein, S. E., and McHugh, P. R. (1975). Mini mental state. A practical method for grading the cognitive state of patients for the clinician. *Journal of Psychiatric Research, 12,* 189–198.

Foster, J. C. and Taylor, G. A. (1920). The applicability of mental tests to persons over 50 years of age. *Journal of Applied Psychology, 4,* 39–58.

Frearson, W. and Eysenck, H. J. (1986). Intelligence, reaction time (RT) and a new 'odd-man-out' RT paradigm. *Personality and Individual Differences, 7,* 807–817.

Friedman, G., Froom, P., Sazbon, L., Grinblatt, I., Shochina, M., Tsenter, J., *et al.* (1999). Apolipoprotein E-epsilon4 genotype predicts a poor outcome in survivors of traumatic brain injury. *Neurology, 52,* 244–248.

Fry, A. F. and Hale, S. (1996). Processing speed, working memory, and fluid intelligence: evidence for a developmental cascade. *Psychological Science, 7,* 237–241.

Fuller, T. (1648, reprinted 1936). Of natural fools. In R. Vallance (Ed.), *A hundred English essays.* London: Nelson.

Fulton, M., Raab, G., Thomson, G., Laxen, D., Hunter, R., and Hepburn, W. (1987). Influence of blood lead on the ability and attainment of children in Edinburgh. *Lancet, i,* 1222–1226.

Furneaux, W. D. (1952). Some speed, error and difficulty relationships within a problem solving situation. *Nature, 170,* 37–38.

Galton, F. (1883). *Inquiries into human faculty.* London: Dent.

Galton, F. (1888). Head growth in students at the University of Cambridge. *Nature, 38,* 14–15.

Galton, F. (1890). Remarks on 'Mental tests and measurements' by J. McKeen Cattell. *Mind, 15,* 380–381.

Gardner, H. (1983). *Frames of mind: the theory of multiple intelligences.* New York: Basic.

Gasser, T., von Lucadou-Müller, I., Verleger, R., and Bächer, P. (1983). Correlating EEG and IQ: a new look at an old problem using computerized EEG parameters. *Electroencephalography and Clinical Neurophysiology, 55,* 493–504.

Gasser, T., Pietz, J., Schellberg, D., and Köhler, W. (1988). Visually evoked potentials of mildly mentally retarded and control children. *Developmental Medicine and Child Neurology, 30,* 638–645.

Gazzaniga, M. S., Ivry, R. B., and Mangun, G. R. (1998). *Cognitive neuroscience: the biology of the mind.* New York: Norton.

Ghebremedhin, E., Schultz, C., Braak, E. and Braak, H. (1998). High frequency of apolipoprotein E epsilon4 allele in young individuals with very mild Alzheimer's disease-related neurofibrillary changes. *Experimental Neurology, 153,* 152–155.

Giannitrapani, D. (1969). EEG average frequencies and intelligence. *Electroencephalography and Clinical Neurophysiology, 27,* 480–486

Giannitrapani, D. (1985). *The electrophysiology of intellectual function.* Basel: Karger.

Glaser, R. and Pellegrino, J. W. (1978). Uniting process theory and differential psychology: back home from the wars. *Intelligence, 2,* 305–319.

Gleitman, H., Fridlund, A. J., and Reisberg, D. (1999). *Psychology* (5th ed.). New York: Norton.

Gloor, P. (1994). Berger lecture: is Berger's dream coming true? *Electroencephalography and Clinical Neurophysiology, 90,* 253–266.

Gold, A. E., MacLeod, K. M., Frier, B. M., and Deary, I. J. (1995). Changes in mood during acute hypoglycaemia in healthy subjects. *Journal of Personality and Social Psychology, 68,* 498–504.

Gottesman, I. I. (1997). Twins: en route to QTLs for cognition. *Science, 276,* 1522–1523.

Gottfredson, L. S. (1997). Why *g* matters: the complexity of everyday life. *Intelligence, 24,* 79–132.

Gould, S. J. (1981). *The mismeasure of man.* Harmondsworth, UK: Penguin.

Gratton, G. and Fabiani, M. (1998). Dynamic brain imaging: event-related optical signal (EROS) measures of the time course and localization of cognitive-related activity. *Psychonomic Bulletin and Review, 5,* 535–563.

Guilford, J. P. (1956). The structure of intellect. *Psychological Bulletin, 53,* 266–293.

Guilford, J. P. (1967). *The nature of human intelligence.* New York: McGraw-Hill.

Gustafsson, J.-E. (1984). A unifying model for the structure of mental abilities. *Intelligence, 8,* 179–203.

Gustafsson, J.-E. (1992). The relevance of factor analysis for the study of group differences. *Multivariate Behavioral Research, 27,* 239–247.

Gustafsson, J.-E. (1999). Measuring and understanding G: experimental and correlational approaches. In P. L. Ackerman, P. C. Kyllonen, and R. D. Roberts (Eds.), *Learning and individual differences: process, trait, and content determinants* (pp. 275–289). Washington, DC: American Psychological Association.

Hachinski, V. and Munoz, D. G. (1997). Cerebrovascular pathology in Alzheimer's disease: cause, effect or epiphenomenon? *Annals of the New York Academy of Sciences, 826,* 1–6.

Haier, R. (1993). Cerebral glucose metabolism and intelligence. In P. A. Vernon (Ed.), *Biological approaches to the study of human intelligence* (pp. 317–332). Norwood, NJ: Ablex.

Haier, R. J., Siegel, B., Nuechterlein, K. H., Hazlet, E., Wu, J., Paek, J., *et al.* (1988). Cortical glucose metabolic rate correlates of abstract reasoning and attention studies with positron emission tomography. *Intelligence, 12,* 199–217.

Hale, S. and Jansen, J. (1994). Global processing-time coefficients characterise individual and group differences in cognitive speed. *Psychological Science, 5,* 384–389.

Hampson, P. J. and Morris, P. E. (1996). *Understanding cognition*. Oxford: Blackwell.

Harvey, I., Persaud, R., Ron, M. A., Baker, G., and Murray, R. M. (1994). Volumetric MRI measurements in bipolars compared with schizophrenics and healthy controls. *Psychological Medicine, 24,* 689–699.

Hearnshaw, L. S. (1979). *Cyril Burt: psychologist*. London: Hodder and Stoughton.

Hebb, D. O. (1949). *The organization of behavior: a neuropsychological theory*. New York: Wiley.

Helkala, E. L., Koivisto, K., Hanninen, T., Vanhanen, M., Kervinen, K., Kuusisto, J., *et al.* (1995). The association of apolipoprotein E polymorphism with memory: a population-based study. *Neuroscience Letters, 191,* 141–144.

Helkala, E. L., Koivisto, K., Hanninen, T., Vanhanen, M., Kervinen, K., Kuusisto, J., *et al.* (1996). Memory functions in human subjects with different apolipoprotein phenotypes during a 3-year population-based follow-up study. *Neuroscience Letters, 204,* 177–180.

Hendrickson, A. E. (1982). The biological basis of intelligence. Part 1: Theory. In H. J. Eysenck (Ed.), *A model for intelligence*. Berlin: Springer-Verlag.

Hendrickson, D. E. (1982). The biological basis of intelligence. Part II: Measurement. In H. J. Eysenck (Ed.), *A model for intelligence*. Berlin: Springer-Verlag.

Herrnstein, R. J. and Murray, C. (1994). *The bell curve*. New York: Free Press.

Hesse, H. (1990, originally published 1943). *The glass bead game*. New York: Owl.

Hettema, J. and Deary, I. J. (1993). Biological and social approaches to individuality: towards a common paradigm. In J. Hettema and I. J. Deary (Eds.), *Foundations of personality* (pp. 1–14). Dordrecht, The Netherlands: Kluwer.

Hick, W. E. (1952). On the rate of gain of information. *Quarterly Journal of Experimental Psychology, 4,* 11–26.

Hill, L., Craig, I. W., Asherson, P., Ball, D., Eley, T., Ninomiya, T., *et al.* (1999). DNA pooling and dense marker maps: a systematic search for genes for cognitive ability. *NeuroReport, 10,* 843–848.

Ho, H. Z., Baker, L., and Decker, S. N. (1988). Correlation between intelligence and speed of cognitive processing: genetic and environmental influences. *Behavior Genetics, 18,* 247–261.

Hobbes, T. (1651, reprinted 1885). *Leviathan*. London: Routledge.

Horgan, J. (1999). *The undiscovered mind*. London: Weidenfeld and Nicolson.

Horn, J. L. (1979). Trends in the measurement of intelligence. *Intelligence, 3,* 229–240.

Horn, J. L. (1994). Theory of fluid and crystallised intelligence. In R. J. Sternberg (Ed.), *Encyclopedia of human intelligence*. New York: Macmillan.

Horn, J. L. and Cattell, R. B. (1966). Refinement and test of the theory of fluid and crystallised general intelligences. *Journal of Educational Psychology, 57,* 253–270.

Horn, J. L. and Hofer, S. M. (1992). Major abilities and development in the adult period. In R. J. Sternberg and C. A. Berg (Eds.), *Intellectual development* (pp. 44–99). Cambridge: Cambridge University Press.

Houlihan, M., Campbell, K., and Stelmack, R. M. (1994). Reaction time and movement time as measures of stimulus evaluation and response processes. *Intelligence, 18,* 289–307.

Howe, M. J. A. (1988). Intelligence as an explanation. *British Journal of Psychology,* 79, 349–360.

Howe, M. J. A. (1990). Does intelligence exist? *The Psychologist, 3,* 490–493.

Howe, M. J. A. (1997). *IQ in question.* London: Sage.

Huarte, J. de San Juan. (1969, originally published 1575, originally translated 1594). *Examen de ingenios, or, A triall of wits (The examination of mens wits).* Amsterdam: Da Capo Press, Theatrum Orbis Terrarum. (This facsimile edition from a copy held in the Bodleian Library, Oxford, is an English translation [by R. Carew] from an Italian translation [by M. Camilio Camiili] of the original Spanish. Published by Richard Watkins, London, 1594.)

Hultsch, D. F., Hertzog, C., Small, B. J., and Dixon, R. A. (1999). Use it or lose it: engaged lifestyle as a buffer of cognitive decline in aging? *Psychology and Aging, 14,* 245–263.

Humphreys, L. G. (1989). Intelligence: three kinds of instability and their consequences for policy. In R. L. Linn (Ed.), *Intelligence.* Urbana: University of Illinois Press.

Hunt, E. (1980*a*). Intelligence as an information processing concept. *British Journal of Psychology, 71,* 449–474.

Hunt, E. (1980*b*). Mechanics of verbal ability. *Psychological Review, 85,* 109–130.

Hunt, E. (1983). On the nature of intelligence. *Science, 219,* 141–146.

Hunt, E. (1999). Intelligence and human resources: past, present and future. In P. L. Ackerman, P. C. Kyllonen, and R. D. Roberts (Eds.), *Learning and individual differences: process, trait, and content determinants* (pp. 3–28). Washington, DC: American Psychological Association.

Hunt, E. and MacLeod, C. M. (1978). The sentence-verification paradigm: a case study of two conflicting approaches to individual differences. *Intelligence, 2,* 129–144.

Hunt, E. B., Frost, N., and Lunneborg, C. (1973). Individual differences in cognition: a new approach to intelligence. In G. Bower (Ed.), *The psychology of learning and motivation,* vol. 7. New York: Academic Press.

Hunt, E., Lunneborg, C., and Lewis, J. (1975). What does it mean to be high verbal? *Cognitive Psychology, 7,* 194–227.

Hunter, J. E. (1983). A causal analysis of cognitive ability, job knowledge, job performance, and supervisor ratings. In F. Landy, S. Zedek, and J. Cleveland (Eds.), *Performance measurement and theory* (pp. 257–266). Hillsdale, NJ: Erlbaum.

Hunter, J. E. and Hunter, R. F. (1984). Validity and utility of alternative predictors of job performance. *Psychological Bulletin, 96,* 72–98.

Hyman, B. T., Gomez-Isla, T., Briggs, M., Chung, H., Kohout, F., and Wallace, R. (1996). Apolipoprotien E and cognitive change in an elderly population. *Annals of Neurology, 40,* 55–66.

Hyman, R. (1953). Stimulus information as a determinant of reaction time. *Journal of Experimental Psychology*, 45, 188–196.

Ibatoullina, A. A., Vardaris, R. M., and Thompson, L. (1994). Genetic and environmental influences on the coherence of background and orienting response EEG in children. *Intelligence*, 19, 65–78.

Iragui, V., Kutas, M., and Salmon, D. P. (1996). Event-related brain potentials during semantic categorisation in normal aging and senile dementia of the Alzheimer's type. *Electroencephalography and Clinical Neurophysiology*, 100, 392–406.

Irwin, R. J. (1984). Inspection time and its relation to intelligence. *Intelligence*, 8, 47–65.

Jack, C. R. Jr., Petersen, R. C., Xu, Y. C., Waring, S. C., O'Brien, P. C., Tangalos, E. G., *et al.* (1997). Medial temporal atrophy on MRI in normal aging and very mild Alzheimer's disease. *Neurology*, 49, 786–794.

Jacomb, P. A., Jorm, A. F., Croft, L., Gao, X., and Easteal, S. (1999). HLA-A and CTGB33 polymorphisms and variation in IQ scores. *Personality and Individual Differences*, 26, 795–799.

Jefferys, R. G. R., Traub, R. D., and Whittington, M. A. (1996). Neuronal networks for induced '40 Hz' rhythms. *Trends in Neurosciences*, 19, 222–228.

Jenkinson, J. C. (1983). Is speed of information processing related to fluid or crystallised intelligence? *Intelligence*, 7, 91–106.

Jensen, A. R. (1980). *Bias in mental testing*. London: Methuen.

Jensen, A. R. (1982a). The debunking of scientific fossils and straw persons. *Contemporary Education Review*, 1, 121–135.

Jensen, A. R. (1982b). Reaction time and psychometric g. In H. J. Eysenck (Ed.), *A model for intelligence*. Berlin: Springer Verlag.

Jensen, A. R. (1984). Test validity: g versus the specificity hypothesis. *Journal of Social and Biological Structures*, 7, 93–118.

Jensen, A. R. (1985). Methodological and statistical techniques for the chronometric study of mental abilities. In C. R. Reynolds and V. L. Willson (Eds.), *Methodological and statistical advances in the study of individual differences* (pp. 51–116). New York: Plenum.

Jensen, A. R. (1987a). Individual differences in the Hick paradigm. In P. A. Vernon (Ed.), *Speed of information processing and intelligence* (pp. 101–175). Norwood, NJ: Ablex.

Jensen, A. R. (1987b). Process differences and individual differences in some cognitive tasks. *Intelligence*, 11, 153–179.

Jensen, A. R. (1993). Why is reaction time correlated with psychometric g? *Current Directions in Psychological Science*, 2, 53–56.

Jensen, A. R. (1998a). *The g factor: the science of mental ability*. New York: Praeger.

Jensen, A. R. (1998b). The suppressed relationship between IQ and the reaction time slope parameter of the Hick function. *Intelligence*, 26, 43–52.

Jensen, A. R. (1998c). Jensen on 'Jensenism'. *Intelligence*, 26, 181–208.

Jensen, A. R. and Munro, E. (1979). Reaction time, movement time, and intelligence. *Intelligence*, 3, 121–126.

Jensen, A. R. and Sinha, S. N. (1993). Physical correlates of human intelligence. In P. A. Vernon (Ed.), *Biological approaches to the study of human intelligence.* Norwood, NJ: Ablex.

Jensen, A. R. and Vernon, P. A. (1986). Jensen's reaction-time studies: a reply to Longstreth. *Intelligence, 10,* 153–179.

Johnson, R. C., McClearn, G. E., Yuen, S., Nagoshi, C. T., Ahern, F. M., and Cole, R. E. (1985). Galton's data a century later. *American Psychologist, 40,* 875–892.

Johnson, D. M., Watson, C. S., and Jensen, J. K. (1987). Individual differences in auditory capabilities. I. *Journal of the Acoustical Society of America, 81,* 427–438.

Jordan, B. D., Relkin, N. R., Ravdin, L. D., Jacobs, A. R., Bennett, A., and Gandy, S. (1997). Apolipoprotein E epsilon4 associated with chronic traumatic brain injury in boxing. *Journal of the American Medical Association, 278,* 136–140.

Josiassen, R. C., Shagass, C., Roemer, R. A., and Slepner, S. (1988). Evoked potential correlates of intelligence in nonpatient subjects. *Biological Psychiatry, 27,* 207–225.

Jung, R. E., Brooks, W. M., Yeo, R. A., Chiulli, S. J., Weers, D. C., and Sibbitt, W. L. (1999a). Biochemical markers of intelligence: a proton MR spectroscopy study of normal human brain. *Proceedings of the Royal Society of London Series B, 266,* 1375–1379.

Jung, R. E., Yeo, R. A., Chiulli, S. J., Sibbitt, W. L., Weers, D. C., Hart B. L., et al. (1999b). Biochemical markers of cognition: a proton MR spectroscopy study of normal human brain. *NeuroReport, 10,* 1–5.

Junque, C., Pujol, J., Vendrell, P., Bruna, O., Jodar, M., Ribas, J. C., et al. (1990). Leuko-araiosis on magnetic resonance imaging and speed of mental processing. *Archives of Neurology, 47,* 151–156.

Juolasmaa, A., Toivakka, E., Outakosi, J., Sotaniemi, K., Tienari, P., and Hirvenoja, R. (1986). Relationship of quantitative EEG and cognitive test performance in patients with cardiac vascular disease. *Scandinavian Journal of Psychology, 27,* 30–38

Kail, R. (1991). Developmental change in speed of processing during childhood and adolescence. *Psychological Bulletin, 109,* 490–501.

Kail, R. and Park, Y. (1992). Global developmental change in processing time. *Merrill-Palmer Quarterly, 38,* 525–541.

Kail, R. and Salthouse, T. A. (1994). Processing speed as a mental capacity. *Acta Psychologica, 86,* 199–225.

Kamboh, M. I., Aston, C. E., Ferrel, R. E., and Hamman, R. F. (1993). Impact of apolipoprotein E polymorphism in determining interindividual variation in total cholesterol and low density lipoprotein cholesterol in Hispanics and non-Hispanic whites. *Atherosclerosis, 98,* 201–211.

Kamino, K., Sato, S., Sakaki, Y., Yoshiiwa, A., Nishiwaki, Y., Takeda, M., et al. (1996). Three different mutations of presenilin 1 gene in early-onset Alzheimer's disease families. *Neuroscience Letters, 208,* 195–198.

Kangas, J. and Bradway, K. (1971). Intelligence at middle age: a thirty-eight-year follow-up. *Developmental Psychology, 5,* 333–337.

Katzman, R., Zhang, M.-Y., Chen, P. J., Gu, N., Jiang, S., Saitoh, T., *et al.* (1997). Effects of apolipoprotein E on dementia and aging in the Shanghai survey of dementia. *Neurology, 49*, 779–785.

Kelley, E. L. (1927). *Interpretation of educational measurements.* Yonkers, NY: World.

Killiany, R. J., Moss, M. B., Albert, M. S., Sandor, T., Tieman, J., and Jolesz, F. (1993). Temporal lobe regions on magnetic resonance imaging identify patients with early Alzheimer's disease. *Archives of Neurology, 50*, 949–954.

Kline, P. (1991). Sternberg's components: non-contingent concepts. *Personality and Individual Differences, 12*, 873–876.

Knibb, K. (1992). A dynamic mask for inspection time. *Personality and Individual Differences, 13*, 237–248.

Korten, A. E., Jorm, A. F., Jiao, Z., Letenneur, L., Jacomb, P. A., Henderson, A. S., *et al.* (1999). Health, cognitive, and psychosocial factors as predictors of mortality in an elderly community sample. *Journal of Epidemiology and Community Health, 53*, 83–88.

Kranzler, J. H. and Jensen, A. R. (1989). Inspection time and intelligence: a meta-analysis. *Intelligence, 13*, 329–347.

Kranzler, J. H., Whang, P. A., and Jensen, A. R. (1988). Jensen's use of the Hick paradigm: visual attention and order effects. *Intelligence, 12*, 379–392.

Kuhlen, R. G. (1940). Social change: a neglected factor in psychological studies of the life span. *School and Society, 52*, 14–16.

Kuller, L. H., Shemanski, L., Manolio, T., Haan, M., Fried, L., Bryan, N., *et al.* (1998). Relationship between ApoE, MRI findings, and cognitive function in the cardiovascular health study. *Stroke, 29*, 388–398.

Kutas, M. and van Petten, C. K. (1994). Psycholinguistics electrified. In M. A. Gernsbacher (Ed.), *Handbook of psycholinguistics.* San Diego, CA: Academic Press.

Kyllonen, P. C. (1993). Aptitude testing inspired by information processing: a test of the four sources model. *Journal of General Psychology, 120*, 375–405.

Kyllonen, P. C. (1996*a*). Is working memory capacity Spearman's *g*? In I. Dennis and P. Tapsfield (Eds.), *Human abilities: their nature and measurement* (pp. 77–96). Hillsdale, NJ: Erlbaum.

Kyllonen, P. C. (1996*b*). Aptitude testing inspired by information processing: a test of the four sources model. *The Journal of General Psychology, 120*, 375–405.

Kyllonen, P. C. and Christal, R. E. (1990). Reasoning ability is (little more than) working memory capacity?! *Intelligence, 14*, 389–433.

LaDu, M. J., Falduto, M. T., Manelli, A. M., Reardon, C. A., Getz, G. S., and Frail, D. E. (1994). Isoform-specific binding of apolipoprotein E to beta-amyloid. *Journal of Biological Chemistry, 269*, 23403–23406.

Laird, J. E., Newell, A., and Rosenbloom, P. S. (1987). SOAR: an architecture for general intelligence. *Artificial Intelligence, 33*, 1–64.

Langsford, P. B., Mackenzie, B. D., and Maher, D. P. (1994). Auditory inspection time, sustained attention, and the fundamentality of mental speed. *Personality and Individual Differences, 16*, 487–497.

Larson, G. E. and Saccuzzo, D. P. (1986). Jensen's reaction time experiments: another look. *Intelligence*, *10*, 231–238.

Larson, G. E., Saccuzzo, D. P., and Brown, J. (1994). Motivation: cause or confound in information processing/intelligence correlations? *Acta Psychologica*, *85*, 25–37.

Larson, G. E., Haier, R. J., LaCasse, L., and Hazan, K. (1995). Evaluation of a 'mental effort' hypothesis for correlations between cortical metabolism and intelligence. *Intelligence*, *21*, 267–278.

Lashley, K. S. (1950). In search of the engram. *Symposia of the Society for Experimental Biology*, *4*, 454–482.

Lazarus, R. S. (1993). From psychological stress to emotions: a history of changing outlooks. *Annual Review of Psychology*, *44*, 1–21.

Lehtovirta, M., Laakso, M. P., Soininen, H., Helisalmi, S., Mannermaa, A., Helkala, E. L., *et al.* (1995). Volumes of hippocampus, amygdala and frontal lobe in Alzheimer patients with different apolipoprotein E genotypes. *Neuroscience*, *67*, 65–72.

Lehtovirta, M., Kuikka, J., Helisalmi, S., Hartikainen, P., Mannermaa, A., Ryynanen, M., *et al.* (1998). Longitudinal SPECT study in Alzheimer's disease: relation to apolipoprotein E polymorphism. *Journal of Neurology, Neurosurgery and Psychiatry*, *64*, 742–746.

Lemmon, V. W. (1927). The relation of reaction time to measures of intelligence, memory, and learning. *Archives of Psychology*, No. 94.

Letz, R., Pieper, W. A., and Morris, R. D. (1996). NES test performance in a large US army veteran sample: relationships with both demographic factors and traditional neuropsychological measures. *Neurotoxicology and Teratology*, *18*, 381–390.

Levy, P. (1992). Inspection time and its relation to intelligence: issues of measurement and meaning. *Personality and Individual Differences*, *13*, 987–1002.

Lezak, M. D. (1995). *Neuropsychological assessment.* Oxford: Oxford University Press.

Li, S.-C., Jordanova, M., and Lindenberger, U. (1998). From good senses to good sense: a link between tactile information processing and intelligence. *Intelligence*, *26*, 99–122.

Lindenberger, U. and Baltes, P. B. (1994*a*). Aging and intelligence. In R. J. Sternberg (Ed.), *Encyclopedia of human intelligence* (pp. 52–66). New York: MacMillan.

Lindenberger, U. and Baltes, P. B. (1994*b*). Sensory functioning and intelligence in old age: a strong connection. *Psychology and Aging*, *9*, 339–355.

Lindenberger, U. and Baltes, P. B. (1997). Intellectual functioning in old and very old age: cross sectional results from the Berlin Aging Study. *Psychology and Aging*, *12*, 410–432.

Lindholm, E. and Koriath, J. J. (1985). Analysis of multiple event related potential components in a tone discrimination task. *International Journal of Psychophysiology*, *3*, 121–129.

Lindley, R. H. and Smith, W. R. (1992). Coding tests as measures of IQ: cognition or motivation. *Personality and Individual Differences*, *13*, 25–29.

Loehlin, J. C. (1992). *Genes and environment in personality development.* Newbury Park, CA: Sage.

Loehlin, J. C., Horn J. M., and Willerman, L. (1989). Modeling IQ change: evidence from the Texas Adoption Project. *Child Development*, 60, 993–1004.

Lohman, D. F. (1994). Component scores as residual variation (or why the intercept correlates best). *Intelligence*, 19, 1–11.

Lohman, D. F. (1999). Minding our p's and q's: on finding relationships between learning and intelligence. In P. L. Ackerman, P. C. Kyllonen, and R. D. Roberts (Eds.), *Learning and individual differences: process, trait, and content determinants* (pp. 55–76). Washington, DC: American Psychological Association.

Longstreth, L. E. (1984). Jensen's reaction time investigations of intelligence: a critique. *Intelligence*, 8, 139–160.

Lubar, J. F., Gross, D. M., Shively, M. S., and Mann, C. A. (1990). Differences between normal, learning disabled and gifted children based upon an auditory evoked potential task. *Journal of Psychophysiology*, 4, 249–260.

Lubin, M.-P. and Fernandez, J. M. (1986). The relationship between psychometric intelligence and inspection time. *Personality and Individual Differences*, 7, 653–657.

Luo, D., Petrill, S. A., and Thompson, L. A. (1994). An exploration of genetic *g*: hierarchical factor analysis of cognitive data from the Western Reserve Twin Project. *Intelligence*, 18, 335–347.

Luukinen, H., Viramo, P., Koshi, K., Laippala, P., and Kivela, S.-L. (1999). Head injuries and cognitive decline among older adults. *Neurology*, 52, 557–562.

Lynn, R. (1990). The role of nutrition in secular increases in intelligence. *Personality and Individual Differences*, 3, 273–285.

Mackenzie, B. and Bingham, E. (1985). IQ, inspection time and response strategies in a university sample. *Australian Journal of Psychology*, 37, 257–268.

Mackenzie, B. and Cumming, S. (1986). How fragile is the relationship between inspection time and intelligence? The effects of apparent motion cues and previous experience. *Personality and Individual Differences*, 7, 721–729.

Mackenzie, B., Molloy, E., Martin, F., Lovegrove, W., and McNicol, D. (1991). Inspection time and the content of simple tasks: a framework for research on speed of information processing. *Australian Journal of Psychology*, 43, 37–43.

Mackintosh, N. J. (1981). A new measure of intelligence? *Nature*, 289, 529–530.

Mackintosh, N. J. (1986). The biology of intelligence? *British Journal of Psychology*. 77, 1–18.

Mackintosh, N. J. (1998). *IQ and human intelligence*. Oxford: Oxford University Press.

MacLullich, A. M. J., Seckl, J. R., Starr, J. M., and Deary, I. J. (1998). The biology of intelligence: from association to mechanism. *Intelligence*, 26, 63–73.

Mahley, R. W., Nathan B. P., and Pitas, R. E. (1996). Apolipoprotein E. Structure, function, and possible roles in Alzheimer's disease. *Annals of the New York Academy of Sciences*, 777, 139–145.

Mann, D. M. A., Brown, A. M. T., Prinja, D., Jones, D., and Davies, C. A. (1990). A morphological analysis of senile plaques in the brains of non-demented persons of different ages using silver, immunocytochemical and lectin histochemical staining techniques. *Neuropathology and Applied Neurobiology*, 16, 17–25.

Mark, R. J., Lovell, M. A., Markesbery, W. R., Uchida, K., and Mattson, M. P. (1997). A role for 4-hydroxynonenal, an aldehydic product of lipid peroxidation, in disruption of ion homeostasis and neuronal death induced by amyloid beta-peptide. *Journal of Neurochemistry*, *68*, 255–264.

Marshalek, B., Lohman, D. F., and Snow, R. E. (1983). The complexity continuum in the radex and hierarchical models of intelligence. *Intelligence*, *7*, 107–127.

Martin-Loeches, M., Gil, P., and Rubia, F. J. (1993). Two-Hz wide EEG bands in Alzheimer's disease. *Biological Psychiatry*, *33*, 153–159.

Masliah, E., Mallory, M., Ge, N., Alford, M., Veinbergs, I., and Roses, A. D. (1995). Neurodegeneration in the central nervous system of apo-E deficient mice. *Experimental Neurology*, *136*, 107–22.

Massaro, D. W. (1970). Perceptual auditory images. *Journal of Experimental Psychology*, *85*, 411–417.

Massaro, D. W. (1973). A comparison of forward versus backward recognition masking. *Journal of Experimental Psychology*, *100*, 434–436.

Matarazzo, J. D. (1992). Psychological testing and assessment in the 21st century. *American Psychologist*, *47*, 1007–1018.

Matthews, G. and Deary, I. J. (1998). *Personality traits*. Cambridge, UK: Cambridge University Press.

Mayeux, R., Ottman, R., Maestre, G., Ngai, C., Tang, M. X., Ginsberg, H., *et al.* (1995). Synergistic effects of traumatic head injury and apolipoprotein-e4 in patients with Alzheimer's disease. *Neurology*, *45*, 555–557.

Maylor, E. A. and Rabbitt, P. M. A. (1995). Investigating individual differences in a serial choice reaction time task: use of auditory feedback and analysis of responses surrounding errors. *Journal of Motor Behavior*, *27*, 325–332.

McCall, R. B. (1994). What process mediates predictions of childhood IQ from infant habituation and recognition memory? Speculations on the roles of inhibition and rate of information processing. *Intelligence*, *18*, 107–125.

McClearn, G. E., Johansson, B., Berg, S., Pedersen, N. L., Ahern, F., Petrill, S. A., *et al.* (1997). Substantial genetic influence on cognitive abilities in twins 80 or more years old. *Science*, *276*, 1560–1563.

McGarry-Roberts, P. A., Stelmack, R. M., and Campbell, K. B. (1992). Intelligence, reaction time, and event-related potentials. *Intelligence*, *16*, 289–313.

McGeorge, P., Crawford, J., and Kelly, S. W. (1996). The relationship between WAIS-R abilities and speed of processing in a word identification task. *Intelligence*, *23*, 175–190.

McGonigle, B. O. and Chalmers, M. (1992). Monkeys are rational! *Quarterly Journal of Experimental Psychology*, *45B*, 189–228.

McGue, M. (1997). The democracy of the genes. *Nature*, *388*, 417–418.

McGue, M., Bouchard, T. J., Lykken, D. T., and Feuer, D. (1984). Information processing abilities in twins reared apart. *Intelligence*, *8*, 239–258.

McGuffin, P. and Martin N. (1999). Behaviour and genes. *British Medical Journal*, *319*, 37–40.

McNemar, Q. (1964). Lost: our intelligence? Why? *American Psychologist*, *19*, 871–882.

Menon, R. S. and Kim, S.-G. (1999). Spatial and temporal limits in cognitive neuroimaging with fMRI. *Trends in Cognitive Sciences*, 3, 207–216.

Meredith, G. (1935, first published 1879). *The ordeal of Richard Feverel*. London: Dent.

Merkel, J. (1885). Die zeitlichen Verhaltnisse der Willensthatigkeit. *Philosophische Studien*, 10, 499–506.

Michael, J. S. (1988). A new look at Morton's craniological research. *Current Anthropology*, 29, 349–354.

Miller, E. (1994). Intelligence and brain myelination: a hypothesis. *Personality and Individual Differences*, 17, 803–832.

Minthon, L., Hesse, C., Sjogren, M., Englund, E., Gustafson, L., and Blennow, K. (1997). The apolipoprotein E e4 allele is normal in fronto-temporal dementia, but correlates with age at onset of disease. *Neuroscience Letters*, 226, 65–67.

Moller, J. T., *et al.* (1998). Long-term postoperative cognitive dysfunction in the elderly: ISPOCD1 study. *Lancet*, 351, 857–861.

Morgan, M. (1998). Discussion. *The limits of reductionism in biology: Novartis Foundation Symposium 213*. Chichester: Wiley.

Morris, G. L. and Alcorn, M. B. (1995). Raven's progressive matrices and inspection time: P200 slope correlates. *Personality and Individual Differences*, 18, 81–87.

Mortensen, E. L. and Kleven, M. (1993). A WAIS longitudinal study of cognitive development during the life span from ages 50 to 70. *Developmental Neuropsychology*, 9, 115–130.

Mortimer, J. A., Van Duijin, C. N., Chandra, V., Fratiglioni, L., Graves, A. B., Heyman, A., *et al.* (1991). Head trauma as a risk factor for Alzheimer's disease: a collaborative re-analysis of case-control studies. *International Journal of Epidemiology*, 20 (Suppl. 2), S28–S35.

Muise, J. G., LeBlanc, R. S., Lavoie, M. E., and Arsenault, A. S. (1991). Two stage model of visual backward masking: sensory transmission and accrual of effective information as a function of target intensity and similarity. *Perception and Psychophysics*, 50, 197–204.

Napoli, C., D'Armiento, F. P., Mancini, F. P., Postiglione. A., Witztum, J. L., Palumbo, G., *et al.* (1997). Fatty streak formation occurs in human fetal aortas and is greatly enhanced by maternal hypercholesterolemia. Intimal accumulation of low density lipoprotein and its oxidation precede monocyte recruitment into early atherosclerotic lesions. *Journal of Clinical Investigation*, 100, 2680–2690.

Nathan, B. P., Bellosta, S., Sanan, D. A., Weisgraber, K. H., Mahley, R. W., and Pitas, R. E. (1994). Differential effects of apolipoproteins E3 and E4 on neuronal growth in vitro. *Science*, 264, 850–852.

Navon, D. (1984). Resources: a theoretical soup stone? *Psychological Review*, 91, 216–234.

Neisser, U. (1967). *Cognitive psychology*. New York: Appleton Century Crofts.

Neisser, U. (1979). The concept of intelligence. *Intelligence*, 3, 217–227.

Neisser, U. (1998). *The rising curve*. Washington, DC: American Psychological Association.

Neisser, U., Boodoo, G., Bouchard, T. J., Boykin, A. W., Brody, N., Ceci, S. J., *et al.* (1996). Intelligence: knowns and unknowns. *American Psychologist, 51,* 77–101.

Nelson, D. L. (1998). Molecular basis of mental retardation: fragile X syndrome. In J. B. Martin (Ed.), *Molecular neurology.* New York: Scientific American.

Nettelbeck, T. (1982). Inspection time: an index for intelligence? *Quarterly Journal of Experimental Psychology, 34A,* 299–312.

Nettelbeck, T. (1987). Inspection time and intelligence. In P. A. Vernon (Ed.), *Speed of information processing and intelligence* (pp. 295–346). Norwood, NJ: Ablex.

Nettelbeck, T. (1998). Jensen's chronometric research: neither simple nor sufficient but a good place to start. *Intelligence, 26,* 233–241.

Nettelbeck, T. and Lally, M. (1976). Inspection time and measured intelligence. *British Journal of Psychology, 67,* 17–22.

Nettelbeck, T. and Rabbitt, P. M. A. (1992). Age, intelligence, and speed. *Intelligence, 16,* 189–205.

Nettelbeck, T. and Vita, P. (1992). Inspection time in two childhood age cohorts: a constant or a developmental function? *British Journal of Developmental Psychology, 10,* 189–197.

Nettelbeck, T., Edwards, C., and Vreugdenhil, A. (1986). Inspection time and IQ: evidence for a mental speed–ability association. *Personality and Individual Differences, 7,* 633–641.

Nettelbeck, T., Rabbitt, P. M. A., Wilson, C., and Batt, R. (1996). Uncoupling learning from initial recall: the relationship between speed and memory deficits in old age. *British Journal of Psychology, 87,* 593–607.

Neubauer, A. C. (1990). Selective reaction times and intelligence. *Intelligence, 14,* 79–96.

Neubauer, A. C. (1991). Intelligence and RT: a modified Hick paradigm and a new RT paradigm. *Intelligence, 15,* 175–193.

Neubauer, A. C. (1997). The mental speed approach to the assessment of intelligence. In J. Kingma and W. Tomic (Eds.), *Advances in cognition and education: reflections on the concept of intelligence.* Greenwich, Connecticut: JAI Press.

Neubauer, A. C. and Bucik, V. (1996). The mental speed–IQ relationship: unitary or modular? *Intelligence, 22,* 23–48.

Neubauer, A. C. and Fruedenthaler, H. H. (1994). Reaction times in a sentence–picture verification test and intelligence: individual strategies and effects of extended practice. *Intelligence, 19,* 193–218.

Neubauer, A. C. and Knorr, E. (1998). Three paper and pencil tests for speed of information processing: psychometric properties and correlations with intelligence. *Intelligence, 26,* 123–151.

Neubauer, A. C., Bauer, C., and Holler, G. (1992). Intelligence, attention, motivation and speed–accuracy trade-off in the Hick paradigm. *Personality and Individual Differences, 13,* 1325–1332.

Neubauer, A., Freudenthaler, H. H., and Pfurtscheller, G. (1995) Intelligence and spatiotemporal patterns of event-related desynchronization (ERD). *Intelligence*, 20, 249–266.

Neubauer, A. C., Riemann, R., Mayer, R., and Angleitner, A. (1997). Intelligence and reaction times in the Hick, Sternberg and Posner paradigms. *Personality and Individual Differences*, 22, 885–894.

Neubauer, A. C., Spinath, F. M., Riemann, R., Borkenau, P., and Angleitner, A. (in press). Genetic and environmental influences on two measures of speed of information processing and their relation to psychometric intelligence: evidence from the German Observational Study of Adult Twins. *Intelligence*.

Newman, M. F., Croughwell, N. D., Blumenthal, J. A., Lowry, E., White, W. D., Spillane, W., *et al.* (1995). Predictors of cognitive decline after cardiac operation. *Annals of Thoracic Surgery*, 59, 1326–1330.

Nichols, M. J. and Newsome, W. T. (1999). The neurobiology of cognition. *Nature*, 402, C35–C38.

Nicoll, J. A. R. (1996). Genetics and head injury. *Neuropathology and Applied Neurobiology*, 22, 515–517.

Nicoll, J. A. R., Robertson G. W., and Graham, D. I. (1995). Apolipoprotein E e4 allele is associated with deposition of amyloid beta-protein following head injury. *Nature Medicine*, 1, 135–137.

Nisbet, J. D. (1957). Intelligence and age: retesting with twenty-four years' interval. *British Journal of Educational Psychology*, 27, 190–198.

Noble, D. (1998). Reduction and integration in understanding the heart. *The limits of reductionism in biology: Novartis Foundation Symposium 213*. Chichester: Wiley.

O'Carroll, R. (1995). The assessment of premorbid ability. *Neurocase*, 1, 83–89.

O'Donnell, B. F., Friedman, S., Squires, N. K., Maloon, A., Drachman, D. A., and Swearer, J. M. (1990). Active and passive P3 latency in dementia: relationship to psychometric, electroencephalographic, and computed tomographic measures. *Neuropsychiatry, Neuropsychology, and Behavioral Neurology*, 3, 164–179.

Olsson, H., Bjorkman, C., Haag, K., and Juslin, P. (1998). Auditory inspection time: on the importance of selecting the appropriate sensory continuum. *Personality and Individual Differences*, 25, 627–634.

Orsini, A., Chiacchio, L., Cinque, M., Cocchiaro, C., Schiappa, O., and Grossi, D. (1986). Effects of age, education and sex in two tests of immediate memory: a study of normal subjects from 20 to 99 years of age. *Perceptual and Motor Skills*, 63, 727–732.

O'Toole, B. I. and Stankov, L. (1992). Ultimate validity of psychological tests. *Personality and Individual Differences*, 13, 699–716.

Owens, W. A. (1959). Is age kinder to the initially more able? *Journal of Gerontology*, 14, 334–337.

Owens, W. A. (1966). Age and mental abilities: a second adult follow-up. *Journal of Educational Psychology*, 57, 311–325.

Paradiso, S., Andreasen, N. C., O'Leary, D. S., Arndt, S., and Robinson, R. G. (1997). Cerebellar size and cognition: correlations with IQ, verbal memory and motor dexterity. *Neuropsychiatry, Neuropsychology and Behavioral Neurology*, 10, 1–8.

Parker, D. M., Crawford, J. R., and Stephen, E. (1999). Auditory inspection time and intelligence: a new spatial localization task. *Intelligence*, 27, 131–139.

Parks, R. W., Loewenstein, D. A., Dodrill, K. L., Barker, W. W., Yoshii, F., Chang, J. Y., *et al.* (1988). Cerebral metabolic effects of a verbal fluency test: a PET scan study. *Journal of Clinical and Experimental Neuropsychology*, 10, 565–575.

Peak, H. and Boring, E. G. (1926). The factor of speed in intelligence. *Journal of Experimental Psychology*, 9, 71–94.

Pearson, K. (1906–1907). On the relationship of intelligence to size and shape of head, and to other physical and mental characters. *Biometrika*, 5, 105–146.

Pedersen, N. L., Plomin, R., Nesselroade, J. R., and McClearn, G. E. (1992). A quantitatively genetic analysis of cognitive abilities during the second half of the life span. *Psychological Science*, 3, 346–353.

Pellegrino, J. W. and Glaser, R. (1980). Components of inductive reasoning. In R. E. Snow, P.-A. Federico, and W. E. Montague (Eds.), *Aptitude, learning and instruction: cognitive process analyses of aptitude*, vol. 1. New York: Lawrence Erlbaum.

Pelosi, L. and Blumhardt, L. D. (1992). 'Memory-scanning' event-related potentials: correlations with verbal and performance scores. *Acta Neurologica*, 14, 304–312.

Pennington, B. F., Filipek, P. A., Lefly, D., Chabildas, N., Kennedy, D. N., Simon, J. H., Filley, C. M., Galaburda, A., and DeFries, J. (2000). A twin MRI study of size variations in the human brain. *Journal of Cognitive Neuroscience*, 12, 223–232.

Perry, N. W. Jr. and Childers, D. W. (1969). *The human visual evoked response: method and theory*. Springfield, Illinois: Thomas.

Petrie, R. X. A. and Deary, I. J. (1989). Smoking and human information processing. *Psychopharmacology*, 99, 393–396.

Petrill, S. A., Thompson, L. A., and Detterman, D. K. (1995). The genetic and environmental variance underlying elementary cognitive tasks. *Behavior Genetics*, 25, 199–209.

Petrill, S. A., Plomin, R., McClearn, G. E., Smith, D. L., Vignetti, S., Chorney, M. J., *et al.* (1996). DNA markers associated with general and specific cognitive abilities. *Intelligence*, 23, 191–203.

Petrill, S. A., Plomin, R., Berg, S., Johansson, B., Pedersen, N. L., Ahern, F., *et al.* (1998). The genetic and environmental relationship between general and specific cognitive abilities in twins age 80 and older. *Psychological Science*, 9, 183–189.

Phillips, L. H. and Rabbitt, P. M. A. (1995). Impulsivity and speed–accuracy strategies in intelligence test performance. *Intelligence*, 21, 13–29.

Phillips, W. A. and Singer, W. (1974). Function and interaction of On and Off transients in vision. I: Psychophysics. *Experimental Brain Research*, 19, 493–506.

Plassman, B. L., Welsh, K. A., Helms, M., Brandt, J., Page, W. F., and Breitner, J. C. S. (1995). Intelligence and education as predictors of cognitive state in late life: a 50-year follow-up. *Neurology*, 45, 1446–1450.

Plassman, B. L., Welsh-Bohmer, K. A., Bigler, E. D., Johnson, S. C., Anderson, C. V., Helms, M. J., *et al.* (1997). Apolipoprotein E e4 allele and hippocampal volume in twins with normal cognition. *Neurology, 48,* 985–989.

Plenz, D. and Kital, S. T. (1999). A basal ganglia pacemaker formed by the subthalamic nucleus and external globus pallidus. *Nature, 400,* 677–682.

Plomin, R. (1999). Genetics and general cognitive ability. *Nature, 402 (Suppl.),* C25–C29.

Plomin, R. and Crabbe, J. (in press). DNA. *Psychological Bulletin.*

Plomin, R. and Loehlin, J. C. (1989). Direct and indirect IQ heritability studies: a puzzle. *Behavior Genetics, 19,* 331–342.

Plomin, R. and Petrill, S. (1997). Genetics and intelligence: what's new? *Intelligence, 24,* 53–77.

Plomin, R., McClearn, G. E., Smith, D. L., Vignetti, S., Chorney, M. J., Chorney, K., *et al.* (1994*a*). DNA markers associated with high versus low IQ: the IQ Quantitative Trait Loci (QTL) Project. *Behavior Genetics, 24,* 107–118.

Plomin, R., Pedersen, N. L., Lichenstein, P., and McClearn, G. E. (1994*b*). Variability and stability in cognitive abilities are largely genetic later in life. *Behavior Genetics, 24,* 207–215.

Plomin, R., McClearn, G. E., Smith, D. L., Skuder, P., Vignetti, S., Chorney, M. J., *et al.* (1995). Allelic associations between 100 DNA markers and high versus low IQ. *Intelligence, 21,* 31–48.

Plomin, R., DeFries, J. C., McClearn, G. E., and Rutter, M. (1997). *Behavioral genetics.* New York: W. H. Freeman.

Poirier, J. (1994). Apolipoprotein E in animal models of CNS injury and in Alzheimer's disease. *Trends in Neurosciences, 17,* 525–530.

Polich, J., Ehlers, C. L., Otis, S., Mandell, A. J., and Bloom, F. E. (1986). P300 latency reflects the degree of cognitive decline in dementing illness. *Electroencephalography and Clinical Neurophysiology, 63,* 138–144.

Poppel, E. (1994). Temporal mechanisms in perception. *International Review of Neurobiology, 37,* 185–202.

Popper, K. (1972). *Conjectures and refutations: the growth of scientific knowledge* (4th ed.). London: Routledge and Keegan Paul.

Posner, M. I. and Mitchell, R. F. (1967). Chronometric analysis of classification. *Psychological Review, 74,* 392–409.

Posner, M. I. and Petersen, S. E. (1990). The attention system of the human brain. *Annual Review of Neuroscience, 13,* 25–42.

Posner, M. I. and Raichle, M. E. (1994). *Images of mind.* New York: Freeman.

Prabhakaran, V., Smith, J. A. L., Desmond, J. E., Glover, G. H., and Gabrieli, J. D. E. (1997). Neural substrates of fluid reasoning: an fMRI study of neuro-cortical activation during performance of the Raven's progressive matrices test. *Cognitive Psychology, 33,* 43–63.

Prescott, J. W. (1975). Developmental neuropsychophysics. In J. W. Prescott, M. S. Read, and D. B. Coursin (Eds.), *Brain function and malnutrition: neuropsy-chological methods of assessment.* New York: John Wiley.

Pueyo, A. A. (1996). *Manual de psicologia diferencial.* Madrid: McGraw-Hill.

Pushkar Gold, D., Andres, D., Etezadi, J., Arbuckle, T., Schwartzman, A., and Chaikelson, J. (1995). Structural equation model of intellectual change and continuity and predictors of intelligence in older men. *Psychology and Aging, 10,* 294–303.

Rabbitt, P. (1992). Memory. In G. J. Evans and T. F. Williams (Eds.), *Oxford textbook of geriatric medicine* (pp. 463–479). Oxford: Oxford University Press.

Rabbitt, P. (1993). Does it all go together when it goes? *Quarterly Journal of Experimental Psychology, 46A,* 385–434.

Rabbitt, P. (1996). Do individual differences in speed reflect 'global' or 'local' differences in mental abilities? *Intelligence, 22,* 69–88.

Rabbitt, P. M. A. and Maylor, E. A. (1991). Investigating models of human performance. *British Journal of Psychology, 82,* 259–290.

Raber, J., Wong, D., Yu, G.-Q., Buttini, M., Mahley, R. W., Pitas, R. E., and Mucke, L. (2000). Apolioprotein E and cognitive performance. *Nature, 404,* 352–353.

Rae, C., Scott, R. B., Thompson, C. H., Kemp, G. J., Dumughn, I., Styles, P., *et al.* (1996). Is pH a biochemical marker of IQ. *Proceedings of the Royal Society of London Series B, 263,* 1061–1064.

Rammsayer, T. (1997). Are there dissociable roles of the mesostriatal and mesolimbocortical dopamine systems on temporal information processing in humans? *Neuropsychobiology, 35,* 36–45.

Raven, J. C. (1938). *Progressive matrices.* London: Lewis.

Raz, N. and Willerman, L. (1985). Aptitude-related differences in auditory information processing: effects of selective attention and tone duration. *Personality and Individual Differences, 6,* 299–304.

Raz, N., Willerman, L., Ingmundson, P., and Hanlon, M. (1983). Aptitude-related differences in auditory recognition masking. *Intelligence, 7,* 71–90.

Raz, N., Willerman, L., and Yama, M. (1987). On sense and senses: intelligence and auditory information processing. *Personality and Individual Differences, 8,* 201–210.

Raz, N., Torres, I. T., Spencer, W. D., Millman, D., Baertschi, J. C., and Sarpel, G. (1993). Neuroanatomical correlates of age-sensitive and age-invariant cognitive abilities: an *in vivo* MRI investigation. *Intelligence, 17,* 407–422.

Reed, T. E. and Jensen, A. R. (1991). Arm nerve conduction velocity (NCV), brain NCV, reaction time, and intelligence. *Intelligence, 15,* 33–47.

Reed, T. E. and Jensen, A. R. (1992). Conduction velocity in a brain nerve pathway of normal adults correlates with intelligence level. *Intelligence, 16,* 259–272.

Reed, T. E. and Jensen, A. R. (1993a). Choice reaction time and visual pathway nerve conduction velocity both correlate with intelligence but appear not to correlate with each other: implications for information processing. *Intelligence, 17,* 191–203.

Reed, T. E. and Jensen, A. R. (1993b). A somatosensory latency between thalamus and cortex also correlates with psychometric intelligence. *Intelligence, 17,* 443–450.

Reed, T., Carmelli, D., Swan, G. E., Breitner, J. C. S., Welsh, K. A., Jarvik, G. P., *et al.* (1994). Lower cognitive performance in normal older adult male twins carrying the apolipoprotein E e4 allele. *Archives of Neurology*, *51*, 1189–1192.

Regan, D. (1989). *Human brain electrophysiology: evoked potentials and evoked magnetic fields in science and medicine*. New York: Elsevier.

Reiman, E. M., Caselli, R. J., Yun, L. S., Chen, K., Bandy, D., Minoshima, S., *et al.* (1996). Preclinical evidence of Alzheimer's disease in persons homozygous for the e4 allele for apolipoprotein E. *New England Journal of Medicine*, *334*, 752–758.

Reiman, E. M., Uecker, A., Caselli, R. J., Lewis, S., Bandy, D., de Leon M. J., *et al.* (1998). Hippocampal volumes in cognitively normal persons at genetic risk for Alzheimer's disease. *Annals of Neurology*, *44*, 288–91.

Reiss, A. L., Abrams, M. T., Singer, H. S., Ross, J. L., and Denckla, M. B. (1996). Brain development, gender and IQ in children: a volumetric imaging study. *Brain*, *119*, 1763–1774.

Resnick, L. B (Ed.). (1976). *The nature of intelligence*. Hillsdale, NJ: Erlbaum.

Resnick, L. B. (1979). The future of IQ testing in education. *Intelligence*, *3*, 241–253.

Riegel, K. F. and Riegel, R. M. (1972). Development, drop and death. *Developmental Psychology*, *6*, 306–319.

Rijsdijk, F. V. and Boomsma, D. I. (1997). Genetic mediation of the correlation between peripheral nerve conduction velocity and IQ. *Behavior Genetics*, *27*, 87–98.

Rijsdijk, F. V., Boomsma, D. I. and Vernon, P. A. (1995). Genetic analysis of peripheral nerve conduction velocity in twins. *Behavior Genetics*, *25*, 341–348.

Rijsdijk, F. V., Vernon, P. A., and Boomsma, D. I. (1998). The genetic basis of the relation between speed-of-information-processing and IQ. *Behavioural Brain Research*, *95*, 77–84.

Robaey, P., Cansino, S., Dugas, M., and Renault, B. (1995). A comparative study of ERP correlates of psychometric and Piagetian intelligence measures in normal and hyperactive children. *Electroencephalography and Clinical Neurophysiology*, *96*, 56–75.

Roberts, R. D., Beh, H. C., and Stankov, L. (1988). Hick's law, competing task performance, and intelligence. *Intelligence*, *12*, 111–130.

Roberts, R. D., and Stankov, L. (1999). Individual differences in speed of mental processing and human cognitive abilities: toward a taxonomic model. *Learning and Individual Differences*, *11*, 1–120.

Robinson, D. L. (1993). The EEG and intelligence: an appraisal of methods and theories. *Personality and Individual Differences*, *15*, 695–716.

Rogosa, D. (1980). A critique of cross-lagged correlations. *Psychological Bulletin*, *88*, 201–210.

Rose, S. (1998). Discussion. *The limits of reductionism in biology: Novartis Foundation Symposium 213*. Chichester: Wiley.

Rose, S. A. and Feldman, J. F. (1995). Prediction of IQ and specific cognitive abilities at 11 years from infancy measures. *Developmental Psychology*, *31*, 685–696.

Rosenbloom, P. S., Laird, J. E., Newell, A., and McCarl, R. (1991). A preliminary analysis of the SOAR architecture as a basis for general intelligence. *Artificial Intelligence*, *47*, 289–325.

Roses, A. D. (1996). Apolipoprotein E in neurology. *Current Opinion in Neurology*, *9*, 265–270.

Roth, E. (1964). Die Geschwindigkeit der Verabeitung von Information and ihr Zusammenhang mit Intelligenz. *Zeitschrift fur Experimentelle und Angewandte Psychologie*, *11*, 616–622.

Royer, F. L. (1977). Information processing in the block design task. *Intelligence*, *1*, 32–50.

Royer, F. L. (1978). Intelligence and the processing of stimulus structure. *Intelligence*, *2*, 11–40.

Royer, F. L. and Gilmore, G. C. (1985). Age and functions of the transient component of ON and OFF responses in visual processes. *Quarterly Journal of Experimental Psychology*, *37A*, 147–170.

Roznowski, M. and Smith, M. L. (1993). A note on some psychometric properties of Sternberg task performance: modifications to content. *Intelligence*, *17*, 389–398.

Rugg, M. D. and Coles, M. G. H. (1995). *Electrophysiology of mind: event related potentials and cognition.* Oxford: Oxford University Press.

Rushton, J. P. (1997). Race, intelligence, and the brain: the errors and omissions of the 'revised' edition of S. J. Gould's *The mismeasure of man*. *Personality and Individual Differences*, *23*, 169–180.

Rushton, J. P. and Ankney, C. D. (1996). Brain size and cognitive ability: correlations with age, sex, social class, and race. *Psychonomic Bulletin and Review*, *3*, 21–36.

Russell, J. A. and Barrett, L. F. (1999). Core affect, prototypical emotional episodes, and other things called *emotion*: dissecting the elephant. *Journal of Personality and Social Psychology*, *76*, 805–819.

Saccuzzo, D. P., Larson, G. E., and Rimland, B. (1986). Visual, auditory and reaction time approaches to the measurement of speed of information processing and individual differences in intelligence. *Personality and Individual Differences*, *7*, 659–667.

Sackeim, H. A., Freeman, J., McElhiney, M., Coleman, E., Prudic, J., and Devanand, D. P. (1992). Effects of major depression on estimates of intelligence. *Journal of Clinical and Experimental Neuropsychology*, *14*, 268–288.

Salthouse, T. A. (1985). Speed of behavior and its implications for cognition. In J. E. Birren and K. W. Schaie (Eds.), *Handbook of the psychology of aging* (2nd ed., pp. 400–426). New York: Van Nostrand.

Salthouse, T. A. (1993). Influence of working memory on adult age differences in matrix reasoning. *British Journal of Psychology*, *84*, 171–199.

Salthouse, T. A. (1994a). The nature of the influence of speed on adult age differences in cognition. *Developmental Psychology*, *30*, 240–259.

Salthouse, T. A. (1994b). How many causes are there of aging-related decrements in cognitive functioning? *Developmental Review*, *14*, 413–437.

Salthouse, T. A. (1996*a*). Constraints on theories of cognitive aging. *Psychonomic Bulletin and Review, 3*, 287–299.

Salthouse, T. A. (1996*b*). The processing-speed theory of adult age differences in cognition. *Psychological Review, 103*, 403–428.

Salthouse, T. A. (1996*c*). General and specific speed mediation of adult differences in memory. *Journal of Gerontology: Psychological Sciences, 51B*, P30–P42.

Salthouse, T. A., and Czaja, S. J. (2000). Structural constraints on process explanations in cognitive aging. *Psychology and Aging, 15*, 44–55.

Salthouse, T. A., Fristoe, B. N., and Rhee, S. H. (1996). How localized are age-related effects on neuropsychological measures? *Neuropsychology, 10*, 272–285.

Sargent, W. (1942). How shall we study individual differences? *Psychological Review, 49*, 170–182.

Sattler, J. M. (1982). Age effects on Wechsler Adult Intelligence Scale-Revised tests. *Journal of Consulting and Clinical Psychology, 50*, 785–786.

Schafer, E. P. W. (1982). Neural adaptability: a biological determinant of behavioral intelligence. *International Journal of Neuroscience, 17*, 183–191

Schafer, E. W. P. (1985). Neural adaptability: a biological determinant of *g* factor intelligence. *Behavioural and Brain Sciences, 8*, 240–241.

Schaie, K. W. (1989). The hazards of cognitive aging. *Gerontologist, 29*, 484–493.

Schaie, K. W. (1994). The course of adult intellectual development. *American Psychologist, 49*, 304–313.

Schaie, K. W. (1996). *Intellectual development in adulthood*. Cambridge: Cambridge University Press.

Schmidt, F. L. and Hunter, J. E. (1998). The validity and utility of selection methods in personnel psychology: practical and theoretical implications of 85 years of research findings. *Psychological Bulletin, 124*, 262–274.

Schmidt, H., Schmidt, R., Fazekas, F., Semmler, J., Kapeller, P., Reinhart, B., *et al.* (1996). Apolipoprotein E e4 allele in the normal elderly: neuropsychologic and brain MRI correlates. *Clinical Genetics, 5*, 293–9.

Schwartzman, A. E., Gold, D., Andres, D., Arbuckle, T. Y., and Chaikelson, J. (1987). Stability of intelligence: a 40 year follow up. *Canadian Journal of Psychology, 41*, 244–256.

Scottish Council for Research in Education. (1933). *The intelligence of Scottish children: a National Survey of an age-group*. London: University of London Press.

Seckl, J. R. and Olsson, T. (1995). Glucocorticoid hypersecretion and the age-impaired hippocampus: cause or effect? *Journal of Endocrinology, 145*, 201–211.

Segalowitz, S. J., Unsal, A., and Dywan, J. (1992). Cleverness and wisdom in 12-year-olds: electrophysiological evidence for late maturation of the frontal lobe. *Developmental Neuropsychology, 8*, 279–298.

Seidman, L. J., Breiter, H. C., Goodman, J. M., Goldstein, J. M., Woodruff, P. W. R., O'Craven, K., *et al.* (1998). A functional magnetic resonance imaging study of auditory vigilance with low and high information processing demands. *Neuropsychology, 12*, 505–518.

Selnes, O. A., Goldsborough, M. A., Borowicz, L. M., and McKhann, G. M. (1999). Neurobehavioural sequelae of cardiopulmonary bypass. *Lancet, 353*, 1601–1606.

Seshadri, S., Drachman, D. A., and Lippa, C. F. (1995). Apolipoprotein E e4 allele and the lifetime risk of Alzheimer's disease. *Archives of Neurology*, *52*, 1074–1079.

Sharp, S. E. (1898–1899). Individual psychology: a study in psychological method. *American Journal of Psychology*, *10*, 329–391.

Sheng, H., Laskowitz, D. T., Bennett, E., Schmechel, D. E., Bart, R. D., Saunders, A. M., *et al.* (1998). Apolipoprotein E isoform-specific differences in outcome from focal ischemia in transgenic mice. *Journal of Cerebral Blood Flow and Metabolism*, *18*, 361–366.

Shepard, R. and Metzler, J. (1971). Mental rotation of three-dimensional objects. *Science*, *171*, 701–703.

Sherrington, R., Froelich, S., Sorbi, S., Campion, D., Chi, H., Rogaeva, E. A., *et al.* (1996). Alzheimer's disease associated with mutations in presenilin 2 is rare and variably penetrant. *Human Molecular Genetics*, *5*, 985–988.

Shucard, D. and Horn, J. (1972). Evoked cortical potentials and measurement of human abilities. *Journal of Comparative and Physiological Psychology*, *78*, 59–68.

Silber, J. H., Radcliffe, J., Peckham, V., Perilongo, G., Kishani, P., Fridman, M., *et al.* (1992). Whole-brain irradiation and decline in intelligence: the influence of dose and age on IQ score. *Journal of Clinical Oncology*, *10*, 1390–1396.

Simpson, C. R. and Deary, I. J. (1997). Strategy use and feedback in inspection time. *Personality and Individual Differences*, *23*, 787–797.

Singer, W. and Phillips, W. A. (1974). Function and interaction of On and Off transients in vision. II: Neurophysiology. *Experimental Brain Research*, *19*, 507–521.

Skuder, P., Plomin, R., McClearn, G. E., Smith, D. L., Vignetti, S., Chorney, M. J., *et al.* (1995). A polymorphism in mitochondrial DNA associated with IQ? *Intelligence*, *21*, 1–11.

Sliwinski, M. and Buschke, H. (1999). Cross-sectional and longitudinal relationships among age, cognition, and processing speed. *Psychology and Aging*, *14*, 18–33.

Smith, C. U. M. (1996). *Elements of molecular neurobiology* (2nd ed.). Chichester: Wiley.

Smith, E. E. (2000). Neural bases of human working memory. *Current Directions in Psychological Science*, *9*, 45–49.

Smith, C. D., Malcein, M., Meurer, M., Schmitt, F. A., Markesbery, W. R., and Pettigrew, L. C. (1999). MRI temporal lobe volume measures and neuropsychological function in Alzheimer's disease. *Journal of Neuroimaging*, *9*, 2–9.

Smith, G. A. and Carew, M. (1987). Decision time unmasked: individuals adopt different strategies. *Australian Journal of Psychology*, *39*, 339–351.

Smith, G. E., Bohac, D. L., Waring, S. C., Kokmen, E., Tangalos, E. G., Ivnik, R. J., *et al.* (1998). Apolipoprotein E genotype influences cognitive 'phenotype' in patients with Alzheimer's disease but not in healthy control subjects. *Neurology*, *50*, 355–362.

Snow, R. E. (1978). Theory and method for research on aptitude processes. *Intelligence*, *2*, 225–278.

Snow, R. E. (1980). Intelligence for the year 2001. *Intelligence*, 4, 185–199.

Spearman, C. (1904). 'General Intelligence' objectively determined and measured. *American Journal of Psychology*, 15, 201–293.

Spearman, C. (1923). *The nature of intelligence and the principles of cognition*. London: Macmillan.

Spearman, C. (1926). Some issues in the theory of 'G' (including the law of diminishing returns). Address to the British Association Section J—Psychology, Southampton, 1925. Bound in Collected Papers, Psychological Laboratory, University College of London.

Spearman, C. (1927). *The abilities of man*. London: Macmillan.

Stankov, L. and Roberts, R. D. (1997). Mental speed is not the 'basic' process of intelligence. *Personality and Individual Differences*, 22, 69–84.

Starr, J. M., Deary, I. J., Inch, S., Cross, S., and MacLennan, W. J. (1997). Age-associated cognitive decline in healthy old people. *Age and Ageing*, 26, 295–300.

Staudinger, U. M. and Baltes, P. B. (1994). Psychology of wisdom. In R. J. Sternberg (Ed.), *Encyclopedia of human intelligence*, vol. 2 (pp. 1143–1152). New York: MacMillan.

Stauffer, J. M., Ree, M. J., and Carretta, T. R. (1996). Cognitive-components tests are not much more than *g*: an extension of Kyllonen's analyses. *The Journal of General Psychology*, 123, 193–205.

Sternberg, R. J. (1977a). Component processing in analogical reasoning. *Psychological Review*, 84, 353–378.

Sternberg, R. J. (1977b). *Intelligence, information processing, and analogical reasoning: the componential analysis of human abilities*. Hillsdale, NJ: Erlbaum.

Sternberg, R. J. (1978). Intelligence research at the interface between differential and cognitive psychology: prospects and proposals. *Intelligence*, 2, 195–222.

Sternberg, R. J. (1979). Six authors in search of a character: a play about intelligence tests in the year 2000. *Intelligence*, 3, 283–293.

Sternberg, R. J. (1985). *Beyond IQ: a triarchic theory of human intelligence*. Cambridge, UK: Cambridge University Press.

Sternberg, R. J. (1990). *Metaphors of mind*. Cambridge, UK: Cambridge University Press.

Sternberg, R. J. (1997). *Thinking styles*. New York: Cambridge University Press.

Sternberg, R. J. (1999). Successful intelligence: finding a balance. *Trends in Cognitive Sciences*, 3, 436–442.

Sternberg, R. J. and Gardner, M. K. (1982). A componential interpretation of the general factor in human intelligence. In H. J. Eysenck (Ed.), *A model for intelligence*. Berlin: Springer Verlag.

Sternberg, R. J. and Gardner, M. K. (1983). Unities in inductive reasoning. *Journal of Experimental Psychology: General*, 112, 80.

Sternberg, S. (1966). High speed scanning in human memory. *Science*, 153, 652–654.

Sternberg, S. (1975). Memory scanning: new findings and current controversies. *Quarterly Journal of Experimental Psychology*, 27, 1–32.

Stewart, A. L., Rifkin, L., Amess, P. N., Kirkbride, V., Townsend, J. P., Miller, D. H., *et al.* (1999). Brain structure and neurocognitive and behavioural function in adolescents who were born very preterm. *Lancet, 353,* 1653–1657.

Stoljar, D. and Gold, I. (1998). On biological and cognitive neuroscience. *Mind and Language, 13,* 110–131.

Stott, D. H. (1983). Brain size and 'intelligence'. *British Journal of Developmental Psychology, 1,* 279–287.

Stough, C., Mangan, G., Bates, T., and Pellett, O. (1994). Smoking and Raven IQ. *Psychopharmacology, 116,* 382–384.

Stough, C., Bates, T., Mangan, G., and Pellett, O. (1995*a*). Smoking, string length and intelligence. *Personality and Individual Differences, 18,* 75–79.

Stough, C., Mangan, G., Bates, T., Frank, N., Kerkin, B., and Pellett, O. (1995*b*). Effects of nicotine on perceptual speed. *Psychopharmacology, 119,* 305–310.

Stough, C., Nettelbeck, T., Cooper, C., and Bates, T. (1995*c*). Strategy use in Jensen's RT paradigm: relationships to intelligence? *Australian Journal of Psychology, 47,* 61–65.

Stough, C., Brebner, J., Nettelbeck, T., Cooper, C J., Bates, T., and Mangan, G. L. (1996). The relationship between intelligence, personality and inspection time. *British Journal of Psychology, 81,* 255–268.

Stough, C., Bates, T., Mangan, G. L., Colrain, I., and Pellet, O. (in press). Inspection time and intelligence: further attempts at reducing apparent motion strategy. *Intelligence.*

Strachan, M. W. J., Deary, I. J., Ewing, F. M. E., and Frier, B. M. (1997). Is type II diabetes associated with an increased risk of cognitive dysfunction? A critical review of published studies. *Diabetes Care, 20,* 438–445.

Sun, Y., Wu, S., Bu, G., Onifade, M. K., Patel, S. N., LaDu, M. J., *et al.* (1998). Glial fibrillary acidic protein–apolipoprotein E (apoE) transgenic mice: astrocyte-specific expression and differing biological effects of astrocyte-secreted apoE3 and apoE4 lipoproteins. *Journal of Neuroscience, 18,* 3261–3272.

Tallal, P. and Piercy, M. (1973). The repetition test. *Neuropsychologia, 11,* 389–398.

Tan, U. (1996). Correlations between nonverbal intelligence and peripheral nerve conduction velocity in right-handed subjects: sex-related differences. *International Journal of Psychophysiology, 22,* 123–128.

Tang, Y.-P., Shimizu, E., Dube, G. R., Rampon, C., Kerchner, G. A., Zhuo, M., *et al.* (1999). Genetic enhancement of learning and memory in mice. *Nature, 401,* 63–69.

Tardiff, B., Newman, M., Saunders, A., Strittmatter, W., White, W., Smith, L. R., *et al.* (1994). Apolipoprotein E allele frequency in patients with cognitive deficits following cardiopulmonary bypass. *Circulation, 90 (Suppl. 1),* 201.

Teasdale, G. M., Nicoll, J. A. R., Murray, G., and Fiddes, M. (1997). Association of apolipoprotein E polymorphism with outcome after head injury. *Lancet, 350,* 1069–1071.

Teasdale, T. W. and Engberg, A. (1997). Duration of cognitive dysfunction after concussion, and cognitive dysfunction as a risk factor: a population study of young men. *British Medical Journal*, *315*, 569–572.

Teng, E. L. and Chui, H. C. (1987). The modified mini-mental state (3MS) examination. *Journal of Clinical Psychiatry*, *48*, 314–318.

Terry, J. G., Howard, G., Mercuri, M., Bond, M. G., and Crouse, J. R. (1996). Apolipoprotein E polymorphism is associated with segment-specific extracranial carotid artery intima-media thickening. *Stroke*, *27*, 1755–1759.

Thapar, A., Petrill, S. A., and Thompson, L. A. (1994). The heritability of memory in the Western Reserve Twin Project. *Behavior Genetics*, *24*, 155–160.

Thatcher, R. W., McAlaster, R., Lester, M. L., Horst, R. L., and Cantor, D. S. (1983). Hemispheric EEG asymmetries related to cognitive functioning in children. In E. Perecman (Ed.), *Cognitive processing in the right hemisphere*. New York: Academic Press.

Thatcher, R. W., Walker, R. A., and Giudice, S. (1987). Human cerebral hemispheres develop at different rates and ages. *Science*, *236*, 1110–1113.

Thomson, G. H. (1939). *The factorial analysis of human ability*. London: University of London Press.

Thorndike, E. L. (1904). *An introduction to the theory of mental and social measurements*. New York: Teachers College, Columbia University.

Thorndike, E. L., Lay, W., and Dear, P. R. (1909). The relation of accuracy in sensory discrimination to intelligence. *American Journal of Psychology*, *20*, 364–369.

Thurstone, L. L. (1938). Primary mental abilities. *Psychometric Monographs*, No. 1.

Tolar, M., Marques, M. A., Harmony, J. A. K., and Crutcher, K. A. (1997). Neurotoxicity of the 22 kDa thrombin-cleavage fragment of apolipoprotein E and related synthetic peptides is receptor mediated. *Journal of Neuroscience*, *17*, 5678–5686.

Towler, D. A., Havlin, C. E., Craft, S., and Cryer, P. (1993). Mechanism of awareness of hypoglycaemia: perception of neurogenic (predominantly cholinergic) rather than neuroglycopenic symptoms. *Diabetes*, *42*, 1791–1798.

Tramo, M. J., Loftus, W. C., Stukel, T. A., Green, R. L., Weaver, J. B., and Gazzaniga, M. S. (1998). Brain size, head size, and intelligence quotient in monozygotic twins. *Neurology*, *50*, 1246–1252.

Tuddenham, R. D., Blumenkrantz, J., and Wilkin, W. R. (1968). Age changes on AGCT: a longitudinal study of average adults. *Journal of Consulting and Clinical Psychology*, *32*, 659–663.

Tulving, E. and Markowitsch, H .J. (1997). Memory beyond the hippocampus. *Current Opinion in Neurobiology*, *7*, 209–216.

Turnbull, W. W. (1979). Intelligence testing in the year 2000. *Intelligence*, *3*, 275–282.

Undheim, J. O. and Gustafsson, J.-E. (1987). The hierarchical organization of cognitive abilities: restoring general intelligence through the use of linear structural relations (LISREL). *Multivariate Behavioral Research*, *22*, 149–171.

Valentine, J., Wilding, J., and Mohindra, N. (1984). Independence of slope and intercept in Sternberg's memory scanning paradigm. *British Journal of Mathematical and Statistical Psychology*, 37, 122–127.

Vernon, P. A. (1983). Speed of information processing and general intelligence. *Intelligence*, 7, 53–70.

Vernon, P. A. (1985). Reaction times and speed of processing: their relationship to timed and untimed measures of intelligence. *Intelligence*, 9, 357–374.

Vernon, P. A. (1986). Inspection time: does it measure intelligence? *Personality and Individual Differences*, 7, 715–720.

Vernon, P. A. (1989). The heritability of measures of speed of information processing. *Personality and Individual Differences*, 10, 573–576.

Vernon, P. A. and Jensen, A. R. (1984). Individual and group differences in intelligence and speed of information processing. *Personality and Individual Differences*, 5, 411–423.

Vernon, P. A. and Kantor, L. (1986). Reaction time correlations with intelligence test scores obtained under either timed or untimed conditions. *Intelligence*, 10, 315–330.

Vernon, P. A. and Mori, M. (1992). Intelligence, reaction times, and peripheral nerve conduction velocity. *Intelligence*, 16, 273–288.

Vernon, P. A. and Weese, S. E. (1993). Predicting intelligence with multiple speed of information-processing tests. *Personality and Individual Differences*, 14, 413–419.

Vernon, P. A., Wickett, J. C., Bazana, P. G., and Stelmack, R. M. (2000). The neuropsychology and psychophysiology of human intelligence. In R. J. Sternberg (Ed.), *Handbook of Intelligence*. Cambridge: Cambridge University Press.

Vernon, P. E. (1950). *The structure of human abilities*. London: Methuen.

Vernon, P. E. (1961). *The structure of human abilities* (2nd ed.). London: Methuen.

Vickers, D. (1995). The frequency accrual speed test (FAST): a new measure of 'mental speed'? *Personality and Individual Differences*, 19, 863–879.

Vickers, D. and McDowell, A. (1996). Accuracy in the frequency accrual speed test (FAST), inspection time and psychometric intelligence in a sample of primary school children. *Personality and Individual Differences*, 20, 463–469.

Vickers, D. and Smith, P. L. (1986). The rationale for the inspection time index. *Personality and Individual Differences*, 7, 609–624.

Vickers, D., Nettelbeck, T., and Willson, R. J. (1972). Perceptual indices of performance: the measurement of 'inspection time' and 'noise' in the visual system. *Perception*, 1, 263–295.

Vickers, D., Foreman, E. A., Nicholls, M. E. R., Innes, N. J., and Gott, R. E. (1989). Some experimental tests of the application of an interval of uncertainty model to a time-limited expanded judgement task. In D. Vickers and P. L. Smith (Eds.), *Human information processing: measures, mechanisms and models* (pp. 253–265). Amsterdam: North-Holland.

Vickers, D., Pietsch, A., and Hemmingway, T. (1995). Intelligence and visual and auditory discrimination: evidence that the relationship is not due to the rate at which sensory information is sampled. *Intelligence, 21*, 197–224.

Wahlsten, D. (1999). Single-gene influences on behavior. *Annual Review of Psychology, 50*, 599–624.

Waldstein, S. R., Manuck, S. B., Ryan, C. M., and Muldoon, M. F. (1991). Neuropsychological correlates of hypertension: review and methodologic considerations. *Psychological Bulletin, 110*, 451–468.

Watkins, W. E. and Pollitt, E. (1997). 'Stupidity or worms': do intestinal worms impair mental performance? *Psychological Bulletin, 121*, 171–191.

Watson, B. U. (1991). Some relationships between intelligence and auditory discrimination. *Journal of Speech and Hearing Research, 34*, 621–627.

Watson, B. U. and Miller, T. K. (1993). Auditory perception, phonological processing, and reading ability/disability. *Journal of Speech and Hearing Research, 36*, 850–863.

Wechsler, D. (1981). *Manual for the Wechsler Adult Intelligence Scale-Revised*. New York: Psychological Corporation.

Whelan, T. B., Schteingart, D. E., Starkman, M. N., and Smith, A. (1980). Neuropsychological deficits in Cushing's syndrome. *The Journal of Nervous and mental Disease, 168*, 753–757.

White, M. (1993). The inspection time rationale fails to demonstrate that inspection time is a measure of the speed of post-sensory processing. *Personality and Individual Differences, 15*, 185–198.

White, M. (1996). Interpreting inspection time as a measure of the speed of sensory processing. *Personality and Individual Differences, 20*, 351–363.

Whitely, S. (1980). Latent trait models in the study of intelligence. *Intelligence, 4*, 97–132.

Wickett, J. C. and Vernon, P. A. (1994). Peripheral nerve conduction velocity, reaction time, and intelligence: an attempt to replicate Vernon and Mori (1992). *Intelligence, 18*, 127–131.

Wickett, J. C., Vernon, P. A., and Lee, D. H. (1994). *In vivo* brain size, head perimeter, and intelligence in a sample of healthy adult females. *Personality and Individual Differences, 16*, 831–838.

Widaman, K. F. (1989). When failure to replicate is not failure to replicate: a comment on Kranzler, Whang and Jensen (1988). *Intelligence, 13*, 87–91.

Widaman, K. F. and Carlson, J. S. (1989). Procedural effects on performance on the Hick paradigm. *Intelligence, 13*, 63–86.

Widaman, K. F., Carlson, J. S., Saetermoe, C. L., and Galbraith, G. C. (1993). The relationship of auditory-evoked potentials to fluid and crystallized intelligence. *Personality and Individual Differences, 15*, 205–217.

Wilbur, R. (1957). *Poems 1946–1956*. London: Faber and Faber.

Willatts, P., Forsyth, J. S., DiModugno, M. K., Varma, S., and Colvin, M. (1998). Effect of long-chain polyunsaturated fatty acids in infant formula on problem solving at 10 months of age. *Lancet, 352*, 688–691.

Willerman, L., Schultz, R., Rutledge, J. N., and Bigler, E. D. (1991). *In vivo* brain size and intelligence. *Intelligence, 15,* 223–228.

Wissler, C. (1901). The correlation of mental and physical tests. *Psychological Review:* Monograph No. 3.

Witelson, S. F., Kigar, D. L., and Harvey, T. (1999). The exceptional brain of Albert Einstein. *Lancet, 353,* 2149–2153.

Wittgenstein, L. (1961). *Tractatus logico-philosophicus.* London: Routledge and Keegan Paul. (Originally published in English in 1922.)

Wolff, C. (1732, reprinted 1968). *Psychologia empirica* (Ed. J. Ecole). Hildesheim: Georg Olms.

Woodruff-Pak, D. S. (1997). *The neuropsychology of aging.* Oxford: Blackwell.

Writing Committee. (1996). The challenge of the dementias. *The Lancet, 347,* 1303–1307.

Yaffe, K., Cauley, J., Sands, L., and Browner, W. (1997). Apolipoprotein E phenotype and cognitive decline in a prospective study of elderly community women. *Archives of Neurology, 54,* 1110–1114.

Yamauchi, H., Fukuyama, H., Katsumi, Y., Dong, Y., Konishi, J., and Kimura, J. (1996). Atrophy of the corpus callosum associated with cognitive impairment and widespread cortical hypometabolism in carotid artery occlusive disease. *Archives of Neurology, 53,* 1103–1109.

Yankner, B. A. (1996). Mechanisms of neuronal degeneration in Alzheimer's disease. *Neuron, 16,* 921–932.

Zeaman, D. (1978). Some relations of general intelligence and selective attention. *Intelligence, 2,* 55–73.

Zenderland, L. (1998). *Measuring minds: Henry Herbert Goddard and the origins of American intelligence testing.* Cambridge, UK: Cambridge University Press.

Zhang, Y. X., Caryl, P. G., and Deary, I. J. (1989). Evoked potential correlates of inspection time. *Personality and Individual Differences, 10,* 379–384.

Zurrón, M. and Díaz, F. (1998). Conditions for correlation between IQ and auditory evoked potential latencies. *Personality and Individual Differences, 24,* 279–287.

Index